- **JAMES A. VAN ZWOLL**

University of Maryland

School Personnel Administration

New York

- **APPLETON-CENTURY-CROFTS**

Division of Meredith Publishing Company

PRINTED IN THE UNITED STATES OF AMERICA

E–89775

. Foreword

THE AMERICAN Public School, along with a very few other institutions, is unique in that its results are produced not by machines, not from the soils or by means of chemistry, computers, or the manipulations of fissionable materials, but by personal service. This being the case, the school administrator, responsible as he is to his Board and the public for an effective educational program which will meet the needs of modern-day society, will deal primarily with humans.

The success of a school administrator will depend more upon his skill in selecting, improving, and dealing with the human element than upon any other factor. Studies and experience in this area indicate that only a small percentage of school administrators lose their jobs because they are inept with budgeting, pupil accounting, building planning, or because of political or religious affiliations. The majority fail because they lack the skill to deal adequately with the human element connected with the school—board members, staff, citizens, and pupils. By far the most important of these, in toting up the final results, is the staff. It is for this reason that emphasis is needed on the personnel phase of the administrator's responsibilities, both in his training and for the guidance and improvement of administrators in service. *There is no more important administrative responsibility than effective personnel administration.*

Since the schools belong to the people and are supported by them, it is inevitable that their welfare and progress will be determined by the results of the educational program and what the public knows about the schools.

Never were truer words spoken than by him who said, "It all begins in the classroom." It is the staff member who, in the last analysis, will interpret and apply the curricula in terms of the needs of the pupils in order to produce the best education. It is this same staff member who, in his many contacts with individuals and professional, social, civic, and

iii

religious groups, will interpret effectively the school's program to the public and build up public confidence in the schools. It is a well known fact to anyone with more than a year's experience in school administration that the staff member—be he teacher, janitor, clerk, supervisor, or principal—is, to some individual or group, the public relations agent for the whole school system. If reactions are favorable or enthusiastic to that individual, you have a good school system. If the relationship is flat, frustrating, or antagonistic, your whole school system suffers.

Since the objective of every administrator is to achieve the best education possible in his community, requiring, as it inevitably does, public support and confidence, *The administrator has the primary responsibility to institute personnel policies and practices which will provide working conditions under which staff members can be well informed about objectives, exercise their competence with reasonable freedom, have a share in planning, take pride in their work, and feel that their efforts are recognized and appreciated.*

In this volume, the author presents a philosophy and a range of sound practices called for by the needs of a good personnel program, rather than by the usual course of indiscriminately including current practices. While the working administrator may not agree with the author in every instance as to what is best practice, the book should stimulate profitable review and reappraisal of personnel policy and practice.

This book has the potential to fulfill a very real need of those who teach in the field of educational administration and of active and prospective school administrators.

Forrest E. Conner
Executive Secretary
American Association of School Administrators
Washington, D.C.

. Preface

THIS BOOK, *School Personnel Administration,* is not in-fallible. It does not provide *the* answers to the major questions pertaining to personnel administration. Its contents will prove in some instances readily acceptable, in some controversial, and in others not at all acceptable. Its purpose is not to serve as a Bible for personnel administration. Its purpose is to extend perspective; to stimulate thinking about personnel problems, practices, and need for evidence upon which to base innovations; and to promote consideration of the functions and functioning of a personnel division along orthodox and not so orthodox lines.

To the extent that the reader finds himself thoughtfully agreeing with, questioning, and disagreeing with the contents of this book as he progresses through it, the work that has gone into producing the text is justified. The book is intended to serve as a catalyst and as a point of departure.

It is expected that, after reading and perhaps even studying the contents of this book, some will find themselves entertaining ideas that have not formerly occurred to them; some will find in it support for their own ideas and a stimulus to experiment with them; and some will be able to say that, being conversant with the book, they have nevertheless charted a course quite different from any intimated in it. Each of these possible outcomes, if it is the product of thoughtfully reflective reading and subsequent investigation, represents the achievement of the objective for writing this book.

School Personnel Administration brings into focus, for the purpose of improving education through the administration of personnel, the practices and findings of private enterprise, government, and the schools. The thesis held is that the field of education may be spared the lag of undergoing the experiences of industry and government by making them vicariously its own and by capitalizing upon them.

Personnel administration is regarded as an activity that has a common base, irrespective of the area of operation—private enterprise, government, or the schools—in which it is applied, although adaptations will often have to be made in accordance with the specific area of operation and its peculiar problems.

Sixteen years of teaching, revising, and supplementing a graduate level course taught at the Universities of Michigan, Iowa, and Maryland, have gone into the production of *School Personnel Administration.* Credit for the book is shared with the many whose works are cited throughout the text; the successive groups of experienced teachers and school administrators who made up the graduate school classes in the personnel administration course; the Esso Standard Oil Company for liberal authorization to make use of materials included in its edition (no longer available) of *Incentives in Industry;* Harold L. Alderton, Assistant Principal in charge of Instruction in Montgomery County, Maryland, for his survey of application forms used by school systems; Fabian A. Meier, President of La Sierra College in La Sierra, California, for his intensive review of teacher recruitment practices; Superintendent Samuel Miller Brownell, Robert E. LeAnderson (Assistant Superintendent for Personnel), Albert Schiff (Director for Personnel), and Adelaine Callery (Personnel Assistant of Detroit, Michigan, for making available for inclusion in the text a set of the personnel forms in use in the Detroit public school system; Superintendents Harold S. Chambers of Forest Hills, Michigan, Howard D. Crull of Port Huron, Michigan, Clarence E. Hinchey of Montclair, New Jersey, and Edmund H. Thorne of West Hartford, Connecticut, for useful information pertaining to their professional experiences; Dean Vernon E. Anderson and Professors J. Paul Anderson, Kenneth O. Hovet, Clarence A. Newell, and Gladys A. Wiggin of the University of Maryland, Malcolm B. Rogers of the University of Connecticut, and Winston L. Roesch of the Northern Illinois University for the professional impact of their ideas; J. Edward Andrews, Administrative Assistant to the Superintendent, Montgomery County, Maryland, for technical editing of the manuscript and for bibliographical assistance; and Ellen S. Lee for the accurate preparation of the manuscript. The responsibility for shortcomings is wholly mine.

James A. van Zwoll

. Contents

. Tables

.1.

The Personnel Activity

WHENEVER an individual is in some kind of association with another the problem of human relations is posed. When the relationship of individuals is one of employer and employee the personnel factor complicates the problem of human relations.

Employer-employee relations are present in industry, government, and education. They constitute an important facet of human relations which deserves to be explored in order that an organization may be given a better chance to attain the objectives that brought it into being and justify its continuance.

The thrust of this chapter, and of the book, will be on personnel in the schools. This thrust will be supported by analogies to governmental and industrial practice. The activities relating to employer-employee relations are dealt with under the caption of *personnel administration.*

PERSONNEL ADMINISTRATION DEFINED

The definition of personnel administration at its present stage of development is derived from the evolution caused by the impact of a number of sociological and ideological forces. A brief verbal sketch of the operation of these forces will provide needed background.

Past Employer-Employee Relationships

Each may draw upon his own recollections of history to provide some perspective of the evolution in employer-employee relations. These recollections are stirred into reality by the silently eloquent monuments to ancient Egyptian achievement, the pyramids constructed under harsh management and with slave labor.

1

All have read of feudal systems in which men were bound to the land, attaining through this kind of bondage some degree of rights beyond those of slaves. The development of craft guilds added to the esteem in which manual work came to be regarded and extended further the labor relations of apprentices, journeymen, and master craftsmen. Later, toward the end of the 1400's and the beginning of the 1500's, yeomen and journeymen guilds were organized to protect workers from exploitation by master craftsmen employers. These guilds were the forerunners of today's unions.

The development of an economy in which money became the medium for exchange—a departure from the barter of goods and services—led to the birth of capitalism in the early 1700's. Under this system further change in employer-employee relations had to take place. Man came to be regarded as having the right to employ his talents in whatever manner he chose.[1] Change in conditions, theory, and practice resulted in continued evolution growing out of adjustments, abuses, pressures, and enlightened thinking.

The recentness of the changes in employer-employee relations is emphasized in the United States by the slavery which was not wiped out until a civil war was fought (1861–65), the violent conflicts between organized capital and organized labor (1890–1914 and subsequently), and for that matter, the continued struggle for supremacy between management and labor. In lands beyond the borders of the "Free World" labor continues to be exploited while the only change in management seems to be in who constitutes the group rather than the relationships which they endorse. Thus in the world of today there are still examples of monumental effort and achievement, reminiscent of ancient Egypt's, in which the individual is held in light regard.

Under the circumstances recalled, it is not surprising to note that thought and practice in the school employment situation approximated that in industrial employment. Hence there was an autocracy in school operation that came to be seriously challenged only as recently as the mid-thirties.[2] Consequently there is still much groping in an effort to

[1] Adam Smith, *An Inquiry into the Nature and Causes of the Wealth of Nations,* J. Shield Nicholson, ed., New York, Thomas Nelson & Sons, 1887, p. 286.

[2] Among the earlier writers to deal specifically with the issue of democracy in school administration are the following:

Oliver H. Bimson, *Participation of School Personnel in School Administration* (Lincoln, Nebraska, O. H. Bimson, 1939).

John J. Cohen and Robert M. W. Travers, eds., *Educating for Democracy* (London, Macmillan & Co., 1939).

Stuart A. Courtis, "Getting Cooperation," *The Nation's Schools,* 21:3:35–36, March, 1938.

Department of Elementary School Principals, Michigan Education Association, "Democratic Participation in Administration," *Eighth Yearbook,* 1935.

Department of Supervisors and Directors of Instruction, "Cooperation: Principles and Practices," *Eleventh Yearbook,* National Education Association, Washington, 1939.

recast relationships that are felt to be not quite right. The understanding of what the relationships ought to be has been demonstrated only too infrequently. The result is often well-intentioned but at least temporarily disruptive change in employment relationships within the school system.

The Definition

Personnel administration is the complex of specific activities distinctly engaged in by the employing agency (school district, other unit of government, or business enterprise) to make a pointed effort to secure the greatest possible worker effectiveness consistent with the agency's objectives. This complex is that part of the total administration—comprising planning, organizing, staffing, directing, coordinating, reporting, and budgeting[3]—which concerns itself primarily with various aspects of staffing problems.

Concern with the problems of staffing has brought about realization that the greatest worker effectiveness is possible only when the worker sees his job as a means and an opportunity for him to achieve his own objectives for himself. Personnel administration is first of all an activity organized and intended to facilitate the attainment of the objectives of the employing agency. Nevertheless in its operation personnel administration places the attainment of the employee's objectives for himself on a plane practically coordinate with that of gaining the goals of the employing agency.[4] The objectives of the employing agency and those of the employee have come to be regarded as being so interrelated that they must be considered to be together and equally within the province of the personnel administration activity.

NEED FOR PERSONNEL ADMINISTRATION

Problems of personnel administration are somewhat proportionate to the size and complexity of the organization. In a school district in which the entire school system consists of a single one-room elementary school with but one employee, the personnel problem is minimal and can generally be solved informally by the board members as the employing agents and the teacher as the one employee.

Even the slight growth from a one-room to a two-room school brings

[3] L. Urwick, "Notes on the Theory of Organization," *Papers on the Science of Administration,* Luther Gulick and L. Urwick, eds. (New York, Institute of Public Administration, 1937), p. 13.

[4] For an example of a definition placing the objectives of the employer and employee on a virtually coordinate basis see Michael J. Jucius, *Personnel Management* (Chicago, Richard D. Irwin, Inc., 1948), p. 7.

with it new problems. Which of the two teachers will be the head teacher? Will it be the one who teaches the upper grades or the one who has been employed in that district the longer? What are the relationships of these teachers to be to each other as colleagues and as head teacher and teacher? What are to be the relationships of each to the board?

It is only a short step to the larger and more complex school organizations which are resulting from the growth of cities and from the reorganization of school districts. In each instance the trend is toward school systems with a number of elementary schools, one or more secondary schools, and often one or more community or junior colleges.

Increase in the size of a school district requires a correspondingly large and complex organization. One evidence of the complexity accompanying growth is the specialization of the personnel. Instead of the one job of "teacher" there are now many different school jobs calling for certifiability as a teacher and also many others for which it is not necessary to be certifiable as a teacher.

In addition to the complexity in the employee situation there is that of the extension of the demands placed upon the schools by the community and groups within the community.

The objectives of the school district are in constant flux and the personnel have become both numerous and varied in terms of a wide range of specialities. Hence the formerly simple problem of personnel administration which lent itself to informal solution in the one-room school situation has assumed proportions which would defy control except for the development of new means for meeting the problems of the changed circumstances.

Objectives of Personnel Administration

Although personnel administration has been credited with having a multiplicity of objectives, all of them are summed up in the one objective of doing whatever is necessary to make certain that all who work within and for an organization have the competency, the will, and the working conditions necessary to doing best the task for which the organization exists.

The objective of school personnel administration is to do whatever is necessary to make certain that all school employees have the competencies needed for their respective jobs, the will to use their abilities in optimum fashion, and the working conditions under which each can exercise and improve his competency in such a way that the educational job of the schools will be done with utmost effectiveness.

Principles of Personnel Administration

Underlying the concept and the practice of school personnel administration are the principles which constitute the basis upon which the personnel activity is founded. These principles may be expressed in terms of the twelve statements that follow:

1. Education is the primary purpose of the schools. The good will and cooperation of all school employees must be secured if the optimum education is to take place. Such good will and cooperation are the byproducts of employment in which working is a gratifying social experience as well as a means for making a livelihood.

2. The objectives of the schools are functionally derived from the people who have created them as institutions to meet those needs that they want fulfilled through formal education. Personnel policies must therefore be consistent with all other policies governing the operation of the educative enterprise in accord with its objectives.

3. The people who have instituted the schools and all employees within the school system have the same basic interest. This interest is the provision of the best education possible, consistent with the clearness of the people's mandate in this regard and the means made available for doing the job.

4. Maximum effectiveness of the means for achieving the people's mandates regarding education requires the best possible selection and coordination of all elements comprising those means. The means are comprised of school employees, plant, and supplies. It is the job of personnel administration to assure the optimum in the selection, assignment in terms of job, physical placement, and equipment of personnel.

5. School employees are not commodities. In the sale of a commodity the seller is divorced in the process from the product sold. Personal services remain integral to the seller, who is termed an employee. Thus all the personal considerations of the employee are part of the problem of personnel administration to the extent that they have implications for the work he does.

6. Employees have a private life and a right to the privacy of their own affairs. Invasion of this privacy, no matter how well-intentioned, can be an exasperating irritant which does harm rather than good. It is necessary to tread cautiously in the personal matters of employees even though they may seem to have implications for worker effectiveness. It is virtually impossible to help a worker who is unwilling to confide and to receive aid.

7. The human factor is a variable. The variability is potentially an asset. It is also the cause for many of the most complex and perplexing problems in personnel administration. Temptations to make concessions to the administrative expediency of promoting conformity must be shunned in favor of recognizing and promoting the unique individuality and consequent possible personal development of each within the school system.

8. The most important single factor in getting the best that a school employee has to offer is how he feels about his work, his associates on the job, and the school system in which he is employed. Without negating in any degree the importance of other factors, this emotional factor nevertheless stands

out in bold relief. It has implications for assuring appreciation of, recognition for, and a share in planning by each employee. Everyone has the need to regard his work as worthwhile and to take pride in it if he is to work at his best.

9. Esteem for the intelligence and potential of the employee group is a basic necessity and may be demonstrated by the employer group through acts of confidence. Among such acts are the provision for a continuous flow of significant information, open lines of communication, and the joint employer-employee deliberation by which a sound working basis of understanding and mutual confidence is established.

10. Employee problems have to be dealt with in terms of the situation or the conditions at hand. At the same time the continued study of the causes of personnel problems will provide, in instances, a clue to the circumstances under which some problems may be avoided or solved. The flexibility of approach, the collection and appraisal of data, and the development and application of the necessary measures to make more readily attainable the objectives of the schools as instituted are the essence of the personnel activity.

11. All participants in an enterprise are entitled to fair dealing. Unfairness and the appearance of injustice are causes of rankling resentment which is a threat to worker effectiveness. Fairness has implications for monetary rewards, work load, the working period, various conditions that are concomitant or auxiliary to the job, and virtually every other element making up the total working situation.

12. The relationships among employees and between them and their employers can to a large extent be summed up. This summing up should be expressed in written policy. Written policy is a means for assuring consistency, promoting a feeling of security, and avoiding pitfalls of expediency.

THE JOB OF PERSONNEL ADMINISTRATION

The job of personnel administration has been suggested by the definition provided, the objectives indicated, and the principles adduced. In essence this job is one of compensating through organization in the complex situation for the loss of the interpersonal relationships which were a major asset of the relatively simple, small school system. These close personal relationships are sacrificed in favor of other advantages offered through bigness. The personnel director and his staff are the organization through which some of the penalties of size are offset and some of the values of smallness are salvaged.

The Problem of Personnel Administration

Probably the chief problem of school personnel administration is to make and keep clear the concept of personnel as employees who make a contribution to the carrying out of policies through which the educational program is to be made effective. The job of carrying out policies is an executive one. In this sense all school employees are part of the executive function and each is, in his own job, just as important as any other employee. The failure of anyone in his job would curtail the effectiveness with which the educational program could operate.

When all employees are thought of as having relatively the same importance in the executive activity there is an implication for an appreciation of one another, for mutual respect, and for the spirit in which all employees will work together. In the larger school districts, however, it is easy to find a schism between those who think of themselves as belonging to the administrative group and those who belong to the classroom teacher group. Similarly, only too often the teacher does not think of the janitor—by whatever title he may be known—as a coworker. The janitor is thought of as a cleanup man, a broompusher.

Probably one of the major problems of school personnel administration is that of working with all personnel—administrative, supervisory, teaching, clerical, janitorial, and all others—to bring about recognition of their associate status in doing their respective parts to make the schools genuinely effective. Stated in other terms, the problem of school personnel administration is to help each one to see himself in his true relationship to the specific job he is doing and to the over-all job of the school system.

The Functions of School Personnel Administration

The specific functions of school personnel administration are derived from the objectives, principles, and problems of school personnel administration. The functions are to:

1. gain and keep the good will of all employees in order to obtain their spontaneous and readily proffered cooperation.

2. reflect in all personnel relationships the way of life of the nation and of the school district.

3. ascertain just what the respective educational jobs are in terms of the expectations of the people and the school system.

4. identify, describe, and classify the respective school jobs in terms of their purposes, the knowledge and skill demanded for each, and the qualifications that the prospective employee must have to do well the work required of him.

5. build a reserve or pool of potential employees through the establishment of a recruitment program designed to make available the caliber of employees needed.

6. select from all available sources the best of the *competent* individuals in terms of specific job requirements.

7. assign those selected for employment so as to make maximum and optimum use of the competencies for which they were hired.

8. take the necessary measures to match the competent employee to the work space (e.g., classroom), equipment, and supplies which will be conducive to maximum effectiveness.

9. show tactful interest in each employee in order to promote the understanding and confidence which must be present if he is to seek and welcome counsel, and aid in problems that have implications for how well he does his job.

10. exercise circumspection to differentiate between those problems in which the employee will accept help and those which he regards as solely his business.

11. stimulate each to develop his potentialities so that the school system may capitalize upon the diversity of individuality.

12. shun assiduously any actions that would be conducive to a monotonous conformity which would repress individual differences and inhibit enterprising deviation in word and action.

13. use appreciation of work done, recognition for the worker to the degree warranted, and the flattery of sincere involvement of the employee in the problems of operating the school system—all in order to get him to sense and recognize the worth of his work and to kindle pride in doing a top job.

14. discover both what information is desired by the employee and what he ought to have in addition, then provide both freely.

15. insure lines of communication which are open upwards, downwards, and sideways, with safeguards in case some channel becomes blocked.

16. engender among employees a warranted conviction that the lines of communication are for their use, that use of them is urged and welcome, and that their use carries with it no threat of penalty or prejudice.

17. gather case data from which to ascertain the kinds of problems there are, what their causes seem to be, and what solutions are suggested in the way of preventive or corrective measures.

18. have the flexibility to devise and use whatever means are called for to meet the problem rather than to fall back on cliches and pat formulas which may be gratifying to the user while helping not at all in solving the problem at hand.

19. take the necessary measures progressively to establish fairness in all employment relations and conditions, eliminating even the appearance of injustice.

20. regard and use the occurrence of each vacancy as a golden opportunity to reappraise the job in terms of its specifics and its relationships within the organization of the school system. This appraisal is made in order to assure the employment of competent personnel on the most functionally defensible basis possible rather than in terms of possible unplanned perpetuation of some current or past status.

21. develop an initially tentative written set of personnel policies which will be modified, deleted from, or added to in the light of experience and as a cooperative personnel and personnel administration project.

THE DEVELOPMENT OF SCHOOL PERSONNEL ADMINISTRATION

School personnel administration has developed in various ways beginning with the exercise of the hiring-firing activities, and all that went on between, by the board of education itself. In some instances a personnel committee of the board of education has served administratively in matters of personnel administration. As the superintendency developed in terms of increasing professional competency, the executive activity became the superintendent's province. Thus today personnel administration is part of the superintendent's duty.

In the smaller school districts the major part of the personnel administrative job is done in its initial and final phases by the superintendent himself. The in-between phases are administered through various other personnel including assistant superintendents, supervisors, principals, department heads, and other school employees.

In recent years even the interviewing, on the basis of which recommendations for employment were made, which once was the exclusive province of the superintendent has become a partnership enterprise. The superintendent obtains the assistance of supervisors, principals, and sometimes teachers or committees of teachers to assist him in screening candidates for a job.

At various times, different school systems have recognized the need for an individual who would devote his major efforts to the problems of personnel administration in the larger and more complex school districts. This did not mean that these personnel directors became solely responsible for personnel administration. Rather, the personnel director relieved the superintendent of the immediate duties attendant upon personnel administration and became a staff officer in the superintendent's central office organization. Thus, as early as 1914, there was an Assistant Superintendent in Charge of Personnel in the Detroit, Michigan, public school system. This office was later changed to Director of Personnel and subsequently back to its original designation.

Scope of the Personnel Administration Activity

The personnel administration activity has an extremely broad field of operation. It has the job of coordinating individuals, jobs, place of work, time of work, and the equipment and supplies for working. This job of coordinating is already an enormous task. Nevertheless, the scope of the personnel activity is broader still. The personnel activity is immediately concerned also with those problems of the employees which have implications for how well they do their work. This may bring the personnel officer into the otherwise personal problems of employees, leaving virtually no bar to or limitations upon the kinds of problems in which he will become involved except that of the employee's unwillingness to make a confidant of the personnel officer.

It may well be that overzealous personnel officers have made employees' business their business to such an extent that well-intentioned efforts to be helpful have come to be regarded as meddling and invasion of privacy. This reaction on the part of the employee serves to limit the scope of the personnel activity. Other limitations are determined by a combination of (1) the nature of the problem, (2) school policies, and (3) the ability of the organization to do something about the problem.

PHILOSOPHY OF SCHOOL PERSONNEL ADMINISTRATION

The philosophy of school personnel administration is first of all identified with the philosophy of the way of life of the society served by the school. Thus in the United States the philosophy underlying the founding, development, and operation of the democratic society is basic also to the administration of school personnel. In addition, school personnel administration is the product of an outright pragmatic philosophy, a philosophy concerned with what works in producing desired outcomes.

Once understood these two philosophies can be harnessed effectively and harmoniously.

The Democratic Philosophy

In the United States the school is an agency created by the people of a democratic society to conserve and transmit the cultural heritage and to generate conditions conducive to that change which is thought of as progress or improvement.

Corollary to the concept of an agency of a democratic society is that of democratic organization and operation within that agency to the fullest extent possible. Conceptually the only limitations upon democratic functioning within the school system will be those imposed by the society through the organization which it has provided to further its objectives. The democratic society does operate in terms of authority, the authority of the adult citizenry expressed through their constitutions, laws, the policies of their boards of education, and their use of the referendum.

Basic to the democratic philosophy is the conviction that the individual has worth, that he is endowed with dignity and that both merit recognition.

The way in which an institution of a democratic society is expected to function in order to assure the perpetuation and further evolution of that kind of society, together with the value placed upon the individual and the consequent esteem in which he is to be held in this society, provides a logical foundation for school personnel administration.

The Pragmatic Philosophy

At this time there is agreement among those who have made a study of personnel administration that such factors as worry, ill health, poor working conditions, personal problems that intrude themselves on the job, low pay, lack of a voice in policy determination, injustice, insecurity, failure to realize in his work one's objectives for himself, a feeling of being like just one more ant in an anthill, and lack of sufficient motivation can singly or in some combination contribute to inefficiency on the job.

The obvious antidote to inefficiency is to identify its causes and to offset them in order to secure the desired outcomes most effectively. It becomes apparent that to look after the welfare of the individual and to give him the recognition that he needs is not merely nice, humanitarian, or even democratic; it is also good business because of the increased instructional output which is the immediate dividend paid upon the capital investment of a practically based school personnel policy and its administration.

ESSENTIALS IN SCHOOL PERSONNEL ADMINISTRATION

The need for, problems and functions of, and the philosophy underlying school personnel administration point up those activities which are minimum essentials to providing and promoting the optimum instructional-learning situation. These essentials are to:

1. do what is necessary to recruit a manpower pool of competent individuals from which to select needed employees.
2. employ competent individuals to do the various school jobs that have to be done.
3. take the necessary steps to retain the competent people employed in the school system and to release them from whatever deterrents there are to their effective functioning in the teaching-learning situation.
4. provide for improvement in the competency of each worker.
5. arrange for working conditions in which each is free to use his competencies most effectively and is stimulated to do so.

POLICIES FOR SCHOOL PERSONNEL ADMINISTRATION

Personnel administration within the schools can approach attainment of its objectives and operation in terms of its functions and philosophy most certainly through a carefully charted course of policies.

The Nature and Function of Policy

Just as road maps are necessary to permit the traveler to lay out his route in order to arrive at his destination by a plan that best suits him, so also is a statement of policies necessary as a guide to the decisions to be made and the measures to be taken in meeting the problems of school personnel administration. Also, just as detours are on occasion necessary to the traveler or some heretofore unperceived attraction makes a change of route desirable, so too, unforeseen difficulties and unique facets to the specific problems of personnel administration demand that deviation from policy can be made when necessary and that policy itself may be modified. Policy is to be regarded as a guide, not as a straitjacket.

The general consistency which policy introduces into the administration of personnel is probably one of the most important of the ingredients contributing to the feeling among employees that whatever is done takes place fairly.

Who Formulates Policy

Whereas the need for policy is the product of people and circumstances, the policies themselves are formulated by various individuals and groups. Policies governing the board of education, both endowing it with authority on the one hand and limiting it on the other, come in one way or another from the people. Policies are further formulated by the board of education to govern its actions and to give direction to the actions of its executive agents, including the superintendent of schools and all other employees who carry into effect board policies.

School administrators on each level formulate policy by which they are governed in their school-related activities. Similarly, within the classroom, the teacher operates in accord with policies formulated by him.

In each of the foregoing instances, direction to the policy formulation may well have been provided by others than the actual formulating or approving body or agent.

How Policy Is Formulated

It has become axiomatic that those who are affected by a policy ought to have a voice in policy determination.

In a newly organized school district, it is conceivable that the past experience of and information obtained from comparable school districts will provide the basis for a statement of policy. In a school district which has its traditions, the informally accepted way of doing things may become formalized into a statement of policy. In each of these instances, the policies may best be regarded as tentative, a point of departure, or a trial set of guides. Ultimately it may be expected that these policies will be modified in terms of experience and the appraisal to which they are subjected.

Appraisal of personnel policies is a function that may take place throughout the organization, involving all employees, administrators, the board of education, and finally in its broader aspects the people of the school district. The extent of involvement will vary with the specific policy under consideration.

Realistic personnel administration will capitalize upon the appraisals that are taking place by creating opportunities for making them known and for making suggestions or recommendations for improvement. In this way all personnel may become involved in the process of policy evolvement or formulation, an ongoing and never completed activity. In this way also, those in the line of authority are made aware of the issues with which the front-line employees, teachers and nonteaching workers, are confronted and of the means by which they envision meeting those issues.

Policy formulation is most functionally a cooperative activity. The formulation should, however, not be confused with approval or authorization of policy. There are areas of policy determination in which majority rule can and should set policy. There are also areas of policy determination in which policy is cooperatively developed, and possibly recommended in terms of a majority proposal, but approval must come from a source of authority.

Whom and What Policy Governs

Subject to the policies governing the entire school system, school personnel policies govern to some degree every organizational division of personnel, including central office administrators and their immediate staff, division superintendencies or principalships responsible for a subdivision of a large school system, principals, all other employees who are members of the teaching profession, professional employees who are members of professions other than that of teaching, and a host of nonprofessional employees of various categories.

Among the specifics governed by personnel policy will be:

recruitment	demotion
employee qualifications	dismissal
selection	pay
hiring	tenure
assignment	health
orientation	safety
supervision	working conditions
inservice training	awards of recognition
rating	fringe benefit service
transfer	leaves of absence
promotion	retirement

Measures of a Satisfactory Personnel Policy

All school personnel policies must first of all be defensible because of the contribution they make to the facilitation of the teaching-learning situation. Subject to this, the criteria for each policy may well be that it:

1. relates closely to the objectives, principles, and functions of school personnel administration.

2. is so simply and clearly expressed that misunderstanding is virtually impossible.

3. has been formulated in terms of problems which are of the same general nature and which recur often enough to warrant a specific policy statement.

4. is facilitative to the solving of problems, not restrictive of their solution. Policy must be a guide in situations to which it applies, not a straitjacket in special situations not intended to be covered by the policy and to which the policy does not apply.

5. is kept uptodate through progressive necessary modification and is kept before those for whom it has significance through certain, positive, and effective means. Ordinarily policy should be readily available in written form and it should be specifically referred to whenever it is invoked.

METHODS OF PERSONNEL ADMINISTRATION

In every situation in which there is an employer and an employee, or where there are multiple workers, some kind of personnel administration is operative. The personnel administration may be unplanned, expediential, and unorganized or it may be the converse of these. It may be autocratic in spirit and essence or it may be democratic. It may be centralized or it may be decentralized or diffused.

Informally vs. Formally Organized Personnel Administration

School districts with an autocratic administration centered about one man are likely to have a capricious, inconsistent, opportunistic, and highly subjective approach to the problems of personnel. As the interest of the school administrator is roused to the potentialities of personnel administration, the probability is that a planned approach to the problems of personnel will take place.

In the small school district, the job of personnel administration devolves upon the superintendent. His conscious appreciation of and application to the problem posed will take the direction of an effectively organized personnel activity. In the large school district, some evidence of the planned approach will be the assignment of responsibility for personnel administration to a specialist who will have a title such as assistant superintendent in charge of personnel or director of personnel.

Under haphazard, or informal, personnel administration, policy may be nonexistent, probably unwritten, and generally uncommunicated. Conversely, one evidence of organization of the personnel activity is the formalization, development, and clear enunciation of policy and a general familiarity of all concerned with that policy.

Autocratic vs. Democratic Personnel Administration

Personnel administration that is imposed through authority from above and in which employees have no real or effective voice whatever is thought of as autocratic. Such personnel administration is termed paternalistic when it stresses the interests and welfare of the employee.

Autocracy in personnel administration may be either frankly out in the open or it may be carefully disguised by a skillfully devised façade or window dressing of activities and operational techniques identified as democratic. Only critically analytic observation and deduction which succeeds in identifying the spirit permeating the administration can determine in the latter case whether it is autocratic or democratic.

Democracy in personnel administration is a matter of the pervading and underlying spirit rather than of outward form. Of the many kinds of evidence pointing toward true democracy in personnel administration, probably the one which is by itself the most conclusive is the existence of open lines of communication which are used in all directions without fear or threat of prejudice or penalty. Lacking this evidence, all other indicators of democracy in administration are meaningless. Supported by this evidence, all other indicators become meaningful inasmuch as they tend to confirm an operative democratic administration.

One of the other indicators of democratic personnel administration will be found in the involvement of personnel in appraising and modifying policy. This involvement will take place in various ways; informally, through committee organization, or both as the case may be. Another indicator will be the subordination of the administrative will or preference to that of the group without subterfuge or the invocation of higher authority in all such matters as may legitimately be left to the group. A third indicator will be that there is true regard for the individual and individuality.

Centralized vs. Decentralized Personnel Administration

Personnel administration, whether autocratic or democratic, may be organized in such a way as to be administered under the immediate direction of the specialist in charge of personnel. Or, it may be organized in such a way that the director of personnel relies on administrative and supervisory personnel, as well as others on occasion, throughout the school system to assume some responsibility for the administration of personnel in one or more of its aspects.

In the first instance, personnel administration is centralized about one person and his office; in the second, it is diffused or decentralized so that the personnel administrator becomes a coordinator and his office a clearing house for the administration of personnel.

The nature of the school system throughout the United States, the way in which schools are organized and administered, the professionalization of teaching personnel, the general competency of the school personnel, and the stimulus of all these in a democratically oriented society toward a democratization of school administration in general—all of these factors contribute to the conclusion that functionalization of the personnel administration activity practically demands a decentralized approach. In this approach the various personnel assume appropriate responsibility for personnel administration in terms of the situation and of the opportunity it affords them to assist in solving specific personnel problems in accord with their special abilities.

SUMMARY

Personnel administration is regarded as a special facet of human relations. It is directed toward getting the most efficient service possible for the attainment of the objectives of the organization within which employer-employee relations exist. Subordinate to securing efficient service but corollary to it is a concern for the employee as an individual with aspirations and problems which have implications for his effectiveness as an employee and which for that reason deserve consideration.

The need for a formalized personnel activity is accentuated by the size of the organization and by the extension of the demands made upon the school system. Its objectives are summed up in terms of matching competent and willing workers to the jobs to be done and of promoting working conditions in which the exercise and improvement of competency are furthered. The principles upon which the activity is based are identified with the nature of the school within the democratic society, the differentiating nature of employee services as contrasted to commodities, the variability of human beings, psychological considerations, and the essentiality of well-defined policies.

The job of personnel administration is basically one of providing through organization a substitute for the close personal relationships existing in the small school system, of developing and maintaining perspective about both the functions of the school system and the part which each job and jobholder has relative to those functions, and to develop the specific functions which represent its particular concerns.

Evolved out of the needs of organization, school personnel administration was a recognized activity early in the twentieth century. An activity of wide scope, personnel administration coordinates all factors within the school system for the promotion of effective service and extends into the sensitive area of the personal lives of school employees.

Identification with the democratic society and way of life provides school personnel administration with a basis in the philosophy of democracy. It has in addition a philosophy based on what works. Policies are seen as road maps, or guides, which provide a framework within which personnel administration ordinarily operates. The policies are formulated throughout the various levels of school operation within the community. Policy formulation is functionally a two-way operation involving all who have an interest. Every organizational division and a series of specific activities are governed by policies.

Informal personnel organization contrasts with formal in terms of appreciation of the potentialities of personnel administration and the status of policy. The existence of open lines of communication which operate effectively in three directions is considered to be an outstanding single criterion of democracy in the administration of personnel. Whether formal or informal, the personnel activity in the public school system practically demands expression through decentralization of the activities associated with personnel administration.

SELECTED READINGS

ARGYRIS, Chris, *Personality and Organization—The Conflict between System and the Individual* (New York, Harper & Row, 1957), Chapter 3.

CUBBERLEY, Ellwood P., *Public School Administration* (Boston, Houghton Mifflin Company, 1916), Chapters 14, 15.

ELSBREE, Willard S. and REUTTER, Edmund E., *Principles of Staff Personnel Administration in Public Schools* (New York, Teachers College, Columbia University, Bureau of Publications, 1959), Chapters 1, 3.

FAKHRY, Ahmed, *The Pyramids* (Chicago, University of Chicago Press, 1961), Chapter 2.

KNEZEVICH, Stephen J., *Administration of Public Education* (New York, Harper & Row, 1962), Chapter 12.

MERRIHUE, Willard V., *Managing by Communication* (New York, McGraw-Hill Book Company, Inc., 1960), Chapters 1–3.

MORPHET, Edgar L., JOHNS, Roe L., and RELLER, Theodore L., *Educational Administration: Concepts, Practices, and Issues* (Englewood Cliffs, N.J., Prentice-Hall, Inc., 1959), Chapter 16.

SIMON, Herbert A., *Administrative Behavior* (New York, The Macmillan Company, 1957), Chapters 8, 10.

TEAD, Ordway, *Administration: Its Purpose and Performance* (New York, Harper & Row, 1959).

WELLS, Harry K., *Pragmatism: Philosophy of Imperialism* (New York, International Publishers, 1954), Chapters 1, 2.

.2.

Organization for Personnel Administration

THE NATURE of the personnel activity suggests somewhat the form it will take in organization. The organization of the personnel activity will be examined in terms of the following major subtitles: (1) the place and function of the personnel administrator, (2) the personnel division, and (3) some major considerations for personnel administration in terms of the development of efficient service.

THE PERSONNEL ADMINISTRATOR

The administrator of personnel is the one who, whether or not he is a trained specialist, has the responsibility for initiation and development in the area of personnel policies and for guidance and supervision in executing those policies. This responsibility grows out of his place in the total organizational structure of the school system and the particular functions of his office.

The Place and Function of the Personnel Administrator

In his capacity as personnel administrator, the personnel officer—superintendent, assistant superintendent in charge of personnel, the personnel director, or anyone holding the office regardless of the title by which he is designated—is in fact a part of the administrative team. Yet his work places him in the role of spokesman on the one hand for the administration and on the other for the employee.

The strength of the personnel administrator lies in his ability to identify himself realistically both with the management team and with those who hold subordinate jobs. The management team may be thought of as consisting of the superintendent; divisional superintendents, and others of the central office staff of deputy, associate, and assistant superintendents; the directors of various activities; the supervisors; the principals; and the department heads. Those holding the subordinate jobs include teachers and the host of others holding jobs which do not require certifiability for teaching (see Chapter 3). These jobs range from the professional, e.g., the lawyer retained by the board of education or the school doctor, to the semi-skilled, e.g., the custodian and the general handyman. Included in the subordinate jobs are also those of the clerical, custodial, food handling and preparational, health, maintenance, secretarial, and transportation personnel.

It will be difficult for the personnel administrator to identify himself equally with the management team and the subordinate employees. He is under considerable pressure, psychological if none other, to be oriented in the direction of the superintendent's office and to fall in line with the desire of that office to command the services and to direct the activities of the entire school system, including those of the personnel division.

Nevertheless, to be truly functional the administrator of personnel needs freedom from the bias of and the pressure for subservience to all pressure groups within the school system—whether the group be management or an association of employees. He must be free to seek information, discover facts, report findings, and make recommendations in terms of his own freewheeling relationships and point of view. His contribution to the functioning of the school system depends on his being in the position to furnish the clearest and most unbiased account and estimate of the personnel situation as he sees it. Deprived of such freedoms, the personnel officer is severely limited in the confidence he can generate, the contribution he can make, and the status he can hope to attain for his office and himself.

The place and the job of the personnel administrator is that of a clinician. Pfiffner [1] holds that it is the clinical approach to personnel administration that is most proper. This means that the school personnel administrator is in a position analogous to that of a doctor. Where the doctor attends to the needs of his patient until the patient is cured or dead, so also the personnel officer must attend to the needs of employees and of the organization until those needs have been met. In both instances experimentation is employed in an effort to alleviate ills for which remedies may not yet exist. The analogy to the death of the patient finds its corollary in the possible resignation of an employee or the

[1] John M. Pfiffner, *The Supervision of Personnel* (Englewood Cliffs, N.J., Prentice-Hall, Inc., 1951), p. 307.

demise of the organization which refuses to make reasonable adjustments. In the school system such demise is expressed through a drastic conflict situation within the school district and often through the replacement of the chief executive officer. It takes a long time to repair the damage done and to heal scars caused by inflexibility toward warranted change.

Examination of the place of the personnel officer suggests that a school system which is large enough to warrant it ought to engage a personnel administrator who has supplemented an aptitude for work in the area of human relations with the best training obtainable for working at the job of school personnel administration.

In addition to the qualifications that a personnel administrator must have, it has become evident from the nature of his job and the place it occupies functionally that the position which he holds must be one of prestige within the school system. He must have staff officer status at least equal to that of other staff officers who are specialists in such activities as the adjustive services, child accounting, curriculum, finance, instruction, plant, public relations, research, and service of supplies. Generally this means that he should have the title of assistant superintendent with the usual staff relationship that such an officer has to the superintendent and to those who are affected by his impact upon personnel policy.

Qualifications for the Personnel Officer

Qualifications which are ordinarily listed as requisite to serving as a personnel manager may be subdivided into abilities and qualities.[2] The abilities are those which have implications for directing others and working with them. The qualities are described in terms of approachableness, common sense, courage, humor, industry and resourcefulness, judgment, leadership, patience, managerial and technical skill, tact, vision, and wisdom. However, Yoder [3] expresses the reservation that generalizations about qualifications are almost entirely meaningless.

It is obvious that ability to work with people and even a liking for becoming involved in their problems does very little toward identifying who should be considered for the very specialized task of administering personnel. Throughout present day social life and especially within the schools such ability and liking would not serve selectively. Every reasonably successful teacher must have the abilities and likings suggested for the personnel officer.

The other qualities suggested are also, for the most part, so general

2 Michael J. Jucius, *Personnel Management* (Chicago, Richard D. Irwin, Inc., 1948), pp. 21, 22.
3 Dale Yoder, *Personnel Management and Industrial Relations* (Englewood Cliffs, N.J., Prentice-Hall, Inc.), 1948, p. 38.

that they are virtually what would be desired of everyone within the organization. In addition they are also qualities that do not lend themselves to ready, accurate, or reliably constant measurement. One exception may be that of the element of managerial and technical skill.

The school personnel officer may be selected from those employees who are certified for teaching, who stand out among their colleagues for their organizational and teaching ability, who have understanding of the organization and operation of the school system—gained through experience and training—and who have taken special training in the field of personnel administration and human relations so that they know both what is required of the personnel division and how to go about the job of administering personnel in the school system.

THE PERSONNEL DIVISION

Organization for the program of personnel administration is needed to provide an effective teaching-learning situation. This organization will be under the immediate direction of the personnel administrator and will be referred to here as the personnel division. In practice it may be known by some other designation.

Organization for Personnel Administration

The specific nature of the personnel division will be determined by the size of organization. It is conceivable that it might be staffed by no more than the personnel officer and a general office assistant who will serve as receptionist, secretary, typist, and filing clerk. In the larger school system it may be expected that size in the over-all organization will be reflected in a correspondingly enlarged personnel division with considerable specialization in terms of subdivisional assistant personnel officers and the supporting clerical, secretarial, and other personnel. The size and complexity of the school system will pretty much dictate the kind of personnel division needed.

In addition to the question of size and staffing of the personnel division, organization of the personnel division generally leads to consideration of line, staff, and other possible ways of functioning.

Line Organization. The organization which represents the flow of authority or the chain of command is referred to as the line organization. Thus in the school system the authority of the citizens of the school district is vested in their representatives, the board of education. The board in turn delegates one part of its authority—that of dealing with carrying out its policies—to its chief executive agent, the superintendent.

The superintendent delegates authority as necessary to such other officers as are provided to meet the needs of the school district. In the large district [4] this may involve some or all of the following: divisional superintendents with responsibility for geographical subdivisions of the school district, district superintendents subordinate to the divisional superintendent but responsible for only elementary or secondary education, building principals, teachers, and nonteaching personnel with a number of different functions.

The line organization leaves no doubt about where responsibility lies and to whom each is responsible. It implies a generalized competency on the part of the respective administrative officials which is rarely warranted and beyond reasonable expectancy. The placement of responsibility is its strength and the implication of general competency its chief weakness.

Staff Organization. This form of organization, sometimes referred to as functional organization, takes into account the inability of individuals to be highly specialized in numerous areas. It therefore makes the various specialists needed available to the operations in which their specialties are required. In its purest sense this would mean in the school system that a principal would be answerable to the superintendent, the finance man, the plant man, the personnel man, the research man, etc., in terms of the facet of the issue at stake. The teacher would find himself in much the same position with added responsibility to the principal and the supervisor.

The presence within the organization of needed specialists provides potential for doing better the work to be done. However, the resulting division of authority, even though it may follow lines of competency or specialization, leads toward the kind of confusion which demoralizes workers all along the line and thus decreases efficiency. The availability of expert direction is the strength of the functional staff form of organization. The uncertainty as to where responsibility rests is its chief fault.

Line and Staff Organization. The apparent way out of the dilemma posed by the line and the staff organizations, respectively, was to retain in the line organization the authority which characterizes it and to make the staff organization an advisory one. Thus there is no doubt as to who is in charge at the various levels of school operation and yet there is provision for extending perspective through the use of specialists who serve as advisors, particularly to the chief executive, the superintendent. Moehlman [5] suggests that these specialists with the advisory function be considered staff officers to whom the title "assistant superintendent" be reserved.

[4] Arthur B. Moehlman, *School Administration* (Boston, Houghton Mifflin Company, 1951), pp. 154–159.
[5] *Ibid.*, footnote, p. 158.

Within the staff segment of the line and staff organization, staff officers serve as the administrative heads of their divisions and have line authority within their respective divisions.

The school systems of the United States, private enterprise, and government have all come to appreciate that the line and staff organization makes clear who is in charge and yet provides for the flexibility that becomes possible when there is opportunity to capitalize upon the needed expertness provided through staff specialists.[6]

The personnel administration activity, it may be concluded, may best serve the school system when it is organized as a staff, i.e., advisory division within the total administrative organization.

Participatory Organization. Reference is made here to a form of organization that has intrigued educators for a number of years. It is the organization through which the various personnel throughout the school system are urged to make their contributions to the administration of the schools by means of suggestion systems, committee activity, and such other schemes for involving personnel as seem feasible. It seems that this has struck some as a new system or organization by which democratization of administration is approached.

When such participatory relationships are diagrammed, instead of following a line of authority as in the line and staff form of organization, they are pictured by concentric circles representing, for example, an over-all community committee and a number of subcommittees.[7] On the whole this follows very much that idea of leadership which upon analysis defines leadership as a shifting and rotating activity which devolves at any one time upon the one who at that moment is commanding attention or holding the floor.

A major premise of this form of organization seems to be that school operation is becoming so large and complex an activity that authority can no longer reside in one individual—presumably the superintendent —but must be "shared" with everyone in order to capitalize upon the abilities and ideas of all.

There can be no quarrel with the desire to organize for capitalization

[6] There are still school systems in which the staff function is not yet clearly understood and defined, resulting in a confused operation in which staff officers operate expedientially in the line of authority.

For additional discussion of the line and staff organizations see:

Walter Dill Scott, Robert C. Clothier, and William R. Spriegel, *Personnel Management,* Sixth Edition (New York, McGraw-Hill Book Company, Inc., 1961), pp. 17–21.

Lewis Meriam, *Public Personnel Problems* (Washington, The Brookings Institution, 1938), pp. 368–380.

Dale Yoder, *Personnel Principles and Policies* (Englewood Cliffs, N.J., Prentice-Hall, Inc., 1959), Ch. 5.

[7] Alfred H. Skogsberg, *Administrative Operational Patterns,* New York, Bureau of Publications, Teachers College, Columbia University, 1950, pp. 39, 40.

upon the abilities and ideas of all. And, in fact, there has been use of such abilities and ideas for as long as schools have been operating. It may be that it would be advisable to provide through organization for such capitalization rather than to rely upon individual initiative, courage, and relationships to the administration.

What must be examined is what the sphere of operation of participatory organization is to be. It would seem that, rather than calling for a completely new type of organization, this participatory organization would represent a formalization of heretofore informal advisory and cooperative relationships in order to extend these relationships to the entire staff, at least on an invitational basis, and to place on the relationships the stamp of official sanction.

The sphere of operation of participatory organization must be outside that of the necessarily delegated line of authority. Once a policy decision has been reached, it becomes incumbent upon those in the line of authority to carry that policy into effect. There can be no voting on whether or not to do what is required. Discussion can take place legitimately for clarification, and eventually to serve as a basis for making recommendations for consideration by the policy-making body. Committees may be organized to serve as study and appraising bodies to make recommendations which may possibly, but not necessarily, affect policy. Committees of this kind must be aware of the fact that their recommendations in regard to policy may be rejected wholly or in part.

There is also a sphere of operation in which there is room for committees to make decisions. It is in this area that administrators on the various levels have the opportunity to demonstrate the degree to which they are truly committed to the democratization of administration. This sphere of operation is illustrated by a situation in which the administrator has no latitude as to *what* he is to do, but does have latitude as to *how* he goes about getting the policy put into effect.

The question of *how* is often one calling for professional judgment. Perhaps much too often the administrator has relied upon his own professional judgment to answer this question when he might better have relied upon the judgment of those who are closer to doing the job. Thus, when professional competency is needed to make the decision, the teachers directly concerned might best be asked to serve as a committee to work out ways and means for doing what the policy demands. In this case the administrator has the primary task of making clear what the policy and its implications are, and the corollary responsibility to accept the decision arrived at by those who were consulted as the affected parties. It should go without saying that under these circumstances the operating agents have the responsibility to the same degree as before for appraising policy and to a greater than ever degree for judging the methods of operation.

It is incumbent upon all the administrative personnel, and particularly upon the personnel officer, that line, staff, and participatory organization be understood. The personnel officer has the obligation, among others, to promote understanding of his function and of the latitude—or lack of it—under which each may or has to operate.

Functional Relationships of the School Personnel

Functionally the classroom teacher is the key individual in the school operation. Consequent to large school system organization, some teachers have been taken out of the classroom and have been charged with responsibilities for organizational, administrative, and supervisory activities which are intended to facilitate teaching and learning. Other agents, who are not and need not be teachers, have come into the educational scene to perform other duties which support the teaching-learning activity. Most numerous of these latter are custodial and clerical personnel.

The need to hold someone responsible, as well as the benefits accruing from coordination and a degree of centralization, has led to line organization. The need to make use of specialization—e.g., in counselling, finance, instruction and curriculum, personnel, plant, public relations, record keeping, and research—has introduced the staff activity on an advisory basis. The further recognition of the competencies represented by the various personnel within the school organization, together with the increase in the complexity of the educational enterprise, has prompted the development of organization through which all personnel have the opportunity to contribute to the improved functioning of the school system in accordance with their varied abilities and within the framework of legal organization. This last development has been a stimulus toward and an outcome of a zeal for democracy in administration.

Thus the functional relationships throughout organization are currently those of authority and subordination, advisement, and cooperation. The problem for all personnel and for the personnel division is to keep clearly defined the area in which each will operate. Confusion will result if advisement is resorted to where authority ought to operate, where authority is exercised unnecessarily where advisement is more in order, where cooperation becomes a misplaced façade to create the semblance of democracy in administration when there is in fact no choice, and when no semblance of democracy in administration exists although the situation is one in which cooperation and participation could operate freely and functionally to the welfare of the educational enterprise.

Authority

Much in the atmosphere of discussion about democracy in administration smacks of rebellion against or negation of authority. It seems sometimes as if the concept of authority is considered to be paradoxical to that of democracy. Actually, careful reflection will reward the thoughtful by recalling that democracy is a form of organization for enforcing the will of the people through the authority vested in officials elected and appointed by the people or their representatives.

The source of authority for the schools is the state and the people of the school district. Through a reservation of powers not delegated to the federal government by way of the Constitution, the states have retained for themselves the education function. Through a preference for local control, most of the 50 states make rather general provision for education by way of their constitutions and somewhat more specific provisions by way of their state laws. For the rest, the states make provision in one way or another for the local school district and its agency, the board of education, to mold the schools to their own needs.

The board of education is on the one hand a state agency inasmuch as it is responsible for administering state requirements, and on the other a local agency in that it develops policies which are binding upon the school district and upon the school administration in terms of meeting local educational needs.

The superintendent is the chief executive agent of the board of education who is charged with that one of the board's functions which particularly requires professional expertness, i.e., the execution or carrying out of board policies. Since carrying policies into effect is a complex job in a large school organization, the superintendent engages a large and varied number of executive assistants, each of whom is charged with carrying out some duties through which policy will be executed. These executive agents range from professional people—some qualified and some not qualified to teach—to semiskilled and sometimes unskilled labor. The most numerous executive agents are, respectively, teachers, custodians, and clerical workers.

Within the school system the superintendent is in charge and has over-all authority and responsibility. Within the school building a similar position of authority and responsibility is held by the principal. A similar position of authority and responsibility is occupied by the teacher within the classroom.

Most questions of authority and democratization within the school system, except in the area of the classroom, seem to revolve about the problem of gaining a greater voice and freedom for the various personnel who occupy positions subordinate to that of the superintendent or principal. Here the question is one that is largely confined to the organization and that can be worked out within the organization. It is necessary in this regard that the spheres within which authority must be delegated and those in which resort may functionally be taken to consult employee groups, which have the expertness needed to make decisions, are clearly defined.

Just as democratization of administration can be reasonably worked out for the employees within a school system once the limitations or areas of latitude and permissiveness are understood in contrast to those in which authority must operate, so also can democratization of the classroom take place if the limitations are identified and kept clearly in mind by those who are going to administer the classroom. The danger is that with some vague idea about being democratic some well-intentioned teacher will ask children to make decisions in areas in which decision making is either the prerogative of the parent or of the professional expert, the teacher himself.

So, it becomes evident that the meritorious pursuit of democracy in school operation is fraught with dangers of misunderstanding about democracy itself and the limitations within which democratization must take place. It is essential that it be understood that authority can operate as a consistent component of democracy. Where authority operates inconsistently with democracy, as it sometimes does, autocracy or authoritarianism flourishes. Where there is no authority at all, a state of anarchy exists or is in the making.

Coordination

The size and complexity of today's school systems have led to increased and inevitable specialization with the likelihood of greater rather than less specialization in the future. As already noted, the kinds of personnel vary from those who are professional to the semiskilled or unskilled. The number of different jobs within the school system requiring qualification as a teacher is great and the kinds of jobs are varied. School jobs held by members of other professions are also numerous and highly varied.[8] School jobs held by employees who are not members of any profession may be categorized under at least five classifications, within which there will be considerable variety and which add up to substantial numbers.[9] They include the following:

1. Secretarial and clerical personnel include bookkeepers, filing clerks, receptionists, stenographers, and typists.

2. Custodial personnel include male and female janitors—the cleanup personnel—those who attend the heating and ventilating system (although these may in some instances be licensed stationary engineers), and groundsmen (particularly where large acreages require gardeners and others to keep grounds, walks, and drives in serviceable condition).

3. Among service personnel the chief are cafeteria and lunchroom personnel who have responsibilities for preparing food, serving, and cleaning up; bus

[8] They include all personnel classified among those who practice in the field of the healing arts, such as doctor, dentist, psychologist, psychiatrist, and nurse; architects; engineers; accountants; lawyers; nutritionists; and social workers. See Arthur B. Moehlman and James A. van Zwoll, *School Public Relations*, New York, Appleton-Century-Crofts, 1957, pp. 328–333.

[9] *Ibid.*, pp. 323–327.

drivers; and those who administer the service of supplies by operating the school system warehousing and delivery systems.

4. Special part-time personnel are frequently employed, often from among the student body, to administer the school book store and candy counter; and others to take part in a continuous or periodic census.

5. Maintenance personnel include automotive mechanics and school garage service personnel, cabinet makers, carpenters, electricians, electronics technicians, glaziers, masons, painters, plumbers, and steamfitters.

It is easy in the large school system for specialized personnel, under the immediate supervision provided for their respective activities, to find themselves in the position of being so close to the trees that they cannot observe the forest. They come to regard their individual tasks as important in and of themselves. This is a point of view that deprives the employee of the working stimulus provided by the perspective of the total job. It is important that each sees his job in the light of the contribution it makes to the facilitation of the teaching-learning situation.

The personnel officer is logically the person to exercise the chief responsibility for the promotion of an understanding and appreciation of the part that each job and worker has in making more effective the instructional process. However, the task is one of such magnitude that a personnel officer who might attempt to do the whole job of coordinating the efforts of all employees for the promotion of an optimum instructional situation would be doomed to failure. It is generally recognized that the work of personnel administration must be done to some extent by virtually everyone within the school system and that a degree of coordination takes place through various supervisory activities. A particularly strong case in point is the coordination of efforts in which the principal of a school engages constantly.

Examination of the functions of the personnel division reveals the inevitability of a decentralized operation of the personnel activity in the dispersed school situation. Nevertheless, in order that the school system may operate as a unit—despite its numerous almost autonomous elementary, junior high, high, and junior college subdivisional operations with their respective principals and deans—it is essential that over-all coordination of the personnel activity be provided through the personnel officer. The personnel officer serves to introduce pattern, design, and direction into the decentralized personnel activities of all who participate to some degree in the personnel activity.

DEVELOPMENT OF EFFICIENT SERVICE

The reason for instituting and maintaining a personnel office in the school system is to make the instructional effort more effective. Among the major considerations of the personnel division will be organization for effective service, stimulation through placement policies, development of professional consciousness, group contacts, administrative contacts, and recognition of creative efforts. Most of these topics will be dealt with in detail in subsequent chapters. However, a brief statement regarding each is developed at this time in order to provide perspective now with reference to the way in which the personnel organization must develop and operate so that it may exist defensibly.

Organization for Effective Service

The personnel activity is primarily concerned with the problem of selecting, recommending for employment, maintaining, and stimulating toward improvement the working force. The problem of doing all of this is complicated in the school scene even more than in many another by the obstacles to recruitment.

Recruitment. Commonly known reasons for not considering going into teaching, such as salaries and the working conditions and relationships with which teachers have to contend, result either in quick dismissal of any thought of teacher preparation or in neglecting to even consider doing so. Schoolmen are aware of the fact that this situation is made all the worse by the negative attitude of discouragement expressed by many a teacher when asked by youngsters whether they ought to think of preparing for teaching.

Teachers have often been their own worst enemies in the struggle to improve the teaching profession. Consequently the ranks of the teacher group have been opened to many who have met too few of the professional requirements for teaching, as well as many who are no credit to the profession because of low levels of ability, understanding, or interest. Discouragement from preparing to teach has virtually forced into other more receptive fields of endeavor many of the really able and has left the schools in the predicament of doing the best they could with the few able who would not be discouraged—or who were possibly encouraged by the more thoughtful teachers and parents—and the many less able who ought not to teach.

The personnel division must organize for a recruitment activity which will promote both quality and quantity in the ranks of prospective teachers. When quality is stressed the teaching profession will have made a beginning in the upgrading which will eventually encourage such numbers that waiting lists will be established and selection can be made from the best of a high-quality group.

The sceptic among present teachers will ask how quality can be attracted. If this sceptic also regards himself as a man of ability who is a credit to his profession and who is dedicated to it in spite of disadvantageous conditions, he must realize that teaching has for him values which outweigh the drawbacks. It is reasonable to suppose that those values will have similar appeal to others of ability. There is, therefore, already existing among able teachers the foundation upon which a strong recruitment activity may be built through efforts organized by the personnel division.

Selection. The personnel organization has the job of selecting personnel for the jobs to be done. Selection does not take place in a vacuum; it takes place with reference to something. Often this means that selection is based on qualities loosely associated with the job in terms of how it was done before the vacancy. Functionally, selection ought to take place in terms of most careful analysis of the job, not so much as it has been but rather as careful examination stipulates that it must be.

It takes real organization to do job analysis from which will come the job description and specifications on the basis of which personal qualifications can be examined to provide the defensible basis for personnel selection and recommendation for employment.

Maintenance. A working force assembled through great effort is an investment and a productive resource of such potential that it merits the care needed to keep it intact for the school district.[10] The maintenance of the work force demands that the personnel division know jobs and know individuals so well that desirable adjustments may be made to fill jobs most advantageously and to retain jobholders most effectively. The improvement of the instructional situation is promoted through adjustments which provide for capitalization upon the potentialities of employees.

Improvement. As change takes place in the society and is eventually reflected in the institutions of that society, and as advances are made in knowledge both with respect to the content of subjects and the methods for teaching effectively, teachers are in danger of operating behind the times because they are unaware of social change and its implications for them or of advances in knowledge about how to affect the behavior of individuals through the learning situation provided.

[10] It is rather incomprehensible that during a time of severe teacher shortage, top-rated teachers have been treated without regard for their legitimate interests; e.g., to teach in the area of their competency, to teach in a school conveniently located with reference to their place of residence, or to be transferred to a school situation more compatible with their personality requirements. Rather, these teachers have been given the choice of remaining where they are or of leaving. Some of the most independent ones, who also had confidence in their ability to succeed in vocations often than teaching, have under these circumstances chosen the alternative of leaving the teaching profession.

The personnel division has the distinct responsibility to organize for an improvement activity by which teachers are kept fully abreast of social change, knowledge of human behavior, and methods for teaching in accord with changes and advances in knowledge. When this activity is or has been neglected, the initial job of improvement will be a discouragingly great one because of the gap that has been permitted to develop between the past and the present. When it is engaged in on a continuous basis, the changes and advancements will generally be found to take place so gradually that the job of improvement calls for evolutionary rather than revolutionary adjustment.[11]

Organization for helping to keep teachers abreast of developments can result in the easy and painless adjustment that parents generally make to the growth of their children. Failure to organize for such adjustment on the part of the teacher is conducive to the crisis situations in which sometimes highly distasteful inservice programs seem to be the only way out of the dilemma.

Placement Policies. A strange phenomenon in teacher placement, serving also as an indictment of the personnel administration that has been operative, is the practice of hiring teachers almost as if all are alike in competency irrespective of training, interest, and personality differences.[12]

This kind of placement is engaged in when personnel administration takes place without understanding, without the exercise of the intelligence and effort necessary to do a defensible placement job, or in subservience to some shortsighted expedient dictated by an administration that is more concerned with immediate convenience than with soundness in meeting the problems of placing or assigning personnel.

The personnel division can and should organize for placement in accord with both the needs of the institution and the competencies of the individual. Such organization is necessary because of the very real work entailed if the placement activity is to take place functionally. The employee who finds his competencies recognized through proper placement policies and operations is thus furnished with a stimulus to regard

[11] This is really analogous to any growth situation in which daily association breeds a familiarity in which growth takes place almost unnoticed. A parent who sees his child daily is aware of growth in a general way. A friend who has not seen the child for several months is likely to remark about the great amount of growth that has taken place in "so short a time."

[12] Both during the depression of the 1930's when there was a surplus of qualified teachers and in the period since World War II when there was a great shortage of qualified teachers, it has been common practice in school districts throughout the United States to employ teachers with high qualifications in some area of teaching and to place them in areas of teaching for which they had little or no competency. Sometimes this has even taken place in such a way as to call, for example, for a teacher competent to teach mathematics to teach English instead, while the teacher with competency in English was assigned to teach mathematics.

his competencies as having value and to enhance that value by use and improvement.

Professional Consciousness. Education shares with many other types of occupations a great craving to be regarded as a profession.[13] Just what differentiates a profession from other occupations is generally not clear. White-collar operation and a service emphasis with altruistic highlights are often the chief hallmarks of a profession to which claim is laid by the aspiring group.

Some who have made a particular study of the problem of what constitutes a profession have come to the conclusion that the common element which makes for professionalism and yet differentiates from what would be nonprofessional defies identification.[14]

In spite of the difficulties of defining "profession," values have accrued to those laying claim to being professional. These values are in terms of the group spirit generated, prestige felt, standards developed, means sought for transmitting the theories and practices of the group, efforts to subscribe to the socially oriented concept of unselfish service rendered beyond the call of duty and at some sacrifice to self. Thus a working concept of professionalism has been developed, going very little if at all beyond the criteria developed by Flexner[15] suggesting that professionalism demands:

1. intellectual operations coupled with large individual responsibilities
2. raw materials drawn from science and learning
3. practical application
4. an educationally communicable technique
5. tendency toward self-organization
6. increasingly altruistic motivation

Reflective consideration of the foregoing criteria suggests the need for at least two activities by which the attitudes of those directly involved may be redirected.[16] These two activities are arduous and extensive training together with personal commitment to an exacting code of ethics.

It is incumbent upon the personnel division to provide through its organization for such development as may be needed of the concept of professionalism, its limitations, its potentialities, and the hard work neces-

[13] Among those who lay claim to being professional are: accountants, architects, business management executives, dentists, engineers, lawyers, medical doctors, ministers and priests, nurses, social workers, surveyors of land, and teachers.

[14] Oliver Garceau, "Some Aspects of Medical Politics" (Ph.D. Dissertation in the Department of Government), Cambridge, Harvard University, 1939, p. 4, and Morris L. Cogan, "Toward a Definition of Profession," *Harvard Educational Review,* Vol. 23, Winter, 1953, pp. 33–50.

[15] Abraham Flexner, "Is Social Work a Profession?" *School and Society,* Vol. 1, June 26, 1915, p. 904.

[16] See Charles L. Stevenson, *Ethics and Language* (New Haven, Yale University Press, 1944), p. 210.

sary to attain the distinction of a warranted label of professionalization.

Group Contacts. The personnel division has occasion for contacts with employees throughout the school system. These contacts will be direct or indirect as called for by the occasion.

Many direct contacts will take place in relationship to the events which are corollary to initial employment, to those requiring adjustive services beyond what the local school administration can provide, and to those which are corollary to separation from service.

If the direct contacts are limited to the foregoing, the personnel division may find itself lacking the confidence of the employee group. Hence it is highly desirable that the personnel division take steps to know the personnel and to be known by them. The personnel division owes, both to the school administration and the various employees, a responsibility for making clear administrative objectives and for seeking employee cooperation through policy execution and appraisal. Employee experience with policies can be a valuable aid toward realistic execution and necessary revision of policy.

In many instances the personnel division, being in an advisory relationship to administration, has an impact upon the individual employee of which that employee is hardly aware since the impact is transmitted through the chain of command. In addition, in its research activities the personnel division may find itself relying upon the submission of data by the personnel through their completion of blanks, their answering of questionnaires, and their reporting through committee delegations.

Indirect contacts are necessary. They may often be made more effective when the employees involved are familiar with the personnel officer and the division which he heads. Organization may be developed for joint meetings between employee groups and the personnel division for the purpose of promoting the feeling of association, the development of confidence, and the building of a foundation for an effective educational operation.

Administrative Contacts. The personnel division can work effectively only to the extent that it commands the confidence equally of both the employees and the administration. The confidence of the administration is necessary in many instances as a matter of survival alone. If the administration should lack confidence in the personnel activity, it can hardly be expected to perpetuate a division which on the financial account shows up as that much overhead.

The personnel division has the particular obligation to develop and maintain such relations that administrative policies are at all times formulated with the best possible appreciation of their implication for all employees affected by them. Corollary to this is the continued informing of the administrators as to the actual effect upon personnel of the policies being executed with recommendations as to the modification that seems desirable in terms of administrative objectives and of the consideration due the personnel.

Recognition of Effort. All constructive efforts which are put forth merit recognition. The kinds of effort put forth may be classified as (1) legitimately required, (2) creative, and (3) others going beyond the call of duty. Each of these will be discussed briefly in terms of the need to provide recognition through organization within the personnel division.

Consideration of teaching as a profession has led to identification of virtually everything a teacher does meritoriously as being part of his job. However, there are job requirements which may be considered minimal in nature which must be met by any teacher who is to be retained on the job. The performance of these tasks is considered here.

All efforts expended in the pursuit of duty are recognized in part by the periodic paycheck. In addition, the administrator—particularly the principal who has appreciation of the individual and genuine understanding of the problems confronted on the job—can take action, sometimes involving no more than a comment, whereby he allies himself to the teacher in the task of education. Thus he creates also the effect of lightening the teacher's burden or of making it more bearable. In such ways the board of education and the building principal take part in the exercise of the personnel function.

Fortunately there are also teachers who have the originality, vision, and inventiveness by which they make an extraordinary contribution in their carrying out of their duties. This contribution may often be unnoted because a teacher thinks of his development of technique, device, or content as merely a part of the job. Consequently the benefits of creative effort are restricted to the occasional classroom instead of being made available to the school system. In addition, the teacher may be really unaware of the potential value of his contribution and actually regard himself as just another teacher, or even as an unsuccessful one.

The personnel division must be organized to take cognizance of the individual teacher's contributions both as they facilitate the learning in his classroom and as they have potential for improving instruction more widely throughout the school system. The recognition may be monetary to a degree and this will no doubt be appreciated. In any case, moral encouragement and working conditions conducive to making further contributions should be provided. Also, the personnel division is logically the one to make the services of the creative teacher available throughout the school system so as to acquaint others with innovations that hold promise, a particularly gratifying and sometimes somewhat frightening form of recognition.

There are also teachers who, whether they are creative or not, expend efforts well beyond the minimum duties required by the job. Some of these are activities which demonstrate interest in children as individuals and in the teaching-learning situation through which change in behavior is stimulated. Because they are so generally taken for granted as a commonly accepted expression of professionalism, such efforts and activities are seldom especially recognized. As particularly important efforts and activities which go beyond the immediate and readily identifiable call of duty, they deserve the identification and recognition by which they are encouraged and extended.

A more usually recognized form of effort expended beyond the call of duty—when not specified as part of the teacher's job—is the sponsorship of activities and the performance of additional duties. This is an area in which the recognition at times is often limited to assignment of duties and possible appreciation. These duties are such as to make no demand on the professional competence of the teacher and are often imposed expedientially as a matter of administrative convenience. Teachers have come to recognize the nature of these duties, to resent them, and to make at least a monetary issue of them. Reward for extra duties has come to be a hotly debated issue in a number of school systems and a form of recognition in others.

The area of somewhat routine extra duties needs much more careful attention from the personnel division than has generally been accorded. The question as to whether professional talent should be distracted from professional channels of operation into those in which no special expertness is required has to be faced squarely. Once the nature of the problem has been clearly defined, it may be that the question of rewards will be at least shared with that of how the problem may be most warrantably solved.

SUMMARY

Irrespective of title or specialization, the one charged with major responsibility in the area of personnel is in fact the personnel administrator. He is part of the administrative team but must on the one hand justify himself before that team and on the other identify himself with those who hold jobs subordinate to the administrators. In this dual role he serves also as a clinician to both parties and to the school system.

In spite of the importance of the personnel officer's job, it is difficult to be definitive about the qualifications needed. School personnel administration may have an edge on personnel administration in other occupations because the general qualifications seem to be very much like those sought in the superior teacher. Add to these general qualifications evidence of particular organizational ability, understanding of school organization and operation, and special training for personnel administration, and the chances are that the person selected can succeed in the job of school personnel administration.

The job of personnel administration is a big one demanding careful organization for the attainment of its objectives. Operating with line authority within the division, the personnel officer and his division functionally have an advisory or staff relationship to the administration, which has the superintendent as its head.

Administrative relationships are either "must" or "may" in nature. Where they are mandatory there is no choice but to exercise line authority. Where they are permissive the administrator on any level has the latitude to secure participation by or involvement of personnel in terms of the expertness which they can bring to bear on the problem in question. One difficulty presented is that differentiation between situations which are mandatory and those which are permissive is not always clear. The result is confusion as to what constitutes legitimate exercise of authority, appropriate subordination, the area of advisement, and the proper realm for cooperation.

Democracy and authority are neither mutually incompatible nor paradoxical. They are on the contrary logical concomitants. Democracy cannot exist without authority. Yet, authority can operate inconsistently with democracy and then there is autocracy—or, for lack of authority, anarchy.

Growth of school systems has led to complex organizations, high specialization for many different jobs, danger that relationships and functions will be seen out of their proper perspective, and the need for a high degree of coordination. The coordination in the realm of personnel is the job of the personnel officer. He needs the assistance of other administrative and executive agents throughout the school system. To a considerable extent his job is that of coordinating the personnel activities of these other personnel.

Getting the most efficient service possible is the major reason for having a personnel division. In order to do its job well the personnel division must be organized to provide for effective service through the recruitment, selection, maintenance, and improvement of personnel. These activities can be largely negated unless they are accompanied by placement or assignment in accord with the competencies for which individuals were initially hired.

Esprit de corps, a sense of prestige, a reaching for ideals and resultant growth, and a search for means of transmitting what is known about learning and teaching constitute the justification for identifying teaching as a profession. Aside from the foregoing, sincere effort to do as well as possible the job required of one might be fully as productive whether or not the professional label were attached to the occupation.

SELECTED READINGS

BRANDT, Richard B., *Ethical Theory* (Englewood Cliffs, N.J., Prentice-Hall, Inc., 1959), Chapters 14, 17.

BURRUP, Percy E., *The Teacher and the Public School System* (New York, Harper and Row, 1960), Chapter 13.

CRESSMAN, George B. and BENDA, Harold W., *Public Education in America* (New York, Appleton-Century-Crofts, 1961), Chapters 1, 5.

HAWKINS, D. J. B., *Man and Morals* (London, Sheed and Ward, 1960), Chapter 1.

HUGHES, James M., *Human Relations in Educational Organization* (New York, Harper and Row, 1957), Chapter 2.

MOEHLMAN, Arthur B., *School Administration* (Boston, Houghton Mifflin Company, 1951), Chapters 2, 16, 28.

PFIFFNER, John M. and PRESTHUS, Robert V., *Public Administration* (New York, the Ronald Press, 1960), Chapter 5.

Rockefeller Panel Report, *The Power of the Democratic Idea* (New York, Doubleday and Company, 1960).

SPITZ, David, *Democracy and the Challenge of Power* (New York, Columbia University Press, 1958), Chapter 1.

THAYER, Lee O., *Administrative Communication* (Homewood, Ill., Richard D. Irwin, Inc., 1961), Chapter 1.

.3.

The Education Job

THE JOB of education was at one time thought of as simple enough to require the employment of one type of individual. This situation has changed and is changing to such a degree that a number of activities have become necessary for better understanding of what is meant by *the job*. Among these activities are those of definition, identification and listing, analysis, description, classification, specification, and rating. These activities are very much and immediately the concern of the personnel administrator.

DEFINITION

The function, the job, or the total obligation to be undertaken by the school system is the education of the child in accord with his needs and the dictates of the society to which he belongs.

Evolution

During the colonial period of American history the entire job of education was entrusted to the school master. In the increasingly rare one-room school systems the teacher is still the sole executor of board policies. In his activities are to be seen the basic and specific functions and interrelationships of such currently familiar figures as the superintendent, principal, classroom teacher, secretary, clerk, and janitor.

The total job of education is much the same irrespective of population or time factors. However the school scene changes. The impact of changing social concepts is reflected in the changed and increased services expected from the schools. Continued industrialization gives rise to population concentrations which promote large school systems and schools. Larger school systems are also the product of reorganizations which have taken place in order to capitalize upon the educational advantages of size.

The job scene emerging is one of increasing specialization. The basic job of education has been broken down in many places into a number of components, each of which has become a job in itself. The jobs range from the professional to those of the semi- or un-skilled laborer.

Elementary School. An elementary school does not have to be very large—policies vary from district to district—to have the following regular specialties represented: principal, clerk, janitor, lower elementary teacher, upper elementary teacher, kindergarten teacher, and often on a full or part-time basis specialized teachers for music, art, physical education, science, industrial arts, and counselling. In fact it begins to look as if the elementary school is being confronted with prospects of further specialization. Even on the elementary school level one is no longer a schoolmaster in the original comprehensive sense.

Secondary School. The high school that operates with less than twelve teachers can hardly be expected to have the comprehensive course offerings by which the needs and interests of youth and society can be met. In fact, in terms of subject matter preparation alone, if a teacher were to teach in only his major and minor fields of preparation, it would take unusually careful selection to make possible an adequately comprehensive secondary school program with only twelve teachers.

On the secondary school level the usual personnel would include at least a principal, counsellor, clerk-secretary, janitor, and a number of subject matter specialist teachers. The idea of a teacher who is a generalist and competent to teach anything in high school is an unrealistic dream entertained by only a few. The practical matter of training such a generalist would involve so much time that the prime of life would be past before teaching could begin, and even then there would have to be areas in which specialization could not be avoided. So, here also the schoolmaster in the original and comprehensive sense no longer exists.

Coordination. The tide of specialization brings with it the problem of putting the personnel components together in such a way as to make them work as a unit. Such coordination is necessary if the endeavors of all employees are to contribute to the primary job of the schools, education. Each worker in his specific and particularized position must do what he can to make the teaching-learning situation effective and to improve it.

All of the administrative officers of the school system have a distinct responsibility for providing for coordination. Further coordination is provided through the supervisory staff. The coordination that is of major concern here is that which is the chief responsibility of the personnel administrator.

Thorough understanding of the basic job, of the nature of all of the component jobs, and of the implications of both for the staffing of the school system is the especial province of the personnel administrator. It is his job to coordinate the respective jobs, working conditions, and personnel in such a way as to attain the best possible working unit.

The greatest steps in the direction of providing the organizational structure and the necessary staff for understanding the jobs to be done and the implications for the kind of qualifications and competencies that the job holders must have seem to have been taken in the larger school systems. As school systems decline in size, there tends to be increasing assumption of job understanding without measures to validate the assumption. Also the means for matching personnel to the jobs tend to be less formalized and more personal.

To the extent that the coordinating activities of the personnel administrator are operative, they seem to have been most highly refined and effectively utilized in that area of school employment in which certifiability to teach is not required.

In the areas of job listing, analysis, description, classification, specification and rating—all highly important to coordination—there is much room for improvement and for application, particularly with reference to the teaching personnel.

JOB LISTING

Before real progress can be made in understanding jobs, the positions that have somehow come into being have to be identified and compiled into a list. Initially such a list is made up informally and without any particular sequence, grouping, or analysis. It may be made up as it occurs to the compiler. The list will never be a constant because functions tend to change when personnel changes take place and because there will be accretions, deletions, and planned changes in jobs.

The Job Listing

Without being all inclusive—something that would be different for each school system—this kind of listing may be illustrated by the following:

superintendent	directors (by specialty)
supervisor	secretary
principal	clerk
teacher (by division and specialty)	bookkeeper
doctor	receptionist
dentist	janitor
nurse	maintenance men (by specialty)
psychologist	driver (bus, truck)
lawyer	food handlers (by specialty)
nutritionist	handymen
assistant superintendents (by specialty)	

This job listing should include every position in the school system by the designations that have come into being and which distinguish one from another. At some later time it may be found desirable to devise more definitive designations or titles. In some instances it may be necessary to mark a position for particular attention at the time of subsequent analysis so that the analysis may contribute to better identification and designation.

Whereas all positions should be carefully designated in the list, the importance of the teaching activity and the number and kinds of teaching positions in a school system suggest that particular attention be given to the identification and definitive listing of each. Teaching positions are distinguished from each other by school division—e.g., elementary, secondary, junior high, senior high, and junior college—by grade level, and by subject specializations.

The complete listing of all positions in a school system is preparatory to and a first step toward gaining an understanding of each through job analysis.

JOB ANALYSIS

Analysis of a job is the study or examination by which that job gets to be seen in terms of its constituent parts. Analysis is basically a taking-apart operation through which each component is separated from the others for investigation and consideration by itself and in terms of its relationships to the over-all job.

The analyst is concerned with four major factors:[1] (1) what the worker does, (2) how he does it, (3) why he does it, and (4) the skill involved in the doing. These factors include the purpose, responsibility, duties, working conditions, physical and mental activities, and skill which characterize positions and differentiate them from others.

[1] Department of Labor, U.S.E.S., *Training and Reference Manual for Job Analysis* (Washington, D.C., U.S. Government Printing Office, June 1944), p. 1.

The Analyst

The analyst cannot hope to analyze many and varied positions in terms of his own knowledge alone. The knowledge and understanding of any one man is unavoidably too limited to make analysis possible by a lone agent. Hence the one who does job analysis must be adept at establishing the relationships with others which will permit him to elicit information that he needs. He must be a keenly observant person who has developed the faculty to make note of the discrete facets of each activity. Further he must have the understanding and insight needed to discern the implications of his findings.

The field of education requires of the analyst also a thorough understanding of the place and function of the school in American society. Conversance with every aspect of school organization, administration, and over-all operation, together with an appreciation of the need to have every action contribute to the well-being of the teaching-learning situation, is another prerequisite to job analysis in a school system.

All of the foregoing virtually stipulate extensive training and experience as a teacher. It is suggested that an individual who has the general personal traits necessary for the job should meet the following minimum additional requirements: a master's degree in education with a major in school administration, an additional year's specialized training in the behavioral disciplines—e.g., psychology, human relations, sociology, political science, and philosophy—leading to certification as an educational specialist, two years of classroom teaching experience, two years in a job in which perspective of the total school operation is gained, e.g., principal, assistant to the principal, vice-principal, or aide to the superintendent.

Method

The means for analyzing a job have been implied in the discussion of the analyst. They consist of interviewing, questioning, observation, and interpretation. What is found has to be interpreted in the report on the breakdown of each position. The approach used is generally that of making notations of what takes place as it occurs and what the time factor is.

JOB DESCRIPTION

The information gained through the job analysis provides the breakdown on each position. This is organized and written as a statement called the *job description*. This statement should be detailed and explicit. Technical language should either be reduced to understandable English in the text or explained.

Language

The matter of the language used is important in any job description. It is a matter of particular importance to the schoolman. As in any specialized field of endeavor, there is in education also a technical language—sometimes called pedaguese—which has meaning for the initiated but which is virtually unintelligible to anyone else.

In order to make certain that the job description really does fit the job it purports to depict, it is important that the description be reviewed by the worker(s) engaged in the job, by those who normally supervise the worker and have consequent familiarity with the job, and by a layman who can be particularly helpful in calling attention to wording which is ambiguous or unintelligible to him. These reviews should be used to rewrite the description until the descriptive statement is unquestionably clear.

Purpose

Job descriptions have the purpose of clarifying the nature of the job in order that the job may be more accurately identified and definitively designated or titled, understood in terms of all that is involved in the doing of it, and classified or grouped in terms of the likeness of their distinguishing facets. In addition, the job description serves as the detailed statement on the basis of which worker qualifications may be specified.

JOB CLASSIFICATION

Positions which have like characteristics form a category, group, family, or class of jobs. The job analysis and description provide the information needed to make the comparisons from which job classifications are derived.

Factors

The first and probably most important act in job classification is to determine the major and outstanding differentiating feature in the performing of the work. The different groupings and subgroupings will be characterized by those duties and responsibilities which they have in common and which set them apart from other jobs.

When the *what, why, how,* and *skill* factors are basically alike, the probability is that all the positions held by the employees doing the work constitute one job classification.

It is currently the classification factors which come from job analysis and description which are definitive about jobs rather than title designations. Within an organization, such as a school system, one by-product of classification, which is highly desirable for the personnel division, is the standardization of terminology and job designations.

Purposes

Through systematization and standardization, job classification purposes to give the school system and its employees an understandable concept of each job and the qualifications required for it.

A corollary purpose is to facilitate the work of the personnel division in doing what is necessary—recruiting, training, selecting and hiring, placing, transferring, and promoting personnel—to match workers to jobs in such a way as to promote the teaching-learning situation which is the heart of the school operation.

A third purpose is the evolvement of a consistent pay scale which is adjusted to the nature of the work, the personal qualifications of the worker, and the background requirements of the employee.

Classifications

Within the school system, classifications might well begin in terms of (1) all jobs for which certification to teach is required and (2) all jobs for which certification to teach is not required.

Jobs Requiring Certification. The classifications will differ with the size of the school district and the nomenclature is not standardized. However, for purposes of illustration, the subclassifications would include (1) administrative, (2) staff or advisory, and (3) teaching jobs.

Administrative jobs would include further subclasses, such as the superintendency, subdistrict administrators, principalships (elementary, junior high, and senior high, or dean of the junior college), vice-principalships, and administrative assistants.

Staff jobs would include those—by whatever title, associate or assistant superintendent and director—who head up the respective advisory services, such as child accounting, finance, instruction, personnel, plant, public relations, pupil adjustment, research and records, and service of supplies, and also all supervisors.

The remaining subclassification is that of the teachers. This group lends itself to further subclassification in terms of school division, grade level, and subject specialization. It is in this area in particular that much more careful work needs to be done in job identification and designation, analysis, description, and classification so that the staffing activities of the personnel division may be facilitated.

Jobs Not Requiring Certification. These will vary in number and kind with the school district and the size of the district. Four of the major subclassifications in this grouping would be (1) office, (2) operation, (3) maintenance, and (4) service jobs.

Office jobs would include positions which could be subclassified as follows: accountant, bookkeeper, secretary, stenographer, typist, clerk, receptionist, switchboard operator. If done under the direction of a competent schoolman who assumes the direct responsibility for all purchasing, much of the work of the purchasing agent could also be performed by noncertificated personnel.

Operational jobs include positions of responsibility for the heating, ventilating, and cleaning of the school building. This group of personnel could well include such subclassifications as licensed engineer (stationary), janitor or custodian, and matron.

Service jobs—concerned with problems of food, health, service of supplies, transportation, and maintenance—lend themselves to further subclassification in terms of the duties of, for example, nutritionist, cook, and food handlers; doctor, dentist, psychologist, psychiatrist, nurse, clinicians; warehouse and stockroom personnel; bus and truck drivers, and gasoline pump and lubrication rack operators; and maintenance men further subclassified by their respective trades (carpenters, electricians, plumbers, steam fitters, masons, auto mechanics, etc.).

Summary. Without being at all exhaustive of the possibilities, the foregoing classifications and subclassifications indicate possibilities of systemtizing and standardizing so that the assurance of effective staffing is improved and the work of the personnel division is facilitated.

JOB SPECIFICATION

Commonly known as a job specification, the activity so designated is in fact a worker specification. Job specification is concerned primarily with the qualifications and competencies that a worker must have in order to be able to do the job in question.

Purpose

The job specification is intended to facilitate the work of the employment function of the personnel division. Hence it is not particularly concerned with all the facets of the job turned up through analysis and drawn up in the description. It is concerned with those qualities and qualifications that a worker must have in order to be considered for a position and with the degree to which the qualities must be present.

The job specification serves the purpose of supplying the employing personnel, those who do the interviewing or the reviewing of applications, with that specific information which they need in order to make the best possible selection and to recommend employment accordingly.

How Drawn

The job specification is derived from the detailed job description. It is in fact a job description in brief and with a slanting toward the particular needs of the employment office.

The Writer. Whereas the job description is written most logically by the one who performed the analysis, the job specification is written by employment personnel. These personnel scrutinize the job description for every indication that would be helpful in screening prospective employees and make note thereof for inclusion in the specification.

Just as the writer of the job description must check and double check his descriptive write-up with those who supervise the doing of the job and with those who hold the positions, so also the writer of the job specification needs the double check of going back to the analyst, the supervisor, and occasionally even the worker in the position of the job in question to make certain that the job specification derived by him accurately portrays the worker qualifications, which are his chief interest.

Content

The literature about job specifications is in general agreement as to the basic requirements of the specification. With some adaptation to fit these requirements to the school personnel scene, the content of the job specifications may be outlined as follows:

    I Job Identification
        Title
        Alternate title
        Relation of jobs to other jobs
        School system
            Division
            Department
            Place of work
   II Description of Duties (brief statement)

  III Employee Qualifications (minimum)
        Physical and health requirements
        Sex, age, height, weight
        Education
        Literacy (reading, writing, and speaking
            knowledge of the English language)

Knowledge of pertinent measuring devices
and techniques
Special knowledge
Experience

IV Working Conditions
Personal tools and equipment
Supplies and equipment furnished
Raw materials worked on or with
Accuracy required
Average achievement (production)
Degree of supervision
Contacts within and outside the
school system
Seasonality of job (9, 9½, 10 or 12 months)
Time requirements
Pay scales, overtime

V Miscellaneous (aids to employment officer)
Possibilities of transfer
Order of promotions to and from the job
Time needed to train raw recruits
Sources of prospective employees
Tests to be used in selection

A job specification outline such as the above could be filled out for each job in the school system, both those requiring certifiability to teach and those not requiring such certifiability. The detail would vary according to the job and should be supplemented as the occasion may require.

Effect

The anticipated effect of careful job specification is improvement of the possibility for the personnel division of the school system to staff the various positions for which it has responsibility with efficiency, expedition, and a certainty that is introduced through the specification.

A part of this improved effectiveness of the personnel division's operation will be reflected in the retention of workers who are regarded as being in line for the transfers and promotions for which their current jobs are the starting point. This will conserve to the school system some teachers who have aspirations to other professional school jobs. It will also conserve nonteaching personnel who see possibilities for self-improvement through recognized procedures for advancement.[2]

[2] The prospect of becoming a fulltime janitor gained one school system a handyman who served as bus driver, helper to the maintenance men, assistant in the stockroom, and substitute janitor. This handyman proved to be both intelligent and responsible. With the growth of the school system, he became qualified in a few years to assume full responsibility for the school system's stock room and service of supplies.

JOB RATING

In school circles rating has generally had only the one connotation, that of personnel rating. Job rating is not personnel rating. It is the evaluation and relating of jobs in some logical order. This order might be from a job requiring the least to one demanding the most training.

The job-rating sequence relates the families or classes of jobs to the over-all job. The relating of jobs to the total operation, e.g., administrative, staff, teaching, clerical, custodial, transportation, and maintenance, provides perspective of the job of the school system and of its personnel needs. The respective kinds of jobs are like pieces in a jigsaw puzzle inasmuch as they make real sense only when they are seen in their true and defensible relationship to the whole.

Purpose

Job rating, grading, or classification has the one main purpose of setting up and providing recognition of the relative worth of each job in the school system. This worth is evaluated in terms of the contribution that the job makes to the over-all job of the school system, the education of the child which is the function of the school.

Uses. Job rating provides advantages in practice that are in some respects subordinate purposes of rating. It introduces the development and application of criteria by which like jobs are evaluated as being alike. It provides the basis for removing the inequalities of classification and remuneration that are otherwise likely to characterize the employment scene.

Through comparison of pay scales for one or more kinds of jobs with similar jobs outside the school system, the administration and the board of education may be made aware of equitable pay scales both on the job(s) in question and, in terms of the relative rating of jobs, of other jobs in the school system which do not lend themselves to ready comparisons outside the schools. This has very real implications for the school's ability to compete with other employing agencies in the hiring of competent personnel. There are further implications for the recruitment activity.[3]

[3] In Washington, D.C. and its environs it is possible for a high school graduate with a knowledge of typing and ability to take dictation to begin with a Grade Four job at about $4000 with annual increments to approximately $4400. With demonstrated ability, this employee can advance at least two grades, to a maximum of about $5500, with the possibility of further advancement to Grade Nine with a salary range up to about $7000. In the Washington Metropolitan area, the recruitment of teaching, clerical and secretarial, operative, and maintenance personnel and their employment are greatly affected by government employment conditions.

Agents

Ordinarily job rating in a school system will be done by a number of individuals. It is possible that in a small school system the superintendent would do the actual job of rating. It is preferable, however, that where the job of rating has not been done before, each individual school set up a committee of those who have analyzed the jobs and of the principal to work out the basis for rating and to arrive at the preliminary ratings. Thereafter, a committee involving representative analysts and principals and a representation from both the office of the superintendent and that of the personnel division would have the responsibility for deciding what the respective job ratings or gradings to be put into effect should be.

Means

The actual rating of jobs will in the final analysis be somewhat arbitrary inasmuch as it is done on the subjective basis of judgment. It is trusted that the judgment exercised will be better than the haphazard consequences of not doing the job of rating. It is also expected that the committee approach and the utilization of analysts, principals and others who supervise the respective workers, and representatives from the superintendent's and the personnel division's offices would contribute to the best possible judgment, one in which necessary compromises will have virtually negated highly personal viewpoints and consideration.

In the smaller school districts, lacking the personnel structure implied above, the committee might well include the superintendent, the principal, and a representative from one or more of the following: the College of Education of a reputable University, the State Department of Education, a consultant from the personnel division of a larger school system which has a well-organized job-rating plan.

In addition to the committee approach, four techniques for job rating are employed in industry and may be applied as well to the school situation. These are the techniques of ranking, classification, point allocation, and factor comparison.

Irrespective of the approach, who does the ranking, or the technique used, the possibility of doing an optimum job of ranking is enhanced by a well-founded, detailed, and carefully written job description.

Ranking. In the small school system, it is possible that the superintendent, with only a few schools and a minimum of supporting personnel, could do a pretty satisfactory job of ranking jobs. With a little assistance from a committee, such as has been suggested, a simple ranking might in relatively simple school organization prove adequate.

Classification. Where, because of the complexities of size, the limitations of the ranking procedure would assert themselves unmistakably, some refinement of ranking has been resorted to through classification.

Classification has been referred to earlier in terms of grouping together into job categories those positions that were comparable. In this classification no consideration was given to the relative values of jobs. The chief concern of the aspect of classification which is part of the job-rating activity is to establish the relationships between jobs in terms of their relative values to the over-all job.

The classification approach may consist of a grouping of jobs, the grouping being derived from the preliminary ranking procedure. Or, jobs might be rated and then, in terms of the ratings, classified or graded. A third possibility is that grades be arbitrarily set up and then jobs fitted into the respective grades in terms of the criteria determined upon —such criteria as educational level and special training, experience, degree of supervision received and/or given, and responsibility.

The same grade might include such personnel as teacher aides, various clerical personnel, and a number of maintenance personnel. A grade, therefore, cuts across job lines. Ordinarily there would be little likelihood of transferring from one job to another within a grade. However, particularly within the nonprofessional jobs, there would often be the expectation that with experience and the necessary additional training the able employee would be able to move into a higher grade of classification for his kind of job or competency.

Both ranking and the refined version of it called classification enjoy the advantage of simplicity and ease of explanation to those who are involved. Both lack, however, the definitiveness by which consistency and equity in personnel administration can be assured.

The Point System. Under the point system, the various jobs are examined for approximately nine and often as many as eleven factors that are common and important to all. The number of points merited by each factor is stipulated for each kind of job. Thus for one job in a school system the factor of education might rate 10 points (representing elementary education); for another it might be 30 (representing a high school education); for a third, 50 (representing graduation from college); for a fourth, 60 for attaining the master's degree; for a fifth, 70 for qualifying for the professional diploma; and for a sixth 80 for completion of doctoral requirements. Obviously something in the way of a handbook or manual is necessary so that the degree to which points may be allocated for any one factor for any one job may be readily ascertained.

In the nonschool situation, the factors frequently included are education, effort (physical and mental), experience, responsibility (for materials and people), skill, and working conditions. In the school situation, it may well be a first concern of the rating committee to examine a number of representative school job analyses and descriptions in order to determine the factors on which to base the rating. Special consideration will undoubtedly have to be given to the inclusions of some factors that are peculiar to the responsibility of the school for the education of children.

A major advantage of the point system is that the factors—possibly the same used in ranking or classification—are identified as the ones to be considered in rating the job. Further, the extent to which the respective factors shall weigh is consistently stipulated for each job. After points have been allocated for the factors selected they may be added to give the relative worth of each job within the complex of jobs characteristic of the school system.

The joker or possible weak spot in the point system is the problem of selecting the right factors and then determining the point value ratios. The right factors are those which have genuine pertinence to evaluating the job. The degree to which they have pertinence is presumably designated by the point value ratio given to the factor. Both the judgment as to the factors to be included and the allocation of a point value are unavoidably tinged with subjectivity and arbitrariness.

The vulnerability of the point system can be reduced through the fullest possible use of such varied judgments as can be evoked through the use of such a committee as has been suggested and by meticulous adherence to, pondering of, and reflection about the information available from job analysis and set forth in the job description.

Factor Comparison. This is a technique in which a number of jobs, ranging from the top to the bottom of the job list totem pole, are selected. These jobs are those whose relative worth in the total organization, the school system, is pretty generally considered to be well and acceptably established. This judgment about the defensible position of the respective jobs may be corroborated in part by their comparability to jobs in competing organizations, both school and nonschool. The jobs selected as representative and defensibly established are regarded as *key jobs*.

The key jobs are studied in terms of several of the larger factors which all have in common. These factors may be those which summarize the nine or more used in the point system. Factors appearing in the literature are generally those of skill, effort, responsibility, and working conditions. It is up to the individual school districts to determine whether these cover the major facets for the schools or whether there are other factors peculiar to the school situation which should take the place of or supplement those listed.

Each factor is given careful consideration in terms of (1) its importance to the job in question and (2) its translation into point or money equivalents. All other jobs are compared with the key jobs which they most closely resemble. Then they are given ratings the same as that of the key job or as much above or below it as seems warranted by the degree and nature of their variance from it.

The factor comparison technique or system has a flexibility and adaptability which are attributes of its use of only a few basic factors which are described in broad terms. This is in contrast to the point system in which fixed sets of values are worked out for each of a considerable number of detailed factors. In factor comparison the scale is the logically arranged list of key jobs with which other jobs are compared or to which they are related. Comparisons are with actual jobs rather than with paper specifications. It is claimed that new and even unlike jobs can be evaluated with ease through the use of the factor comparison technique.[4]

SUMMARY

The job or over-all function of the school in the democratic society of the United States is defined as the total obligation for the education of the child in accord with his needs and the dictates of society.

This comprehensive job was described as evolving into a considerable number of component specialized jobs. Job and specialty proliferation at all levels was produced by the growth of school districts as a result of industrialization, urbanization, and school district reorganization.

Size brought with it advantages in school programs and problems in the coordination of personnel efforts. Activities which have come into being to facilitate the work of the personnel division in providing needed leadership in coordination included job listing, analysis, description, classification, specification, and rating.

Preparing the list of jobs is the first step toward understanding the jobs in the school operation. A subsequent step is the analyzing of positions, a process described as breaking the position down into its constituent parts, covering the *what, why, how,* and *skill* of worker activities.

Analysis provides the wherewithal for the job description, a detailed statement prepared by the analyst for ready understanding by any literate person.

The job descriptions lend themselves to the preparation of job classifications, the grouping of similar positions into definitive job categories. The outcome sought is systematization and standardization by which to improve school functioning. The two large categories of school jobs under which all others may be subsumed are those (1) requiring certification to teach and (2) not requiring such certification.

[4] Edward N. Hay, "Characteristics of Factor Comparison in Job Evaluation," *Personnel,* Vol. XXII, No. 6, May, 1946, pp. 370–375.

Although all the information needed by the employing agents can be found in the job description, the needs of the employing agents are more effectively served by the job, or rather worker specifications which are prepared by the personnel who review applications and interview prospective employees. Specifications derived from job descriptions highlight the interests and needs of the employing officers.

Finally, perspective of the worth of each job in relationship to other jobs and the over-all job of education is provided by job rating. The evaluation, grading, or rating of a job advances from the elementary ranking to classification and the more precise use of the point system. Considered somewhat rigid and unadaptable, the point system is overshadowed by the technique of factor comparison. In factor comparison all jobs are compared with and related to selected *key* jobs and derive their own rank or rating from this comparison.

School personnel administration has far to go in the development for school use of the activities and techniques covered in this chapter and in the application of them to the school employment scene. Diligence in doing so promises improved personnel administration and consequent increased efficiency in school functioning.

SELECTED READINGS

CHANDLER, B. J., and PETTY, Paul V., *Personnel Management in School Administration* (Yonkers-on-Hudson, World Book Company, 1955), pp. 485–6.

HALSEY, George D., *Handbook of Personnel Management* (New York, Harper and Row, 1947), Chapters 2, 3, 16.

JUCIUS, Michael J., *Personnel Management* (Chicago, Richard D. Irwin, Inc., 1948), Chapters 4, 5, 18.

MERIAM, Lewis, *Public Personnel Problems* (Washington, The Brookings Institution, 1938), Chapter 1.

MOORE, Harold E., and WALTERS, Newell B., *Personnel Administration in Education* (New York, Harper and Row, 1955), Chapters 5, 6.

MOSHER, William E., and KINGSLEY, J. Donald, *Public Personnel Administration* (New York, Harper and Row, 1941), Chapter 19.

PIGORS, Paul, and MYERS, Charles A., *Personnel Administration* (New York, McGraw-Hill Book Company, Inc., 1951), pp. 255–62.

TEAD, Ordway, and METCALF, Henry C., *Personnel Administration* (New York, McGraw-Hill Book Company, Inc., 1933), Chapters 17, 18.

WAITE, William W., *Personnel Administration* (New York, The Ronald Press Company, 1952), Chapters 4, 10.

WATKINS, Gordon S., and DODD, Paul A., McNAUGHTON, Wayne L., and PRASOW, Paul, *The Management of Personnel and Labor Relations* (New York, McGraw-Hill Book Company, Inc., 1950), Chapter 9 and pp. 523–33.

YODER, Dale, *Personnel Management and Industrial Relations* (Englewood Cliffs, N.J., Prentice-Hall, Inc., 1948), Chapter 5 and pp. 413–23, 755–59.

.4.

Recruitment

ACUTELY aware of the need for personnel—because of the perspective gained through job analysis, description, and classification, and the manning tables which have designated how many employees are needed in each kind of job—the personnel administrator considers how he is going to go about getting the personnel he needs.

After scrounging for personnel from all available sources and through a variety of approaches, the personnel administrator becomes keenly conscious of the need to prepare the ground for the staffing activity through a well-organized and functionally operative program of recruitment.

Recruitment is the preliminary appraisal of individuals as potentially desirable school employees followed by an activity of getting those people so interested that they will be attracted by the possibilities of school employment and will follow through by getting the necessary training for a school job.

Recruitment will be explored in this chapter in terms of the need for this activity, its purpose, its extent, the agents and agencies involved, the means employed, and the development of the sources of supply.[1]

NEED FOR RECRUITMENT

Particularly since 1946, the great shortage of qualified personnel to fill the different kinds of school vacancies in the vital activity of education has driven home the need for a well-planned operative program of recruitment.

[1] Through the courtesy of Dr. Fabian A. Meier, much of the material in this chapter has been adapted from his unpublished doctoral dissertation, Recruitment for Teaching (College Park, Maryland, The University of Maryland, 1955). Where possible, credit is given throughout for direct references.

Demand

The demand for school personnel is determined basically by two elements, the class size being considered a constant. These are the number of children of school age and the number of teachers leaving teaching. Subordinate factors are over-crowded classrooms, double sessions, and provision of qualified personnel in place of the unqualified ones employed.

Children. Since 1954 the number of children born has exceeded 4 million annually. During the 1930's the children born annually constituted about 1.9 per cent of the population. During the 1940's, the ratio fluctuated between 1.9 and 2.6 per cent, stabilizing somewhat in 1949 at 2.4. During the 1950's, the ratio stabilized at about 2.4 per cent. With a population currently near the 190 million mark and projected to 200 million by 1966, and with an increasing trend toward attending school through the senior high school in some kind of program—approximately 90 per cent of secondary school age youth are enrolled in school—school memberships promise to approximate the school-age population.

It looks as if elementary school (K-6) enrollments may stabilize somewhere in the 28 million vicinity while secondary school (7–12) enrollments continue to grow to approximately 22 million by 1969. This is for both public and nonpublic schools. Nonpublic school enrollments have approximated 12–14 per cent of the total for some time, thus public school personnel needs would have to be computed in terms of about 44 million elementary and secondary youth.

Teachers. In 1959 there were over 43 million children in the 5–17 age group. By 1969 it is wholly conceivable that there will be approximately 50 million children in grades K-12 inclusive. With an average of 30 pupils per classroom teacher, this would call for 1,667,000 classroom teachers with the usual supporting administrative and supervisory, clerical, custodial, and other school personnel for the public and nonpublic schools of the United States.

Somewhere between 8 and 11 per cent of the teachers employed in the public schools have been leaving the classroom annually in recent years. At a 10 per cent loss, there would be a need in 1960 for 143,608 new teachers merely to replace those leaving the practice of teaching. By 1965 this need would have progressed to 163,521.

The total of new teachers needed annually, as shown in Table 4-1, is more than twice the number who enter teaching yearly now. In terms of a projection of the anticipated number of college graduates ranging from 355,100 in 1960 to 512,600 in 1965, meeting the demand for teachers would require that 55 per cent of the graduates in 1960, diminishing

TABLE 4-1
Teachers Needed, 1960–65*

Year	For Increase in Enrollments	For 10 per cent Replacement	Total New Teachers	Teachers Retained	Total Teachers
1960	52,306	143,608	195,914	1,292,472	1,488,386
1961	40,414	148,839	189,253	1,339,547	1,528,800
1962	38,193	152,880	191,073	1,375,920	1,566,993
1963	36,447	156,699	193,146	1,410,294	1,603,440
1964	31,773	160,344	192,117	1,443,096	1,635,213
1965	29,020	163,521	192,541	1,471,692	1,664,233

* Derived from The Fund for the Advancement of Education, *Teachers for Tomorrow,* Bulletin No. 2, 1956, p. 54.

gradually to 37.6 per cent in 1965, would enter teaching on the elementary and secondary school levels in the public and nonpublic schools of this country. Currently about 26–30 per cent of college graduates are entering upon school teaching in the public and nonpublic schools of the United States.

In addition, it has been estimated [2] that there are approximately 235,000 elementary school teachers who are not college graduates and approximately 90,000 teachers in the elementary and secondary public schools who are emergency teachers.[3] Conservatively estimated, probably a minimum of 60,000 of these teachers need very much to be replaced. Many of the noncollege graduates, however, are both certified, experienced, and in many an instance valuable teachers.

The scene of teacher demand is one of great need. It can either be most discouraging or it may be stimulative of the kinds of effort that will attract to teaching young people who are not now considering doing so. Some of these may contribute to increasing the percentage of college graduates who take up teaching. Others may increase the number of those who enter college with the intent of preparing for teaching.

Nonteaching Personnel. The data on nonteaching personnel is virtually nonexistent. It is, however, common knowledge that school districts are seldom in a position to compete successfully with other employing agencies, including private enterprise and municipal, county, state, and federal governments. Consequently, in the area of nonteaching personnel, the schools are in the position normally of seeing the most competent

[2] *Teacher Supply and Demand in Public Schools, 1958,* Report of the Eleventh Annual National Teacher Supply and Demand Study, Research Division, National Education Association of the United States, April, 1958, pp. 15, 17.

[3] The Fund for the Advancement of Education, *Teachers for Tomorrow,* Bulletin No. 2, 1956, p. 65.

men and women employed by others while they are faced with the necessity of selecting, from those who are left, individuals who seem not most competent but least incompetent.

The possibility of and the need for recruiting young men and women to serve the school system in the host of nonteaching jobs that exist has not been generally recognized. This is almost virgin territory with all the implications of such territory for exploratory work and experimentation. Also, as with such territory, the possibility for making great gains—this time for the improvement of the teaching-learning situation—is unquestionably very great.

THE PURPOSE OF RECRUITMENT

The immediate purpose of recruitment is to secure the personnel that the school system needs. Recruitment that stops with the effort to fill vacancies falls short, however, of the potential of the recruiting activity. Corollary to the filling of jobs is the purpose to fill jobs with truly competent workers, teaching and nonteaching, at the time of need for personnel.

The personnel needed by a school system vary greatly in the preparation needed to qualify for the respective jobs. The prospective school employee must therefore be initially selected, informed about the possibilities and advantages of school employment, and attracted toward school employment to permit him to undergo the necessary training to qualify for the job.

The training period for the various kinds of jobs determines the minimum lead time that has to be considered in recruitment; e.g., since teachers ordinarily require four to five years of training to qualify for teaching, recruitment for teachers should begin sufficiently early to permit the prospects to make up their minds about becoming teachers and then to complete the program of preparation.

Through the recruiting activity, then, there is a preliminary selection of promising youth, an informational and counselling service to acquaint them with the values of school employment, and a training period. All of this is by way of creating a personnel pool or reserve upon which to draw, as the need occurs, with the assurance that the schools will thus be more likely to be staffed with competent personnel than in the past.

EXTENT OF RECRUITMENT

To the degree to which a carefully planned program of recruitment has come into being, it has been pretty much restricted to those jobs which require certifiability to teach. Inasmuch as all jobs within a school system are part of the unit activity, education, and all are contributing to the facilitation of instruction and learning, it is just as important to assure high competence among the supporting personnel as it is to make provisions for getting competent teachers.

The recruiting activity or program must therefore be extended to make provision for developing a supply of competent personnel from which the school system may select the best when the need for personnel arises. These provisions are incomplete unless they include all prospective employees who are to be members of the teaching profession as well as those who need not be members of the teaching profession.

AGENCIES FOR RECRUITMENT

The need for recruitment has become so obvious that four agencies, which have a very real stake in the outcomes, have become active in recruiting. These agencies are the education associations (state and national), institutions for teacher training (colleges and universities), school districts, and state departments of education or public instruction.

The National Education Association

The Future Teachers of America was formally established by the Representative Assembly of the NEA in 1937. However, the NEA had issued the first charter for a high school FTA club in 1936. Twenty years after their formal establishment, FTA clubs had increased to 3717 and had a membership of 155,000.

The NEA has been active in a number of ways in assuring an adequate supply of teachers. This is in accord with the function of the professional association to provide for the advancement of the cause of education and for the improvement of its own membership.

Future Teachers of America. At first the FTA was organized under the auspices of the Publications Division of the NEA. It was transferred to the sponsorship of the National Commission on Teacher Education and Professional Standards (also NEA) in 1955.

Until 1956 the FTA clubs were found both in high schools and on college campuses. In 1956 it was decided at a work conference that the FTA designation should be reserved to the high school clubs while clubs for institutions of higher education should be known as the Student National Education Association.

These two groups, the FTA and the SNEA, provide for those interested in teaching a common bond through which their interest may be further stimulated and developed. It has served also to provide a unity out of which has grown a pride of membership and of preparation for the teaching profession. In view of the demand for teachers, it is obvious that further extension of such clubs and increases in membership are imperative.

National Commission on Teacher Education and Professional Standards. This commission, commonly referred to as NCTEPS or TEPS, was organized in 1946. One of its goals is the balancing of teacher supply and demand through a vigorous program of selective recruitment. This emphasis on selectivity is in keeping with its purpose of improving the professional status of teachers.

The organization of state TEPS commissions has been encouraged by the national organization with the result that practically every state has a state organization for TEPS. In view of the nature, purposes, and goals of the NCTEPS, it seems most logical that the FTA and Student NEA clubs should come under the sponsorship of this commission.

Teaching Career Month. In 1958 the NEA sponsored the first nationwide observance of April as Teaching Career Month. The observance was launched with a major CBS network TV program on education and an education series in *Life* magazine (beginning March 24 and continuing into April).

Among the objectives of Teaching Career Month is "To encourage larger numbers of qualified youngsters to become teachers." The other five objectives support the recruitment motif through a stress on the importance of education, an appeal to the pride of those in teaching, and an effort to raise the prestige of teaching.

In addition, the NEA, through its Division of Press and Radio Relations, makes available specific materials intended to be of help in planning for Teaching Career Month.

The State Education Associations

State education associations have sponsored recruitment programs in a number of states. The Kansas State Teachers Association developed the program which, with some modifications, is operative now. The committee charged with the program became in 1948 the Kansas Commission on TEPS. An outstanding characteristic of the program is the cooperation called for by deans and department heads in colleges and universities; high school principals; officers of Delta Kappa Gamma, Phi Delta Kappa, the FTA, local teachers associations; and the chairman of the TEPS commission. Through these agents contact is made with the student in an effort to encourage his further interest in becoming a teacher.

The Florida Education Association, in cooperation with the State Department of Education, developed a recruitment program in which the

TABLE 4-2
Ten Recruitment Activities Most Frequently Reported
by Ninety-five Institutions

Activity	Total Number Institutions Reporting Activity	% of Type A Institutions Reporting Activity*	% of Type B Institutions Reporting Activity**
Faculty members of the department or college of education participate in "Career Days," "Career Nights," or similar programs in the high schools	87	92.8	89.7
Faculty members serve or are available as speakers for professional and lay groups concerning teacher shortage	80	83.9	84.6
High school seniors visit college for campus open house, class visitation, or other program designed to encourage college attendance	73	71.4	84.6
A Future Teachers of America chapter has been organized on the campus [now SNEA]	72	66.0	89.7
Students informed as to demand for teachers on elementary and secondary level to prevent imbalance of supply on any level	72	71.4	82.0
Contact promising high school seniors as suggested by teachers, counselors, or principals by letter, recruitment pamphlets or brochures, etc.	71	67.8	84.6
Representatives of the college meet in the various high schools with high school students interested in teaching	71	67.8	84.6
Contacts with administrators are maintained to promote closer relations and cooperation and to remind administrators of their obligation in recruitment if they wish teachers for their schools	66	71.4	66.6

College has prepared or has available for distribution printed materials such as folders, pamphlets, brochures, or booklets concerning teaching as a profession	65	58.9	82.0
Scholarships are available for prospective teachers	62	64.2	66.6

* Includes fifty-six state universities and land grant colleges.
** Includes thirty-nine teachers colleges and colleges of education.
Source: Check-list returns from ninety-five state-supported teacher training institutions.

State Coordinator of Teacher Recruitment serves as chairman of the Recruitment and Future Teachers Committee of the Florida Education Association. The recommendations of this association emphasize that the success of the program of recruitment depends on the execution of plans locally and on the arousal of interest and the elicitation of support by many individuals and organizations.

Under the auspices of the Iowa State Education Association, each county association president is responsible for appointing a teacher selection committee. These committees inform (1) administrators and teachers of the need for selective recruitment and (2) students of the opportunities in teaching. Provision is made to acquaint prospective teachers with available scholarships and to recommend the outstanding prospects for them.

In addition, each state education association publishes a journal in which the problems of teacher demand and supply are brought before the membership for use in recruitment activities.

Teacher Training Institutions

On the whole it would seem that institutions of higher education have much room for improvement of the program to recruit students for teaching. In general their efforts are most helpful in two areas: the sponsorship of SNEA's and the provision of scholarships. A more complete perspective of the recruiting activities in which institutions of higher education engage is provided by Table 4-2 prepared by Meier.[4]

Two programs of recruitment by institutions of higher education have pointed up some possible courses of action for the improvement of recruitment.

The New Jersey State Teachers College Program. The six teachers colleges of the state, together with the State Department of Education, worked out a program of recruitment whereby constructive cooperative efforts to attract youth to teaching replaced the disruptively competitive

[4] Fabian A. Meier, Recruitment for Teaching (Unpublished doctoral dissertation). (College Park, Maryland, University of Maryland, 1955), pp. 135–137.

activities which seemed to result in placing institutional growth ahead of the state's need for teachers.

A pilot program in one of the institutions became the basis for the state-wide program. Policies for operating the program were developed by a planning committee representative of all the institutions. In each institution a member of the staff was charged with responsibility for recruitment and was relieved accordingly of some of his other duties. Each college representative was given a district of the state within which to work and represented himself in his district as the spokesman for, not his own college, but the Teachers Colleges of the State of New Jersey.

Provision was made in New Jersey to work through the guidance programs of the secondary schools, junior as well as senior high. Career conferences provided opportunity to discuss a number of the kinds of issues which concern prospective teachers. A number of charts were prepared as springboards for the discussions and recruitment materials were placed in the hands of the conferees.

The Wayne State University Program. Located in Detroit and drawing students both from this large city and from pretty much all of Michigan, as well as from other states and lands, this University has organized an extensive recruitment program.[5]

The Wayne program has three dominating characteristics. Making use of a coordinator of the over-all recruitment activity, it has an on-campus involvement of the university administration, the staff of the college of education, the student body, and campus organizations. It makes its appeal to high school seniors and liberal arts college students, as well as to several youth groups, through high school counsellors, teachers, university advisors, FTA and SNEA groups, the PTA, clergymen and others who are in a position to identify youth who seem to have the qualities needed for teaching, and community youth groups. And finally, it has an extensive list of activities including the observation of Education Day, organization of FTA and SNEA clubs, visits to high schools by faculty members and by advanced education students and new teachers, departmental publications outlining opportunities, sponsorship of recruitment conferences in the schools, dissemination of information about scholarship, and use of press, radio, and television, as well as billboards, stickers, and displays to get the recruiting message across.

Teachers Colleges. Aside from such other activities as they may engage in to attract students to the preparation of teaching, the state teachers colleges of all the states do provide at least an economic attraction. In practically every instance, e.g., the tuition charges at the state teachers

[5] Details about this program have been reported in *Lay-Professional Action Programs to Secure and Retain Qualified Teachers* (Washington, National Education Association, 1954), pp. 108–116.

TABLE 4-3
Ten Recruitment Activities Frequently Reported
by Ninety-five Institutions

Activity	Total Number Institutions Reporting Activity	% of Type A Institutions Reporting Activity*	% of Type B Institutions Reporting Activity**
Orientation program for new students emphasizes opportunities in teaching profession	57	60.7	58.9
Faculty members and student advisors are given latest information on teacher supply and demand in the state	57	57.1	64.1
College yearbooks are placed in high school libraries and counselor's offices	56	53.5	66.6
Students are kept informed as to need for teachers by articles in school paper, bulletin boards, or other means	54	55.3	58.9
College has sponsored or participated in radio or TV programs planned to stimulate interest in teaching	51	46.4	64.1
College or university publicity office publicizes need for teachers	50	41.0	69.2
Circulate information to high schools about scholarships available for prospective teachers	46	48.2	48.7
Talks during Freshman Week about advantages of teaching	42	48.2	38.4
All high school seniors in our state or area receive a college catalog, bulletin, or some type of communication from the college	37	42.8	33.3
College students now preparing to teach visit home or other high schools to participate in discussions or conferences with high school students concerning teaching	27	21.4	38.4

* Includes fifty-six state universities and land grant colleges.
** Includes thirty-nine teachers colleges and colleges of education.
Source: Check-list returns from ninety-five state-supported teacher training institutions.

TABLE 4-4
Ten Recruitment Activities Least Frequently Reported by Ninety-five State Institutions

Activity	Total Number Institutions Reporting Activity	% of Type A Institutions Reporting Activity *	% of Type B Institutions Reporting Activity **
A teacher-recruitment committee of the faculty, either formally or informally organized, to give study to the problem and to suggest plans for possible recruitment activities	27	26.7	30.7
Alumni association organized to encourage promising high school students to consider teaching	26	4.2	46.1
Prominent educators or others address students in assembly about careers in teaching	25	30.3	20.5
A post-baccalaureate or "Conversion" program which enables liberal arts graduates or those not qualified for certification to begin teaching on "Limited Credentials" after attending summer school, and complete certification requirements at a later date . . .	25	21.4	33.3
Information about opportunities in teaching distributed to liberal arts students	24	26.7	23.0
Establish contact with college students uncertain as to vocational choice to present opportunities in teaching	20	21.4	20.5
A broad survey course in history and philosophy of education showing importance and significance of education in modern society required of all students	17	12.5	25.6
Students suggest names of other individuals not now preparing to teach or undecided as to vocational choice who might be contacted	17	7.1	33.3

Directed correspondence of our college freshmen with prospective students from their own high schools	6	3.5	10.2
Our territory divided into districts and staff members with time and funds are responsible for program of public relations with the schools of these districts	4	1.7	7.6

° Includes fifty-six state universities and land grant colleges.
°° Includes thirty-nine teachers colleges and colleges of education.
Source: Check-list returns from ninety-five state-supported teacher training institutions.

college are lower—and often much lower—than those at the state university.[6] In some states, there is no tuition charge for those students who pledge themselves to teach for a stated period of years, generally two.

The School District. The individual school districts have a tremendous stake in the attraction of potentially good teachers into teaching. Needing good teachers, school districts cannot afford to leave to others the pre-selection which is recruitment. They virtually must take decisive action to assure themselves of an adequate supply of competent teachers. In fact, their need stipulates their extending their efforts to the recruitment also of the nonteaching personnel which the school needs greatly.

Teacher Recruitment. The school district's concern for attracting into the teaching profession individuals who could become good teachers is explored in terms of the activities described below.

As important an activity as any in recruitment is the regard which teachers themselves express for their profession. It may be expected that one who is engaged in teaching will be a spokesman for its attractions and an agent for upgrading the group to which he belongs by doing what he can to improve its membership. However, to do so the teacher must assume the realistic position of understanding exactly why he is a teacher. This understanding involves a careful appraisal of all the values, including advantages, disadvantages, and gratifications.

Teachers are often individuals with competencies which would permit them to succeed in a number of other kinds of endeavor. Many such teachers have come into teaching from such endeavors; others have left teaching in the expectation of finding greener pastures elsewhere only to discover that they have left the really green fields for less attractive ones in terms of what they want out of life. These teachers generally have discovered that important as economic gain is, there is something even more important which keeps them in or brings them back to teaching.

[6] The interested might well make an initial comparison of state teacher college and state university tuition in his own state.

Nevertheless, being human, teachers too have the tendency to emphasize the negative—no doubt with the hope of resultant positive action—and have been known to advise youngsters to put aside their desire to teach in favor of almost anything else. It would be helpful to the recruitment activity and to the improvement of the entire teaching profession if the gripes would be kept within the family or between the profession and those who have a responsibility for correcting a bad situation, and if the dominant values that bring and keep teachers in the profession were emphasized both within the group and in contacts with prospective teachers. If this is impossible, at least a balance between the advantages or gratifications and gripes of teaching deserves to be struck.

The complexities of the large school system have made it necessary for the guidance of classroom teachers to be supplemented by that of those trained for counselling. One part of the counselling activity is concerned with vocational choice. It is imperative that counsellors provide a proportionate perspective of school employment needs and opportunities while presenting the total vocational outlook.

The encouragement of FTA clubs, cooperation with teacher-training institutions and PTA's, and observance of special days, weeks, or months which call attention to teaching are within the province of the local school district.

Inasmuch as it has been established [7] that liking to work with young people is the most frequently stated reason for wanting to teach, it seems advised that youth be given opportunities to associate and work with youngsters so that they may discover whether working with them might be so gratifying to them that they would want to become teachers.

A number of school systems have made use of some kind of experience program whereby advanced high school students who were interested were given the opportunity of learning the facts about teaching and of gaining some experience through their association with and assistance to teachers.

Danville and Decatur, Illinois, are school systems with such programs.[8] Students, usually seniors, help the teacher in the routine things necessary to prepare for teaching, assist in administering tests, do remedial teaching under the close supervision of teachers, and work with groups of children in reading or telling stories and in directing recreational activities.

[7] Probably the most extensive study dealing with motivation for entering teaching is that of Robert W. Richey and William A. Fox, *A Study of Some Opinions of High School Students with Regard to Teachers and Teaching* (Bloomington, Indiana University, 1951), p. 51.

[8] See Katherine Stapp, "High School Course for Future Teachers," *The Journal of Teacher Education*, 4:77–78, March, 1953, and "Preface," *The Teachers College Journal*, 25:70, March, 1954. Also, "Decatur's Done Something about Recruitment," *Illinois Education*, 35:228, April, 1947.

Schenectady, New York; Elkhart, Indiana; and Sheboygan, Wisconsin, are representative of what are termed *Cadet Teacher* programs.[9] The cadet programs include careful selection of those who are interested— e.g., from the upper third of the class group—study of a text that gives perspective on teaching, visiting and observation in schools, directed observation and teaching, and experience evaluation. In the phase of directed observation and teaching, the cadet teacher does what he can to assist the teacher. This will involve routine in gathering, organizing, and distributing materials and extends to doing limited teaching.

Possibly the activity which gives the greatest evidence of the importance attached to and the attention given recruitment with the school districts is the host and variety of specifically designed recruitment brochures that are coming off the press.[10] These brochures are often put out in attractive format, highlighted with color and well illustrated, and with a message that is presented briefly and concisely. These publications are useful for recruitment to the teaching profession. They are probably designed more specifically for attracting to the respective school districts applicants who are qualified for employment.

The Inglewood Unified School District in California and the Clayton, Missouri, brochures were excellent examples of what can be done in good taste to put out a publication that will be sure to be read and which will have the basic information needed to arouse the interest desired. They join with others in their presentation of the following kinds of information:

geographical location	cultural, educational, and recreational
kind of community	opportunities
population	related benefits
school enrollment	sick and sabbatical leave
assessed valuation	group insurance
number of schools and kind	credit union
class size	retirement
length of school day	miscellaneous items
days in school year	board of education point of view
salary schedule	administrative philosophy
tenure provisions	application request form

---

9 Harry J. Linton, "Teacher Recruitment in 1953," *The School Executive*, 73:68–69, January, 1954; Anne McAllister, "Cadet Teaching in the Elkhart Public Schools," *The Teachers College Journal*, 25:62–66, March, 1954; John W. Hahn, "The Sheboygan Cadet Teaching Program," *Lay Professional Action Programs to Secure and Retain Qualified Teachers*, Washington, The National Education Association, 1954, p. 54.

10 There will hardly be a school district of any significant size that has not developed something in the way of a recruitment brochure. Brochures from the following school districts have been reviewed: Washington, D.C.; Baltimore County, Maryland; Newark, Delaware; Newark, New Jersey; New York City, Buffalo, and Rochester, New York; Columbus, Ohio; Indianapolis, Indiana; Clayton, Missouri; Corpus Christi, Texas; Fontana and Inglewood, California; and Seattle, Washington.

The personnel division will find the time spent on turning out a condensed statement of the important items to be included and on attractively tasteful composition a rewarding investment.

Recruitment of Nonteaching Employees. The school district is faced also with the problem of recruiting nonteaching employees. The various kinds of office personnel needed can be made aware of opportunities in the school system during their training in high school and, where it exists, the junior college. This awareness may be followed up by an experience program, summer employment, and advisement as to the advantages accruing to this kind of school employment.

Another large category of nonteaching employees is that of the custodial personnel. It seems that on the whole there is an assumption that it is somewhat ridiculous to attempt the recruitment of young people for custodial work. Perhaps closer cooperation between the counselling division and the personnel division will reveal that many a young person who, by reason of endowment or inclination, has to be limited in his aspirations could be attracted to custodial work in which he can gain the gratification of making a contribution to society through the part he plays in the operation of the school system.

When it is considered that many of those skilled in the building trades are employed only during the time that construction is booming, it becomes obvious that there would be among them some who would be glad to gain for themselves the year-around employment security offered by school employment. School systems which are sufficiently large to have a maintenance force can become more selective of their maintenance staff through the application of recruitment techniques.

It becomes apparent that all kinds of school jobs, particularly those for which a number of personnel are used, provide recruitment possibilities. The recruitment activity is advocated in these instances as a means for assuring the personnel needed and of upgrading the personnel employed in the school system. This recruitment is particularly within the province of the school system and of its counsellors. Its success is not dependent on, but it is greatly enhanced by the provision of benefits akin to those accorded to the teaching personnel. This is accomplished in part in some states through the inclusion of all school personnel within a school employees retirement plan.

The State

There have been casual references to the incidental impact of some state provisions upon recruitment. Thus state scholarships, state provisions for a greater subsidy of teacher training than for other higher education, and state provisions for a retirement program all have significance for the recruitment activity.

Probably the most important single agency in the state organization for the planned recruitment of teachers is the state's agency or department of education or of public instruction.

Since education is recognized as a function of the state, the state has a responsibility for the recruitment of school personnel. This is recognized to a degree through the teacher training institutions provided. However, the effective functioning of the teacher training institution depends on a knowledge by the state agency of the teaching personnel situation—how many teachers there are, what their qualifications are, and what the need for new teachers is in terms of replacements and of additions. This calls for a research and appraisal activity which is logically followed by a plan that includes provisions for a recruitment program.

The recruitment functions of the state department of education have been summarized as follows:[11]

1. Organization and sponsorship of a state-wide conference or regional meetings within the state on teacher recruitment.

2. Coordination of and leadership in recruitment activities within the state.

3. Furnishing consultant or advisory services to high schools, colleges, lay and professional groups.

4. Preparation and publication of recruitment materials.

5. Development of special incentives or means of attracting individuals to the teaching profession.

6. Promotion of experiences for students designed to encourage consideration of teaching as a career.

These functions are to large extent operative in the Florida Department of Education statement [12] which describes its recruitment functions as follows:

1. To furnish a state coordinator of teacher recruitment whose work is to cooperate with and to furnish the leadership for local school systems, colleges, and lay groups in developing an effective teacher recruitment program.

2. To appoint, upon the recommendation of the county superintendents, county coordinators of teacher recruitment to work in cooperation with the state coordinator in developing a county-wide selective teacher recruitment program.

3. To provide leadership to all school systems in the development of teacher personnel policies and practices. This will improve teacher morale and enhance the prestige of the profession.

4. To prepare and distribute literature regarding teaching as a career.

5. To encourage public schools to give experiences with children to students considering teaching as a career.

[11] Fabian A. Meier, *op. cit.*, p. 67.

[12] *School Improvement through Selective Teacher Recruitment* (Tallahassee, Florida, The Florida Department of Education, January, 1954), pp. 15–16.

6. To work with the Florida Education Association to provide an effective teacher recruitment program.

7. To urge teachers to re-examine their attitudes toward teaching and the teaching profession and to encourage them to demonstrate their interest and enthusiasm in teaching by words and action.

8. To keep local schools informed about the number of teachers needed in the various fields.

9. To have a speakers' bureau—a group of competent, informed people strategically located throughout the state who are prepared to speak to groups of young people and of lay people on the status of the teaching profession, on current shortages of qualified teachers, and on teaching as a career.

10. To inform and to interest the ablest young people in the State scholarship program for prospective teachers.

Recruitment Officers. Connecticut was one of the first states to give evidence of the importance it attached to the recruitment activity through the appointment in 1949 of a fulltime official in the state department of education with responsibility for recruitment. Within five years of this action 16 states had such officials and another 10 were considering their appointment.[13] These officials are known as assistant superintendents, directors, coordinators, or supervisors of recruitment.

A program of the importance and scope of the recruitment activity can be expected to operate efficiently only when there is provision for a state department official with primary responsibility for recruitment.

Publications. Brochures, pamphlets, and other materials suitable for teacher recruitment have been published by the following 29 states:[14]

Alabama	Kansas	New York
Alaska	Kentucky	North Dakota
California	Louisiana	Ohio
Delaware	Maine	Oklahoma
Florida	Maryland	Oregon
Georgia	Massachusetts	Pennsylvania
Hawaii	Minnesota	South Carolina
Idaho	Nebraska	Texas
Illinois	New Hampshire	West Virginia
Iowa	New Jersey	

The publications are generally either produced through the efforts of the state department of education or through the cooperative efforts of the state department and the state education association. The activity of the state department is most logically directed towards supplying the local school districts and the teacher-training institutions with the information and leadership they need in order that they may initiate and maintain a successful recruitment operation.

13 Fabian A. Meier, *op. cit.*, p. 79.
14 *Ibid.*, p. 83.

Conferences. Among states which have had or planned to have conferences on teacher shortages were:[15]

Arizona	Maine	Oklahoma
California	Maryland	Oregon
Connecticut	Michigan	Pennsylvania
Delaware	Minnesota	South Dakota
Florida	Montana	Texas
Georgia	Nebraska	Utah
Illinois	Nevada	Vermont
Indiana	New Jersey	Virginia
Iowa	New York	Washington
Kansas	North Dakota	West Virginia
Louisiana	Ohio	Wyoming

Some indication of the worthwhileness of such state conferences is found in the intention of nine states which have engaged in such conferences to do so again. The stimulus provided by central agencies, such as the state and the national government, is proved too by the fact that some conferences have been planned in connection with a White House conference on education.

Participants in the conferences are drawn from agriculture, business, civic groups, industry, labor, the professions, including education and the clergy, and service clubs. A conference on the problems of education unavoidably has implications for personnel considerations and awareness of the need for a well-organized program of recruitment. The expected result is willingness on the part of citizens to share in the solution of the problem of getting and keeping teachers for their schools.

Mobilization of Former Teachers. In a number of states it has been recognized that former teachers, those who were trained for teaching and have had experience, provide a potential which—with some refresher work to bring them up-to-date—could help to reduce the teacher shortage and to improve the total teacher personnel scene.[16] Some of these are state, county, and individual school district mobilization plans which have taken place in:

Arizona	Kentucky	South Carolina
Connecticut	Maryland	Utah
Florida	Nebraska	Vermont
Illinois	New Jersey	Virginia
Indiana	Ohio	Washington
Kansas	Oklahoma	West Virginia
	Pennsylvania	

[15] *Ibid.*, p. 53.
[16] *Ibid.*, p. 82.

Limited information about the effectiveness of attempts to get teachers to return to teaching suggest that such plans are promising. In Montgomery County, Maryland, such a plan accompanied by a 12-week refresher course requirement produced in one year 100 applicants from whom 70 were acceptable and 50 were hired. This program was repeated subsequently with similarly encouraging results.

Conversion Programs. Many a person completes his college education without a vocational plan clearly in mind. Upon graduation such find themselves well versed in their fields of preparation but with limited opportunities to use their knowledge for the earning of a livelihood. State departments of education and teacher training institutions have seen here the possibility of supplementing the subject matter preparation of such college graduates to qualify them for teaching. Various plans were put into effect to assure as well as possible the further professional development of these individuals to the point of complete conversion.

Thirty-six states operated some kind of conversion program.[17] Limited certification to teach was generally given upon completion of a special session designed to prepare for teaching. Four—Indiana, Massachusetts, Nevada, and Rhode Island—required such college graduates to meet all or a major part of the certification requirements.

Cadet Teacher Programs. Operated within the local school district as part of its high school program of recruitment, the cadet program has also received official sanction from a number of state departments of education. Such a program was organized, for example, under the auspices of the Iowa State Department of Public Instruction with provision for high schools that wanted to participate to apply to the State Department for membership in the Iowa Cadet Teachers Corps. Within a year of its birth, the Cadet Teachers Corps had 49 chapters in operation.

Some form of a cadet teacher program was found in almost all the states, exceptions being Arizona, Maine, Missouri, New Mexico, Rhode Island, Utah, and Virginia.[18] Situations such as this do not remain static and these states may have ceased to be exceptions by this time.

Scholarships for Teacher Education. An economic inducement is sometimes provided in areas of particular need to stimulate the preparation of individuals for employment in such areas. Teacher education also has this kind of stimulus to consider teaching as a field of preparation and vocation. With few exceptions, the state legislatures have made scholarship funds available for those who prepare for teaching. In addition, of course, many institutions of higher education have scholarships available

[17] *Ibid.,* p. 91.
[18] *Ibid.,* p. 96.

for their students, including those who prepare for teaching. Acceptance of a scholarship in a number of instances places the student under an obligation to teach for a specified number of years.

The possible value of a scholarship program as an aid to recruitment seems beyond question. An examination of the scholarships made available provides one cue as to why the program is so ineffective as to leave many scholarships unclaimed. Where medical education scholarships ranged from $200 to $1250, teacher preparation scholarships ranged from $75 to a maximum of $500;[19] and this during an era of a minimum cost of approximately $1800 per year for higher education. To be significant as a recruitment device, a scholarship has to be sufficient to make it possible for those who could otherwise not go on to proceed with a program of higher education.

Loan Funds. It may be that society, represented by the state, will regard itself as limited in the number and the amount of the scholarships it provides. It may even question to a degree whether the scholarship plan is really sound.

The point has been made that, although society is also the gainer by the training of teachers, the teacher himself is also a very real beneficiary. He has the advantages of a college education and the preparation for a vocation which promises those suited to teaching security, respect, increasingly a salary which affords a living, and the gratification peculiar to teaching. Hence the prospective teacher ought to be willing to pay for the advantages that are brought within his grasp.

The opportunity to become a teacher can be brought within the reach of even the most economically benighted through the provision of a loan. The states have the opportunity to do much along this line. They might well take their cue from the National Defense Education Act of 1958 through which loans are granted to college students. Interest rates are low and do not apply until one year after the borrower ceases to be a full-time student. Those who enter upon a public school teaching career are remitted a part of their obligation at the rate of 10 per cent per year, up to 50 per cent. Through such provisions broadened by adaptation on the state level, it might be anticipated that recruitment for teaching would be given a very positive stimulus.

MEANS FOR RECRUITMENT

Many of the means for carrying on the recruiting activity have been intimated in the foregoing. However, in order to call them more clearly to attention, they are briefly summarized in the following listings of who does the recruiting and the activities through which recruiting takes place.

[19] *Ibid.,* pp. 99, 101, 108.

Who Does the Recruiting

Recruiting may be done by anyone who has the interest of education at heart. The people who may be expected to take part in the recruitment activity are:

State department officials
Teachers and school administrators
College and university faculty and administration
Advanced education students
New teachers
Secondary school students already interested in teaching
Alumni of teacher training institutions
PTA, Chamber of Commerce, and other local organizations
Education associations—local, state, and national
Citizens advisory commissions

Recruitment Activities

The possibilities are almost unlimited. The following list is selected from practices in use:

research
planning
interpretation
conferences (state and local)
cooperation with school systems, colleges, lay groups, and the education
    associations
use of a speakers bureau
panel discussions
film presentation
publicity by press, radio, and TV
advertising
observance of career week or month
publication and circulation of pamphlets, brochures, and reports
observation and visitation in schools and teacher training institutions
provision and issuance of scholarships
initiation and administration of loans
mobilization of former teachers
conversion of college graduates to qualified teachers
workshops and training programs
internships for college graduates
cadet teaching experience programs
issuance of a proclamation [20]
coordination of all the foregoing

[20] A proclamation by the Governor of Florida, in recognition of the importance of education and the need for teachers, established the week beginning November 15, 1954, as Future Teachers Week and encouraged young people to consider the advantages of teaching as a profession.

The number and variety of the foregoing partial list of possible recruiting activities intimate the need to provide for the organization and administration through which the activities may become parts of a logical and effective plan of recruitment. Such coordination is provided at the state department level through an assistant superintendent of public instruction in charge of teacher recruitment by this or some other title.

DEVELOPMENT OF THE SOURCE OF SUPPLY

In a sense this section summarizes what has been intimated about the sources from which teachers will be drawn. Where this has been only intimated before, it is herewith emphasized. The secondary schools, colleges, former teachers, college graduates not prepared for but interested in teaching; all are potential sources of teacher supply. The potentialities are realized as a result of a planned recruitment program.

The Secondary School

Since the preparation of teachers is a time consuming activity which cannot begin purposefully until the individual has decided that he wants to be a teacher, the first source to be considered is the secondary school pupil. This includes the junior as well as the senior high school student. This is a particularly important source since the indications are that many youths with the ability to complete successfully a college program do not go on to college. Among them there are no doubt many who would be a real credit to the teaching profession.

Some of these youth could undoubtedly be attracted to teaching if they knew more about the opportunities in and advantages of teaching. Others might be attracted if they could see their way economically to prepare for teaching. This, it seems, is the great and almost untapped resource that must be developed.

The College

In the institutions of higher education there are many students who either have no vocational objective or who will be changing their original objectives. These students can generally have their programs readjusted with scarcely any disruption to prepare them for teaching provided they have made up their minds before beginning their junior year of college work. Even thereafter, there are possibilities for adapting college students, even those who have completed another program, with relatively little effort—effort well invested in salvaging and giving direction to a college education—so that they may qualify for teaching.

Thus, the college also is a promising field for the recruitment activity.

Former Teachers

For one reason or another, teachers do leave the profession without a well-defined plan to return to it. To some of these ex-teachers it comes as somewhat of a surprise, and often a welcome one, to find that—now that the reasons for their having been out of teaching are no longer compelling—they could re-qualify themselves for teaching with reasonable assurance of being seriously considered for employment.

In view of the very large number of those who prepare for teaching and never accept employment as teachers and of the very great loss of teachers who have taught for only a few years, it seems that this source is another that promises well for the recruiting activity.

Conversions

Aside from those whose interest is aroused during or immediately after their college student days, there are men and women who have had careers outside the schools and who would like during their retirement years—ages 40–45 and up—to teach. It has been an interesting phenomenon of the post World War II years to note that former officers in the Army and Navy of the United States, among others, having qualified for retirement have taken the necessary steps to prepare and qualify themselves for teaching. Among them there have been those who have proved real assets to the teaching staff of the school system.

As long as the source provides recruits who will upgrade the profession, that source must be regarded as one well worth cultivating.

SUMMARY

The recruitment of carefully selected and well-qualified youth for teaching is regarded as a highly important activity that deserves much greater attention than it has received. Whereas consciousness of the need for a recruiting activity is the product of a demand for teachers far in excess of the supply, it has also become apparent that there will always be a need for the recruiting activity as the means for upgrading the teaching profession by attracting to it better qualified individuals.

It is also recognized that while recruitment has been thought of chiefly in terms of attracting qualified people to teaching, it has just as defensible an application for attracting to school employment the many nonteaching employees needed to support the teaching personnel.

Interest in and activity for recruitment has been manifested by the national, state, and local education associations; teacher training institutions, local school districts, the state and its department of education or of public instruction, and by lay groups such as the Parent Teacher Association, Chamber of Commerce, Citizens Advisory Committees, and others.

The means for recruitment were discussed in terms of the agents and agencies through which recruitment takes place and in terms of a lengthy list of selected activities. Both of these contributed to the conclusion that an effective and well-planned program of recruitment demands the services of a full-time coordinator on the state level.

The source of teacher supply is developed through the agents and activities described throughout the chapter. The source is seen as existing in the junior and senior high schools, the junior and four-year colleges, the group of those who are prepared for teaching but who for some reason are not engaged in this profession, and in those who wish to transfer from some other career to that of teaching and are willing to take the necessary steps to qualify themselves.

Throughout, the stress has been on arousing interest in teaching among those who will contribute to the improvement of the teaching profession through their decision to become members thereof. Further, like stress has been laid upon the possibilities of upgrading nonteaching personnel in other facets of school employment through similar pre-service selection, guidance, and such training before or on the job as may be necessary.

SELECTED READINGS

CHANDLER, B. J. and PETTY, Paul V., *Personnel Management in School Administration* (Yonkers-on-Hudson, New York, World Book Company, 1955), Chapter 4.

DOELE, Helen R., A Study Associated with the Recruiting of Elementary School Teachers by the State of New Jersey. Doctor's thesis (New York, New York University, 1955), 184 pp. Abstract: *Dissertation Abstracts* 16:289–290; No. 2, 1956.

ELAM, Stanley M., Public Relations: An Experimental Evaluation of Student Recruitment Techniques in a Teachers College. Doctor's thesis (Urbana, University of Illinois, 1955), 192 pp. Abstract: *Dissertation Abstracts* 15:2112–13; No. 11, 1955.

ELSBREE, Willard S. and REUTTER, E. Edmund, *Staff Personnel in the Public Schools* (Englewood Cliffs, N.J., Prentice-Hall, Inc., 1954), Chapter 1.

MOORE, Harold E. and WALTERS, Newell B., *Personnel Administration in Education* (New York, Harper and Row, 1955), Chapter 8.

NEA Research Division, National Education Association of the United States, *Teacher Supply and Demand in Public Schools,* current issue.

NEA Research Division, "The Postwar Struggle to Provide Competent Teachers,"

National Education Association *Research Bulletin,* XXXV:3, October, 1957.

NELSON, Lester W., "Improvements Needed in Secondary Schools," *The Annals* (American Academy of Political and Social Science), Vol. 325, September, 1959, pp. 87–94.

RICHEY, Robert W., *Planning for Teaching* (New York, McGraw-Hill Book Company, Inc., 1958).

U.S. Department of Health, Education, and Welfare; The Office of Education, *What Some Communities Are Doing to Recruit Elementary Teachers,* Education Brief No. 31 (Washington, The Office, March 1956), 16 p.

U.S. Department of Health, Education, and Welfare; The Office of Education, *Efforts of State Groups in Recruitment and Selection of Teachers,* Education Brief No. 32 (Washington, The Office, July 1956), 22 p.

YEAGER, William A., *Administration and the Teacher* (New York, Harper and Row, 1954), Chapters 3, 4.

YEAGER, William A., *Administration of the Noninstructional Personnel and Services* (New York, Harper and Row, 1959), pp. 59–62.

.5.

The Training of School Personnel

ALL SCHOOL personnel require some degree of training. Some, such as the custodial staff, can get the training needed after their employment by the school system. Others, such as the broadly-taken clerical staff, require advance training in specific skills and techniques including the taking of dictation, the use of various kinds of office machines, and the keeping of books or accounts. Maintenance personnel require the training by which they acquire competency in their respective trade skills. Teaching personnel are expected to have college training with emphasis upon general background subject matter mastery, and the development of ability to teach. School administrators require, in addition to the preparation for teaching, further training in various specialized aspects of school administration. And, all school employees are expected to improve their competencies while in the employ of the school system.

The total problem or job of training for school employment will be explored in terms of principles, objectives, determinants, means, and possible improvements.

PRINCIPLES

The following principles[1] may be expected to be operative in the various aspects of the training of school personnel:

1. Education is the primary purpose of the schools.
2. The people who have instituted the schools and all employees within the school system have the same basic interest.

[1] For the full statement of these principles, see number 1, 3, 4, and 5, Chapter 1.

3. Maximum effectiveness of the means for achieving the people's mandates regarding education requires the best possible selection and coordination of all elements comprising those means.

4. School employees are not commodities.

It is incumbent upon all school personnel to become educated to their parts in the total educative process conducted by the school. School employees cannot functionally compartmentalize their behavior so that clerical worker, custodian, maintenance man, and teacher work in virtual disregard of each other. All are parts of the school system which society has instituted for the education of youth.

The selection and coordination of personnel in order to provide a high degree of effectiveness of each and of the school system require that the training of employees before their employment and its continuance thereafter be made a matter of primary concern.

Probably one of the most sensitive areas of interpersonal relations is that in which the question of one's competency is raised. Nevertheless, the requirements of the school system as a social institution of the people demand that measures be taken to assure that the existing level of competency will not be lowered and to make provisions for improvement of competency.

Putting the principles to work means that those responsible for personnel administration must select the trained personnel needed, train all others initially, and make warranted provisions for growth on the job—and do all this with real regard for the individual as well as for the welfare of the schools.

OBJECTIVES OF PERSONNEL TRAINING

The over-all objective of all training of school employees is an efficiently operating educational system. The immediate and subordinate objectives are improvement in the competency of the employee, employee gratification resulting from an extension of interests, and sometimes the preparation of the employee for transfer or promotion to another job within the school system.

These objectives will be examined with respect to each, the teaching and nonteaching type of employee.

Improvement in Competency

It should be predicated that every school employee is hired because he is qualified to do the work involved in his job. It is, however, expected that his qualifications can be better adapted to the particular requirements of the specific job which he has taken and of the school system which has employed him. It is also assumed that further experience, experimentation, and supervision will promote greater competency.

Teachers. At one time the teacher was expected to know little other than what he had to teach. It was not uncommon for the teacher to keep only a step or a lesson ahead of his charges. Now, on both the elementary and secondary school levels, teachers are expected to bring to their tasks a comprehensive preparation. Those who come into teaching short of the necessary comprehensive training have the task of gaining and then maintaining an adequate general background.

Experience as a teacher helps to develop the confidence that a good teacher needs. Thus time on the job may be expected to be a factor in improvement. However, time can also confirm a teacher in familiar practices which could be bettered. Development of the confidence that is the product of experience coupled with inquiry and experimentation may legitimately be expected of every teacher.

With the passage of time there are generally advances in knowledge within the fields of what is taught and how to teach. Among the teacher's improvement goals is that of keeping apace of developments in his subject field and in the understanding of how to influence human behavior, i.e., how to teach effectively.

Most important among all the categories of school personnel, the teacher shares with others the need to develop the tolerance to be expected of the well educated and the mature. This is an objective for improvement which will aid the teacher to teach more effectively on the one hand and on the other to establish with all his colleagues, professional and nonprofessional, the optimum working relationships which make possible the good school.

Nonteaching Personnel. Both those with and without technical skills— office, maintenance, custodial, and other service personnel—should be constantly alerted to the need to see their individual tasks as part of one job, the improvement of the school setting so that the conditions for learning will approach the ideal. Attainment and maintenance of this point of view with respect to their respective jobs is the general objective of personnel training for improvement in competency.

In addition to general improvement, a goal in the training and improvement of school personnel is the further development of the skill that each has in his work and perhaps even the development of additional skills.

Extension of Interests

Membership in a democratic society really implies keeping abreast of the times, broadening perspective, and projecting ideas. To live in the past in terms of interests and perspective is to be already dead. To keep abreast of the times in terms of some *single* interest condemns to narrowness of perspective. Failure to project limits existence to an unrecoverable past and an infinitesimal present. Living seems virtually synonymous with an extension of interests. Nevertheless, observation reveals the necessity of taking positive steps to make certain that such extension will take place.

Teachers. All those who are classified as teachers—whether they are in administrative, supervisory, or classroom assignments—are faced with the problem of the demands which their immediate jobs make upon them and with the consequent difficulty of setting aside time for the extension of their interests. Yet, the place of the school in our society is such that it ceases to be functional unless it keeps apace of the society of which it is a part and the changes that take place in it.

As teachers, school personnel have an even greater responsibility for broad interests and keeping up with the times than are imposed upon all adults in terms of their citizenship. The nature of the school and the implications of their tasks add to the demands already made upon teaching personnel, for their initial and further training, the challenge to expand their interests and to become well informed.

Nonteaching Personnel. Working in an environment of education and to the extent that they actually do have contact with and responsibility for children, the nonteaching personnel may have the goal of expanding their interests and knowledge. To some extent this objective is the outcome of the environment,[2] an environment that can be influenced deliberately to provide an encouraging atmosphere for such expansion.

The school situation lends itself to making the nonteaching personnel more aware of their citizenship opportunities and obligations. The results may be expected to be both more intelligently active citizens and more effective school employees. This effectiveness will be demonstrated through their understanding and support of the school system, their attitudes and efforts on the job, and their relationships with and influence upon the pupils in the school.

Change of Position

The great variety and number of jobs within a school system provide many opportunities for a change of position without a change of employment. It is possible to transfer from one kind of job within the school system to another provided one has the competencies required to warrant the change. Such competencies may be developed by the employee in his pursuit of what he considers to be advancement. His efforts may

[2] It is not uncommon to find that a custodian with but little formal education has, by reason of his school job, become interested and proficient in some of the school subjects, such as Latin, History, and Mathematics.

also be promoted by a personnel administration which seeks to make the best use of the potential of the total working force of the school system.

Teachers. There are a number of logical or possible directions in which a teacher may go within the school system. Among the possibilities are a change of major subject field or leaving the classroom to become a counsellor, helping teacher, supervisor, vice-principal or principal, administrative assistant to the principal or superintendent, a specialist in some area of administration—such as child accounting, finance, instruction, personnel, plant, pupil services, and research—or the generalist job of the superintendency itself. In each instance, qualification for the job in mind is the product of initial training followed by pertinent experience.

Nonteaching Personnel. It is possible for the nonteaching personnel to hold the objective of transfer not only to another and possibly advanced nonteaching job but also to a teaching job. Most likely the realization of the objective to transfer from any nonteaching job to some other job within the school system will require the development of the necessary qualifications through some kind of training program.

Their school employment associations may have provided, for example, the clerical personnel with an insight into the opportunities and advantages of teaching. As a result, particularly the younger ones may have developed vocational interests which may be encouraged and directed by the personnel officers. Supplementary training makes possible a change in position from even a nonprofessional to a professional job within the school system. This extreme possibility illustrates the need for that training which is necessary to qualify one for any change of position within a school system.

DETERMINANTS IN TRAINING

The agencies which exert the major influence upon the training of teachers are the state departments of education (otherwise known as departments of public instruction or as the education agency), school districts, institutions for teacher training, and the professional organizations through which teachers express themselves. These agencies will be examined briefly with respect to their impact upon the training of those who are interested in becoming teachers.

State Department of Education

The state department of education is in effect the administrative or executive branch of the state board of education. Whereas the certification of teachers is a function of the state board, it is the state department or one of its divisions through which the state board generally carries into effect its certification policies. Also, the state board of education is influenced by the professional personnel who administer the state department of education and its certification division. Thus, control of certification is theoretically in the lay hands of state board members but is often practically controlled within the state department of education.

Through its specification as to the requirements to be met for the various certificates it issues, the state department virtually stipulates what minimum training the teacher must have. In this way it also determines the minimum teacher-training program of teacher-training institutions.

Any discussion of improvement of teacher training and of the teaching profession of necessity raises question about the actual significance of all certification requirements. There are some that are extremely difficult to defend, the more so in terms of the practices in which certification officials sometimes engage. One state department official in charge of certification stated that it didn't matter what the content of a course required for certification was as long as the title of the course conformed to the stated certification requirements. In another instance the certifying officer is so arbitrary that prospective applicants for certification have found it necessary to protect themselves by getting commitments in writing. Commitments made in conference were often disavowed after the conditions set forth had been met.

Functionalization of certification combined with administrative policies to introduce consistency in certifying would immediately affect teacher training throughout the country.

School Districts

In their efforts to be outstanding, many school districts have set their standards for employment well above the state requirements for certification. The effect of their employment standards is reflected in the course offerings of teacher-training institutions. The practices of school districts which are constantly looking for ways in which to improve instruction have in turn been reflected after awhile in increased certification requirements.

The importance of the ability of school districts to influence the training of teachers through their requirements, quite apart from those for certification, can hardly be over-emphasized. There is sometimes a tendency to look to the state authority for leadership in improving standards. However, if this leadership is not forthcoming, it has become obvious that improvement can still be achieved through local effort. In fact, it is local effort that eventually makes possible successful action on the state level.

Institutions for Teacher Training

Influenced by state certification requirements and by additional demands of local school districts, teacher training institutions are initially constrained to develop courses of study in accord with state and local specifications. In addition, the teacher-training institution provides the perspective and insight of its own staff and may impose its own requirements beyond those already stipulated for graduation from a program in teacher preparation.

It is not always clear to students that certification is the prerogative of the state authority and that graduation from a program, e.g., one in teacher training, is the province of the teacher-training institution. The two may operate so harmoniously as to be indistinguishable from each other, or it may be that a specific choice has to be made either to work for certification, subordinating graduation, or for graduation subordinating certification. This becomes particularly evident on the graduate level when one is concerned on the one hand with getting, for example, a master's degree and on the other with qualifying for another type of certificate, e.g., a principal's.

It is expected that institutions of higher education will have to face up to their responsibilities to much greater degree than they have in training teachers. Offerings must be developed in terms of a defensible rationale and far beyond the necessary, desirable, but rather pedestrian vision of the field practitioner.

The Professional Organization

The impact of the professional organization upon teacher training is generally somewhat less direct than that of the three agencies already discussed. Nevertheless, its impact is felt through various divisions concerned with, for example, colleges for teacher education, school administrators, educational research, audio-visual instruction, educational policies, ethics, exceptional children, public relations, teacher education and professional standards, several subject matter areas, elementary and secondary school principals. These divisions or departments frequently have their own publications addressed first of all to their own interest group membership.

Probably much of the impact of the professional organization is akin to that of the Office of Education (United States Department of Health, Education, and Welfare). In each instance the agency serves as a clearing house for keeping the profession informed about what is going on nationwide. This alone serves to affect thinking, stimulate experimentation and change, and make its impact upon teacher training. In addition, the professional organization commands the services of many well-qualified professional people who assume further responsibility for leadership for improved teacher training.

MEANS FOR TEACHER TRAINING

Teacher training takes place through two approaches, preservice and inservice training.

Preservice Training

Predicating their preparation of teachers on state certification requirements, local demands, and college programs, teacher training divisions of colleges, teachers colleges, and colleges or schools of education in universities prescribe a training program intended to prepare youth for teaching. Requirements vary but generally include a number of the following courses: history and philosophy of education, one or more methods (how to do it) courses, psychology of education, a course in tests and measurements, and a course in which prospective teachers are given the opportunity first to observe various teachers at their normal day's work and next to do teaching (practice teaching) under the supervision of a teacher approved for the purpose by the teacher training institution.

The changes which have taken place in teacher training are particularly highlighted by the scene in practice teaching. Within the past 30 years the scene has shifted from the laboratory school connected to the teacher training institution to the field situation of the regular everyday public (and sometimes nonpublic) school. Also, instead of a few hours of practice teaching, e.g., one period per day for one week, it is not uncommon to find that observation and practice teaching is a full-time assignment for half a semester or more.

Responsibility for the field experience aspect of teacher training is reserved to the training institution which has one or more staff coordinators who recommend for approval by the college those teachers who seem particularly suitable for supervising the teaching experience of novices. Generally these teachers are made part-time members of the teacher-training institution and are paid by that institution for the training services they provide.

Inservice Training

All training gotten after one has become a teacher has come to be called inservice training. This training falls into two major categories. Whereas some inservice education is very informal, other inservice training has become very formalized.

Little need be said about informal inservice training except that it takes place as one teacher communicates ideas to another, as any teacher learns through experience, and as a teacher keeps himself up to date with the literature and developments both in his subject matter field and in the field of education. It seems that in some ways at least, since it is reflective of the teacher's interests and initiative expressed in voluntary actions, this type of inservice training is highly indicative of that spirit which is called professional.

Formalized Training. There is continued training of school personnel, both teaching and nonteaching, through formal provision within the school system and through the programs of institutions of higher education.

Within the school system all supervision of personnel has the function of providing inservice training with the objective of promoting and maintaining competency. Particularly in teaching, it is imperative that the teacher keep up with the changes in his teaching field (the chemistry and physics of today are a far cry from those of 30 years ago and as great changes have taken place in the social field). Likewise the teacher must keep apace of developments in the behavioral sciences. Teaching is the application of the science of affecting behavior.

Another form in which formalized training is found within the school system is the programs which personnel are virtually, if not actually, required to follow. Sometimes the program consists of a sterile series of lectures which are intended to convey evidence—by the physical presence of teachers compelled to attend en mass—that improvement of the teaching personnel is taking place. Sometimes the program consists of a lengthy menu of offerings from which teachers are expected to make a selection according to their interests and needs. Teachers enroll for the courses of their choice and appear regularly for their inservice classes. Such programs can on the one hand provide real opportunities for teachers with needs which can be met through the program. On the other hand, such programs can produce results which make a farce of inservice education and cast a stigma upon it. The potential of a program of inservice training course offerings lies in its appeal, not in coerciveness. It is axiomatic that a horse may be led to water but cannot be made to drink against his will. The forcible immersion of the "heathen" is no longer expected to bring about conversion. Yet, making teachers attend some kind of inservice training program is still often considered a feasible means for improving professionalism and its corollary competency.

A third formalized program for teachers who have entered upon teaching service is that provided in the graduate programs of universities. In some instances these programs are available to full-time teachers who can register for late afternoon and evening classes; in others they are available only on a full-time basis to teachers who take a leave of absence or who attend during summer sessions only. This type of program is of particular advantage to teachers who wish to compensate for a deficiency, prepare for a specialization in education, and extend their perspective in some direction.

Not too readily distinguishable from any who make use of the foregoing are those teachers who seek only the advantage of a degree or its equivalent, not in order that they may improve themselves but rather only in order that they may improve their economic status by qualifying for a salary increment. The presence in our graduate schools of those who have an economic yearning unaccompanied by one for learning places the graduate school at a disadvantage and does very little for education at any level. It sometimes seems that there are teachers who show marked intelligence and ingenuity in the efforts they put forth to get an advanced degree without getting at the same time the education which it is intended to represent.

A fourth program for the inservice training of teachers is that organized by local, state, and national education associations in the form of a centralized meeting or convention. Lectures, panel presentation, group discussions, entertainment, and commercial displays of school supplies, equipment, and construction materials and plan layouts are typical of these conventions.

This fourth kind of inservice program is of such scope and complexity that its careful and formal organization is a necessity. The support of the state department of education and of the school districts is also given through provisions for closing the schools so that teachers may attend. However, there is an informal concomitant to this program in the growth in service provided through the almost casual interchange of ideas between those who make or renew acquaintance.[3]

Informal Inservice Training. Members of the teaching profession who are professional in their interests and outlook improve in service throughout their careers because of their own memberships in organizations, reading of professional and other publications, associations, and reflective thinking. These mediums are a practically unmeasurable but undoubtedly great potential for improving teaching. It is somewhat of an indictment of those who make up the teaching force, or of those who exercise control over inservice training, that rather great reliance for improvement of teaching seems to be placed in pressure approaches and that little faith seems to be put in those means which require initiative, voluntary action, and perseverance on the part of the teacher.

---

[3] There are those who consider this informal exchange, the exhibits, job seeking, and personnel recruiting to be the top values of the convention.

THE IMPROVEMENT OF TEACHER TRAINING

The foregoing discussion of the determinant agents and agencies in the training of teachers and the means through which they operate almost suggests the problems to be met in order that improved training may take place.

Certification

Inasmuch as certification of teachers calls for expert knowledge which is within the province of the teaching profession alone, there is the problem of changing the provisions whereby control of certification now lies within lay or lay-dominated boards.

To the degree that and as long as lay boards operate largely through certification divisions of state departments of education, there is also the problem of having these departments operate as functionally as they can within the limits imposed upon them. Even within these limitations there is often the possibility to use judgment professionally, reduce arbitrariness, and develop an improved policy structure for certification.

There exists the threat that—if state boards continue to exercise responsibility for teacher certification as in the past and the teaching profession fails to assume functional control over the admission of others to their ranks—one or more other lay bodies now organized or organizing will invade and take over certification. What the real interests of self aggrandizing lay interest groups are in their assumption of certification responsibilities will be almost impossible to determine and need not remain constant.

Local Requirements

In recognition of the minimum nature of state certification requirements and of their frequent inadequacy, school districts have often called for qualifications beyond those of the state.

The local school district is an excellent area in which the profession, expressing itself through the school administration and through the local education association, can demonstrate its competency to set the standards for eligibility to teach. One problem facing the local school district is that of getting the education association to become involved and to make that involvement a truly meaningful one. A problem facing both the school district and the professional organization in the event of their mutual involvement in setting higher standards for teacher employment is the determination of just what will be really significant in assuring that better teachers are to be employed.

Academic Requirements

Although determined to a degree by the requirements of the state certifying body and of local school districts, the training programs of the teacher-training institutions have the perfect right to a degree of self determination.

The teacher-training program must reflect the understanding, experience, and special insight of its faculty if it is to command respect in its own right. There is little doubt that this will mean abandonment of the primary requirement that seems to have dominated teacher-training programs, that the training be completed within a four-year period.

The general requirement that teachers have a broad general background, somewhat along the lines of a liberal arts education; the awareness, particularly on the secondary school level, that teachers must have a thoroughgoing knowledge of their teaching subject field(s); and appreciation of the fact that teaching is generally an acquired skill or art which requires the development of the background upon which to build a usable understanding and appreciation of the means by which human behavior may be influenced; all of these predicate an extension of the training period.

In one teacher training institution the music education department insisted on a greater share of the 120 hours of the undergraduate program. A review of all other factors indicated that this was impossible. However, the suggestion that this department's needs might be met by having its graduates stay on for an additional summer session, semester, or year to get the training that the department considered necessary was considered unrealistic because of the four-year tradition.

It may be pointed out that education has sufficient precedent for extending its training period on the undergraduate level to whatever is necessary to turn out qualified teachers. The medical, dental, and legal professional schools have long ago extended their periods of training in accordance with their concepts of need. Schools of library science began by offering the bachelor of library science as a five-year program. For over a quarter of a century engineering schools, in deference to the impact of technological developments and scientific discovery, have extended a number of their programs—aeronautical, mechanical, and electrical in particular—to a five-year training period on the undergraduate level. To these, in deference to the necessity of bringing up to date the civil engineering curriculum because of the increased store of available knowledge, it is proposed [4] to add Civil Engineering as a five-year program of undergraduate study.

It seems sometimes assumed that leadership toward change must come

4 John B. Scalzi, "A Minimum Education for Professional Civil Engineers," *Civil Engineering*, Vol. 29, No. 10, October, 1959, p. 54.

from some vague place of authority "above." There really is nothing to prevent the teacher-training institution from requiring more than the state or the more demanding local school districts before it will confer its stamp of approval upon prospective teachers trained by it.

Professional Requirements

The professional organization could have an even greater impact upon the preparation of teachers than it now has. This impact could conceivably come about through professional requirements which would have to be met before one could affiliate with the organization. Of necessity these requirements would have to be at the same time reasonable, defensible, and high enough to make membership something to be desired and of which to be proud.

Here too it may be emphasized that criteria for selective membership may be set up and put into operation on any level, local, state, and national. There is no excuse for neglecting to take action merely because one or more of the other level agencies are expected to provide the leadership. It is wholly conceivable that the local, state, or national professional organization's standards would be so high that local boards of education would stipulate that no one could be employed in the professional jobs unless he would be eligible for membership in the education association.

Supervision

It is highly questionable that teachers of competency, the kind who make the case for teaching to be a profession, should be closely supervised. The occasionally encountered practice of utilizing supervisors chiefly to orient beginning teachers to their jobs during the first two to three years —the probationary years—of their teaching and to help other teachers only upon request when they have special problems on which they need assistance generally makes sense.

It is quite conceivable that the specialized supervisory activity should be greatly contracted once the school system is assured that it is employing competent teachers. This assurance, now provided as a result of supervision throughout the probationary period, might well come to be provided through an extension of training via a system of internships and residencies not unlike those employed in the training of medical doctors.

Faculty Meetings

The schools face a real problem inasmuch as faculty meetings are undoubtedly necessary. The problem is to have no more meetings than are truly necessary. Observation indicates that it does not take long before periodicity, i.e., operating according to schedule, takes precedence over functionality, i.e., having only meetings that fulfill a real need. At a loss for what to do with a scheduled time for meeting, program committees do their best to come up with something that, it is hoped, will have a salutary effect upon those who are called to meet.

The holding of meetings, as well as some of the other compulsory inservice training activities, can become more suggestive of a defensiveness and need for compensatory activity than of the confidence that professionalism merits.

Programs for Inservice Training

The same kind of problem confronted with respect to faculty meetings faces the programs for inservice training. Some are filled with considerable dead wood, indicating more of a desire to commandeer a portion of a teacher's time than to help that teacher improve himself. The requirement to attend a course offering in the inservice program without reference to teacher need leads teachers to scrutinize the long list of possible courses. The criterion for selection soon becomes that a course should make a minimum demand on the time and energies of the teacher. Hence, such a course as penmanship is soon filled. An elementary school penmanship teacher starts the record player and then walks about making caustic remarks about teachers who have now attained the third-grade level of writing.

Teachers enrolled in such a course as that just described met the technical and time requirements for inservice education. By no stretch of the imagination or of adept rationalization could they expect to become as a result more professionally competent teachers. Can inservice training be cleared of all its dead wood? Can it be organized to meet teacher need? Can it operate functionally on any other than a voluntary basis with the fulfilment of need as the only reward to be gained? These questions highlight the problems faced in inservice training of teachers.

Graduate Programs

The value of graduate programs in institutions of higher education is to provide opportunities to develop further skills, gain additional knowledge, and prepare for a change of professional occupation. These outcomes of graduate training are on the positive side. On the negative side is the degree that has been gotten, not with the intent of improving the recipient but only with the intent of qualifying him for a salary increment. This latter is a perversion of the function of higher education.

A part of the perversion alluded to results in some instances from the preparation of teachers for other professional duties, e.g., administrative jobs. Nevertheless, returning to their regular classroom duties with a technical qualification for administration but no appreciable improvement as classroom teachers, these teachers now are generally eligible for a salary increment. This situation is the product of a rather lightly considered "preparation-based" salary schedule. An immediate improvement would be the requirement that the program pursued has primary pertinence to the job to be done. In this case the specialization in administration would produce no increment until the teacher was transferred to an administrative job for which his training does have implications.

SUMMARY

The training of all school personnel is intimately affected by the origins and the purposes of the schools. The reasons for training are the attainment, maintenance, and improvement of competency, extension of interests, and preparation for a transfer or promotion. These reasons apply to both teaching and nonteaching personnel.

Training of nonteaching personnel varies from that which takes place strictly on the job to that which calls for specialized skill or knowledge, often acquired in high school or junior college or in qualifying for membership in a trade union.

In addition there are a number of jobs for which certification as a teacher is prerequisite. There are a number of agencies and agents which have a major impact upon training for those who are to be certified as teachers. These agencies are the state certifying board, the state department of education, school districts, institutions for higher education, and the professional organizations through which teachers gain the strength of unity.

Teacher training takes place chiefly by two means, preservice training and inservice training. The preservice training takes its cues from the agencies which are concerned with the preparation of teachers. The inservice training may be divided into two categories, formal and informal.

Informal inservice training is reflective of the growth which is incident to teaching, contact with teachers and others, reading, and thinking. Formal inservice training within the schools runs the gamut of excellent and highly worthwhile programs geared to teacher needs and provided on a voluntary basis to those programs which are sterile, time consuming, and highly coercive by mandate or by implication.

Formal training provided teachers in service by teacher training institutions and graduate schools provide opportunity for improvement and for change of position. These programs are organized by the institutions of higher education on the assumption that enrollments will be voluntary. However, their offerings are affected by the kinds of incentives which motivate those who take the courses. These motivations also run a gamut, from genuine desire to get as much from a course as possible to doing no more than is necessary to get some credit. Unavoidably, the courses given suffer from the presence of those whose interest is strictly monetary.

Local, state, and national education associations also provide for in-service training through conventions which provide for an exchange of ideas, association with others, and exhibits of educational supplies and equipment.

There is obviously much room for the improvement of teacher training. Certification, for example, would seem most logically to belong in the hands of a state certification board staffed by highly professional teachers. It might well be realized that no local, state, or national educational organization is really barred from raising its standards above those of the other organizational levels. Failure to act because of lack of leadership from another organizational level of operation is inexcusable.

The teacher-training programs in institutions of higher education have been limited in their potential by some hidebound notion that teacher training must be confined to a four-year undergraduate program. Just as other disciplines have found that with advancements in the realm of knowledge it became necessary to extend the training period on the undergraduate level, so also it is inevitable that teacher training must yield to the requirements for assuring competency in general background, special subject fields, and knowledge of human behavior and how to influence it.

The training of teachers could also be affected much more greatly than at present through the improvement of the requirements for membership in education associations so that such membership may become a symbol of teacher competency.

Another look needs to be taken at supervision and its place in education and at faculty meetings and their functionality. Unless this is done the schools are in danger of perpetuating practices which are of doubtful if not negative value.

Withal, it is the responsibility of the personnel division to give close attention to the training required of those who are to be employed in the schools and to the provision for improved service to the schools by all of the personnel.

SELECTED READINGS

"American Civilization and Its Leadership Needs, 1960–1990," *The Annals* (of the American Academy of Political and Social Science), Vol. 324, September 1959, pp. 1–123.

BLAUCH, Lloyd E., *Education for the Professions* (Washington, United States Government Printing Office, 1955).

BRUBACHER, John S., "Resolving the Conflict Between Academic and Professional Training of Teachers," The University of Michigan *School of Education Bulletin,* Vol. 30, No. 6, March, 1959, pp. 81–88.

DIXON, W. Robert, "Postwar Developments in Secondary Directed Teaching at the University of Michigan," The University of Michigan *School of Education Bulletin,* Vol. 29, No. 6, March, 1958, pp. 87–91.

HODENFIELD, G. K., and STINNETT, T. M., *The Education of Teachers* (Englewood Cliffs, N.J., Prentice-Hall, Inc., 1961).

LIEBERMAN, Myron, *Education as a Profession* (Englewood Cliffs, N.J., Prentice-Hall, Inc., 1956), Chapter 7.

SARASON, Seymour, DAVIDSON, Kenneth, and BLATT, Burton, *The Preparation of Teachers* (New York, John Wiley & Sons, Inc., 1962). 124 pages.

SCHLICHTEN, E. W., "The Idea and Practice of Teacher Certification in the United States," *Teachers College Record,* Vol. 59, April, 1958. pp. 411–426.

STOOPS, Emery, and M. L. RAFFERTY, *Practices and Trends in School Administration* (Boston, Ginn and Company, 1961), Chapter 19.

"Teacher Personnel," *Review of Educational Research,* 28:3, June, 1958, Chapters 1, 3.

"The Administration of the Soviet Higher Education System," *Journal of Engineering Education,* 49:9, May, 1959, pp. 846–854.

TRUMP, J. Lloyd, *Images of the Future* (Urbana, Illinois, Commission on the Experimental Study of the Utilization of Staff in the Secondary School, 1959), pp. 31–33.

YEAGER, William A., *Administration of the Noninstructional Personnel and Services* (New York, Harper and Row, 1959), Chapters 1, 4, 5.

.6.

The Selection of School Personnel

THE SELECTION of personnel for any kind of job is an important and difficult task. This is true for all kinds of public and private enterprises even when they use all available scientific techniques to insure optimum selection of employees. The problem of the schools is complicated because of the importance of child-teacher relationships and the general lack of precise knowledge as to just what constitutes a good teacher. This complication serves to highlight the very great importance of doing all possible to select school personnel so as to assure the best qualified personnel for the various kinds of school jobs.

OBJECTIVES

The primary objective of sound personnel selection is to make possible a level of school operation which is consistent with the nature and the function of the school system and to do so with a minimum loss of time and effort for orientation and subsequent training. Selection is that phase of putting into effect the objective of personnel administration that is concerned with the discovery and employment of personnel who have the ability, will, and necessary initial competency to do the work assigned them.

A secondary objective of a desirable and effective system of personnel selection is the reduction in the need for supervisory services. This has the effect of either reducing the number of supervisory personnel or using supervisors more advantageously. Thus, for example, supervisors of instruction could rely on the competency of teachers employed through effective selection procedures and forego supervising all but a relative few who either are on probation or request assistance under special circumstances.

Similarly a reduction in supervisory activities is possible among the nonprofessional school personnel where there is competency. Many a school principal has found to his joy that the janitor(s) in his building could be relied upon to do whatever had to be done without close supervision. Others have discovered on the contrary that a janitor who lacks competency and the responsibility that is part of it can handicap the instructional activities of the school by his need for supervision.

The objectives of efficiency of operation, reduction in costs resulting from inefficiency, and reservation of monies for further improvement of instruction are the pursuit of the personnel division and are furthered through sound personnel selection.

PRINCIPLES

The principles underlying a sound program of personnel selection are:[1]

1. Education is the primary purpose of the schools.
2. The objectives of the schools are functionally derived from the people who have created them as institutions to meet those needs that they want fulfilled through formal education.
3. Maximum effectiveness of the means for achieving the people's mandates regarding education requires the best possible selection and coordination of all elements comprising those means. The means are comprised of school employees, plant, and supplies. It is the job of the personnel administration to assure the optimum in the selection, assignment in terms of job, physical placement, and equipment of personnel.
4. All participants in an enterprise are entitled to fair dealing. Unfairness or the appearance of injustice is cause for rankling resentment which is a threat to worker effectiveness.

Emphasis on Instruction

Selection of personnel can take place first of all in terms of factors pertaining to competency only when proper consideration is given to the fact that education is the primary purpose of the schools. Such other factors as age, family connections, finance (hiring on the basis of who can be paid the least), marital status, nationality, politics, pressures, race, religion, residence, and sex must either be subordinated to the primary consideration or eliminated.

[1] See Chapter 1, principles 1, 2, 4, and 11.

Meeting the Intent of the People

The school has evolved in the United States as an institutionalized expression of the will of the people that the children be educated in those matters that are of importance to them, the society in which they live, and the democracy which has become the pursuit of the people of this land since its early settlement over 300 years ago.

It is incumbent upon the schools, as institutions of a democratic society, to operate in terms of policies—including personnel and personnel selection policies—that are consistent with the objectives of the schools as determined progressively by the people. This is in effect another way of emphasizing the need to select personnel in terms first of all of the public welfare as expressed through formalized education.

Assuring Optimum Selection

Making certain that the best available personnel are secured for the school system is a major concern of the personnel administrator and the division through which he works. Selection of the best available but not competent may be defensible, if unfortunately unavoidable, in the non-teaching jobs of the school. In the teaching jobs it has become increasingly obvious that the best available is not good enough unless competency is also present. This really means that no selection can defensibly take place if competent teachers are not available. The contraction of services is preferable to adulterating the ranks of those who teach through the admission of those who have no competency to do so.

Here it may be noted that the teacher has need of two attributes, among a host of others. On the one hand he must have knowledge; on the other he must have skill to impart knowledge, to teach, to influence behavior, or however one wants to put it.

Fairness

The people of the school district, the children in the schools, the personnel within the school system, and all those who seek to become employees of the schools have a right to fair treatment. Part of fairness is that all the people of the district and the school staff be assured that the best of the competent teachers and the best available nonteaching staff will be supplied for the operation of the schools. This suggests the setting up of equitable regulations or policies to assure optimum selection. And, fairness to all who aspire to serve through employment by the schools means that each will be accorded equal treatment in terms of the policies set up.

THE IMPORTANCE OF CAREFUL SELECTION

Careful selection of personnel is highly important to the functioning of the school in accord with its historical development as an expression of the wishes of the people with respect to the education of their children. Only through careful selection of personnel, particularly the teaching personnel, can the schools hope to retain—or regain—the confidence of the people. Careful selection can be productive of more effective school operation, reduction in or better use of supervision, and the possible release of funds—otherwise spent on ineffective services and the supervision they entail—for the improvement of instruction. And, it may be anticipated that a policy of careful selection will affect morale positively.

PERSONNEL SELECTION PROCEDURES

Some indication as to the procedures to be followed in selecting personnel has been supplied through the foregoing statements of objectives and principles. A more definitive development of procedures is presented in terms of policies, personnel requisitions, the securing of applicants, applications, the selection activity, and appointment.

Policies

It is unavoidable that the Board of Education of a school district will serve as a selective agency in the employment of its chief executive officer, the superintendent. To do this in the most irreproachable and equitable way, the board will have to set up the rules by which it plans to make its decision. It has something to go by in terms of the state requirements for certification, the publications of the American Association of School Administrators,[2] eligibility for membership in the American Association of School Administrators, specific training for the administration of a school system, experience gained locally or through observation of neighboring school districts, and employment practices of a particularly reputable or successful school district in which the board of education and the superintendent may be consulted. The basis decided upon for the selection of the superintendent constitutes a policy of the board which it adopts and executes.

Under the leadership of the superintendent, aided by the professional staff, other policies regarding the necessary qualifications of employees of various kinds should be formulated for approval by the board of education. Here the job of determining qualifications is a professional one in

[2] American Association of School Administrators, *Professional Administrators for America's Schools* (1960); *Profile of the School Superintendent* (1960); and *Something to Steer By* (1958) (Washington, The National Education Association).

which the decisions require professional competency. The board of education is in the position to raise questions, to call for clarification, to make suggestions, and then to take action in accord with the recommendations that the professional leader makes in view of all that has taken place.[3]

Again, the starting place for all policies governing the selection of school employees is the school code of the state with its requirements for teacher certification and for qualifications of a number of other employees. However, whereas the state's requirements are drawn up on a minimum basis to provide a floor for practice throughout the state, each school district has the responsibility to determine how high above the minimum floor its own standards are to be.

Policy may well concern itself with such factors as training, experience, certifiability where pertinent, personal qualities to the extent that they can be identified significantly, health, who is actually to do the selection, and the major processes to be undergone—such as the application, interview, observation, evaluation of credentials, offer of employment, and use of tests.[4]

Although it is relatively easy to indicate the major items to be included in policy statements, it cannot be emphasized enough that policies at their best are nevertheless subject to improvement. Further, changing conditions may make policies so obsolete that they have to be scrapped and replaced in terms of the situation that has evolved. Policies that are used slavishly without constant and stringent reappraisal and needed modification can be expected to meet the needs of the schools about as well as the horse and buggy can meet today's transportation needs in the United States.

The Personnel Requisition

The use of requisitions for obtaining needed equipment and supplies has been highly formalized in accord with the requirements of a financial accounting system. It is just as essential that there be a well-organized system for accounting for the employees of the school system. Whereas such accounting takes place informally and reasonably effectively in a small school system, it has to be highly organized to serve effectively in the larger school districts. In the larger school systems it is necessary to make certain that the need for personnel is made clear and that the nature of the personnel needed is well defined. Selection of teaching and

---

[3] "The standards of qualifications of all agents shall be determined by the Superintendent and approved by the Board of Education." *The Public School Code* (of the Hamtramck, Michigan, Public Schools), (Hamtramck; The Board of Education, 1928), p. 30.

[4] Sample selection policies are provided in *School Personnel Policies* by the Commission on Teacher Education and Professional Standards, 1956, of the Ohio Education Association (Columbus, The Association, 1956), pp. 34, 35.

nonteaching personnel must begin with a clearcut understanding of the nature of the job to be filled. The personnel requisition is a means for specifying personnel needs.

The Convenience of the Job Specification. Where job specifications have been carefully and extensively developed,[5] it may be possible to use a requisition form which designates when there will be a vacancy, how many individuals are needed, just what job—in terms of the specifications set up—is involved, and any additional information that the department head or principal considers necessary.

When no reference to job specifications can be made, it is necessary to supply detail as to the job in question, the number of employees needed, what the nature of the job is and what this implies for the qualifications of the employee sought, and when the individual employed should report for work.

Routing the Requisition. The requisition of employees may take place informally by word of mouth or by an interoffice communication. It should proceed from the department head to the principal and thence to the superintendent's office. In the superintendent's office, the requisition should be routed to the personnel division for action.

Securing Applicants

The need for personnel is accompanied by the need to provide for locating those who might be interested in the job. The potential candidate will be found in the ranks of those who have experience in a like job or of those who are inexperienced. It is generally easier to find a means of communicating with experienced than with inexperienced persons. Experienced persons know where to look for jobs and with whom to list themselves as available. The inexperienced still have to learn the tricks of the trade for getting the employment in which they are interested.

Experienced Workers. The functionally operating personnel office will have a file of employees that are looking for a change of location, status, or type of job. This list may well be the first source to be investigated in the filling of all teaching and nonteaching types of jobs. Through the use of such a list it becomes possible to correct the inequities that occur as expediential assignments are made. Thus the chance of improving operating efficiency is offered whenever a shift, addition, or replacement of personnel is in the offing.

[5] For a review of the job specification, see Chapter 3.

Teacher-training institutions, teacher agencies, other school districts, and graduate training schools are the major sources of experienced personnel. Contact is established with one or more of these agencies in order to discover suitable personnel.

Especially since 1942, the schools have resorted to the use of advertising, not only in professional journals but also in the classified advertisement columns of the local newspapers, for both professional and nonprofessional workers.

Inexperienced Workers. Teacher-training institutions, teacher agencies, and advertisements are the main means of getting applicants from the pool of inexperienced potential school employees. The personnel office takes the necessary steps to secure such contacts as will produce applicants.

State Agencies. The state department of education and the state education association are two agencies that have a large stake in making provision for the effective operation of the schools. This stake has been recognized in the provision in many states of recruiting officers in the state departments and of recruitment activities under the auspices of the education association. It would seem a logical next step if both these agencies were to cooperate in setting up and operating a clearing house for the placement and transfer of school employees, perhaps particularly teachers.

The existence of state agencies for locating potential school personnel would be a great boon both to the school districts of the state and to the school employees who wish to change jobs.

Recruitment Literature. Much of the so-called recruitment literature is concerned with the seeking of applicants who are qualified for employment and the attracting of those applicants to the school district in need of personnel. The literature generally paints a rosy picture of the kind of community, the schools, the staffing, working conditions, and the salary schedule. Aside from getting this literature posted in teacher training institutions and sending it to placement agencies, the recruitment brochures cannot generally become effective until a person has become initially interested. It is possibly the first follow-up literature in response to a request for information. The brochure often contains also an application form for one who becomes sufficiently interested to take the next step.

The Application

The application form is intended to provide the employing agency with a knowledge of who is interested in being considered for employment for the job vacancies existing. Ordinarily the information needed in order to consider someone for employment is so extensive that it is wasteful of the time both of the applicant and of the personnel division to get this information from everyone. Hence the preliminary application form has been developed as a basis for initial screening while the formal application serves as a basis for ultimate selection.

The Preliminary Application. For the prospective employee this application will call for the basic personal information which will indicate the general qualification or lack thereof for the job in question. For the professional worker this will include: name, occupation, education (college, degrees, majors, minors), experience, health, and such other specific items as may be considered of primary concern. For the nonprofessional worker the same basic information will be necessary, with the expectation that for a number of jobs there will be no college level education.

Where feasible the preliminary application may be followed in questionable cases by an interview to determine whether formal application should be filed. Otherwise, the personnel division will eliminate from further consideration everyone who does not meet the basic job requirements. It will also either eliminate doubtful applicants or give them an opportunity to file a formal application, depending probably to some extent on the number of applications received and the number of those who look promising. And, it will encourage those who definitely seem to meet basic requirements to file formal application.

The Formal Application. All who survive the screening of the preliminary application are invited to complete the more extensive formal application. The information required by this application varies considerably from one school district to another. This information was most generally found [6] to fall into the three categories of personal, educational, and experience data. A glance at the accompanying tables will show the specific items of information that were most often called for among the thirty-eight school districts that submitted application forms.

The value of the kind of information provided in Tables 6-1 to 6-3 lies in the opportunity to analyze each item of information for the specific value, or lack of it, for the school system that is drawing up its own application form. It may also serve as the point of departure for considering items which have particular pertinence to the local school district. The fact that many school districts require an item of information need not be evidence of anything except that many have this item on their blanks; it is not necessarily evidence of the importance of the information. Conversely, it is well possible that information requested by only a few districts may for those districts be of great significance.

[6] Harold L. Alderton, Selection of Teachers, an unpublished seminar study (College Park, The University of Maryland, June, 1958), 29 pp.

TABLE 6-1

PERSONAL DATA
REQUESTED ON APPLICATION FORMS[*]

SCHOOL DISTRICT	Name, Address – Telephone	Present & Permanent	Birth Date–Age–Place	Citizen of U. S.	Marital Status–Date Married	Children – Ages	Date of Application	Physical – Health, Defects	Height & Weight	Sex	Race	Photograph	Social Security No.	Church Memb. or Pref.	Member Communist Party	Where Lived as Child	Fathers Prof. or Occup.	Fathers Name & Address	Former Name & Address	Related to Board Member	State Resident	Court Convictions	Bonded	Who Notify in Accident	Any Other Income	Member Retirement System
1. Arlington, Va.	X	X		X			X	X	X		X	X														
2. Atlanta, Georgia							DO NOT USE APPLICATION FORM																			
3. Atlantic City, N. J.	X	X	X	X			X	X	X					X												
4. Augusta, Maine								DO NOT USE APPLICATION FORM																		
5. Baltimore, Md.	X	X		X	X		X		X	X			X							X						
6. Bennington, Vt.	X	X		X	X	X		X																		
7. Boston, Mass.	X	X			X																					
8. Buffalo, N. Y.	X	X	X				X	X		X																
9. Camden, N. J.	X	X	X	X	X		X	X					X						X							
10. Charleston, S. C.	X	X					X	X	X		X	X	X	X												
11. Charlotte, N. C.	X	X		X			X	X	X	X	X	X	X	X												
12. Chattanooga, Tenn.	X		X	X	X		X	X	X		X	X		X												
13. Chicago, Ill.	X	X	X	X	X		X	X		X	X															
14. Cincinnatti, Ohio	X	X	X	X	X	X	X	X	X	X	X	X				X	X			X						
15. Detroit, Mich.	X	X	X	X			X						X			X		X								
16. Dade Co., Fla.	X	X	X	X	X	X	X	X	X	X	X	X	X									X	X	X	X	
17. Hartford, Conn.	X	X		X			X	X					X													
18. Indianapolis, Ind.	X	X	X	X	X	X		X			X		X		X				X							
19. Johnstown, Pa.	X	X		X			X	X	X		X															
20. Louisville, Ky.	X	X	X	X	X		X	X		X	X		X	X		X			X							
21. Madison, Wisc.	X	X		X	X	X	X	X			X															
22. Milwaukee, Wisc.	X	X	X	X		X					X															
23. Minneapolis, Minn.	X	X	X	X	X														X							
24. Montgomery Co., Md.	X	X	X	X	X	X	X	X	X	X	X	X	X			X		X	X							
25. Montpelier, Vt.	X	X	X	X			X	X	X	X	X		X			X										
26. Nashville, Tenn.	X	X		X						X	X	X	X													
27. New Haven, Conn.	X	X	X	X		X					X															
28. New York City, N. Y.	X	X	X			X						X		X		X				X						
29. Philadelphia, Pa.	X	X	X	X		X			X																	
30. Pittsburgh, Pa.	X	X	X	X		X	X	X																		
31. Providence, R. I.	X	X		X	X		X	X	X		X															
32. Raleigh, N. C.	X	X		X	X		X	X	X	X	X		X													
33. Savannah, Ga.	X	X		X	X		X	X	X		X	X	X	X												
34. St. Louis, Mo.	X	X	X	X	X	X	X	X	X	X		X	X									X	X			
35. St. Paul, Minn.								NO BLANK SENT																		
36. Syracuse, N. Y.	X	X	X	X										X												
37. Washington, D. C.	X	X	X	X			X	X	X	X	X	X														
38. Wilmington, Del.	X	X	X	X	X	X	X	X	X	X	X			X												

[*]Ibid., pp. 7 and 8.

TABLE 6-2

EDUCATIONAL DATA
REQUESTED ON APPLICATION FORMS*

SCHOOL DISTRICT	State Certificate	Type of Certificate	Other Certificates	Grade or Position Desired	Teaching Experience	Training-Elem. College	List Credits	Can You-Art, Music, Etc.	Hobbies-Talents-Excur.	References	N.T.E. Score	Transcript	College Grad. From	Practice Teaching	Honors, Etc.	Continued Study	Curriculum Study, Etc.	When Can Start	Prof. or Frat. Organization	Administrative App.	College Placement Bureau	Other Work or Duties	Transportation	What Reading Recent	Extra Duty - Coach, Etc.	Do You Expect to Cont. Educ.
1. Arlington, Va.	X			X	X	X	X	X	X	X		X		X				X								
2. Atlanta, Ga.						NO BLANK SENT DO NOT USE BLANK																				
3. Atlantic City, N. J.	X	X		X	X	X	X	X																		
4. Augusta, Maine					DO NOT USE BLANK																					
5. Baltimore, Md.	X	X		X	X	X	X	X	X	X	X	X				X	X	X	X							
6. Bennington, Vt.				X	X	X	X	X	X	X	X					X	X	X							X	
7. Boston, Mass.	X	X		X	X					X		X						X								
8. Buffalo, N. Y.	X	X	X	X	X	X	X	X	X	X					X			X								
9. Camden, N. J.	X	X	X	X	X	X	X	X			X	X					X									
10. Charleston, S. C.	X	X	X	X	X	X	X	X	X	X	X	X					X									
11. Charlotte, N. C.	X	X	X	X	X	X	X	X	X	X	X	X		X	X		X	X	X	X	X	X	X		X	
12. Chattanooga, Tenn.	X	X		X	X	X	X				X	X														
13. Chicago, Ill.	X	X	X	X	X	X		X		X																
14. Cincinnatti, Ohio	X	X	X	X	X	X			X	X					X		X	X	X	X						
15. Detroit, Mich.				X	X	X		X	X	X					X	X		X								
16. Dade Co., Fla.	X	X	X	X	X	X	X	X	X	X	X				X	X	X					X				
17. Hartford, Conn.		X	X		X	X	X	X	X	X			X			X	X		X							
18. Indianapolis, Ind.	X	X	X	X	X	X							X			X	X									
19. Johnstown, Pa.	X	X	X		X	X	X		X	X								X								
20. Louisville, Ky.	X	X	X		X	X	X	X	X				X			X										
21. Madison, Wisc.				X	X	X		X	X	X															X	X
22. Milwaukee, Wisc.	X	X	X	X	X	X		X	X	X							X									
23. Minneapolis, Minn.	X	X	X	X	X	X	X	X	X	X		X		X												
24. Montgomery Co., Md.	X	X	X	X	X	X	X	X	X	X	X					X	X	X	X	X			X			
25. Montpelier, Vt.				X	X	X	X	X	X							X										
26. Nashville, Tenn.	X	X	X	X	X	X	X	X	X	X	X															
27. New Haven, Conn.	X	X	X	X	X	X		X	X	X						X										
28. New York City, N. Y.	X	X	X	X	X	X	X			X	X				X	X			X							
29. Philadelphia, Pa.		X	X	X	X	X		X			X															
30. Pittsburgh, Pa.	X	X	X		X	X		X	X	X																
31. Providence, R. I.	X	X		X	X	X		X	X	X					X	X	X	X	X	X	X					
32. Raleigh, N. C.	X	X	X	X	X	X		X	X							X										
33. Savannah, Ga.	X	X		X	X	X	X	X	X	X	X		X	X	X		X		X							
34. St. Louis, Mo.	X	X		X	X	X		X	X																	
35. St. Paul, Minn.						NO BLANK SENT																				
36. Syracuse, N. Y.	X	X	X	X	X	X	X	X	X	X	X															
37. Washington, D. C.	X	X		X	X	X	X	X	X			X	X	X		X			X							
38. Wilmington, Del.	X	X	X	X	X	X			X						X		X	X								

*Ibid., pp. 11 and 12.

TABLE 6-3

EXPERIENCE DATA
REQUESTED ON APPLICATION FORMS[*]

SCHOOL DISTRICT	Work Other Than Teaching	Military-Armed Service	All Experience	Present Teach. Position	Remarks	Salary Now	Salary Desired	Type Job Desired	Club – Youth Work	Travel	Adult Community Soc. Service	Testimonials	Past Address
1. Arlington, Va.	X				X								
2. Atlanta, Ga.		NO	BLANK	USED									
3. Atlantic City, N. J.	X	X					X						
4. Augusta, Maine		NO	BLANK	SENT									
5. Baltimore, Md.	X	X	X		X								
6. Bennington, Vt.	X	X		X	X	X	X			X	X		
7. Boston, Mass.		X	X										
8. Buffalo, N. Y.	X	X	X		X			X					
9. Camden, N. J.	X	X	X		X	X	X						
10. Charleston, S. C.			X	X	X								
11. Charlotte, N. C.	X	X	X		X	X							
12. Chattanooga, Tenn.						X		X					
13. Chicago, Ill.	X	X	X	X	X								X
14. Cincinnati, Ohio	X	X	X					X		X	X		
15. Dade Co., Fla.	X	X											
16. Detroit, Mich.	X	X						X					
17. Hartford, Conn.	X	X	X	X	X				X	X			
18. Indianapolis, Ind.	X								X	X	X		X
19. Johnstown, Pa.	X				X	X	X	X					
20. Louisville, Ky.	X	X	X			X							
21. Madison, Wisc.						X	X						
22. Milwaukee, Wisc.	X	X	X		X								
23. Minneapolis, Minn.	X	X	X	X	X								
24. Montgomery Co., Md.	X	X			X			X					
25. Montpelier, Vt.	X		X		X	X	X	X					
26. Nashville, Tenn.	X												
27. New Haven, Conn.					X	X	X						
28. New York City, N. Y.	X	X		X	X			X					
29. Philadelphia, Pa.	X		X	X				X					
30. Pittsburgh, Pa.	X	X		X		X		X					
31. Providence, R. I.	X	X	X		X	X	X		X		X		
32. Raleigh, N. C.	X		X	X		X		X					
33. Savannah, Ga.	X	X		X	X	X	X	X				X	
34. St. Louis, Mo.	X	X	X						X				
35. St. Paul, Minn.		NO	BLANK	SENT									
36. Syracuse, N. Y.	X	X	X		X	X	X	X					
37. Washington, D. C.	X	X	X	X	X			X					
38. Wilmington, Del.	X	X	X	X	X		X	X		X			

[*]Ibid., pp. 15 and 16.

Selection of Personnel

Those who are selected for employment by the schools are chosen from those available on the basis of practices and procedures that give some promise of securing personnel who would be an asset to the school system. At best the procedures or bases for selecting personnel cannot be drawn up reliably until the characteristics of good teaching have been better identified and a system has been devised for measuring the degree to which a teacher applicant has these characteristics. In this connection McIntyre has said:

> The literature, of course, is not entirely silent on the subject of teacher selection, but the person who is looking for selection devices that have been validated against accepted criteria might as well abandon the search. There are none.[7]

In spite of the handicaps under which a selection process must currently operate, school systems have developed bases for selecting personnel. These may be used in part, adopted wholly, or supplemented to provide the elements of a selection procedure. In this case also, the frequency with which an item appears as a basis for selection is no evidence of its merits or relative value in the selection procedure. As a matter of fact, probably fully as important as the basis is the way in which it is used. It is very likely that for some time to come it will be necessary to rely heavily on the professional judgment of the top level professional men in the school system.

In a survey of thirty-eight school districts, Alderton [8] concluded that the bases shown in Table 6-4 played an important part in the selection of teachers. He also found that in twenty-five instances those who administered the personnel program placed high on their lists of characteristics to be considered:

personality	experience
appearance	scholastic record (high)
special talents	interest in people, children
age	desire for knowledge
sex	regard for teaching as a career

Of these ten items, at most six lend themselves to fairly accurate appraisal. Whether these six are as important as the four which do not lend themselves to such appraisal is unknown. The factor of personality is no doubt a very important one. What personality will be sought is far from clear. The appraisal of teachers with extremely different personalities, sometimes opposites, has failed to prove a difference in effectiveness

---

[7] Kenneth E. McIntyre, "How To Select Teachers," *The NEA Journal,* Vol. 47 No. 4, April 1958, p. 250.

[8] Alderton, *op. cit.,* p. 25.

TABLE 6-4

BASES FOR SELECTION
OBTAINED FROM
INFORMATION REQUESTED ON APPLICATION FORMS*

Y—National Teachers Examination Score
N—National Teachers Examination

SCHOOL DISTRICT	Application Blank	Personal Interview	References	Min. 4 Yrs. College Tr.	Proof of Req. Ed. Training	State Certificate	Birth Cert.–U. S. Citizen	Health–Phys. Exam	Written Tests or N. T. E.	Transcripts	Practical Exam	Observation of Teach.	Experience	Loyalty Oath	Age Limits	College Placement Bur.	Who's Who (College)	Letter of Application	Residence – Location	Letter of Moral Character	Photograph (Separate)	Eligibility
1. Arlington, Va.	X	X	X	X		X			X	X		X										X
2. Atlanta, Ga.		X		X		X			N	X			X									X
3. Atlantic City, N. J.	X	X	X	X			X	X		X		X										X
4. Augusta, Maine		X	X	X						X												X
5. Baltimore, Md.	X	X		X	X	X	X	YN	X	X	X	X		X	X							X
6. Bennington, Vt.	X	X	X	X		X		X		X		X	X									X
7. Boston, Mass.	X	X	X	MA	X	X	X	X	X	X	X	X		X	X							X
8. Buffalo, N. Y.	X	X	X	X	X	X	X	X	X	X							X					X
9. Camden, N. J.	X	X	X	X	X	X	X	X	X			X										X
10. Charleston, S. C.	X	X		X																		X
11. Charlotte, N. C.	X	X		X		X				X		X	X									X
12. Chattanooga, Tenn.	X	X	X	X	X	X	X		X		X		X	X	X		X	X				X
13. Chicago, Ill.	X	X		X	X		X	X	X	X				X								X
14. Cincinnatti, Ohio	X	X		X	X	X	X	X	X		X			X								X
15. Dade Co., Fla.	X	X	X	X	X	X			X			X	X	X						X		X
16. Detroit, Mich.	X	X	X	X		X	X		X	X												X
17. Hartford, Conn.	X	X	X	X	X	X			X	X		X	X					X				X
18. Indianapolis, Ind.	X	X	X	X		X			X	X		X										X
19. Johnstown, Pa.	X	X	X	X		X	X	X		X												X
20. Louisville, Ky.	X	X	X	X		X		X		X												X
21. Madison, Wisc.	X	X	X	X	X	X		X		X		X	X		X							X
22. Milwaukee, Wisc.	X	X	X	X		X	X	X		X												X
23. Minneapolis, Minn.	X	X	X	X	X	X		X	X													X
24. Montgomery Co., Md.	X	X	X	X	X	X	X	X	X		X		X		X							X
25. Montpelier, Vt.	X	X	X	X			X					X										X
26. Nashville, Tenn.	X	X	X	X		X			N	X					X							X
27. New Haven, Conn.	X	X		X		X			X					X	X						X	X
28. New York City, N. Y.	X	X		X	X	X	X	X	X	X					X							X
29. Philadelphia, Pa.	X	X		X		X	X	X	X		X				X							X
30. Pittsburgh, Pa.	X	X		X	X	X	X	X	N					X	X				X		X	X
31. Providence, R. I.	X	X	X	X	X		X	Y	X		X	X		X							X	X
32. Raleigh, N. C.	X	X		X													X					X
33. Savannah, Ga.	X	X	X	X	X				Y	X	X	X										X
34. St. Louis, Mo.	X	X		X		X	X	X	N	X					X							X
35. St. Paul, Minn.		X	X	X						X							X					X
36. Syracuse, N. Y.	X	X	X	X	X	X	X	X	X	X	X											X
37. Washington, D. C.	X	X	X	X	X	X	X	X	X	X	X	X			X	X						X
38. Wilmington, Del.	X	X		X		X	X	X		X					X	X						X

*Alderton, Op. Cit., pp. 19 and 20.

even when the judgment was made by the same appraiser. It seems that effectiveness is predicated on the teacher in question having discovered or developed a technique suitable to his personality.

Serious questions as to the real import of the characteristics upon which to base selection can readily be raised about each of the ten listed. These questions, together with the lack of an accurate device for measuring the extent of the presence of the characteristics, re-emphasize the degree to which selection takes place in terms of doing the best one can under great handicaps.

In a profession, such as teaching is, intelligence is a presumed factor of great importance. It would be valuable if it were known what the impact of intelligence upon the effectiveness of teaching is. What would happen to education if the I. Q. of teachers were to be raised ten points all along the line? The inability to answer this question is eloquent of the virginity of the soil in the area of teacher selection and appraisal.

Some of the steps in selecting personnel have been dealt with under the subheadings of policies, the personnel requisition, securing applicants, and the application. The next step is the evaluation of the items in the application presented. This may be done by an individual, the superintendent in the smaller school districts or the personnel officer and his staff in the larger school systems.

Who Selects? If the job specifications have been so drawn as to truly specify the qualifications needed to fill the job, then certainly the initial screening of the applications can be done in the central office. Practice varies considerably from such central office screening to the involvement of principals, supervisors, and committees of teachers. The involvement of many is sometimes part of an effort to democratize administration or a sop to democratization; at other times it may be merely a technique for shifting some of the administrative burden.

When job specifications are not truly specific, then it may be necessary for the central office to call for help from those who are in a better position to analyze the factors presented in relationship to the job to be done. Under optimum circumstances, the personnel office will attempt to assure that its practices do not unnecessarily add to the burdens of teachers and other school employees.

Generally those considered eligible for consideration are placed on a list in a ranking from the most eligible to the least. Credentials of the most promising applicants are studied and appraised in order to discover the degree to which they support the information in the application. These credentials come from a number of sources.

Credentials. For teachers these will generally include a dossier from the placement office of the college or university in which they prepared for teaching. All prospective employees, with the possible exception of teachers who have not yet taught, should expect that their previous employment records will be examined. And, all will be expected to provide professional or job references and also character references.

Credentials, aside from the academic transcript, are to large extent suspect. There is not sufficient guarantee to the writer of references that what he submits will truly be kept confidential. This results in the writing of statements which lack balance inasmuch as they present only what is favorable. Employing personnel are aware of the weakness of references included in the dossier and also of those submitted by present or former employers and by those who vouch for character.

Not wishing to harm anyone by adverse remarks that would be in order and hoping that the job applicant will make good if given another chance, many who write references actually endanger the welfare of many youth in their concern for the welfare of one adult. It is refreshing to find balanced statements which permit the employing agency to weigh the factors involved for itself. It may be that the chance of an honest statement which will give the unfavorable as well as the favorable facts retains for references a place in the selection procedure.

Observation. When the positions of those who head up the eligibility list are confirmed by the applications and the credentials submitted, it is advisable where and when possible to provide for observation of applicants without their knowledge that the observation is with reference to another job. In fairness to the applicant the observation should provide opportunity to evaluate him in a number of different situations. Any teacher may have a nonrepresentative session or even day. Observation that confirms the place of the teacher on the eligibility list calls for the next step, the taking of such tests as the school system employs in its selection process.

Testing. The area of testing is broad and complex. Among the factors subject to testing and of importance to personnel selection are attitude, clerical ability, interest, mechanical comprehension, mental ability, personality, and trade skill.

Attitude. Great emphasis is placed upon this characteristic for all employment. It may be appraised by means of any of a variety of tests devised for the purpose. These tests may employ a considerable degree of standardization with a free or forced choice of answer. The application of attitude testing to the selection of school personnel would call for the definition of those factors which are considered important and for the development of a scale to appraise the degree to which the desired attitudes are present.

Lovelace[9] analyzed the attitudes of a number of teachers who had been designated by their principals as being in the top 25 per cent of their group as contrasted to the attitudes of the other 75 per cent. Not only would the attitudes identified not serve for the selection of teachers because of the degree to which they are the products of on-the-job experience, but in addition, there is no assurance of the validity of the selection of the two groups of teachers. This accentuates the key problem in the entire issue of teacher selection and appraisal.

Clerical Tests. The General Clerical and the Minnesota Clerical[10] tests provide some basis by which to supplement other bases for selecting clerical or office personnel.

Interest. The historical use of interest tests or inventories to favor the individual rather than the employer places a sort of traditional barrier upon the use of this test for selection purposes. In addition to this, it seems that its use would be questionable also because of the relative ease with which answers may be faked, e.g., in order to secure a job that is at stake. This test is therefore of greatest apparent value in the vocational guidance through which interest in school employment may be revealed.

Mechanical Comprehension. The George K. Bennett test or an adaptation[11] thereof can be valuable in predicting technical specialties, e.g., truck driving. This might be of particular interest to the school system as a means for improving upon its selection of truck and bus drivers.

Mental Ability. Such devices as the Stanford-Binet or Wechsler scales, the California Test of Mental Maturity, and the Army General Classification Test have been developed to measure intelligence. The realistic and defensible use of these tests demands the acknowledgment that intelligence is but one of a number of individual characteristics to be considered when making a practical decision about a prospective employee.

Personality. Particularly with respect to those who have close contact with and a part in the development of children, personality is generally stressed as of great importance. How an individual reacts to others, how others react to him, and how he conducts himself under a variety of circumstances are the generally presumed dimensions of personality. These factors may be appraised through observation (including the use of autobiographical and other documentary materials), projective tech-

9 Neil R. Lovelace, "An Analysis of Certain Attitudes of Selected Elementary and Junior High School Teachers, an unpublished doctoral dissertation" (College Park, Maryland, The University of Maryland, May, 1951).

10 Both of these tests are published by The Psychological Corporation, New York.

11 Philip E. Vernon and John B. Parry, *Personnel Selection in the British Forces* (London, University of London Press, 1949) p. 230. (A form of the Bennett test was reported as having a validity of 0.59 in the selection of British army truck drivers.)

niques (such as the Rorschach test approach), situational tests, and the application of sociometrics.

Despite available approaches, there has as yet been no real breakthrough in the development of any personality test that could warrantably be used as an accurate gauge for the selection of school personnel. The tests available nevertheless have value, if used intelligently and with reservation, for getting a less hazy concept of the individual under consideration.

Trade Tests. Applicants for a number of maintenance jobs in the school systems may well be subjected to tests which will serve as a check on claims of competency.[12] These tests can often help to identify the novice, apprentice, journeyman, or expert in the field of the job for which application is being made.

National Teachers Examination.[13] Providing a test of cultural and professional background and of mental ability, this examination consists of a battery of tests. All teachers subjected to the battery take the *Common Examination.* Nine separate tests in the *Optional Examination* provide for the measurement of achievement and competency in the areas of proposed employment as a teacher.

There is no clear evidence either as to the value or the lack of value of the National Teachers Examination. Again, it seems that the examination can serve as a desirable screening device if used with judgment and as part of the entire complex of selection procedures.

Interviewing. The information secured through the several steps of procedure employed by the school district in its entirety provides the basis for an interview which is expected to serve as the final check before employment. The interviewer must have the available information about the applicant well in mind before he undertakes the interview.

The interview is not a check on the validity of the information secured; it is rather an opportunity to fill in some of the blank spots and to round out the picture of the applicant, to fill him in on some of the aspects of the school district while noting his reactions to the information provided, and to give him an opportunity to ask questions about which he will have to be satisfied before he can accept employment.

"The interview . . . is probably the most important single part of the whole selection process."[14] It is so important because it is generally the decisive stage in selection. Consider how many marginal school employees, hired during a shortage of qualified personnel, nevertheless

---

12 The United States Employment Service has developed a number of such trade tests.

13 Published by the *Educational Testing Service,* Princeton, New Jersey.

14 George D. Halsey, *Handbook of Personnel Management* (New York, Harper and Row, 1947), p. 82.

gained tenure status although they are no asset to the school system. One function of the employment interview is to reduce a little more the element of chance in personnel selection and thus improve the chance to secure for the schools personnel who are assets to the educational enterprise.

It is necessary to set up safeguards so that abuses will not make interviewing worthless. Even run of the mill interviewing, however, has been found to have sufficient value so that school systems which had eliminated interviews because of their weaknesses found it desirable to reinstate them.[15] Many of the weaknesses of interviewing may be overcome. There is general agreement with respect to what constitutes a satisfactory interview. Of prime importance are recognition of function, environment, and the manner in which the interviewer does his task.

"The functions of the employment interview are: to get information, to give information, and to make a friend."[16] The latter two functions are frequently overlooked. To be effective personnel administration in all its phases, including that of selection, must operate for the employee as well as the employer. In the schools, it is particularly important that all who are interviewed—whether or not the outcome is employment— have kindly regard for the organization and administration of the system.

The place for interviewing should be conducive to establishing and maintaining the atmosphere for confidential relations, placing the applicant at ease, and promoting ready and free speech. This means that the physical conditions should be private, quiet, and reasonably comfortable without being opulent.

Following attention to function and environment is the matter of how to conduct the interview. Probably the first requirement is that there be sufficient time so that time pressures may be suspended while the interview becomes the most important consideration for the moment. Next is the attitude of the interviewer. He must be as aware of individual differences as schoolmen are wont to be in their vaunted dealings with youth. He must also be critical of his own biases so that they may be deliberately counteracted. A friendly atmosphere is even more the creation of the interviewer than it is of the physical environment.

The interviewer must retain control of the interview at all times. This will be assured to the degree to which there is a definite plan for the interview, care in formulating questions, a design for getting the applicant to do the talking while keeping comments by the interviewer to a

15 In Elks County, Nevada, a school district of 17,000 square mile area, the Board of Education became unhappy with its policy of employing teachers without personal interviews. Members were convinced that the interview would have served to screen out some selections that proved unfortunate.

16 W. V. Bingham, "The Three Functions of the Interview in Employment," *The Management Review*, Vol. XV, No. 1, January, 1926, p. 36.

minimum, note taking as it seems necessary, and a plan for concluding the interview.

A checklist of questions may provide a guide to the plan for and the sequence of the interview. Prepared questions may be injected as the occasion permits into an apparently informal conference in which the plan of the interview is not obvious. Or, the interview may be an unguided one in which the applicant is encouraged to speak freely about whatever seems pertinent or important to him and is thus induced to reveal himself as he truly is.

Questions asked during an interview should generally be designed to stimulate the applicant to reply in narrative fashion and should be restricted to seeking information that is not readily available except by interview.

The taking of notes is considered by some to inhibit the freedom with which the applicant will speak. By others it is considered to add significance and importance to the proceedings. If notes are taken, it would seem advisable to limit them to occasional important items and to supplement them immediately after the interview so as to retain answers and impressions as faithfully as possible. However, today it is well to consider the possibility of utilizing recording devices which may be installed in such a way as to violate none of the foregoing conditions for a satisfactory interview while adding the dividends of making it possible to go over the interview at leisure and to evaluate the interviewing technique with an eye to improving upon it.

Finally the interview must be brought to an end. It is well for the interviewer to have in mind a plan for bringing the interview to a natural sort of conclusion. This may be done in any of several ways. One technique is to summarize the major points of the interview and to give the applicant a final opportunity to amplify upon conclusions and to ask final questions.

A follow-up interview shortly after the successful applicant has been employed will be of value in boosting the morale of the new employee and in furnishing insight from a fresh point of view on working conditions within the school system.

APPOINTMENT

Successful exhaustion of the selective procedure culminates in selection. The successful applicant is notified that the job is his subject to whatever conditions still have to be met, probably only the passing of a physical examination by a medical doctor employed and paid by the Board of Education.

The notification of appointment or the job offer is generally accompanied by a contract form. The contract should stipulate the conditions to be met in order to validate it. Aside from such stipulations, the contract in effect just puts into the form of a legal agreement those matters that have been made clear throughout the entire selection process.

SUMMARY

The selection of school personnel is considered to be a most important task through which effective school operation is stimulated and by which savings in time and personnel may be effected.

Through carefully worked out procedures—involving policy, the securing of applicants, the use of a well-devised application form, and the use and evaluation of credentials, references, tests, observation, and interview—efforts are directed to securing for the schools the best available of the competent applicants.

Even with the highest refinement of selection procedures, there is need to rely considerably upon the judgment of those who have the responsibility for making the final recommendations. In this connection it is well to note that although there are a number of tests which can be helpful, it is difficult to know where to set the cut-off point above which applicants should be considered further and below which they are eliminated. If used as just another aid in a whole complex of approaches to the problem of selection, tests may be very valuable. If undue importance is attached to one or more tests, their use may be more harmful than beneficial. There is still much to be done in the development of tests before they can be made predictive of success in the complex and many faceted job of teaching.

Appointment is the logical outcome of the selective process. The appointment binds both parties, employer and employee, by a contract that embodies the essentials of the selective process.

SELECTED READINGS

BARR, Arvil S., and JONES, Robert E., "The Measurement and Prediction of Teacher Efficiency," *Review of Educational Research,* Vol. 5, June, 1958, pp. 256–264.

CRONBACH, Lee J., *Essentials of Psychological Testing* (New York, Harper and Row, 1960), Chapters 7–18.

DOWNIE, N. M., *Fundamentals of Measurement* (New York, Oxford University Press, 1958), Chapters 6–16.

ELSBREE, Willard S., and REUTTER, E. Edmund, *Staff Personnel in the Public Schools* (Englewood Cliffs, N.J., Prentice-Hall, Inc., 1954), Chapter 3.

GUILFORD, J. P., *Personality* (New York, McGraw-Hill Book Company, Inc., 1959), Chapters 1–15.

JUCIUS, Michael J., *Personnel Management* (Chicago, Richard D. Irwin, Inc., 1948), Chapters 7–9.

KEARNEY, Nolan C., *A Teacher's Professional Guide* (Englewood Cliffs, N.J., Prentice-Hall, Inc., 1958), Chapters 10, 15.

MOEHLMAN, Arthur B., *School Administration* (Boston, Houghton Mifflin Company, 1951), Chapters 16, 28.

MOORE, Harold E., and WALTERS, Newell B., *Personnel Administration in Education* (New York, Harper and Row, 1955), Chapter 8.

PIGORS, Paul, and MYERS, Charles A. *Personnel Administration* (New York, McGraw-Hill Book Company, Inc., 1951), Chapters 6, 12.

RYANS, David G., "Some Validity Extension Data from Empirically Derived Predictors of Teacher Behavior," *Educational and Psychological Measurement*, Vol. 18, 1958, pp. 355–370.

STOOPS, Emery, and RAFFERTY, M. L., *Practices and Trends in School Administration* (Boston, Ginn and Company, 1961), Chapter 20.

WATKINS, Gordon S., and DODD, Paul A., McNAUGHTON, Wayne L., and PRASOW, Paul, *The Management of Personnel and Labor Relations* (New York, McGraw-Hill Book Company, Inc., 1950), Chapters 11–13.

YODER, Dale, *Personnel Principles and Policies* (Englewood Cliffs, N.J., Prentice-Hall, Inc., 1959), Chapters 13–15.

.7.

The Contract and Job Assignment

ONCE SELECTION has taken place, it is to the advantage of both the board of education and the prospective employee to put their agreement about employment into written form. This form is known as the contract. It is further to the advantage of the school system and the employee that the steps of the selective process be assured optimum effectiveness through job assignment or placement in accord with the basis upon which selection was made. These two facets of employment, embodying (1) the mutual agreement of employer and employee and (2) the implementation of the spirit of the agreement, will be explored in this chapter.

Contract and job assignment logically call into play several of the principles of school personnel administration, three of which are directly pertinent.[1] The first of these demands that coordination by which personnel are assured assignment in terms of the competency for which they were hired. This is clearly a matter for both contract and job assignment. The second emphasizes the fact that personnel are not commodities to be disposed without regard for personal considerations. It points up that personal considerations have implications for the work done by the employee. The third calls attention to the necessity for fair dealing. Through its provisions—regarding monetary rewards, work load, the working period, various conditions concomitant or auxiliary to the job, and virtually every other element making up the working situation—the contract is the instrument for insuring that each party to the contract gets what he bargained for.

[1] See Chapter 1, principles 4, 5, and 6.

117

THE CONTRACT

"A contract is a promise, or a set of promises, for breach of which the law gives a remedy, or the performance of which the law recognizes as a duty."[2] Chief Justice John Marshall of the United States Supreme Court ruled that, "A contract is an agreement in which a party undertakes to do, or not to do, a particular thing."[3] Agreement, of course, connotes obligations on the part of all parties to the agreement.

Limitations

A contract is the legal agreement whereby the spirit of the various steps that have led to employment may be captured and preserved with fairness to both parties. This means that the intent of the agreement will be presented in terms of the major outline but without much of the detail. The very spirit of the agreement could be vitiated by an over-specificity which would bring about rigidity. In addition it is generally presumed that upon entering into contract with such agencies as a city, state, or school district, all know the law. It is also recognized that agencies of government are restricted by law in their powers and can legitimately contract only with due regard for the limitations placed upon them. It is expected that what is stipulated in law need not be expressed in the contract.

Another limitation upon a contract is the requirement that all parties to the contract have the legal capacity to contract, i.e., those signing for the employing agency are properly authorized to do so and that the employee meets all the requirements for eligibility to sign a contract. Should it prove, for example. that a teacher has signed a contract and proves later not to have the necessary qualifications to meet certification requirements, that teacher was not eligible to enter into contract and the contract is not binding upon the board of education.

Form of Contract

A contract may be express, implied in fact, or implied in law. For the most part school employees, especially the professional employees, are somewhat familiar with the express contract, a form in which terms of employment have been stipulated and agreed to by all parties concerned. Generally, and desirably, this express contract is in written form

2 This is the American Law Institute definition. See Samuel Williston, *A Treatise on the Law of Contracts* (New York, Baker, Voorhis and Company, 1936), Vol. I, p. 1, or Francis W. Marshall, *Popular Guide to Modern Legal Principles* (New York, Wm. H. Wise & Co., Inc., 1953), p. 80.

3 Sturges v. Crowningshield, 4 Wheat. 122.

and must be signed by the authorized agent of the board of education and by the employee. It is possible to have an oral express contract. This is understandably undesirable because of the vagueness introduced and the misunderstandings or interpretations that may result even with the best of faith.

A contract is considered to be implied in fact when, although there is no acceptance of an offer and no assent to specified terms, the circumstances are such that a contract is inferable from them, for example, the job to be done is performed by someone with the knowledge of the one for whom it is to be done and without his objection. The inference in this instance is that without an express contract, a meeting of minds has nevertheless taken place.

A contract which is implied in law is in fact not a true contract. There is no actual or inferable meeting of minds but such benefits as one of the parties may receive without being entitled to them may be made the basis for a civil suit. There would be little occasion for any implied contracts to project themselves into the school personnel scene.

Categories of Contracts

Contracts issued to teaching personnel fall into two major categories, limited and continuing or indefinite. Each of these is subject to qualification in terms of state or local provisions for tenure.

Limited Contracts. These are the contracts which are issued for some specific term, such as one year, three years, five years, or such other period as both parties agree upon.

Continuing Contracts. These are also known as indefinite and permanent contracts since there is no terminal date stipulated in the contract. One of these has the automatic continuing provision that the contract remains in effect if by some specified date (usually late March or early April) there has been no notice that the contract will not be renewed. This gives the employee assurance of notification early enough to enable him to apply for work elsewhere. However, it does not give him the sense of security which tenure is intended to provide.

The other continuing, indefinite, or permanent tenure contracts come into operation upon the satisfactory completion of a probationary period of usually two or three years. These contracts are subject to reconsideration or to cancellation if the service rendered should become unsatisfactory or if other conditions of the tenure law are violated. The Maryland law typifies provisions for terminating the continuing contract. Sometimes the phrase "or other just and good cause" is either added to or substituted for the stated causes for dismissal. A statement of the Maryland provision follows:

Any county board of education may, on the recommendation of the county superintendent, suspend any teacher, principal, supervisor, or assistant superintendent for immorality, dishonesty, intemperance, insubordination, incompetency, or willful neglect of duty, and may recommend to the state superintendent of schools the revocation of the certificate of such person, stating in writing the grounds for such recommendations, and giving an opportunity, upon not less than ten days' notice, to be heard in defense, in person or by counsel, and the state superintendent of schools may order such investigation as he may deem necessary. If he approves the recommendation, the teacher's certificate shall be revoked and the teacher shall be dropped from service.[4]

When tenure, or continuing contract, provisions are written into state law they may be changed or revoked only by action of the state legislature. When tenure is provided only through local board of education policy, it may be revised or revoked through action of the local board of education.

More than half of the fifty states, plus the District of Columbia, have either statewide tenure provisions or continuing tenure subject to a Spring notification clause. In most of the remaining states continuing tenure is operative in a number of their local school districts. In only a few states is there no provision for continuing contracts. It is probably only a matter of time until all states will have provisions for mandatory continuing tenure on a statewide basis or permissive continuing tenure by local option.

State Education Authority

Increasingly the State Board of Education or the State Department of Education (otherwise known as the State Department of Public Instruction or the State Education Agency) tends to provide a contract form. This situation is in flux. Currently nearly 80 per cent of the fifty states provide contract forms. Of these some specify that these forms are to be used while others provide the form as a guide or point of departure for the local school districts. Contracts are used in all states. Even in those states where no form is specified there is provision for local school districts to issue contracts. Many of these local districts, particularly the larger ones, do contract with their employees for the services to be rendered.

It is essential that the state education authority exercise its prerogative to devise the best contract form possible in terms of state minimum requirements that have to be protected. It is desirable that the state also

4 Maryland State Department of Education, *The Public School Laws of Maryland* (Charlottesville, Va., The Michie Co., 1958), Art. 77, Sec. 64, By-law 14.

provide leadership in the development of contract forms by calling attention to the kinds of requirements that should be spelled out. The state form might be adopted in all districts in which its provisions sufficed; in all others it would be expected that the contract would be supplemented or modified to meet local requirements in addition to those of the state.

A survey of the state contracts suggests that there is much room for improvement. On the whole the provisions of the contract seem to provide at least superficial protection for the state and the school district, often at the expense of the security of the school employee. It is extremely doubtful that failure to protect the employee's interests will truly benefit the school system. One example of the lack of protection accorded the employee follows:

When employment was stipulated for the school year and the school year was specified as 180 school days, school started early in September. Taking a school year when school would have started September 7 and allowing for holidays—Thanksgiving day week-end, Christmas–New Year interim, Washington's birthday, snow days, Easter or Spring interim, and Memorial Day—the 180 school days would have been completed by June 10 to 17 (depending on the number of snow days).

Traditionally, as a matter of convenience to the board of education in its payroll procedures, it became practice to pay teachers monthly for each of the calendar (not school) months during which they taught (a school month would be defined as a 20-day period of instruction). Some of the calendar months in the above example might have as few as 10 or as many as 23 school days. Actually under this procedure teachers received their pay somewhat ahead of time on some paydays but at the end of the year, unless a special payroll was prepared, their final check was paid about three weeks late.

Teachers did not object because they received what had been agreed upon and what was a convenience to the board proved to be a convenience also to the teachers. Instead of having to budget for nearly a three-month period of unemployment—erroneously referred to as a summer vacation—teachers now found that they had to budget for only a two-month summer layoff.

The next development was that teachers were called in on a Saturday morning, before the week school opened, for a final briefing. This briefing became extended to as much as two weeks or more of induction or pre-school inservice training. This extension of the school year was accomplished through fiat and without additional pay for the increase in the length of the commandeered time. Next a period of a week to 10 days was added to the close of the school year, and in some instances a day per month is set aside as a non-school day for teacher meetings. Again there was no pay for the added work period. These extensions are now being hailed by some administrators and their ill-informed board members as just the requirement that teachers work for the 10 calendar months for which they are paid. Aggressive superintendents have even said that they saw no legal limitation to prevent having teachers serve the entire 12 months without increase in pay. Thus have 9 school months been stretched into 10 calendar months at teacher expense.

The foregoing example illustrates the degree to which teachers are the victims of inadequately informed boards of education and of administrators who either are as poorly informed or seek to exploit teachers. The contract is the instrument through which school employees should be assured that an extension of the service period will result in added compensation on a pro-rated basis.

Another of the protections to which all employees, and especially such professional specialists as teachers, are entitled is the assurance that they will be expected to work in accordance with their competencies and not otherwise. In both of these respects, the personnel administrator has an obligation to school employees which requires much reenforcement.

One of the greatest threats to the school personnel situation is indicated in the foregoing example, i.e., the alchemy which a teacher undergoes when he becomes an administrator. Only as the superintendent and other administrators take measures to remain first of all teachers can the teaching profession and the school systems avoid the cleavage between management and labor which results in conflict, unionization, and the struggle for power that has often characterized industrial labor-management relations.

Local Education Authority

In the instances in which local school boards issue contracts other than the form provided by the state, there is great variation in the form and content of the contract.[5] The form varied from a small file card confirming the appointment and the salary of the employee to a detailed contract outlining the many and specific duties of the teacher and the regulations binding upon him.

Conditions of Employment. Incorporating the same provisions found in the state contract forms, the local school districts tend to emphasize in addition certification, participation in the retirement provisions subscribed to (sometimes both state and local), submission of health certificates, and a number of conditions among which are such considerations as: marital status, loyalty oaths, outside employment, residence, membership in professional organizations, use of alcohol and tobacco, attendance at social functions, submission of poll tax receipts, and presentation of auto liability insurance policies. Violation of a condition in the contract jeopardizes the contract for the violator.

[5] From an unpublished survey of 129 school district contracts issued in 36 states; a study by Edwin C. Riggin, University of Maryland, 1959.

The School Term. Practice in designating the school term varied among the 129 districts. Of 47 specifying length of school term, 25 did so in terms of months (8–10), 10 in terms of weeks (37–40), and 12 in terms of days (180–200).[6] In 35 school districts length of school term was not specified at all and in another 47 this was provided for at the time the contract was signed.

It is to be noted that there seems to be an assumption that a month or a week will mean the same to everyone. Within the school organization a school-week is thought of as five school days and a school month as consisting of 20 school days. Clarification of just what period of time is covered by the contract is an obligation of the board of education and the school administration to both school employees and the supporting public. Failure to specify the length of school term deprives employees of the protection implicit in the concept of a contract.

Pay Provisions. Generally there is provision in the contract to indicate the beginning salary or wage. Where there is a salary schedule, this is part of the policy structure which is properly part of the contract. In many a school district a statement of all personnel policies is provided at the time of employment, together with the contract form, supplying the employee with the policies which become binding upon him by his signing the contract.

Variations in pay provisions were found in terms of cost of living increments, change in salary by a 30-day notice, additional pay for attendance at any professional meetings including workshops when conducted on other than a school day, and school board maintenance of a life insurance policy for the teacher for as long as he is employed by the school district.

The payroll intervals were also generally indicated, although a number of districts were found to have no pay period prescribed and some left this to be filled in at the time of signing the contract. Monthly payments for a 12-month period were the most common. Other monthly payments were for the school year, 10 months, or 9 months. A number of school districts also paid semimonthly for the school year, for 20 or for 24 payments. Others paid biweekly for the school year, 19, or 26 payments. Some had 11 or 13 pay-days for the school year. One school district of those surveyed paid once every 19½ days (presumably school days) throughout the school year.

Duties. Although the entire selection process revolves about the competencies of the prospective employee to do a specific job, not one of the

---

[6] Qualifiers were sometimes added, such as: At least eight months; not to exceed 10 months; 37 weeks plus two days (four days) for teachers' meetings, workshops, etc.; and 180–190 days.

129 contracts surveyed specified the subject(s) to be taught by teachers. The matter of duties for teachers was generally covered by the broad and nondefinitive provision that they: teach according to the rules and regulations of the board of education, or discharge faithfully the duties of a teacher. Other provisions occasionally found were with reference to keeping records, attending meetings, preserving school property, participating in extracurricular functions, following the course of study, exercising discipline, doing prescribed reading for professional advancement, etc.

The broad provisions covering teacher duties is possibly administratively convenient. However, the personnel administrator is concerned with coordinating the competency of the individual to the job to be done. There is little value in a procedure, for example, that provides for meticulous selection of the most qualified person among competent applicants for a mathematics and science teaching vacancy if the person so selected is, under the broad provisions of the contract, to be assigned to teaching a combination of language and social studies for which he has no particular competency.

Overspecificity in a contract may hamper school administration unduly; however, underspecification nullifies the value of the selective process, deprives the teacher of the opportunity to demonstrate his effectiveness as a teacher in the field of his competency, and lowers the efficiency of instruction. It is quite likely that in the example above, even a run-of-the-mill language and social studies teacher would teach more effectively in this area than would a top-notch math-science man.

Provisions for specificity as to duties to be performed are owing to all school employees, including nonteaching workers. Careful selection may generally be expected to result in the employment of individuals who, understanding what is required of them, will work in terms of the spirit of their jobs rather than the letter of the contract. To generate such a spirit is a major function of personnel administration. The good faith demonstrated in a contract that is fair to both the school system and the employee is an important step toward engendering a desirable working spirit.

Minimum Contract Provisions

There was general agreement among the states as to 8 items to be covered in the contract form.[7] These are:

1. When contracts are to be drawn
2. Who does the contracting

[7] Evelon D. Weyant, "The Factors in Teacher Contracts as Determined by a Survey of the School Laws of Twenty-five States," an unpublished seminar report (College Park, University of Maryland, 1958).

3. Who must sign
4. What penalties follow a breach of contract
5. What period is covered by the contract
6. What the compensation is
7. How the contract may be modified or terminated
8. That the contract shall be written

In addition to the foregoing items, it has been found that other specifics are often included as follows:[8]

1. The time limit for submitting the signed contract
2. The number of working days to be covered by the contract
3. The beginning salary (and an accompanying policy statement with particular reference to the length of the school year, salary schedules, and payment plans)
4. The specific kind of job for which the employee has been hired
5. The date when the contract is to go into effect
6. Date of signatures
7. Place of signatures
8. An affidavit, appearing just before the signature of the new employee, attesting that he has signed with full knowledge of the policies and regulations that accompanied the contract form

The minimum provisions indicated by the foregoing 8 items and 8 additional specifics will no doubt have to be supplemented, or phrased, in terms of the particular circumstances of the individual states and school districts. However, contracts may generally be greatly improved through specification of the working days required and by stipulation of the duties for which the individual is employed.

School districts have been increasing the actual days a teacher is required to be on the job without a prorated increase in pay. Also, the flagrant disregard of the professional competency for which a teacher is employed might be lessened if the grade level (elementary school), the subject areas (secondary school), or other specialization for which the teacher has been selected were made a part of the contract.

ASSIGNMENT OF PERSONNEL

The recruitment, training, and selection of teachers are part of a pattern by which the importance of these school personnel is given recognition. The same principles which have brought this pattern into existence pertain also to the nonteaching personnel. In view of the concern for these activities which lead to the employment of school personnel, it seems only logical that the workers so secured would be assigned to tasks consistent with their qualifications. Common practice violates

[8] *Ibid.*, and also the foregoing sections on the State and Local Education authorities.

that logic so frequently that it is necessary to deal with the matter of the assignment of personnel in a very specific manner. This section will deal with this issue in terms of practice, reasons for assignment inconsistent with competency, and means for eliminating malpractice in assignments.

Assignment Practice

In practice, assignments are made in a variety of ways. Many assignments are made in terms of the competency of the individual employed and in accord with the basis for his selection. There is no need to do more than emphasize the desirability of assigning employees in this fashion. However, there is also the malpractice of assigning employees without regard for their competencies. This malpractice must be brought into the open, recognized as generally harmful in its impact upon education, analyzed as to its causes, and diagnosed so that remedies may be devised and put into effect.

A few cases of malpractice in assignments are presented. The administrator, school employee, and student will without doubt be able to supplement these cases with numerous examples out of his own direct or vicarious experiences.

Case No. 1, Administrative. A teacher of metal shop was employed because of his qualification to teach metal shop, particularly the area of sheet metal work. As a teacher in metal shop, this man did work justifying the selection process which led to his employment. Within 2 years, he was made assistant superintendent of finance and school plant within the same school system. He could not possibly have been selected for this job on a qualifying or competitive basis. He had to delegate the finance activity almost completely to a 21-year old secretary-bookkeeper who had been with the school system 2 years and whose training did not extend beyond high school. The basis for the assignment was predominantly the questionable, if not wholly erroneous assumption that the school plant function is first of all concerned with maintenance and that a metal shop man has the "practical" background to look after maintenance.

This school was deprived of a good teacher, got a very poor assistant superintendent to start with, suffered in both its finance and plant activities for some years, and—to the extent that this man became a passable assistant superintendent eventually—provided expensive training for the job, on the job, and at the expense of the school system.

Case No. 2, Teacher. A board of education for a small school system lost a mathematics-science teacher. Without any other thought than that a mathematics-science vacancy existed, the board of education and the administration went through an exhaustive selection process to secure the best qualified math-science man they could get. They received 67 applications from qualified men and women in this field. These applications were carefully screened, credentials were examined, and applicants were interviewed. Thus the top man out of 67 qualified men was selected and hired.

On the Saturday before school was to begin all the faculty were called to the school. A history-social studies teacher with no science qualification was given a science teaching assignment to supplement his other teaching; mathematics teaching assignments were spread among a number of other teachers with no particular regard for competency in this subject. All assignments were thus made progressively until only the new math-science teacher had to be assigned. He was told that as the new teacher in the school, he would teach the subjects not already assigned—English, Literature, and Art—subjects which he had no particular competency to teach.

At the end of the school year, the math-science teacher was offered renewal of contract. His acceptance rested upon what the teaching assignment for the next year was to be. He was told it would be just about the same; whereupon he resigned.

In this school children were taught, in the areas of math and science, by teachers who had no particular competency in these subject fields while a competent teacher was available within the school. The children who received instruction in English, literature, and art from the math-science man were given the best that the teacher could contrive to do in an area in which he lacked qualification. Instruction suffered in a number of areas because of job assignment which was not in accord with the basis of teacher selection. Many children were deprived of effective instruction. The school lost a highly qualified, carefully and expensively selected, and professionally conscientious teacher.

Case No. 3, Secretary-Bookkeeper. A girl who had followed the commercial curriculum in high school graduated and was employed as a bookkeeper in a local industry. The school system needed a secretary-bookkeeper. No bona fide selective procedure was followed. The superintendent's secretary, knowing of the job to be filled, interceded with the superintendent with the result that her sister was attracted away from her job in the local industry to become the secretary-bookkeeper in the board of education offices. The girl proved intelligent and adaptive. She learned quickly, through on-the-job training by the assistant superintendent in charge of finance, to keep the books in accord with the uniform financial accounting practices developed for local and state school systems in the United States. Then a new assistant superintendent was employed.

After two years in the school system, the secretary-bookkeeper was now held responsible for deciding what entries to make even when there was the possibility of an item being operation, maintenance, or even instruction. The new assistant superintendent, not qualified to make the determination himself and unable to give needed supervision, placed upon his secretary-bookkeeper the responsibilities of a professionally trained school finance man. The girl suffered a nervous breakdown and, after a period of working under the unsatisfactory conditions described, resigned to accept employment in industry.

The school system was placed in jeopardy through the unjustifiable delegation of an assistant superintendent's responsibility for school finance to a secretary-bookkeeper who, competent in the job for which she was hired, was wholly unqualified to assume the professional responsibilities thus thrust upon her. The school suffered the consequences of this unreasonable demand upon the secretary as her efficiency on the job was undermined by the strain under which she was placed and by the dissatisfaction that was engendered by the imposition of an assignment beyond her qualifications. The school system lost a desirable employee. What this secretary-bookkeeper had learned on the job, at the expense of the school system, was lost to the school system. A better job assignment might have permitted the school system instead to capitalize upon what had been learned in the two years on the job through the retention of a valuable employee.

Case No. 4, School Nurse. In one of the large school systems of the United States, serving a population of a little less than a million, nurses are employed under the terms of a contract which enumerates their responsibilities as nurses and then adds a clause calling upon them to perform "any other duty assigned by the principal." The result was that health services are neglected because the "other duties," such as handling switchboards, operating cafeteria cash registers, handling the lost- and found-department, and doing clerical work, received primary consideration.

School nurses are employed in terms of their competency as nurses. They, like teachers, are especially trained for a particular professional function. Yet, under the provisions of their employment they were given assignments which called upon them to subordinate their professional functions and competencies to providing services for which their training had no application. A high school graduate could have done as well many of the tasks assigned.

The school system failed to provide the health services which were considered to be part of its over-all program. For lack of time to devote to nursing services because of the "other duties" nurses were unable to have children released from classes to attend clinics, waiting lists for clinical services became much too long, nursing supplies were curtailed, and nurses themselves developed a nonfunctional concept of their own jobs. The justification for school health services lies in the contribution they make to the teaching-learning situation of the school. Neglect of the health services deprived the school system of effectiveness in its provisions for education and secured services for which the board of education apparently had no provision in its budget. These services, provided through the misuse of nurses, were to a large extent gotten under false pretenses although by a technicality they were provided for by the clause in the contract.

Case No. 5, School Janitor. Selected for his character because of his association with children, for his industry, and for a modicum of adeptness as a general handyman, the school janitor or custodian is employed primarily in most instances to provide for the heating and ventilating, cleaning, and minor maintenance of the school building. Keeping a school clean is a large part of the janitor's job.

One janitor proved to be exceptionally good at repairing and refinishing furniture. Thereupon he was given not only all the school furniture of the school in which he served but also school furniture from other schools. This work was assigned him without any alteration in his status or duties as a janitor. As it was impossible for him to do both his regular janitorial work and the school furniture renovation, the cleaning of the building was the function put off.

Assignment to duties that interfered with the prime function of the janitor led to a school building situation in which the cleanliness conducive to good teaching and to the development of an appreciation of cleanliness on the part of the children was neglected. The chief reason, the facilitation of instruction, for the employment of the janitor was made secondary to another task for which he was not employed and which constituted at best a minor aspect of his overall job. The teaching-learning situation was again jeopardized.

The above 5 cases are roughly representative of an all too common practice in assigning jobs in such a way as to render the chief function of the school, education, less effective than it could be. These 5 cases are also representative in terms of the general causes for otherwise seemingly inexcusable blunders in assigning jobs. These causes will be reviewed briefly.

Causes of Inconsistent Assignment

It may well be that the all-encompassing reason for malpractice in assigning personnel to jobs within the school system is administrative convenience or expediency. Disregard of individual competencies permits the simple approach to personnel placement of merely having an individual (irrespective of qualification) assigned to each work station.[9] The causes in the foregoing cases will shed further light on the specifics involved in administrative convenience and expediency.

Case No. 1, Administrative. Here the superintendent was inexperienced and inadequately trained for his job. Under the circumstances it is not surprising that he had little grasp of what qualifications were essential to performing the duties of an assistant superintendent in charge of finance and plant. By considering school finance as something that would come by osmosis and plant as primarily a maintenance job which a sheet metal shop man could do because he is a practical type, he drew up a mental job description and specification that lent itself to an unexacting selection of personnel.

Case No. 2, Teacher. The simplest approach to a vacancy is to focus on the one job immediately affected rather than on the total job and employee scene. Then, having hired in terms of so myopic a consideration

[9] This would be somewhat analogous to using the various figures in a chess game for whatever one wanted to use them at the moment, without regard for the very specialized functions of the respective pieces. The chess player realizes the impossibility of playing the game intelligently under such circumstances. The school administrator must develop appreciation of the impossibility of operating the schools functionally under such circumstances.

of the vacancy, the administrator becomes aware of problems of scheduling, pressures of teachers who have seniority and the ear of the administrator, and possibly competencies of other teachers who have not been adequately assigned. Under such various conditions, the new teacher is made the scapegoat to whom is assigned whatever is left rather than the subjects he is qualified to teach. The administrative psychology frequently seems to be that it is better to have an unqualified person on the job than no teacher at all.

Case No. 3, Secretary-Bookkeeper. The employment of an assistant superintendent unqualified in school finance left a competent employee without the support of a responsible person to make the decisions which an assistant superintendent is paid to make. It was convenient to ask a secretary-bookkeeper, with no more than a high school education and with only two years in school work, to assume these responsibilities even though she did not have the qualifications to assume them and was not paid any more to assume the added responsibilities. Here the incompetency of the assistant superintendent and the convenience of the administration were the direct causes for an unjustifiable job assignment.

Case No. 4, School Nurse. If there are routine matters that cannot be put off, they almost invariably take precedence over the primary functions when those functions can be put off. The switchboard must be attended, records must be kept, someone must provide for a lost and found department, and someone must take the money as the children come through the cafeteria line. These are obviously matters that cannot be put off. Now, the matter of health is, although of prime importance, one of the things that lends itself to being put off.[10] Here it is evident that administrative expediency demanded that the routine "musts" were to be given priority over the functional duties and responsibilities of school nurses.

Case No. 5, School Janitor. There was furniture to be renovated. Here was a man who developed a skill in doing this kind of work. Without thought as to the implications of what was being done, the janitor became a maintenance man on janitor's pay and that without being relieved of janitorial duties. As he could not do all the janitorial work and also the furniture renovation, the job which he got to like the better and which the school administrator valued assumed the greater importance

10 What principal has not found that he had to neglect his most important duties in order to meet a deadline on a routine matter of relatively little educational import? This is what occurred in the situation pertaining to the malpractice of assignments in school health.

and the janitorial function was neglected. When it was noticed that the school was not clean, the explanation that the janitor did such a fine job of renovating furniture was expected to satisfy. It is easy to see with what facility the minor maintenance work of a janitor developed into the major job of renovating school furniture, a job to which mere janitorial services were subordinated.

Eliminating Malpractice in Assignment

The causes for the malpractice give the cue to the means for eliminating it.

Case No. 1, Administrator. Here it is emphasized that job analysis, description, and specification are so important that they cannot be left to the ill informed. The new and inexperienced superintendent may call upon such resources as the state department of education and the nearby university where he can get the help he so desperately needs. This is more to his credit than to blunder independently and it is better for the school system. The next step is to exploit the selection procedure to secure for the school system the best of the competent individuals available, thus avoiding the employment of an unqualified assistant superintendent or other employee.

Case No. 2, Teacher. A first rule when a vacancy occurs is that this event be regarded as a golden opportunity to diagnose the job-employee situation to discover whether the situation calls merely for a replacement or for a general shakedown, reorganization, and reassignment of personnel. Next, the schedule for the following school term should be set up to make certain that the personnel to be available can be assigned in terms of both the job to be done and the competencies for which they were employed. Where difficulties occur, the time to make adjustments is before hiring. It may mean the hiring of a person with completely different qualifications. Care in reviewing personnel needs, and a reasonable bit of planning should serve to eliminate much unjustifiable assignment of individuals.

The administrative psychology that it is better to have an unqualified teacher than none at all is open to question. Would it not be better to suspend a school offering whenever competent teachers therefor are not available? The school's position would be strengthened if it could be said that whatever is taught is taught by competent personnel. The courage to contract school offerings is rare among school administrators.

Possibly another means available to teachers is their own insistence, and support in this regard from their professional organizations, upon assignment in accord with the basis upon which they were selected. This is particularly practicable during times of teacher shortage.[11]

Case No. 3, Secretary-bookkeeper. This is a more involved case. It goes back to Case No. 1 inasmuch as one of the factors was the employment of an assistant superintendent of schools who was not qualified in the area of either finance or plant. The suggestion for correcting this has already been made. In addition, the selective procedure employed was hardly a satisfactory one although the selection proved defensible as long as there was appropriate supervision. Again, definitive job descriptions and specifications for his secretary-bookkeeper's job would have proved enlightening to the assistant superintendent of schools and protective to the secretary-bookkeeper. If the employee was to be charged with responsibility beyond her competency, she ought also to have been remunerated in accord with the responsibility. Probably all of the causes could have been eliminated through proper employment of qualified personnel in the first place and through the observance of fair play in the second.

Case No. 4, School Nurse. There are two means for rectifying the situation described. The major functions to be served by the personnel have to be well defined and assured of priority consideration. Routine tasks that tend to take precedence over other activities must be provided for specifically through the employment of personnel in accord with the need. There is no legitimate defense for the utilization of professionally qualified personnel—whether teaching, nursing, or other—for subprofessional duties. It is incumbent upon school administrators to provide for the performance of all duties on a sound financial and personnel basis or to determine on the basis of educational values which duties have to be suspended for lack either of finances or qualified personnel.

Case No. 5, School Janitor. This instance is very similar to the preceding one. Developments indicate that there is need in the school system for a maintenance man to renovate school furniture. In that case it is necessary to recruit and select one who is competent to do the job and to pay him the going wage for such work. If a currently employed janitor has demonstrated the desired competency in his minor maintenance duties, he may be transferred to do maintenance work. Then it becomes necessary to employ another to serve in the capacity of janitor. If the maintenance work is insufficient for full-time employment, it may be possible

[11] Mention of this in a personnel class met with the rejoinder from one, an assistant superintendent in a large school district, to the effect that he questioned whether teachers should take advantage of the shortage to "throw their weight around" in matters of assignment in accord with their competency. Apparently it is all right for administrators to throw their weight around in assigning without regard for competency.

to employ janitorial help on a part-time basis to make up for the time given by the regular janitor to maintenance work.

SUMMARY

Contract and job assignment are interrelated facets of the personnel activity. The contract is supposed to be a definitive statement of the agreement arrived at by the employer and the employee, outlining the duties and obligations of each and thus providing each protection against misunderstanding and assurance that the intent of the agreement will be sustained.

Contracts for school employees are either required or permitted in the 50 states. Many are prescribed by state departments of education. With few exceptions, a review of contract forms in use indicates that they lend themselves better to protection of the employing agency, the board of education, than to assuring the employee that he will be required to do the kind of work for which he has been hired and for the length of time that was implicit at the time of employment. There is room for much greater definitiveness which is necessary to provide for fairness to the employee and also to the school system which can only capitalize on its manpower assets to the full as assignments of jobs are in accord with the qualifications of the individual employee.

Malpractices in the assignment of personnel extend throughout the school system among administrative, teacher, office, school nurse, janitorial, and other personnel. Underdeveloped personnel practices, general disregard for individuals and their competencies, administrative convenience and expediency, and failure to use state department and university services are among the main causes for indefensible assignment of employees to jobs for which they have little or no qualification.

The remedies for malpractice in job assignment is virtually implicit in the causes for such assignments.

Much of the problem of assignment might be resolved if schoolmen did not try to do the impossible. If money is lacking, the schools attempt nevertheless to operate as if there are sufficient funds. If there are insufficient personnel, there is an attempt to make up the deficiency in numbers or qualifications through unfair allocation of extra duties through which professional personnel are required—often on the ludicrous basis of thus proving their professionalism—to assume subprofessional jobs. Nonprofessional individuals, in like fashion, are called upon to do some special task in addition to their regular duties.

Thus, recognizing the problem, school administrators have the obligation to take measures to make the contract definitive, as protective of the employee as of the school district, and equitable. This can take place only if vacancies are carefully analyzed, personnel hired in terms of the competencies needed, and job assignments made so as to co-ordinate worker qualifications with job requirements.

A satisfactory contract and a defensible job assignment promote the interest of both the public and the employee. Neglect of either of these interests places the other in jeopardy. It is incumbent upon sound personnel administration to recognize the individuality of employees and their special competencies, to assign work accordingly, and thus to overcome an administrative proclivity to regard school employees as educational, or other, jacks of all trades.

SELECTED READINGS

ANDERSON, Earl W., *The Teacher's Contract and Other Legal Phases of Teacher Status* (New York, Teachers College, Columbia University, 1927).

BLISS, Walton B., and DRURY, Robert L., *Teachers' Contracts and Sick Leave* (Columbus, Ohio, Ohio Education Association, 1957).

CHAMBERLAIN, Leo M., and KINDRED, Leslie W., *The Teacher and School Organization* (Englewood Cliffs, N.J., Prentice-Hall, Inc., 1958), Chapters 3, 10.

CHANDLER, B. J., and PETTY, Paul V., *Personnel Management in School Administration* (New York, Harcourt, Brace, and World, 1955), Chapters 10, 12.

ELSBREE, Willard S., and REUTTER, E. Edmund, *Staff Personnel in the Public Schools* (Englewood Cliffs, N.J., Prentice-Hall, Inc., 1954), Chapter 16.

EYE, Glen G., and LANE, Willard R., *The New Teacher Comes to School* (New York, Harper and Row, 1956), Chapter 10.

KEARNEY, Nolan C., *A Teacher's Professional Guide* (Englewood Cliffs, N.J., Prentice-Hall, Inc., 1958), Chapter 11.

MOORE, Harold E. and WALTERS, Newell B., *Personnel Administration in Education* (New York, Harper and Row, 1955), Chapter 10.

NEA Research Division, *NEA Research Memo 1958–16; State by State Abstract of Tenure Laws* (Washington, D.C., The National Education Association, November, 1958).

YEAGER, William A., *Administration of the Noninstructional Personnel and Services* (New York, Harper and Row, 1959), Chapter 4.

YODER, Dale, *Personnel Management and Industrial Relations* (Englewood Cliffs, N.J., Prentice-Hall, Inc., 1948), Chapter 20.

.8.

Orienting the School Employee

THERE is no doubt about the necessity to orient employees to their jobs. However, orientation practices have given a connotation to the activity which has made them a topic for controversy. Hence it has become necessary to state what orientation is, discuss its objectives, provide the setting for a defensible orientation program, examine practices engaged in for orienting employees to their jobs, and indicate the means by which orientation may be made effective.

ORIENTATION DEFINED

Limited concepts of orientation cannot withstand the test of reflection about it. Orientation of the school employee is that process by which he becomes aware of the various facets of the school employment for which he has been engaged and the implications of these facets for him.

The process of becoming aware is a part and a product of every experience in and pertaining to the school scene. Thus orientation to the school job is derived from a host of factors beginning with the individual's earliest concepts of the society in which he lives and of the school to which he is early introduced. When one becomes sufficiently interested in teaching or other school employment to consider it as a vocation, orientation receives the added boost of this more than general interest which is a stimulus to inquiry into and investigation of the educational system and its various facets.

Once committed to an interest in becoming a teacher, the prospective teacher is made more fully aware of the educational scene through such organizations as the Future Teachers of America and the Student N.E.A. Preparation for teaching in a teacher training institution contributes to further awareness of the school as an institution, the jobs—teaching and other—in the school, and the functions and functional relationships of the jobs.

Upon completion of training, a new phase of orientation receives emphasis as notices of job possibilities are explored and the prospect becomes involved in a selection procedure which can give him about as much information about the school system as that system is seeking to get about him.

Finally, each school job—teaching and nonteaching—with its many similarities to others nevertheless has its own nuances of local setting, organization, and operation. Each job experience is an orientation to both the local and the general educational scene.

THE PURPOSE OF ORIENTATION

A review of the orientation or induction programs of a number of school districts throughout the United States[1] suggests that the purposes of a program of induction are to:

Make the employee feel welcome, secure, and a member of the team
Inspire the employee
Help employees to adjust to the current situation
Develop confidence on the part of the newcomer
Provide direction for the school year ahead
Acquaint each with all with whom he will be associated
Generate social relationships and good will
Solicit membership in professional organizations
Know the community
Distribute such materials as handbooks, codes of ethics, etc.
Permit the press, radio, and TV to get publicity material
Assign teachers to their classrooms
Make necessary preparations for beginning school
Provide information useful to the new teacher
Furnish some inservice training (philosophy and objectives of education, school policies and practices, apprenticeship and workshop activities, how to get instructional materials, and information about salary schedule, pay procedures, deductions, tenure, leaves, credit unions, probation, retirement, etc.).

[1] Arizona (Tucson), California (Los Angeles, Pasadena, San Bernardino), Indiana (Indianapolis), Illinois (Brookfield, Glencoe), Kansas (Kansas City), Maryland (Baltimore, and the Baltimore, Montgomery, and Talbot County systems), Minnesota (Rochester), Missouri (St. Joseph and Webster Grove), Montana (Great Falls), New Jersey (Livingston and Rutherford), New York (Rochester and White Plains), Ohio (Cincinnati and Lakewood), Oklahoma (Norman and Tulsa), Oregon (Portland), Texas (Lockhart), Utah (Provo), and Virginia (Culpepper County).

A comparison of the preceding list of purposes with that prepared for induction into industry[2] indicates a close relationship which may cause one to wonder to what degree the school orientation is an adaptation of management's program for inducting workers into industry. The purposes are to bring to the new employee:

A feeling that he really belongs
Knowledge of the organization
An awareness of his privileges
The necessity of safe practices
A concept of job requirements
Realization of his responsibilities
The marked importance of HIS job

Whether the area of concern is the schools, government, or industry, there is agreement that the induction activity is desirable and serves sound purposes.

PRINCIPLES AND SETTING FOR ORIENTATION

The definition and purposes of orientation provide background for a consideration of those principles of personnel administration which are pertinent. Five principles[3] will be considered as this chapter is developed. However, at this time each of these principles will be stated in condensed form and discussed briefly with respect to its pertinence to orientation.

1. Education is the primary purpose of the schools. The good will and cooperation of all school employees must be secured if the optimum education is to take place.

It follows that an induction program which does in fact serve to enhance and facilitate education and promotes good will and cooperation will be beyond reproach. Experience with orientation programs will remind many of the sterility, over-organization, coerciveness, and lack of consideration for the individual by which the antitheses of goodwill, resentment is fostered. Otherwise highly desirable provisions for orientation too often suffer from the unnecessary and time-wasting parts of the program. Too little attention is given to the goodwill aspect of the principle.

2. The people who have instituted the schools and all employees within the school system have the same basic interest. This interest is the provision of the best education possible.

A number of the purposes listed indicate the need to assure under-

2 The Missouri State Office of the War Manpower Commission, a mimeographed release. See also Dale Yoder, *Personnel Management and Industrial Relations* (Englewood Cliffs, N.J., Prentice-Hall, Inc., 1948), p. 210.

3 See Chapter 1, Principles numbers 1, 3, 7, 8, and 10 for the full statement of the principle.

standing of the common interest of all school employees. An inspirational address to serve as a reminder of the concern for providing top education is surely in order to initiate the new school year. It may well be remembered by an anxious school administration, however, that teachers have been trained to a knowledge of their work, responsibilities, and relationships within the school organization. They have generally had, in addition to preparation in other areas of competency, training in educational methods, educational psychology, and the history and philosophy of education. It is highly questionable that time should be used during the orientation period to cover again the familiar ground.

3. *The human factor is a variable. The variability is potentially an asset. Temptations to make concessions to the administrative expediency of promoting conformity must be shunned in favor of recognizing and promoting unique individuality and consequent possible personal development of each within the school system.*

Without indicting orientation programs as such, it is necessary to call attention to the danger that this program can serve as the occasion for mass indoctrination, the inhibition of creativity and originality, and stultifying intimations that the way to get ahead is to avoid doing anything that might disturb someone, particularly administrators or supervisors. The problem to be met is how to encourage truly individual development even when this does complicate administration.

4. *The most important single factor in getting the best that a school employee has to offer is how he feels about his work, his associates on the job, and the school system in which he is employed. Everyone has the need to regard his work as worthwhile and to take pride in it.*

Through orientation the employee is inducted into his work, works in relationship with his administrative, teaching and nonteaching associates, and develops some feeling about his job and the school. Feelings are often neither rational nor logical. It doesn't so much matter whether the feeling generated is merited or even understandable. What does matter is that whatever feeling it is, it will have very real implications for the kind of job done.

This principle leads to the conclusion that activities which make it possible for the various employees to get to know, understand, and appreciate each other are essential. Further, it suggests that all employees—administrative, supervisory, teaching, and nonteaching—should see their own and each other's jobs as interacting pieces in the personnel jigsaw puzzle operations of the school system. This is a function of the orientation process and a necessity so that each may come to an appreciation of the high importance of his job.

5. *Employee problems have to be dealt with in terms of the situation or conditions at hand. Flexibility of approach and the development and application of the necessary measures to make more readily attainable*

the objectives of the schools are essential aspects of the personnel activity.

Some questions seem pertinent here. Is it characteristic of orientation programs that they do take into consideration varying conditions? For example, is the same orientation program suitable for well- and fully-trained teachers and also for those employed as marginal and emergency certificated teachers? Is the same orientation program desirable for the hometown teacher and also for the one who will be a stranger to the district? Are new employees treated as if they have no general knowledge to fall back upon but must get a minimum at some briefing session called orientation day or week? Is it either necessary or desirable to cram orientation down the professional throats of teachers or could certain orientation services be scheduled and made available on a need and voluntary use basis?

A consideration of the foregoing principles and the questions raised provides a setting for the next step, the examination of orientation practices.

ORIENTATION PRACTICES

Orientation does, of course, take place in every school system. It begins with the first contact that the prospective employee has with the system in terms of what he learns from the job notice, recruitment literature, application form, interview, and contract. It continues as he takes up residence in, interacts with, and becomes part of his new environment.

Some school districts make little deliberate effort to induct new teachers into their new situation. The new teacher may be left completely to his own devices for getting oriented. His first opportunity to meet others in the school to which he is assigned and to find out about the way in which that school operates may be the first day of regular school.[4] The new employee is plunged into a situation in which survival depends on the resourcefulness of the individual to make necessary adaptation to the unknown.

Other school districts, keenly aware of the problems facing the new employee, exploit the common means noted above to make them serve as fully as possible the orientation objective and then supplement them with helpful literature in the way of courses of study; a handbook of school district and school philosophy, objectives, regulations, schedules, and methods of operation; and special instructions and correspondence which will be helpful to the employee in anticipation of his arrival in the school district to take up his duties.

[4] For an account of an extreme example see Clarence A. Weber, *Personnel Problems of School Administrators* (New York, McGraw-Hill Book Company, Inc., 1954), pp. 55–56. See also Glen G. Eye and Willard R. Lane, *The New Teacher Comes to School* (New York, Harper and Row, 1956), pp. 66–68.

Practices of organized orientation programs will be reviewed for consideration as to the promise they hold for some specific school or school district. It is not suggested that the practices described represent what ought to be present in every school district. Who sponsors orientation, what kinds of programs there are, when and how long the orientation period is, and who participate in organization will be explored.

The Sponsor

Sponsorship of the orientation activity is undertaken by one or a combination of organizations or individuals. Most generally these are the board of education, the professional teacher association, and the Parent Teacher Association.

Board of Education. Functionally the orientation activity must conform to and be provided for by board policy. The importance of board policy is emphasized by two considerations, educational and budgetary. Educationally, it is advantageous to the school district that teachers adjust with a minimum loss of time to the organization and operation of the schools. Budgetarily, it is the obligation of the board of education to make provision to pay teachers for the orientation time which is so much to the advantage of the educational program. Sneaking orientation time into the contract period without commensurate compensation is not worthy of any board of education or its professional administrators.

The school district's stake is such that the board of education is responsible for an orientation policy which becomes part of the administrative responsibility of the superintendent of schools.[5] Ordinarily the superintendent will get a number of his staff to work with him on the development of a program. One of the most logical people to be immediately involved is the one who directs the personnel activity. Associated with the superintendent in the sponsorship and development of the orientation program will be other central office personnel, supervisors, principals, counselling staff, library staff, curriculum coordinators, and teachers.

Teachers Association. Teacher organizations have recognized the opportunity provided through the orientation activity to be of service to beginning teachers and also to solicit their membership in the local, state, and national professional associations. Thus they have served either to sponsor the orientation program or to join with the school administration in providing sponsorship.

The teachers association, as a professional organization, is concerned with the improvement of school and teacher effectiveness as well as with

[5] Clarence A. Weber, *op. cit.,* pp. 62–64.

the welfare of the teacher group.[6] Concern with the functions of the professional organization would prompt the association to sponsor the activity by itself if necessary and to affiliate itself in this activity with the school administration when possible.

The P.T.A. The P.T.A. has a concern for child welfare which logically finds its expression in interest in and cooperation with the schools.[7] As it is generally anticipated that all teachers, also those new to the school system, will participate in P.T.A. activities, this organization is also interested in welcoming the new teacher both to further its interest in the child and his educational welfare and to encourage membership in the joint parent-teacher association.

Occasionally the P.T.A. alone sponsors the orientation activity. Otherwise it joins with the school system and/or the professional teacher association in helping teachers to become adjusted to their new situation.

Kinds of Programs

The mention of orientation conjures up a period of time, usually just before the formal opening of school to the pupils, during which teachers—particularly new ones—are inducted into the mysteries of the coming year's operations. The pre-opening orientation period is a wholly defensible kind of orientation activity. However, it is generally limited to the professional employees. There is also the need to provide for orientation of nonprofessional employees. And, then too, in both instances there is inescapably the need to realize that orientation cannot be capsulized to take place during some relatively brief initial period after which the obligation to induct has been met and the activity can be consigned to limbo. Rather, it is likely that the most important part of orientation still remains to be done after the initial period and that it will take place over an extended period of time, in fact, as long as the employee remains with the school system.

The Initial Program. Organized for the professional, this orientation program is designed to serve selected purposes through a combination of some of two kinds of activities, the one social in its emphasis and the other professional.

The social activities serve the excellent purpose of getting people acquainted, an essential if they are truly to work together intelligently. Among social activities frequently found—and the list is not exhaustive —are: informal gatherings; a community breakfast in which leading

[6] Arthur B. Moehlman and James A. van Zwoll, *School Public Relations* (New York, Appleton-Century-Crofts, 1957), pp. 130–131.

[7] *Ibid.*, pp. 381–387.

citizens of the community participate as hosts or guests; luncheons, possibly with the local chamber of commerce or one or more of the service clubs; a school picnic, either for professional personnel or for all personnel; a tour of the community to provide some knowledge of it and acquaintance with its scenic spots; and something recreational, such as an evening at the civic theatre or with a symphony orchestra.

Obviously the social activities can be extended almost indefinitely. The problem is to determine which of them will suffice for a beginning and whether others may serve their purpose better if scheduled as the school year progresses.

The professional activities are intended to provide needed help to teachers who are new to the school system so that they may begin their new tasks with confidence. Among such professional activities are the welcoming address; lectures; discussions, either by the total group or smaller groups which address themselves to selected problems; workshops, conducted with the help of supervisors and teachers who are experienced in the school system; tours of the school system to acquaint teachers with the range of schools and facilities in which they may be expected to find a place for themselves; assignment of room—and sometimes, belatedly and indefensibly, assignment also of grade level or subject area; and preparation of the classroom and of lesson plans in anticipation of the first day(s) when the children will attend school.

As in the case of the social activities, there is always opportunity to think of desirable things which could be worked into the orientation period. Again the problem is to be selective, so that the menu of orientation activities will be held to a digestible level. Some orientation activities may best take place on a voluntary and counselling basis in accord with needs recognized by both those who are to be oriented and those who must organize the orientation program. Many of these latter activities will serve best if spread throughout the school year.

Nonteaching Employees. These employees are frequently neglected in what is termed the orientation program. This does not mean that they do not receive help in becoming oriented to their jobs. As in the case of the professional employees, they are oriented in a general way by whatever they know about school organization and operation. In addition, the job notice, application form, interview, and contract serve as orientation mediums.

Often further orientation of nonteaching employees is left from this initial stage to the administrative officer with whom he will be associated —accountants and bookkeepers are associated with the superintendent's office, clerical and secretarial personnel with the board of education office staff or the school principal, maintenance men with the assistant superintendent in charge of school plant (and, where pertinent, the transportation supervisor), custodial help with the administrator of the building to which they are assigned or, in the case of a large building, to a chief custodian who is responsible to the administrator.[8] This orientation takes place ordinarily right on the job.

It seems reasonable to believe that if orientation during a planned pre-school period is desirable for those who are specifically trained for the particular school job to which they are coming and who know considerable about the organization and operation of a school system, there is even more of a case to be made for an orientation period for new school employees who lack the background of special preparation for and knowledge of the school operation.

Also, in view of the unit concept of school operation in which all personnel are regarded as part of the executive activity with just one function, to facilitate instruction,[9] it would seem desirable to make provision for the orientation of nonteaching employees to be included in at least some facets of an initial orientation period for all new school employees. Such inclusion would provide them, together with all other employees, the opportunity to become acquainted, appreciative of the importance of their related tasks, and psychologically attuned to contributing to the united efforts required to make school operation effective.

The Continuing Program. At least by intimation it has been suggested that orientation cannot be achieved even by the best organized pre-school orientation session. In fact, there is no question about it, much orientation does take place as employees work into their jobs, becoming familiar on the job with the specific problems of the job—problems which have little real meaning until they are encountered.

In virtually all school systems, whether they consider their activities as orientational or not, further orientation does take place through what are termed supervisory and inservice training activities. Much is to be said in favor of these activities when they are truly functional and when they work in the spirit of helping people to adjust so that they can become more effective school employees. Of particular value are the informal relationships established among teachers whereby they become aware of a variety of points of view, practices, and problems.

These continuing orientation activities are easiest to justify (not rationalize) when they are extensively used by personnel, new and experienced, on a voluntary and need basis. Where they operate on a coercive basis, even the testimonies of those served must be considered inconclusive at best. An orientation program can best demonstrate its

[8] William A. Yeager, *Administration of the Noninstructional Personnel and Services* (New York, Harper and Row, 1959), pp. 69–72.

[9] Arthur B. Moehlman, *School Administration* (Boston, Houghton Mifflin Company, 1951), p. 207.

functionality by the extent to which employees make independent use of its services.

Length of Orientation Period

There probably is no clear answer to how long the pre-school orientation period should be. In view of what has gone before, it would seem that since trying to crowd too much into a program will lead to surfeit, it would be advisable to apply the maxim of stopping while still ahead.

A curious but understandable difference seems to exist between the administrator and supervisor versus the teacher concept of a desirable pre-school orientation period. Ordinarily those who represent the central office seem pleased with what they think they were able to do in the time scheduled and are convinced that with an even longer period of time they could have gone on to new heights. The teacher conversely seems to believe that there is a limit to what he, as a stranger to the school system, can be expected to absorb, retain, and digest during the initial orientation period.

While administrative and supervisory personnel seem often to yearn for more initial orientation time, extending to as much as a month, teachers tend to indicate that if the program would include the minimum essentials, it could be reduced to an initial and more effective period ranging from a minimum of one half day to a maximum of three days.

On the whole authors in the field of school personnel administration do little more than indicate practice by citing a few examples of initial orientation sessions. Their selection of examples does not necessarily indicate their endorsement. Eye and Lane [10] commend the one-month pre-session workshop for new teachers which they cited for Rochester, Minnesota, while they also present a schedule for a short (five day) pre-session meeting. Yeager [11] opines that whereas "Ordinarily, two or three days are devoted to the program. A week may not be too long. . . ." In general there is consensus among those who have reflected on the topic of orientation in that the program is thought of as having three phases; preliminary, pre-session, and continuing. Attention is directed to the need to give more attention to the continuing aspect of the orientation program.

It would seem desirable that those who assume responsibility for orientation programs develop a criterion of functionality instead of length of program as the measure of merit. This would undoubtedly lead to programs which would vary in length with the particular needs of the school district but which would probably find a median of two or

[10] Glen G. Eye and Willard R. Lane, *op. cit.*, p. 359.
[11] William A. Yeager, *Administration and the Teacher* (New York, Harper and Row, 1954), p. 161.

three days for a pre-session realistically satisfactory as long as orientation is provided for on a continuing basis throughout the school year.

Participants in Orientation

Ordinarily all who have been mentioned as taking part in planning orientation represent also the categories of those who participate in the orientation activity. These include:

Board member
  (president or chairman)
Superintendent of schools
Assistant superintendents
  (particularly for instruction and
  personnel)
Principals
Supervisors
Teachers

President or chairman
  (local education association)
President (School District
  P.T.A.)
Local leader of private enterprise
Representative of local government
  (mayor, city or county manager,
  chairman of city or county council)

Role of Participant. During the pre-school orientation period the activity of the board member, superintendent, assistant superintendent(s), presidents of the education association and P.T.A., local leader of private enterprise, and the representative of local government will probably be limited to a brief statement of welcome on one occasion or another during the induction session.

The principals, supervisors, and other teachers, and also the assistant superintendent in charge of personnel have the specific function to help personnel new to the school system to become acquainted with their immediate associates, duties, and working environment. Much of their activity will take place in the school building to which the teacher is assigned.

The assistant superintendent in charge of personnel has a particular responsibility to help new personnel to solve the problems which confront them relative both to their jobs and to their lives in the new situation. He has the responsibility to recognize and help resolve job-related problems. Also to the degree that his services are welcome, he must be available to help resolve the personal problems of new employees.

Making Orientation Effective

An analysis of and some reflection about the objectives of orientation listed at the beginning of this chapter indicate that not one of them can be met during a period of initial induction whether that period is one half day or a whole month. In every instance the purpose can be met only if there is provision for continued orientation throughout the regular school year. It is evident that real orientation takes place progressively and that what can be done initially will be elementary if not superficial and may, in some instances, better be deferred until school is well underway.

An effective orientation of new employees will follow the spirit of the principles enunciated and will take place through preliminary, pre-session, and continuing programs.

The Principles. 1. *The program must be one which commands the good will and cooperation of the school employees.* This means that the program must be noncoercive and assured of success because of the needs of new employees which it is developed to meet. It is a program which avoids self-exaltation of existing staff and is therefore also kept to a practical minimum. It is a program which compensates all participants for the time spent, recognizing that new employees have added expenses for coming to the school district in advance of the opening of school and that existing staff—except for 12-month employees—must give up their own time and pursuits to take part in orientation. Contrary to clichés to the effect that assuming duties without recompense proves professionalism, not being paid is no criterion for being professional.

2. *The basic interest of all school employees is the provision of the best education possible.* The effective orientation program will take into account the training of teachers in subject matter, the historical and philosophical basis for education, and the methods for and theories of learning. This will eliminate from the program unnecessary duplication, saving time and effort for what is essential.

3. *Human variability is potentially an asset.* Education in a democracy has an obligation to recognize individual differences among personnel and to recognize the asset value of variability and even idiosyncrasy. The effective induction program will promote the spirit of individualism and of the individual responsibility which is probably one of the basic facets of professionalism. Without necessarily penalizing the team approach and cooperation, the orientation program might be an excellent place to emphasize that the image of the organization man is not consistent with the organization and operation of a system of public education in and for a democracy. There are occasions for cooperative effort and there are times when the individual must stand to be counted even when he is a lone voice. Conditions must assure him the exercise of this expression as a right to be favorably regarded and not penalized.

4. *The need to regard one's work as important and to take pride in it represents that important factor, how one feels about his job.* Ordinarily it seems that much more time might be spent on helping the new employee to understand and appreciate not only what his own job is but also how his job relates to and is supported by his professional and non-

professional colleagues. The place to begin this is within the individual building where, for example, the new teacher is oriented to the realities and the assumptions relating to the teachers who have had his prospective pupils and those who are going to inherit those pupils.

The new teacher must realize exactly what the implications of the work of the custodian, secretary, and principal are for his own success as a teacher. The custodian, as a new employee, may find it particularly difficult to think of himself as more than one who does the school building's housekeeping. He must learn to regard his task as having justification only to the extent that it improves the conditions under which learning may take place.

Preliminary Orientation. Once the contract has been assigned, the director of personnel has a basis for continuing the orientation begun with the recruitment literature and continuing through application, interview, and the job offer. Further and more specific information may be made available about the community, its cultural, recreational, and religious resources, and the addresses of their representatives. Information about housing may be provided and an offer made to give assistance in securing facilities. Specific information as to the teaching or other assignment, if not already provided in the contract, should now be provided.

A handbook containing the policies for the school district and one pertaining to the specific school in which the new employee will work should be provided. A copy of the course of study (where applicable) and of the textbooks to be used by the new teacher should be sent with an indication of usual expectations as to their use and instructions for preparing lesson plans for the first several lessons.

Any special announcements and bulletins should be sent to new employees just as they ought to be sent to former employees. In addition, when established personnel have offered their services for this purpose, the new employee may be referred to one of the experienced staff for such further help as he may need.

All handout material should be forwarded at such a time that new personnel may have time to read and re-read it at leisure with consequent improved opportunity to digest it. Thus is avoided the feeling of engulfment that the new teacher experiences as he receives such materials more rapidly than he can possibly read them during the first few days of an induction period.

Pre-session Orientation. There is a place for the pre-school opening period of induction. If this part of the induction program is to be effective, it must be kept to a level that can be assimilated by the inductee. Since there is so much orienting that has to take place eventually, there will be temptation to add to the program. This temptation must be resisted because overloading the orientation period will defeat the very objectives of orientation and, no matter how much extended, will never comprise all needed orientation activities. It may as well be faced that orientation cannot take place during the pre-session period often designated for the purpose.

A simple, functional, and not overly long pre-session induction program might provide for:

1. an inspirational welcome address, less than 20 minutes, by the superintendent of schools. This may be supplemented by a few words of welcome (limit, five minutes per person) from, for example, the president of the board of education, a leading municipal official, the presidents of the local education association and the P.T.A.

2. meeting the principal of the school to which the new employee will be assigned.

3. room assignment for teachers and introduction to office or custodial facilities for nonteaching employees.

4. introduction to the instructional materials center.

5. meeting a few of the teachers, such as those who teach in the same grade or subject fields and those who have neighboring rooms.

It is wholly probable that all of these activities, depending on when they begin, can be scheduled into one morning or a day.

The Continuing Program. The lengthy orientation programs to which reference has been made and which seem to be so popular with administrators and supervisors are no doubt scheduled because they recognize the inadequacy of the preliminary and pre-session programs as they are described above. This inadequacy is obvious. However, it is highly dubious that this inadequacy may be overcome through lengthened orientation programs. Rather, it is suggested, the aspects of orientation that have not been provided by preliminary and pre-session orientation may be provided for logically, functionally, and progressively as the school year proceeds.

Again, it is to be noted that coerciveness is a poor basis for any orientation. Thus, provisions for continued orientation may most desirably be made on the basis of such need that the activities scheduled are utilized voluntarily at a level that warrants their continuance. The advocates of coercive activities are reminded that a horse may be led to water but cannot be made to drink; likewise physical presence at scheduled activities, and even participation against one's will, are no evidence of the effectiveness of the activity.

Among activities which may be included, at least tentatively and experimentally, in the continuing orientation program are:

1. demonstration teaching by some teacher considered to be outstanding in the grade level or subject of special interest.

2. observation of other experienced teachers in their regular classroom teaching.

3. supervision by the principal and supervisor who make the new teacher their prime concern.

4. lectures.

5. workshops in which there is freedom from pressure and an atmosphere which welcomes the exchange of ideas.

6. introduction to teacher committees (functional, not façades, it is hoped).

7. get acquainted events—such as luncheons or dinners, picnics, dances, and other social events—may well be spread throughout the school year to help new employees become acquainted. These events may start with the individual school and be extended by the departments and divisions of the school system. The education association also may assume a definite responsibility for some of the get acquainted events.

8. breakfasts or luncheons with civic groups, such as the chamber of commerce and the service clubs, may much better be arranged as the school year progresses than to be crowded into the first week in the school district when too much activity produces a haze rather than a picture of the community.

9. tours of the school system, commercial and industrial scene, residential sectors of the community, and scenic, cultural, and recreational resources of the community also may best be introduced gradually and one at a time after the new employee has had time to adjust himself somewhat to his new environment.

With full appreciation of the important roles of all participants in the orientation program, it must be noted that as a matter of fact the new employee will most likely consult a fellow worker in the same kind of job in which he finds himself, not a superior. For new teachers, this means that the teacher across the hall or in the next room is perhaps the potentially most influential means of orientation. This highlights the importance of each teacher being made fully aware of his responsibility within the school system for that facet of personnel administration known as orientation.

SUMMARY

Orientation of the school employee is the process by which he becomes aware of the facets of his school job and the implications of those facets for him. The purposes of orientation are numerous but all resolve into one, that the employee have the way paved for his becoming as early as possible an effectively operating agent within the school system.

Some principles of personnel administration which pertain particularly to the induction of new employees emphasize the function of the school, the need for employee good will and cooperation, the unity of employee interest, the variability of human beings and the asset value thereof, the importance of how an individual feels about his job, and the differences in the orientation needs of each and the consequent need for flexibility in meeting the needs of the respective employees.

Orientation practices were reviewed. These cannot be considered as models to be followed but they may serve as mediums to be adopted, adapted, or rejected following consideration for any one specific school situation.

Those who are frequently found to be participants in the orientation program were summarized and their roles in providing welcome; acquaintanceship with duties, associates, and environment; and help in solving job related and personal problems were stated.

Finally, it was suggested that a program of orientation must be thought of as being tri-partite, beginning with the provision of all kinds of information that can be put into the new employees' hands before he arrives, followed by a pre-session orientation period which is limited to those prime essentials which can be effectively included in as brief a period as one half to a whole day, and carried on progressively through a range of activities as the school year unfolds. Thus it is possible to avoid surfeit and assure a maximum of assimilation.

Without in any way detracting from the importance of all other participants in the process of orientation, it is suggested that the singly most important individual to help the new employee is his fellow-worker, pointing up the necessity for each to appreciate his potentialities for influencing that improvement of the teaching-learning situation which depends on orientation.

SELECTED READINGS

CHANDLER, B. J., and PETTY, Paul V., *Personnel Management in School Administration* (Yonkers-on-Hudson, N.Y., World Book Company, 1955), Chapter 6.

ELSBREE, Willard S., and REUTTER, E. Edmund, *Staff Personnel in the Public Schools* (Englewood Cliffs, N.J., Prentice-Hall, Inc., 1954), Chapter 5.

EYE, Glen G., and LANE, Willard R., *The New Teacher Comes to School* (New York, Harper and Row, 1956).

KEARNEY, Nolan C., *A Teacher's Professional Guide* (Englewood Cliffs, N.J., Prentice-Hall, Inc., 1958), Chapter 8.

MOORE, Harold E., and WALTERS, Newell B., *Personnel Administration in Education* (New York, Harper and Row, 1955), Chapter 9.

"Orientation of New Teachers," *The N.E.A. Journal*, 47:5, May, 1958, pp. 292–299.

PIGORS, Paul, and MYERS, Charles A., *Personnel Administration* (New York, McGraw-Hill Book Company, Inc., 1951), Chapter 13.

SCOTT, Walter Dill, CLOTHIER, Robert C., and SPRIEGEL, William R., *Personnel*

Management (New York, McGraw-Hill Book Company, Inc., 1961), Chapter 18.

WEBER, Clarence A., *Personnel Problems of School Administrators* (New York, McGraw-Hill Book Company, Inc., 1954), Chapter 4.

YEAGER, William A., *Administration and the Teacher* (New York, Harper and Row, 1954), Chapter 8.

YEAGER, William A., *Administration of the Noninstructional Personnel and Services* (New York, Harper and Row, 1959), pp. 69–72.

YODER, Dale, *Personnel Principles and Policies* (Englewood Cliffs, N.J., Prentice-Hall, Inc., 1959), Chapter 16.

.9.

Motivation and Incentive

DURING a recession period, when the percentage of the unemployed reached an unprecedentedly high level, there was a man of independent wealth, curiosity about the determinants that affect the attitudes and behavior of workers, and a *willingness to finance a limited investigation to* satisfy his curiosity. He carefully sought out and hired men who were especially needy, whose plight was particularly desperate. Eager to earn money to meet their personal and family needs, the men reported for work and were put to digging in their employer's yard. Under his supervision, they dug holes and filled them until much of the yard had been so excavated and filled.

As the work progressed a change of attitude took place. At first glad to be working regardless of what they had to do, the men began to question the value of what they were doing until finally they put down their tools and refused to dig holes only to fill them again. Thereupon the employer told them that there was a legend of family wealth buried during an historically critical era and never recovered. He set forth that there was reason to believe that if the legend was true, the family silver, jewels, and coin must be somewhere within his yard. He added that it was his concern either to find the wealth or discredit the legend. Thereupon the men fell to with greater vigor than before.[1]

The thrust of the anecdote is that the worker needs purpose or interest to sustain his effort. There were present here both motivation and incentive. These will be defined, the methods used in industry and government will be presented, their implications for productivity will be explored, and the applicability of conclusions about motivation and incentives to the education scene will be discussed.

[1] As recounted by William Clark Trow, Professor of Educational Psychology, University of Michigan, 1938.

MOTIVATION AND INCENTIVE DEFINED

Whereas incentive is given as a synonym of motive, the synonyms for incentive do not include motive but do include such words as goad, incitement, and spur.[2] This differentiation in synonyms suggests a distinction that enters into the definition, the distinction between the internal basis of the motive and the external basis of incentive.

Motivation

Motivation is the activation of an inner drive which may be conscious or subconscious. This drive produces within the individual the sensation of physio-, neuro-, psycho-, and/or socio-logical needs which may have been latent but are now awakened and crave fulfillment.

The strict interpretation of this definition of motivation suggests that to speak of motivating another means little more than stimulating an awakening to a need which is already part of him. Motivation cannot be instilled. The technique for motivating, or stimulating to an awakening to the sense of need, probably does not lend itself to blueprinting but will vary with the individuals involved.

Incentive. Incentive is the product of an externally applied stimulus or spur. This stimulus provides the promise of some reward which is regarded by the individual as having value for him.

The rewards employed as incentives are often categorized as financial, extrafinancial, and nonfinancial. These three categories include many devices by which to appeal to the individual to extend himself so that he may attain the reward attending his efforts. These devices will be dealt with in the following pages.

Working Definition. A working definition, for the purposes of personnel administration, probably does not generally need to make the sharp distinctions of the definitions of motivation and incentive. In practice the distinctions shade into each other so that it is difficult sometimes to distinguish clearly between motive and incentive.

By way of example, an individual begins working to meet his physical need for food, shelter, and clothing. He is given incentives to make him productive beyond the meeting of his needs. As a result he develops tastes for a greater variety of foods, more commodious shelter, clothes for a variety of occasions, and adds the need for transportation. These developments result in his gaining social status providing an inner drive, which is now added to his pursuit of his physical needs. Thus

2 Consult such sources as Webster's Dictionary, Roget's Thesaurus, and H. C. Warren, *Dictionary of Psychology* (Boston, Houghton Mifflin Company, 1934), p. 134.

inner motive and external incentive are found in alliance with one another to affect the behavior of the individual.

For the purposes of the discussion that follows, the means by which individuals are awakened to their needs or incited to seek rewards are regarded, without differentiation, as motivators and incentives. For the sake of convenience, both will be included under the designation of incentive.

THE PROVISION OF INCENTIVE

Incentives generally fall into categories of financial versus non-financial, with occasional reference to extrafinancial incentive, or of positive versus negative motivation.

In every instance the needs, interests, and desires of man decide whether the incentive provided will be effective and to what extent. Having ascertained the needs, interests, and desires of the employee, the director of personnel is prepared to select from a long list of tried incentives those which may be expected to be most effective under the circumstances.

Positive Incentives

These are the incentives that ordinarily tend to fulfill the desires of the worker. They cut across the lines of financial and nonfinancial classifications of incentives, being sometimes the one and sometimes the other. They operate in terms of rewards which may be monetary, status with peers or superiors, or personal sense of achievement or justice. These are regarded as positive and also constructive.

Ordinarily an incentive playing upon an employee's fears would be considered negative and destructive. However there is one possible exception. The constructive incentive of a fear of the consequences of wrongdoing, a fear which reinforces other positive incentives to do what is defined as right, may be considered positive.

Negative Incentives

These are the incentives that ordinarily operate on the basis of fear and are destructive inasmuch as they prey upon the worker, causing him to be so anxious, fretful, and worried that his efficiency on the job is decreased. The destructive aspect of fear in this instance is the product either of this incentive operating with insufficient reinforcement from constructively or positively operating stimuli or of capriciously arbitrary action—by a superior or a fellow worker—which provides a threat to the welfare of the employee or to the attainment of his objectives.

Financial Incentives

The pay received for work is a common financial incentive. This pay may be related to the time worked (hours, days, etc.), the quantity of acceptable quality units of production (piece work), a formula by which extra productivity is rewarded, or premium rates for overtime, weekend, or holiday work.

In addition awards for profitable suggestions, profit-sharing bonuses, and stock ownership provisions are among financial incentives that are effectively employed in industry and to some extent in government.

Extrafinancial Incentives. Including bonus and premium payments, Waite [3] adds a category of vacations, holidays, and terminal pay; the group of incentives commonly referred to as the "fringe" benefits; and the provisions for employment and income stability. Although these incentives are not positively reflected in the regular periodic pay envelope, nevertheless over the long haul they are definitely part of the financial incentive picture.

Conclusions. Economic or financial incentives may prove effective when the pay scale is inadequate to meet the needs of the worker. Once, however, the individual's needs can be met by his income, the financial incentive may be expected to become progressively weaker. Mayo [4] reviewed a situation in which four financial incentive plans were used without success until a more pressing nonfinancial problem of rest periods was solved. He concluded therefore that those who put financial incentives first are likely to be wrong.

Nonfinancial Incentives

Among an almost endless list of possible nonfinancial incentives, the following thirty are mentioned consistently in the literature covering such stimuli:

acceptance—by fellow workers, superiors, society
affection—the liking of and for others
automation—use of machines to facilitate work
committees—to provide a voice in operations
competition—with others and one's own former achievements
conferences—staff and between the individual and his supervisor
contests—a form of competition

3 William W. Waite, *Personnel Administration* (New York, The Ronald Press Company, 1952), pp. 328–334.
4 Elton Mayo, *The Social Problems of an Industrial Civilization* (Cambridge, The Harvard University Press, 1945).

equipment—actually the physical facilities, including machines and tools for doing best the work to be done

fellowship—the opportunity to enjoy companionship under other than working conditions as well as on the job

hours—a working period geared to the conditions, e.g., of noise, speed, pressure, and tension

in-group spirit—often spoken of as belonging, identifying with the organization in its objectives and operations

job satisfaction—finding in the work itself the incentive for doing one's best

placement—assignment to work in terms of competence

pleasure—enjoyment of the task which is labeled work

praise—commendation given when deserved

privilege—equity rather than equality in treatment

recognition—having notice taken of oneself and one's achievements

rest periods—as required by the working conditions

security—job and wage stability, absence of destructive fears

selection—functional, and therefore catering to personal pride in being the successful candidate for the job

self-respect—working under conditions which permit one to live with himself

service—the feeling or knowledge that one's efforts are significant or provide a worthwhile service

status—among one's fellow-workers, superiors, and in the community

suggestion plans—providing for capitalization upon the knowledge, ingenuity, and creativity of the employee

supplies—having the use of those expendables, in the necessary quantity and uniformity of quality, that will expedite production

training—getting instruction to maximize skills and develop potential

transfer—in accord with developed competence or observed potential

work—sufficient to keep one busy and challenged

working conditions—heat, lighting, sanitation, and ventilation conducive to productive effort

It is readily noted that the list of thirty incentives may be divided into two major categories, involving recognition and working conditions. In several instances an incentive may belong to either category or both, depending on what the intent was and how it was taken by the employee.

Conclusions. The large number of incentives that have individual recognition or status implications is suggestive of the importance of status as a key to behavior.[5] When a fair and adequate wage policy is in effect, it seems that nonfinancial incentives may prove more effective than financial. However, it also seems that, whatever the interest of the personnel director, the success of the incentive requires that it serve as the

[5] Dale Yoder supports a statement about the importance of status with a lengthy bibliography of well known names in Anthropology, Management and Industrial Relations, and Sociology in his *Personnel Management and Industrial Relations* (Englewood Cliffs, N.J., Prentice-Hall, Inc., 1948), p. 78.

means for attaining a genuine comprehension and appreciation of all with respect to the identity of interests of both management and the worker.[6] An incentive system which is no more than a means for exploiting people in order to raise production levels has no real promise of success.

INCENTIVES AND PRODUCTIVITY

An incentive system either bucks or provides new direction for the tendencies of employees. To have a chance of being successful it must have the following favorable conditions: sound personnel policies administered by competent personnel workers and supported by an enlightened management, the management planning and supervision that itself serves as an inducement to high level performance, a fair and adequate wage scale, and a personnel selection process in which the general interest of the prospective employee is in line with the interest that the job is expected to command.[7] With these four components in operation, further incentives of both the financial and the nonfinancial kind may be expected to improve productivity provided the selection of the incentive is soundly based upon the specific problems to be solved.

An increase in the production of private industry, averaging from 2 to 2½ per cent annually since the beginning of the 1900's has been attributed to considerable degree to incentive plans which took into account the problems of both production and human relations.[8] This is particularly understandable in view of the inclusion of automation and the provision of adequate working space and facilities as elements in the structure of an incentive system.

In a series of case studies, Britton [9] found that wage incentives could be conducive to significant production improvements and were credited on occasion with a doubling of productivity. The evidence of success for an incentive system, and sometimes the basis for its development, depends largely on the ability to make sound time and motion studies and the existence of a satisfactory means for cost accounting and control.

[6] See also Ordway Tead and Henry C. Metcalf, *Personnel Administration* (New York, McGraw-Hill Book Company, Inc., 1933), p. 186.

[7] See also John M. Pfiffner, *The Supervision of Personnel* (Englewood Cliffs, N.J., Prentice-Hall, Inc., 1951), Chap. 13; Walter D. Scott, Robert C. Clothier, William R. Spriegel, *Personnel Management* (New York, McGraw-Hill Book Company, Inc., 1961), Chap. 23; William W. Waite, *Personnel Administration* (New York, The Ronald Press Company, 1952), p. 334; and Gordon S. Watkins, Paul A. Dodd, Wayne L. McNaughton, and Paul Prasow, *The Management of Personnel and Labor Relations* (New York, McGraw-Hill Book Company, Inc., 1950), Chap. 16.

[8] Charles E. Britton, *Incentives in Industry* (New York, Esso Standard Oil Company, 1953), p. 5.

[9] *Ibid.*, Appendix, seven cases.

Conclusions

The conclusions to be drawn about incentives and their effects upon productivity are summarized by Britton [10] and reproduced below:

The worker's desire to be "one of the boys" often prevents his developing creativeness, personal efficiency, pride in work and job aggressiveness. He wants to be treated as an individual, yet, in an effort to protect his security in the group, he hesitates to put his best foot forward and use the abilities which would establish his individuality. The resolving of this conflict seems to call for a general re-education of most employees and many managements in the fact that individual differences (in ability, job performance, productivity) should be recognized and rewarded and that mass mediocrity is a cancer in our free enterprise system.

Incentives embrace many methods of reaching the worker, creating in him the desire to do his best work, and making the fullest possible use of his individual abilities. . . .

Wage incentive plans are based on piece rates rather than time rates. The majority of the world's workers are paid on time basis. The theory of wage incentives (the linking of output to earnings) is to some "inherently objectionable," to others, "inherently desirable."

The incentive principle is generally acceptable to management, but past errors in the design and application of wage incentive plans led to abuses which in many cases turned management against them. . . . Labor approves of the incentive principle but is strongly opposed to wage incentive plans except in piece work industries, such as shoe and textile, where incentive work is traditional.

For every successful plan put in operation during a recent five-year period, there were, according to one survey, three that failed or developed major weaknesses and required drastic revision. Failures have often been due to the fact that management has been content to refine and adapt plans used by other companies instead of developing their own wage incentive plans.

Installation of a wage incentive plan requires advance setting of work standards (through time and motion study, standard data, etc.) to provide:

a. an objective basis for effective appraisal of a fair day's work
b. data which will differentiate between producers and non-producers
c. a basis for evaluating the potentialities of the plan.

Development and application of a wage incentive plan is slow and expensive, requiring years of pre-planning, a substantial addition of personnel to the industrial relations staff, and continual maintenance and revision. A wage incentive plan requires a sound basis of good employee relations, sound management and supervision, and a program of nonfinancial incentives. Wage incentive plans properly conceived, installed, administered and maintained for workers whose output is measurable have resulted in lower costs, lower selling prices, higher profits and higher wages. . . .

The following five major conclusions were reached by Britton:

[10] *Ibid.,* pp. 83–85.

*Good leadership provides the most effective incentive to increased produc-
tion.* Nothing has been found to take the place of good supervision and management; incentive plans are supplementary to leadership. . . .

*Local conditions determine whether a company should adopt a specific
incentive plan, and dictate the type required.* Local study to discover employee
needs and desires should be made before an incentive plan is chosen. . . .

*Non-financial incentives seem to be the most effective type for a normal
situation.* That is, in a normal economy where workers receive reasonable
wages and enjoy a measure of security, non-financial incentives have been the
most successful. . . . A man's time, his presence on the job, a measured quantity
of work may be bought. Job satisfaction, enthusiasm and pride in work, impossible to buy, can be developed only by an enlightened management constantly
striving to find methods for creating teamwork. . . . Being on the right job,
having a good working spot, and receiving recognition for work well done, are
all important non-financial incentives. . . .

*Financial incentives, other than direct wage incentives, are essential to
good employee relations but are comparatively weak as incentives to increase
production.* Indirect financial incentives (such as a fair wage classification
system, a sound promotional procedure, and fringe benefits) may be said to
improve employee output negatively; that is, where they do *not* exist, morale and
productivity suffer. . . . There is little evidence that financial incentives (other
than specific wage incentive plans) have succeeded in increasing the worker's
desire to produce more.

*Wage incentive plans are more suitable for use in other industries than
petroleum refining, but include valuable incentive procedures which may be
used independently.* Because wage incentive plans base the worker's pay
directly on his output, some yardstick must be available for measuring output
and relating quality to earnings. Furthermore, the worker must be able to exert
a measure of control over his performance, which presupposes a constant even
flow of materials, independence of production processes and a more or less
repetitive type of work. For these reasons, wage incentive plans have not
proved practical in the process industries.

INCENTIVES AND SCHOOL PERSONNEL

The concept of motivation is familiar to school employees, particularly to teachers who have been conditioned to the idea of motivating
children to study, learn, and take action, and who have themselves been
subjected to activities that were intended to motivate, stimulate, influence,
provide leadership, or serve as incentives. It seems sometimes as if the
idea of motivation is so familiar in school circles that school personnel
are led to believe it to be peculiar to the field of education. There is
therefore the danger that a myopic view of motivation will be developed
in which the nature of motivation and the experiences of other enterprises are overlooked.

It is because of the value of the experiences of others with the problems of motivation that the intensive background of the preceding pages has been provided. Just as in every other field, so too in the field of education it is necessary to identify and analyze the problems peculiar to it and to arrive at the specific solutions called for by the school situation. Nevertheless, it is expected that when the problems and solutions of the school scene are examined in the light of those in other fields, schoolmen may avail themselves of shortcuts made possible by the experiences of others. They will be enabled to concentrate their efforts on constructive efforts, avoiding the trial and error approaches which have been demonstrated as unrewarding in other fields and adapting the findings of others whenever possible to the school situation.

Principles Governing Motivation

In some way every one of the twelve principles for personnel administration [11] has implications for some facet of the problem of motivating or providing incentives. These twelve principles deal with the purpose of the schools, employee interest and attitudes, policies governing the employee and his voice in their development, clear understanding of the nature of the job, placement in accord with competence and job requirements, regard for the individual and individual differences, job satisfaction, psychological and physical working conditions conducive to high level performance and fairness in pay, work load, and the length of the working period.

If motivation is regarded as something internal to the individual, then it follows that about all that another can do toward motivating someone else is to create and arrange conditions and circumstances by which to bring about an awakening of those inner factors that do motivate one to action.

It is not at all certain that the conditions intended to awaken inner drives will actually accomplish their task. Motivation seems to reach expression under the most unpredictable climates. Nevertheless, it would seem necessary that the awakening to inner drives be attempted in order to promote a level of performance that will bring the schools nearer to attaining the objectives which justify their existence. The effort to arouse to motivation is expressed in part through a system of incentives.

Incentives Used in School Systems

Schools and school systems have always operated in terms of some incentives as well as the motivation which induced one to become a

---

[11] See "Principles of Personnel Administration," Chap. 1. It is recommended that these principles be reviewed with special attention to their implications for motivation and in the light of this chapter dealing with motivation and incentives.

teacher or other type of school employee. A number of these incentives are so familiar to the employee that he may even forget to regard them as such. Among them are salaries and wages, salary schedules, tenure, retirement, recognition, status, leaves, and physical conditions of a suitable place to work, equipment with which to work, and the needed supplies. Each of these will be given consideration.

Salaries and Wages. Actually the salaries and wages of the various kinds of school personnel have been such as to eliminate them largely from the incentive scene. The best that can be said about them is that at the lower end of the scale, the nationwide scene has been such as to distinguish the teacher as a member of the economically marginal college graduate worker group. The financial rewards for teachers and other school workers obviously have not been an incentive or inducement to people of ability to seek school employment. The inducement to the many able men and women who became school employees had to be something other than the paycheck.

Yet, before the general acceptance of salary scheduling, boards of education and superintendents, threatened with the loss of an employee whom they had come to prize, did make offers of pay increments to induce those employees to stay on. In this sense, salary and wage increments were used as incentives. Similarly, if an individual happened to be sought after by a school system, the job offer was sweetened by a salary that was made sufficiently high to serve as an inducement to accept employment. These practices led to high differentiation and subjectivity in the administration of salaries or wages in which there was much occasion for others to feel that comparisons indicated an absence of fairness.

Part of the issue of salaries and wages for both professional and non-professional workers in the school system is that of some provision to compensate them for work done in addition to the duties for which they were employed and qualified. Recognition of the demands made upon some school personnel, beyond the regular working day and sometimes aside from their competencies, demands that in fairness to the employee a policy of compensation in money or time be provided.

Teachers have often been induced to do all manner of tasks, unrelated to their functions or competencies, from participation in some kind of community-school activity and directing school productions to taking tickets at the gate. The final inducement, intended to overcome any reservations or objections, is only too generally that one "must be professional about such things." There is, of course, nothing professional about doing tasks outside one's professional competency, nor is it unprofessional to be paid for work done. It is well possible that some school employees would be willing to do side-tasks if the incentive of pay for work done would be held out to them.

Salary Schedules. In recognition of the very real administrative problems accompanying a salary determination which followed no observable or defensible pattern, salary scheduling was introduced and adopted progressively until practically every school system of any significant size in the country has and operates in terms of a salary schedule.[12]

The fact that an employee could forecast his economic advancement in terms of the salary schedule under which he worked provided an incentive both to enter and to remain in school employment.

Together with the consideration given salary schedules came the recognition of the conceptual desirability of pay increments in accord with merit. Through a consideration of position, preparation, and experience in combination, a degree of recognition was given automatically and yet in terms of the merit implications of these factors. Beyond this, merit awards were superimposed upon the other forms of automatic schedules to "recognize and reward exceptional ability and to set up goals that may be attained after all the formal requirements have been met."[13]

Even during the period of the 20's it was recognized that "there are now no real standards, except personal judgment, for the evaluation of merit."[14] In spite of long-term and dedicated efforts by some, there has really been no breakthrough in the attempt to develop a valid and reliable technique for measuring teacher effectiveness.[15]

Merit pay has been introduced in a number of school districts only to be abandoned in many instances after a relatively short experience with it. Not only have the problems of administering the program and of employee morale been very great, but, it is to be suspected, school systems are discovering what industry has also discovered: wage incentive plans are suitable in occupations in which the worker's pay is based on his output. Therefore, a yardstick must be available to measure output and to relate quantity and quality to earnings. Also, the worker must be able to exert a measure of control over his performance—in other words, the difference in performance between one worker and another must be truly to his own credit or lack of it, not to a difference in the materials with or the conditions under which he works—that is, uniformity in the quality of the materials and constancy in their availability, independence of production processes (he is not affected by others in the process), and

[12] Early in the 1900's, E. S. Evenden and F. W. Ballou prepared for publication by the National Education Association reports on *Teachers' Salaries and Salary Schedules* (1918–19) and *Salary Schedules, 1920–21* (Cities over 100,000 population), respectively.

[13] Arthur B. Moehlman, *Public School Finance* (Chicago, Rand McNally & Company, 1927), p. 133.

[14] *Ibid.*, p. 134.

[15] D. Lee Castetter, Lloyd S. Standlee, and Nicholas A. Fattu, *Teacher Effectiveness: An Annotated Bibliography* (Bloomington, Institute of Educational Research, School of Education, Indiana University, 1954), 104 p.

relative repetitiveness in the work.[16] In addition, it seems as if a merit pay plan is often resorted to as a means for evading the provision of warrantable salaries or as a device for getting popular approval for what is to be truly an additional step in the automatic scale disguised as a merit step and later referred to as a career-recognition plan; something quite different.

Quite obviously, at this time the yardstick for measuring merit has not been developed for teaching nor can the conditions for working—control over his own performance—as described above be applied to the teaching field under current conditions. Many social and human variables and the heterogeneity of even the most homogeneous groupings attempted in schools defy at this time any attempt to attribute differences in results to the performance of the teacher in such a way as to provide a defensible basis for a merit pay scale.

Under existing circumstances it would seem that although continued efforts to develop a sound basis for a merit pay scale are to be commended, employees in the field of education will have to content themselves with being part of the majority of the world's workers[17] who are paid on a time basis until a sound merit pay plan is devised.

Tenure. As an incentive, tenure provides a positive influence conducive to the level of job performance attainable when enervating fear and anxiety about job and economic security are absent. Provision for tenure is one way to set the stage for activation of the inner drives called motivation.

By itself tenure probably does not ordinarily serve as a strong enough incentive. It must be re-enforced by others of such incentives as are discussed in these pages.[18]

Retirement. It has become desirable in all occupations and necessary in those that are not well paid to provide, in addition to job and economic security during an employee's working years, economic security for the retirement years. When this was done by way of a pension, the dependency of the employee and the paternalism of the employer could easily overshadow the appreciation that was present and the recognition that was being given.

Under the provision of a retirement plan to which both the employer and the employee contribute in accord with a stipulated plan; the employee receives recognition progressively, has the opportunity to regard the provisions for his retirement as an earned right—not a dole—

---

16 See the fifth conclusion by Britton as quoted on p. 159.

17 See paragraph three of the conclusion by Britton as quoted on p. 158.

18 Tenure is here discussed only as an incentive. A discussion of the pro's and con's of tenure will take place in Chapter 17.

which is in part the product of his own thrift, and is assured a degree of economic security during his declining years when he is no longer gainfully employed. When the contributions to the retirement plan are made by the employer alone under contract provisions, the employee still can regard the plan as one made possible by his productive efforts; something earned, not charity.

The provision for the future, the recognition implicit in the retirement plan, and the self respect engendered by the formula for assuring annuities upon retirement are all part of a pattern of incentives which begin to operate with the choice of career and continue throughout employment.

Recognition. During recent years the importance of recognition has come to be acknowledged. The ways in which recognition may be given are virtually limitless. Often a word of appreciation or gesture of commendation will go a long way in meeting the need for recognition.

More formally, recognition is expressed by city, county, or school district officials, civic organizations, Parent-Teacher or Home and School Associations, the local education or teacher association, groups of alumni, or others.

The recognition accorded school personnel has included, among others, the following:[19]

Acknowledgment of recognition given by other agencies

Awards—financial, gifts, and token

Certificates of award

Dedication—of a school, auditorium or gymnasium, or other facility to the memory of an honored school employee

Dinners—for selected employees in terms of length of service, retirement, or some special service(s) rendered

Expression of appreciation—possibly on some public occasion

Job titles—prestige often goes with a title, thus recognition may be given through the awarding of a title that will add prestige to the deserving employee

Passing of resolutions of gratitude spread on the minutes of the board of education and publicized in the local press

Plaque with names of teachers with, for example, 15 or more years of service in the school district

Provision of time to do creative or constructive work

Receptions in honor of the employee or group of employees

Scroll with inscription

[19] Although common throughout the United States, these specific practices were found singly or in some combination in Washington, D.C., Illinois (Glencoe), Indiana (Griffith), Maryland (Montgomery, Prince Georges, and Wicomico Counties), Minnesota (Rochester); and at the Universities of Chicago and Michigan a $1000 award has been made to each of several outstanding professors.

There is no doubt that recognition given as it is merited will encourage extended efforts to improve performance and aids in creating the atmosphere necessary for motivation to become operative.

Status. Actually a facet of recognition, status is implicit in the nature of respective jobs within the school system. Thus a custodian, clerk, secretary, bookkeeper, teacher, department head, assistant to the principal, assistant- or vice-principal, supervisor, coordinator, director-, assistant-, associate-, and deputy-superintendent, and superintendent all have status according to the job designation. To improve one's status may mean either recognition for high level performance within one's occupation group or moving from one group to one with more desirable status. Status may be in terms of job or in terms of the authority of position. The importance of status is illustrated by the experience of one school district. Four assistant superintendents were given pay increases at the same time that their titles were changed to "director." Their duties remained as before. First, the affected personnel made no move to have the new title designation replace the old on their office doors. Second, they expressed dissatisfaction at their loss of the status title, "Assistant Superintendent." And, third, three of them left within a short period for jobs in other school systems.

The feeling that status is attainable or has been achieved serves both as an incentive toward productive effort and inducement to remain a part of the organization.

Leaves. A policy on the basis of which absence from work is permitted without jeopardizing either the security of the job or the income of the employee provides for a working situation which decreases stress on the individual and permits him to absent himself from work when it would be to his advantage and that of his employer, e.g., in case of illness.

The provision of this incentive to work has particular significance for the school system inasmuch as school employees work so closely with children that the stresses occasioned in the absence of a leave policy would too often be reflected in the teaching-learning situation. In the instance of illness, the harm to the instructional situation could be added to by the exposure of children to the illness of the school employee.

Leaves, then, provide a means through which school employees are placed in positions of decreased stress and given the incentive of a resulting gratification with achievements when on the job.

Physical Conditions. The school site, building, equipment, and supplies are part of the physical conditions which either facilitate or handicap instruction. Conditions that facilitate instruction are part of the atmosphere for awakening the motivating drives and are therefore included under the incentives to be supplied.

The design of the facilities so that rooms are planned in terms of the purpose to be served, sanitary conditions, heating, cooling, ventilation, humidity control, lighting, and acoustics are important factors in creating the atmosphere and conditions for teaching and learning.

Job satisfaction is sometimes mentioned as being the best motivator of all. A teacher who has to work with insufficient or inadequate equipment is deprived of the conditions conducive to job satisfaction. For example, the teacher who had to perform demonstration experiments for science with the use of a borrowed blow torch in the absence of a more suitable type burner, to teach biology with inferior microscopes, or to conduct social studies classes without the maps, charts, globes, and references which are an asset is likely to become frustrated because of the lack of the equipment which would serve as an added incentive to effective teaching.

Neither is it unknown in school circles that a shortage of such supplies as chalk, paper, and books or the provision of these in inferior quality has virtually caused teachers to give up or to accept the necessity of a less satisfactory standard of performance than might have been held if the supply situation were remedied.

Motivated as they are, teachers and other school employees will undoubtedly do their best under the circumstances confronting them. This best may actually give birth to a creativity that might otherwise not have emerged. However, doing one's best under such circumstances is virtually certain to be short lived. Working under handicaps of physical conditions of any kind must be accompanied by the assurance that those physical conditions will be made to facilitate instruction. Then this knowledge, together with the provision of desirable physical conditions will serve as an incentive to continued effective teaching and learning.

Conclusions. Teachers and the professional personnel of the school system have a sense of purpose which comes from and serves as a source of motivation and provides incentive. Similar sense of purpose and stimulus through the application of incentives may be promoted among the nonprofessional employees through orientation, a sound administrative program, functional supervision, and on-the-job learning.

Motivation itself has to be from within. One does not motivate another. It is possible, however, to apply incentives to spur others on to greater effort and to create psychological and physical conditions intended to awaken motivating drives.

Positive incentives, tending to fulfill individual desires are contrasted and preferable to the negative incentives based on fear of capricious and arbitrarily determined penalties.

Among the positive incentives, wage and other financial incentives are likely to be less important than nonfinancial and indirect financial incentives. This will probably be true provided salaries and wages are at a respectable level and represent compensation commensurate with work done.

The provision of incentive by way of a merit pay plan would require years of pre-planning, adequate staffing of a personnel division, and continued study, evaluation and revision of the bases for appraising a fair day's work, differentiating between effective and noneffective teachers, and evaluating the effects of the plan upon instruction. Further, development of a merit pay plan, to the extent that it is found feasible, requires a basis of good employer-employee relations, mutual confidence and respect, and joint development of the plan.

Whether operating in terms of financial or nonfinancial considerations, an incentive system must have as its setting a body of sound personnel policies, administration of these policies by a competent personnel staff, and support of the incentive and personnel program by an enlightened administration.

One of the major problems within organization is that of developing the cooperative relations necessary to effective school operation while at the same time stimulating and encouraging each individual to develop and capitalize upon his own genius. An incentive program is intended to produce a workable balance between needed cooperative groupism which does threaten to submerge the individual and the creative individualism which chafes at the need for and harness of joint operation or concerted action.

SUMMARY

A distinction is made between motivation and incentive. It is concluded that about all that can be done in regard to motivation is to set and regulate the climate intended to activate the drives of employees. Incentives are regarded as the externally applied spurs or goads which operate through some form of reward commensurate with effort and effectiveness.

Incentives geared to the desires of employees are thought of as positive. Those operating on fear are generally regarded as negative. Positive incentives provide desired rewards. Negative incentives threaten feared penalties. Whether positive or negative, incentives may also be categorized as directly or indirectly financial or as nonfinancial.

Direct financial incentives could be provided through a wage or salary incentive plan when conditions for doing so are favorable. This seems currently inadvisable for teachers. Incentives for both teaching and nonteaching employees on the basis of extra pay for extra work seems a reasonable and desirable financial incentive.

Indirect financial incentives are expressed through such mediums as tenure, leave, and retirement provisions. The nonfinancial incentives are expressed through a number of forms for recognizing the efforts and achievements of employees and for providing the conditions conducive to effective work.

SELECTED READINGS

ARNSPIGER, V. Clyde, *Personality in Social Process* (Chicago, Follett Publishing Company, 1961), Chapters 4, 6, 7.

BRITTON, Charles E., *Incentives in Industry* (New York, Esso Standard Oil Company, 1953), 91 pp.

DUBIN, Robert, *Human Relations in Administration* (Englewood Cliffs, N.J., Prentice-Hall, Inc., 1951), Chapters 3, 15.

GRIFFITHS, Daniel E., *Human Relations in School Administration* (New York, Appleton-Century-Crofts, 1956), Chapter 2.

JUCIUS, Michael J., *Personnel Management* (Chicago, Richard D. Irwin, Inc., 1948), Chapters 19, 23, 26, 27.

KEARNEY, Nolan C., *A Teacher's Professional Guide* (Englewood Cliffs, N.J., Prentice-Hall, Inc., 1958), Chapters 9, 13, 15.

MOORE, Harold E., and WALTERS, Newell B., *Personnel Administration in Education* (New York, Harper and Row, 1955), Chapters 11, 12, 14.

MOSHER, William E., and KINGSLEY, J. Donald, *Public Personnel Administration* (New York, Harper and Row, 1941), Chapters 20–26.

PFIFFNER, John M., *The Supervision of Personnel* (Englewood Cliffs, N.J., Prentice-Hall, Inc., 1951), Chapters 13, 14.

WOODWORTH, Robert S., *Dynamics of Behavior* (New York, Holt, Rinehart, and Winston, 1958).

YEAGER, William A., *Administration and the Teacher* (New York, Harper and Row, 1954), Chapters 16–18.

YEAGER, William A., *Administration of the Noninstructional Personnel and Services* (New York, Harper and Row, 1959), Chapters 5–7.

YODER, Dale, *Personnel Principles and Policies* (Englewood Cliffs, N.J., Prentice-Hall, Inc., 1959), Chapter 22.

ZIRBES, Laura, *Spurs to Creative Teaching* (New York, G. P. Putnam's Sons, 1959).

.10.

Morale

MORALE MEANS something to almost everyone. A low level of morale quickly invokes concern. Also, a high level of zealousness on the parts of employees, whether they work as individuals or as members of a group, calls forth commendation of their morale. Nevertheless the administrator who would like to promote good morale confronts a puzzling problem. Suddenly morale becomes something neither well defined nor understood. The reasons for its being good or bad seem, upon study and reflection, not wholly clear. Also, there just are no refined measures for determining the level of morale or the exact reasons for whatever level there may be.

A degree of perplexity caused by the morale problem is indicated by the numerous writings which deal with morale and factors pertaining to it. A survey of the literature reveals a struggle to identify what it is that causes one sort of morale situation rather than another.

Score cards, lists of morale factors, emphasis upon positive thinking, attitude inventories, assumptions, basic needs of individuals, personal and working conditions, diagrammed dimensions of morale, and freedoms represent the thought, surveys, or research done in the area of morale among employees. A review of these underlines the elusiveness, unidentifiability, and nebulousness of morale while at the same time it exhibits the significance attached to this will-o'-the-wisp. There is a sense of urgency to identify morale and a concern about discovering how to affect it positively.

To bring the issue of morale into perspective, the discussions and findings of 25 authors[1] are summarized below under eight headings:

[1] Franklin S. Barry and Richard C. Lonsdale, "School Administration Staff Practices: Influences upon Administrative Morale," *School Executive*, 76:76–78, October, 1956. James A. Bennett and Emery Stoops, "Seven Freedoms for Teachers," *School Executive*, 76:43–45, October, 1956. Thomas H. Briggs, "Morale," *The Educational*

Summary of Morale Factors

Heading	Factor
Organization	Decentralization of responsibility and authority Provision for participation
Administration	Leadership by administrators The according of recognition
Environment	Physical and psychological
Worker Correlates	Pay Job satisfaction Identification with the group
Operation	Security—social, economic, and physical Communications—adequate and functioning Personal relationships in and out of organization Positiveness of attitudes—derived from beliefs, values, and experiences
Objectives	Realization of personal and institutional objectives Clarity of policies as guides to reaching objectives Social organization for attainment of objectives
Work Load	Formal and informal Orientation of new employees and load implications Accessibility of administrators and supervisors as psychological load lighteners Mental health Fairness and the feeling of equitability
Other	Management of men—giving orders, disciplining Physical fitness Ability to listen General goodwill

Headings or groupings are presented in the order of citation by most writers. The sequence within each grouping is without intended design or significance.

In addition to the foregoing, four projects[2] to survey morale to a large extent substantiate the eight-point summary. In general the four projects pretty much agreed on the basic importance of five items and the sup-

Forum, 22:147–51, January, 1958. B. J. Chandler, "Merit Rating Not Detrimental to Teacher Morale," *The Nation's Schools*, 61:58–9, April, 1958. Rex V. Call, "Faculty and Morale," *Journal of Higher Education*, 29:267–71, May, 1958. Loren A. Critser and Ralph V. Backman, "How May the Principal and the Faculty Promote Wholesome School Morale?" *Bulletin of the N.A.S.S.P.*, 40:234–38, April, 1956. J. W. Getzels and E. G. Guba, "Social Behavior and the Administrative Process," *The School Review*, 65:423–41, Winter, 1957. Harvey Handel, "Keeping Morale Where It Should Be," *The School Executive*, 76:86–7, June, 1957. C. Gordon Higgins, "Is Your Morale Showing?" *Virginia Journal of Education*, 49:11–13, January, 1956. J. T. Hunt, "School Personnel and Mental Health," *Review of Educational Research*, 26:502–21, December, 1956. E. C. Hunter, *What New Orleans Teachers Think of the Public-Schools* (New Orleans, Tulane University, 1957), 96 pp. Oliver F. Johnson, "Pat on the Back

porting importance of an additional twelve items. These items are tabulated below.

Elements that Affect Morale

Basic to Morale:

  Administrative cooperation, assistance, and support

  A just and adequate salary plan

  Job assignment in terms of competency and interest

  Evidence of administrative confidence in teachers

  Friendly, cooperative, and professional attitudes on the part of fellow-workers

Supporting to Morale:

  Pleasing physical working conditions, adequate equipment and supplies

  A worthy retirement plan

  Recognition of merit by administrators

  Position security through tenure provisions

  Freedom from out of school tensions

  An adequate sick leave policy

  Existence of a practical written educational philosophy for the school system

  Community acceptance of financial and moral responsibility to maintain an adequate educational program

  Freedom to approach administrators and supervisors for help and counsel without prejudice or danger of penalty

  Equality of status within the staff

  Cooperative and appreciative parental attitude

  Courteous and respectful pupil attitude

Helps Teachers Too," *The American Teacher Magazine*, 41:21, October, 1956. Harley Lautenschlager, "The Role of the Principal as a Morale Builder," *Peabody Journal of Education*, 34:258–62, March, 1957. Joseph P. Lyford, "Social Science Teachers and the Difficult Years," *Bulletin* of the A.A.U.P., 43:636–45, December, 1957. Alexander A. J. MacKimmil and Kent W. Leach, "In What Ways May the Principal and the Faculty Promote Wholesome School Morale?" *Bulletin* of the N.A.S.S.P., 44:39–43, April, 1957. Lowell Ogden and Emery Stoops, "Staff Morale: What Is It? How Do We Get It?" *Educational Administration and Supervision*, 43:487–91, December, 1957. Don H. Otto, "Supervisory Counselling and Teacher Morale," *The Teachers College Journal*, 29:42–3, December, 1957. Frederick L. Redefer, "Teacher Morale and Quality of Education," *The Nation's Schools*, 59:53–5 and "Toward a Theory of Educational Administration," *School and Society*, 87:135–7, March, 1959. Lester J. Roth, "Occupational Analysis and Teacher Morale," *The Journal of Educational Sociology*, 32:145–51, December, 1958. Martin Silverman, "Principals—What Are You Doing to Teacher Morale?" *Educational Administration and Supervision*, 43:204–10, April, 1957.

2 Peter D. Shilland, "A Teacher Morale Survey," *The Educational Forum*, 13:479–86, May, 1949. L. E. Leipold and Joseph W. Yarbrough, "What 1600 School People Think about Teacher Morale," *American School Board Journal*, 119:29–30, December, 1949. Lyle M. Spencer, Frederick Gehlmann, and Edith F. Maris, *What Los Angeles Educators Think of Their School System* (Los Angeles, The Board of Education, 1953). Betty M. Petraitis, A Local Opinion Poll on Teacher Morale (Unpublished study, University of Maryland, College Park, Maryland, 1954).

These seventeen elements affecting morale move through a spectrum from the immediate working situation, through an area of fringe benefits, and to the general area of pupil and adult attitudes toward school personnel.

The summary of morale factors, as well as the list of elements affecting morale, suggest a definition, at least for working purposes.

DEFINITION

Morale is the term used in personnel administration to sum up conveniently the mental and emotional state of the employee. The dominant facets of this mental-emotional state are employee self-confidence, personal and group discipline, and contentment.

The development and maintenance of employee self-confidence, discipline, and contentment is so much a part of the whole cloth of personnel administration that virtually every principle of personnel administration has morale implications.

PRINCIPLES

Among the principles of personnel administration[3] there are five that are particularly pertinent to morale.

1. Education is the primary purpose of the schools. The good will and cooperation of all school employees must be secured if the optimum education is to take place. Such good will and cooperation are the byproducts of employment in which working is both a gratifying social experience and a means for making a livelihood.

2. Maximum effectiveness of the means for achieving the people's mandates regarding education requires the best possible selection and coordination of all elements comprising those means. The means are comprised of school employees, plant, and supplies. It is the job of personnel administration to assure the optimum in the selection, assignment in terms of job, physical placement, and equipment of personnel.

3. The most important single factor in getting the best that a school employee has to offer is how he feels about his work, his associates on the job, and the school system in which he is employed. . . . this emotional factor . . . has implications for assuring appreciation of, recognition for, and a share in planning by each employee. Everyone has the need to regard his work as worthwhile and to take pride in it if he is to work at his best.

4. Esteem for the intelligence and potential of the employee group is a basic necessity and may be demonstrated by the employer group through acts of confidence. Among such acts are the provision for a continuous flow of significant information, open lines of communication, and the joint employer-employee deliberation by which a sound working basis of understanding and mutual confidence is established.

[3] Chapter 1, particularly principles 1, 4, 8, 9, and 11.

5. All participants in an enterprise are entitled to fair dealing. Unfairness or the appearance of injustice is cause of rankling resentment which is a threat to worker effectiveness. Fairness has implications for monetary rewards, work load, the working period, various conditions that are concomitant or auxiliary to the job, and virtually every other element making up the total working situation.

The awareness of these principles and a conscientious effort to put them to work are conditions which must be met in order to set the stage for the high morale that is every employer's desire.

SETTING THE STAGE FOR HIGH MORALE

Morale cannot be created, ordered, delivered, or guaranteed. The most that can be done is to do all that is possible to create the conditions which favor high morale and to correct the conditions which threaten high morale. The cue to these conditions is implicit in the factors, elements, and principles already listed. These will be explored under the eight headings of the *Summary of Morale Factors*.

Organization

Increasingly there is a trend toward fewer but larger school districts. Often bigness is accompanied by a tendency toward centralization. To some extent the school system is protected from the extremes of centralization. Its locales for operation provide for a decentralization which also makes possible a considerable degree of individual employee participation within the over-all organization of the school system.

Decentralization. Largeness of organization causes a depersonalized distance between the chief executive and the large body of operating personnel, the employees doing the on-the-spot job of the schools. The organization of a personnel division is partial recognition of the need to compensate for impersonal bigness and the problems it brings.

The fact that schools are located in the various population centers of the school district favors decentralization to overcome the disadvantages of school system size. The principal of each school serves in the place of the superintendent in his relationships with the personnel of the school. An important part of his job is to recognize his responsibility and exercise his authority to give personal and individual attention, consideration, and assistance to the various employees in that school— the teachers, clerks, custodians, foodhandlers, etc.

Decentralization may well be a key to securing the good-will and cooperation which contribute to making one's job a gratifying social experience as well as a means for earning one's living.

Participation. It is axiomatic that the individual should have the opportunity to participate in the development of those policies by which he will be governed. When an employee accepts a job, he accepts also its restrictions as imposed by existing policy. However, policy is not functionally static; rather it is dynamic and always subject to change. Hence there is a promising opportunity to have the employee express his identification with the school through participation in making policy changes.

The employee is part of the team to execute or carry into effect policy and must be so recognized. Provision for participation elicits cooperation or a share in planning that is productive of good will, engenders a feeling of having a stake in the functioning of the school system and a sense of the importance of his particular job in the total scheme of education, and establishes a basis for the understanding and confidence produced by the joint action of administrative and field personnel.

Administration

Personnel administration is a staff activity within the administrative organization headed by the superintendent of schools. The provision of an office for personnel administration is tacit admission that the conditions for improved production are a responsibility of and can be affected by the administrator and what he does.[4] Among these conditions is the level of morale. Looming large in the role that the administrator can play relative to morale is what he does to provide leadership and the extent to which he accords recognition.

Leadership. Within a decentralized pattern of operation, the administrator has a position of leadership which he cannot legitimately abdicate. The leadership activity may be exercised autocratically or democratically, according to the resultant of all the forces to which the administrator is subject—forces within and outside himself.

Autocratic leadership requires no elaboration since it provides for the making and execution of policies in accord with administrative dictates. The area of voluntary operation on the part of nonadministrative teaching and nonteaching employees is minimal. It may generally be expected that morale will be low under an oppressively autocratic administration. If the autocratic administration is benevolent and paternalistic, the level

---

[4] Walter A. Anderson, Dean, School of Education, New York University, "The Effects of Administrative Behavior on Teacher Morale," (An address given before the American Association of School Administrators at Philadelphia, Pennsylvania, March 27, 1961). Howard S. Bretsch, "Achieving High Morale in a School System," *The University of Michigan School of Education Bulletin*, 29:35–37, December, 1957. Frederick L. Redefer, "Toward a Theory of Educational Administration," *School and Society*, 87:135–137, March 28, 1959. Jack A. Culbertson, Paul B. Jacobson, and Theodore L. Reller, *Administrative Relationships* (Englewood Cliffs, N.J., Prentice-Hall, Inc., 1960), pp. 418–26.

of morale could be fairly high and reflective of a considerable amount of personal loyalty.

A lip service to democratic leadership seems sometimes to connote an abdication of the position of leadership. However, the chief executive agent of the board of education in a democratically conceived school system may not and cannot divest himself of any of his responsibility for the operation of the school system. He has to make decisions and he cannot evade the consequences of decisions made.

There is an area of school policy making which allows the superintendent very little latitude. This is the area in which policy is formulated, adopted, and prescribed by the board of education or the state legislature.

Once a board of education approves a policy and demands its execution, the superintendent surely has no immediate recourse except to take the necessary steps to make the policy effective. Even under such circumstances employee morale can be given a lift by the administrator's explanation of the situation. However, whereas some policies originate with the board of education and are formulated within that body, there are also policies in the making of which the employees of the school system may legitimately be involved.

As the professional leader to the board of education, the superintendent who is democratically inclined has the obligation to make a strong case for and to urge the board of education to provide for the involvement of employees within the school system in policy initiation and formation. The bona fide involvement of employees in policy making, whenever that is practicable, on a voluntary basis is one hallmark of morale-boosting democratic administration.

Whereas approval of policy is the realm of the board of education, the determination of the means for carrying out policy is the realm of the professional. Here again is an opportunity for the administrator to demonstrate the degree to which he has committed himself to democratic administration. This he may do by placing the problem of developing means before those who will have to do the actual field job of putting the policy into operation.

When a policy affects a specific group of employees, the involvement on a voluntary basis of those employees in the development of the means for making the policy effective makes good sense and serves as an indicator of interest in administering democratically.

A third, and probably singly the most significant hallmark of democracy in administration has already been discussed (Chapter 1). This is a working system of communications in which there is free interaction vertically and laterally, with no fear of penalty or prejudice. Such a system of communication serves to inform all and welcome from each the honest appraisals which are the sound basis for progress and improvement. Morale inevitably suffers when channels of communication are blocked or become inoperative.

Some cautions seem in order. In practice there often seems to be an attempt to involve everyone within the organization irrespective of the pertinence of the involvement. Coerciveness frequently rears an ugly head, manifesting itself in fact or in a pervading atmosphere. And, involvement becomes, on occasion, a means by which an administrator gets nonadministrative employees to do his administrative tasks. These are a few of the pitfalls confronting an administrator who is democratically inclined but who confuses form with function.

The intelligent employee sees through form with comparative ease. If form and function are not consistent with each other, a loss rather than a gain of employee goodwill is in prospect. Goodwill may be expected to develop as confidence is generated through the understanding which results from effective communication and from the joint efforts of administrative and field employees in the school system.

Recognition. Morale is a necessary condition for motivation to operate at its best and for incentives to become effective. Not only an expression of democratic leadership, but also one of the most important factors in the provision of the conditions for motivation and a real incentive itself is the awarding of recognition.

The worker who has performed well and conscientiously gets a lift from recognition in whatever sincere form it is conferred. It may be that all that is called for is a nod, a smile, or a word of appreciation. Or, the recognition may in instances require formal action in the way of an award or assignment to a position of increased responsibility.

Whatever its form, it is necessary that the bestowal of recognition does not become a meaningless formality without reference to a worthy act. The employee will be appreciative of sincere recognition. He will scorn recognition awarded when he knows that he did not deserve it. There is danger of formalizing the action of providing recognition and making of it a hollow gesture without significance.

The real reason for providing recognition is that it contributes to the self-esteem of the individual as he gets deserved personal attention in a big operation in which individuals are easily lost. It re-emphasizes the importance of the job. And, it gets credit to the school and the individual worker who is on the educational firing line where the real job of influencing child behavior takes place. Earned recognition will do much for how an employee feels about his job, his associates, and the school system.

Environment

Surroundings, the place to work, the equipment and supplies necessary to do one's work, and one's associates on the educational scene constitute the environment. On a minimum basis this means largely that the bare necessities are provided. This is the physical environment.

Beyond the provision of the bare necessities for performing the tasks to be done are the considerations that are conducive to making the working situation effectively pleasing. This is to considerable degree a psychological-environmental consideration.

An environment which is pleasing—in terms of providing adequate area, lighting, air-conditioning, humidity control, and ventilation; suitable furnishings and equipment; and agreeably appropriate coloring— constitutes to a large extent the physical and psychological conditions for making the teaching-learning situation effective.

The facilitation of instruction and of learning is the prime reason for creating the particular environment of the school. Efforts to make the environment effective by making it pleasing signify the value the administrator attaches to the task of education and the concern he has for the employee and the pupil.

Although there is no direct evidence that the physical environment does affect morale,[5] there is no gainsaying that the provision of a suitable environment is in fact an expression of value placed upon the work and consideration for the worker. When part of other and more basic provisions for good morale, the provision of a pleasing environment conducive to effective learning serves as a morale booster and an expression of administration's function to minister to the physical and psychological needs of school employees.

Worker Correlates

Under this heading will be considered pay, job satisfaction, and identification with the group as factors having morale implications.

Pay. Monetary reward is frequently several items down the list of factors of primary significance to the worker. This may reflect some feeling that the material should be subordinated and that the job should be transcendent. In spite of the tendency to place other factors before pay, in both the summary of morale factors and the list of elements, pay did obtrude itself as a major consideration for high morale.

There really is no question about the importance of pay. Up to the point of subsistence, pay may be even more important to the individual than the job itself; and, if pay is insufficient to provide a living, all but the independently wealthy worker may be expected to give up the work of his choice for something more remunerative.

Beyond the subsistence level pay becomes relatively and progres-

[5] Elton Mayo, *The Human Problems of an Industrial Civilization* (Boston, Harvard University, Graduate School of Business Administration, 1946), pp. 1–54.

sively less important. However, the fact that social status in the United States is largely accorded on an economic basis tends to adduce to pay a significance that may not be ignored. Thus, when pay is at a low level there is the likelihood that the work and the worker will be held in correspondingly low regard.

Lack of individual status and social prestige because of the economic standing of school employees could easily have demoralizing side effects upon the entire education enterprise.

Aside from pay level, it is recurrently observable that the manner of providing for pay increases can become so great an issue that morale suffers. This has been experienced during the pre-salary-schedule days when pay increases were awarded on an individual and often personal basis. It is experienced again wherever merit pay plans are foisted upon teachers in the absence of satisfactory means for measuring merit.[6] The problem undoubtedly relates to fairness or justice. High morale may be reasonably expected only when employees are free from fear and convinced that they are working in an atmosphere of justice.

All employees are entitled to fair dealing. Unfairness or the appearance of injustice produces rankling resentment which threatens worker effectiveness and high morale.

Job Satisfaction. Unless the employee can realize his own objectives for himself there is little reason for him to work on a high morale level. His own objectives for himself may probably be summed up in terms of (1) the satisfaction he gets from doing work he enjoys and considers worthwhile, (2) feeling or knowing that what he does is appreciated by others within and outside the school system, and (3) the pay he gets which will permit him to finance his own material, spiritual, and aesthetic needs.

The personnel activity provides for getting, placing, supervising, adjusting, recognizing, and rewarding personnel. Performed on a functional basis, these facets of the activity assure the gearing of competencies to jobs. Thus may one condition for job satisfaction and correlative high morale be met. Actually, as already discussed, pay is a part of the job satisfaction package inasmuch as the worker's self-realization is involved and pay is an expression of the school system and the public's appreciation of the importance of his job and of his efforts as a school employee.

Identification with the Group. Morale is surely a phenomenon that may be displayed by the individual. However, it is more often discussed as a phenomenon of group spirit. To the extent that morale is associated with groupism, it seems clear that it is heightened by group solidarity.

6 "Why Few School Systems Use Merit Ratings," *NEA Research Bulletin* 39:61–63, May, 1961.

The impact of group solidarity upon morale imparts to professionalism much of its value (Chapter 2), that of generating group spirit, gaining prestige for the group, developing standards, seeking means to transmit theory and advance practice, and rendering unselfish service beyond the call of duty and at some personal sacrifice.

It has been suggested[7] that a general indication of lack of group solidarity and of consequent low morale is displayed by the readiness with which school personnel not only fail to close ranks against those who are not of the profession but even join them in their diatribes against education, the schools, and teaching.

One important step in promoting group solidarity is the development and identification of clearcut goals toward which all employees can direct their efforts. It has been indicated that cooperation and participation in developing goals give the employee or the member of the professional group a sort of stake in the education venture.

Especially in the professional aspects of school operation it is important that individual and group efforts be recognized as having developed out of knowledge and experience over a long period of time and as being consequently representative of the best-known practices.

It is not surprising to find morale shattered when administrative leadership takes the direction of discounting current practices as they have evolved out of the past in favor of almost anything that may be branded as new and has some kind of gimmick or glamor appeal.[8] What morale level can be logically and legitimately expected of teachers who have not been involved in policy determination, lack understanding of a projected change, and are nevertheless required by administrative edict to work under greatly different conditions in which they have no confidence and for which they are not prepared?

Group solidarity, an oft-mentioned ingredient of high morale, may be generated to a degree by the expressed and demonstrated confidence of school administrators in the general competency and effectiveness of teachers who were trained in the best known practices and who have modified their own practice through experience and their varied activities

---

[7] Daniel E. Griffiths, *Human Relations in School Administration* (New York, Appleton-Century-Crofts, 1956), p. 147.

[8] This phenomenon found expression in the urgency to have schools and teachers look Progressive during the 1930's irrespective of their genuine commitment to the progressive school of thought. The same occurred in the 1950's as a tidal wave pressure for Core programs demanded conformity from those neither sympathetic to nor competent to teach in terms of Core. Indiscriminate use of TV teaching provides another example of promotion rather than readiness. Pressure has built up to get administrators to commit themselves to team teaching and to have teachers converted overnight and by edict in their theory, competency, and practice. Similarly the pressure is on to regard subject programming and the use of teaching machines as a nostrum for the needs of education, a nostrum to be adopted before its side-effects or its proper use have been determined experimentally.

in keeping abreast of further developments in the understanding of how to influence human behavior.

Change is unavoidable and as desirable as the progress that makes it necessary. If provided for on a continuous and progressive basis, change can take place under conditions of unruffled evolution and growth rather than by shock conditions of revolutionary abandonment of one practice in favor of another. Revolutionary change makes those who are not ready for it feel threatened, produces uncertainty, and has a negative impact upon morale. Evolutionary change may be accompanied by a maintained and even raised morale.

Administrators with a band-wagon complex for the new, at least by implication, declare to the teachers that they have little confidence in them or what they do. When teachers lack confidence in, or the confidence of, school administrators, group solidarity may resolve itself into teachers united against administrators—hardly the condition for high morale or for the professionalism which regards all school personnel as contributing to a unit activity and all administrators as first of all teachers.

If morale is to be high, it is imperative that the employee feels appreciated, is recognized, shares in the planning by which he will be affected, and is made to feel that others within the school system, parents and adults in the community, and pupils in the schools place appropriate value on his job as contributing to the functioning of the important social institution, the school.

Operation

In the operation of the school system further evidence of the value placed on the work of the schools and of regard for the worker take the form of measures to assure security, communications, agreement, harmonious personal relationships, and positiveness of attitudes.

Security. It is generally assumed that the confidence, self-discipline, and contentment indicative of and conducive to high morale are furthered through measures that make the employee feel secure.

Personnel administration that is concerned with the morale implications of feelings of security may well ask what a projetced action will mean for the employee as: 1) a member of the group(s) with which he identifies himself within and outside the school, 2) an individual with economic needs and obligations, and 3) one who can feel or be physically threatened.

An action which does, or appears to, improve the status of an employee—e.g., a change of position, pay classification, or title—strengthens his social position within the school system and possibly within the community in which he lives. The morale implications of this, or the converse situation, are self-evident.

Personnel actions which relieve the stress of employee concern about personal affairs, particularly his economic needs and obligations, leave the employee free to concentrate on doing what is necessary to give a good account of himself on the job. Indicative of provisions to bolster economic security are insurance, leaves (sick and other), loans or pay advances, medical care, retirement plans or pensions, salary schedules, tenure, and unemployment benefits.

Within the school system there is ordinarily little threat of physical harm. Nevertheless security against physical harm cannot be wholly or summarily dismissed. It is incumbent upon the school administration to make certain that it does not itself threaten either the physical or the psychological well-being of its personnel either directly or indirectly. It may begin by removing as many as possible of the hazards to safety from the school scene and continue by making certain that it will no more use a psychological bludgeon than it would a physical one.

It is also the responsibility of the administration to make certain that there is no threat to an employee or group of employees by another employee or group of school employees. This may be done through the medium of a functioning system of communications and through a system of disciplinary action to which the administration and the employees have jointly committed themselves.

Finally the administration is responsible for taking such measures as are locally necessary to meet such threat as some pupils present to teachers. This means gaining for education and the institutions and agents through which it is fostered the regard of adult and juvenile citizens and insisting upon actions to corroborate the regard. A first step might be administrative treatment of school employees with regard.

Communications. It is a prime thesis of democracy that it can only operate with a promise of success if the members of the group have the knowledge that is necessary for intelligent action. This is a matter of communications and has been dealt with at some length in a preceding section of this chapter, under administrative leadership.

Personal Relationships. The personal relationships within the school organization revolve about the function of the schools and of all school personnel to facilitate and further learning. This makes all personnel colleagues in the facilitation process.

The colleague relationship is sometimes called the unit concept of school operation. It is important that this concept be held in mind by all personnel. It is particularly essential that administrators take pains to use every opportunity possible to emphasize the fact that they are first and above all teachers. Failure to do this threatens the unit concept with the same internal conflict that has characterized management and labor too long.

Despite the unit concept there will probably always be personality conflicts growing out of individual differences. The administration may do much to prevent or overcome these by efforts to staff the respective schools or their departments with those who can work together harmoniously.

Positiveness of Attitudes. In an analysis of teacher attitudes, Lovelace[9] came to the conclusion that, "The more effective teachers tend to have a more positive attitude than do the less effective. . . ." It seems reasonable to assume that attitudes conducive to high morale would have to be positive.

The principal and supervisor may affect attitude by addressing themselves to the question of what they can do to make themselves welcome instead of regarded as intruders, acknowledgedly conversant with teacher problems, and advocates of a balance between the points of view that teaching success is predicated upon 1) good teacher-pupil relationships and 2) mastery of subject and the means for influencing change in pupil behavior.

Objectives

The job satisfaction that is expressed in high morale is in part the product of an overlapping of interests between the employing agency and the employee. The employing agency, the school, has a job to be done and is interested in employing personnel to bring about realization of its objectives, the education of youth. The employee, similarly, has an interest in using his knowledge, skill, and inclinations to bring about a realization of his own objectives. Ideally the same working situation serves to bring about simultaneously the realization of the objectives of the school and of the school employee.

The effectiveness with which organizational and employee objectives are reached at the same time may be improved by joint efforts to identify needs, set immediate and ultimate goals, and define what may be expected from each of the parties to the enterprise.

Policies. The chart of the course to be followed, policies can do much to establish guidelines by which both employer and employee determine and appraise their conduct. A clearly defined course of action, or framework

9 Neil R. Lovelace, An Analysis of Certain Attitudes of Selected Elementary and Junior High School Teachers (Unpublished doctoral dissertation, College Park, University of Maryland, 1951), p. 3 of the abstract.

within which to act, is helpful in setting the climate for high morale. (See also the preceding section in this chapter, under Participation.)

Organization. The organization of the school system for the attainment of the educational objectives of the school district lends itself to operating without the usual disadvantages of great size even though the school district may be large in terms of area, population, or both. (See also the preceding section in this chapter, under Decentralization.)

Within the individual school there is great opportunity to capitalize upon the opportunity to become acquainted. As the working relationships of all employees within the school gain the basis of mutual understanding, appreciation, and confidence, they lend themselves to the ease and naturalness in human relations that is identified with a high morale situation.

Work Load

There is probably little so frustrating as the feeling of having so much to do that one does not know where to begin, has little chance of gaining perspective, and probably cannot accomplish very much in spite of genuine effort. This will be true whether the load is a formal one of many and large classes or an informal one which so fills nonclass hours as to leave no time for reflective thought. The situation described is one that can be expected to be conducive only to low morale.

New Employees. Teachers new to teaching or merely new to the school system work at some disadvantage as compared to those oriented to the school system. In order to promote conditions for high morale, it is advisable to provide them with the best possible working conditions, as light a teaching and other load as is feasible, and assignments within their competencies. It is desirable at the same time to let them know what the normal working conditions are, the loads carried by other teachers and that will be expected of them, and the intent always to assign in terms of competency with the reservation that special situations do at times have to be met by emergency measures which will be kept temporary and to a minimum.

Load Lighteners. Aside from care in making assignments, there is a limit to what one can do about actually decreasing load, even with a judicious use of innovations continuously emerging. However, load may be lightened psychologically. The accessibility of administrators, supervisors, and other teachers and the demonstration of their willingness to listen and to help by providing perspective and counsel can serve to ease the yoke of the burden and to instil the confidence which accompanies high morale.

Mental Health. Morale is often identified with mental attitude. A listing of attitudes or characteristics that are identified with mental health may on the one hand alert the administrator to the existence of mental health problems and on the other suggest of themselves measures to be taken to improve the situation.

Characteristics of Mental Health

Good	*Poor*
Ability to face reality	Aggressiveness (over)
Assurance	Conflict
Cheerfulness	Dogmatism
Confidence	Escapism or social withdrawal
Contentment	Hostility
Feeling of accomplishment	Jealousy
Firmness	Inadequacy or inferiority
Happiness	Insincerity or superficiality
Humor	Irritability
Joy	Melancholia
Love or friendliness	Moroseness
Security	Persecution complex
Sense of well-being	Tension
Tolerance	Worry

Perhaps the key to the characteristics of good mental health is the happiness or *joie de vivre* which might be termed the barometer of mental health. To considerable extent the key to poor mental health is probably tension. Without a doubt, the expectation of high morale would rest with personnel exhibiting predominantly the characteristics of good mental health.

Personnel administration measures for providing for recognition and security are steps in the direction of creating conditions for good mental health. Measures like these, supplemented by enlightened acceptance and treatment of disturbances and by friendly and sympathetic association, can do much to alleviate poor mental health, maintain good mental health, and set the stage for high morale.

Fairness. Morale is threatened when employees are or feel they are dealt with unfairly. Conversely, even seemingly harsh measures are taken in stride without a lowering of morale—perhaps even with a stiffening of morale—when the conclusion of the employee is that the action taken was fair.

Opportunities for justice or injustice to operate run through the entire warp and woof of school organization and operation, from selection to retirement and come to mind with particular force when morale is under consideration.

Other Factors

At the remote end of the spectrum of morale factors mentioned by the authors cited are a number of items which have to some extent been dealt with under other headings.

Management of Men. On few occasions is it necessary to give orders. The same results may be obtained with better feelings all around by requesting the performance of a task or by making a suggestion. The performance of tasks requires the organization through which the work may be done in orderly and effective fashion. This calls for a sort of social organization of the schools in which there is a group discipline to which employees subscribe just as the members of a society subscribe to social control.

Under conditions of high morale, it is likely that the social control within the school organization is so acceptable that self- and group-discipline make the exercise of other discipline a rarity. When the organizational discipline is onerous and not subscribed to by the employees, it is likely that discipline problems will loom large and that administrative disciplinary actions will be frequent. An alertly intelligent administration will make certain that rules will be kept to a minimum, be reasonable in the eyes of both the administration and the employees, will be adhered to with firmness and fairness, and will be consistent with high morale expectations.

Physical Fitness. To the extent that performance on the job, attitude, and even mental health may be affected by the state of one's physical condition, morale may also be influenced by physical fitness. In the school situation, the physical well-being of the pupils is an added concern of the schools and may not be endangered by irresponsible disregard of employee physical condition.

Personnel administration in the schools has the obligation for morale and other reasons to make certain of the physical fitness of its personnel as a condition for employment initially and thereafter as a service to check on and help to maintain employee fitness.

Ability to Listen. It is sometimes said that one of the best counselling services that can be rendered is to give the counsellee a chance to say what he wants to say to someone who listens well. In school personnel administration, there may be great therapeutic value in providing the employee the opportunity to relieve himself of what is troubling him by talking to someone who exercises a well developed ability to listen.

It has been said in tribute to such listeners that they "always seem to have time to listen." The troubled person has been known to go away feeling better, not always because of any direct help he has received but often because, "after having had my say, things seemed better." Thus is the way paved for improved morale.

General Goodwill. Much of morale may be summed up in the attitude of the worker toward his job, the administrator, and his fellow workers. A great deal of this summation is concerned with what is currently referred to as human relations. And, the human relations that may be expected to pervade a situation of high morale will most likely be epitomized by a pervading goodwill among all employees within the school, school system, or other organization.

THE MEASUREMENT OF MORALE

As a mental-emotional attitude or state of being, morale does not at this time lend itself to precise or direct measurement. The measurement of morale is actually a noting and evaluation of a number of indices which are expressed through:

1. The quantitative and qualitative level of employee performance—to the degree that performance can be measured.
2. The spirit in which tasks are performed.
3. The topics of free conversation.
4. The gripe level.
5. The use, or abuse, of leave privileges.
6. The amount of illness, particularly when ascribable to psychosomatic causes.
7. Turnover—leaving a school or the school district's employ.

The indices enumerated provide bases for gauging the morale level of the employee group as one or more of the following means is used to build a fund of information for appraisal purposes:

1. Records of performance, including unit cost data. This would apply chiefly to the noninstructional tasks of the school at this writing.
2. Interviews to take place during, upon termination of, and after cessation of employment.
3. Some system for getting employee suggestions.
4. Observation.

The use of the indices and means mentioned should provide some image of the morale situation, giving some idea of its nature, shape, and dimensions, together with an idea of what are the disturbing elements in and the possible solutions to the problems of morale.

SUMMARY

Regarded as paramount in importance, recognized when high and a matter for concern when low, morale does not lend itself to precise definition or measurement. A working definition incorporates concepts of mental attitude and emotional state, revealing themselves in zealousness, confidence, discipline, and contented satisfaction.

All the principles of school personnel administration have some implication for morale. However, the implementation of these principles does not assure high morale nor does it guarantee the retention of morale. Nevertheless, there are administrative practices which have such morale implications that they must be observed because they, in effect, set the stage for high morale.

Morale has the doubtful distinction that it can easily and quickly be dashed from a pinnacle and virtually shattered, even when the sum of conditions is favorable to high morale, by a seemingly insignificant action or condition.

The importance of morale is such that an effective personnel administration will be constantly on the alert to discover threats to high morale and to provide preventive or corrective measures as necessary to promote conditions for high morale.

SELECTED READINGS

ARNSPIGER, V. Clyde, *Personality in Social Process* (Chicago, Follett Publishing Company, 1961), Chapters 8, 9.

BERNARD, Harold W., *Mental Hygiene for Classroom Teachers* (New York, McGraw-Hill Book Company, Inc., 1961), Chapters 5, 18, 19–21.

CHAMBERLAIN, Leo M., and KINDRED, Leslie W., *The Teacher and School Organization* (Englewood Cliffs, N.J., Prentice-Hall, Inc., 1958), Chapter 19.

CULBERTSON, Jack, JACOBSON, Paul, and RELLER, Theodore, *Administrative Relationships* (Englewood Cliffs, N.J., Prentice-Hall, Inc., 1960), Chapters 5, 6, 8.

DIMOCK, Marshall E. and Gladys O., and KOENIG, Louis W., *Public Administration* (New York, Holt, Rinehart, and Winston, 1958), Chapters 21, 22, 26.

GLOVER, John G., *Fundamentals of Professional Management* (New York, Simmons Boardman Publishing Corp., 1958), Chapters 12, 13, 14.

JUCIUS, Michael J., and SCHLENDER, William E., *Elements of Managerial Action,* (Homewood, Illinois, Richard D. Irwin, Inc., 1960), Chapters 14, 15, 18.

MOORE, Harold E., and WALTERS, Newell B., *Personnel Administration in Education* (New York, Harper and Row, 1955), Chapter 3.

NIGRO, Felix A., *Public Personnel Administration* (New York, Holt, Rinehart, and Winston, 1959), Chapter 12.

SPRIEGEL, William R., *Principles of Business Organization and Operation* (Englewood Cliffs, N.J., Prentice-Hall, Inc., 1960), Chapter 26.

STAHL, O. Glenn, *Public Personnel Administration* (New York, Harper and Row, 1956), Chapter 11.

.11.

The School Employee
and His Job

THE TASK of the schools has been discussed (Chapter 3). Also, the school employee has been examined with respect to training, selection, orientation, motivation, and morale. However, both the job of the schools and the role of school personnel in getting that job done may well require further consideration of school employees, professional and nonprofessional, as they are observed with respect to their performance on the job and to the way in which they relate to their jobs. This will be done in terms of the types of employment, principles pertaining, job attitudes, some status factors, and professionalism.

TYPES OF EMPLOYMENT

School employees may be classified under one or another of two major categories; one of these is teaching and the other is services that support teaching.

In some instances the classification of school employees is simple, e.g., clerical and custodial help are clearly personnel who provide a service to teaching whereas teachers who are engaged in the instruction of children clearly belong in the teaching classification. Somewhat more ambiguous is the position of teachers who have been removed from the actual teaching situation to one of administration, coordination, supervision, or counselling. Classification of these members of the teaching profession is of necessity somewhat arbitrary and can no doubt be defended or rationalized by the classifier regardless of the category in which they are placed.

The Teacher and Teaching

A little space will be devoted to bringing into perspective the teacher and selected aspects of the teacher's job.

The Teacher. At one time it seemed as if teaching was a means by which the individual improved his position in society. The child of the blue-collar worker achieved the status of the white-collar group via teaching. A half century ago this seemed to be the pattern. Today approximately 40 per cent of the teachers are from the white-collar segment of society, a considerable number from families of teachers.[1]

Also, at one time marriage voided the contract of the woman teacher and barred her from employment as a teacher. Today over two-thirds of all teachers, men and women, are married.[2]

It is common to find men in over one-half the secondary school teaching positions. The elementary school is still generally and predominantly staffed by women teachers although efforts are made in numerous instances to get more men into the elementary schools.

The Teacher's Workday. With slight variations the working day at school for the elementary school teacher is 7½ hours; for the secondary school teacher, 8 hours. This school day is about one hour longer than that of the pupils. In addition, the median number of hours devoted to school duties outside the regular school day comes to 2 hours per day for the 5-day school week, making a total of 48 to 50 hours as a teacher's work-week.[3]

The School Year. There are generally about 180–190 school days in the calendar year. A very few school districts employ teachers for a 12-month period, generally with one month's paid vacation in addition to school holidays, and with duties or activities stipulated or approved by the board of education for the summer weeks. The majority of school districts do not pay teachers for the summer period, making it therefore a seasonal lay-off rather than a vacation.

The period of summer lay-off is utilized by many teachers to improve themselves professionally through advanced and refresher work at colleges and universities, travel, and independent reading. More than one-third of the men teachers and one-tenth of the women teachers use

[1] "The Status of the American Public School Teacher," *NEA Research Bulletin,* Vol. XXXV, February, 1957, p. 10.

[2] *Ibid.,* p. 11. (Note: A parent who recently inquired about the marital status of the teachers in a 12-classroom elementary school was told by the principal, somewhat wryly, that she was the only single person on the school's staff.)

[3] *Ibid.,* p. 30 and "How Long is a School Day," *NEA Research Bulletin,* Vol. 39, February, 1961, pp. 8 and 9.

their summer lay-off time to work at whatever jobs they can get to supplement their school-year income.

The supplementation of school-year income is not confined to summer employment. Approximately 10 per cent of the men and 4 per cent of the women teachers also work on extra jobs either in or outside the school system to add to their regular school earnings.[4]

The Work of the Teacher. The major task of the teacher is to teach. This he does through management of the environment, stimulation of pupil interest and enthusiasm, and such guidance and direction as is needed in order to promote learning.

Work Load. For economic reasons the teacher is generally assigned a number of pupils approaching a median of 31 in the elementary school and 27 in the secondary school.[5] The number of pupils in a class is one factor in the work load of a teacher. In addition there are such factors as the number and kinds of classes; preparation and planning requirements; methods employed; facilities and equipment needed, used, and cared for; pupil adjustment and counselling responsibilities; record keeping and other related or clerical duties; extra-curricular duties assumed or imposed; and local and state requirements for or incentives toward professional improvement.

The actual work load of teachers pretty much defies precise measurement or even accurate comparison. Probably the greatest concern about teacher load, translated into an effort to solve the enigma, is represented by the Douglass formula.[6]

In spite of an effort to incorporate into one formula the variables that affect teacher load, the Douglass formula seems to provide chiefly a measure for relative comparisons in which small differences merit little consideration whereas great disparities would be expected to alert the administrator to the need to analyze the situation carefully in order to determine whether action was called for and what action to take.

Supporting Personnel

Personnel drawn from the teaching profession, other professions, clerical occupations, the trades, and semiskilled or at times unskilled labor groups provide services which support the major task of the school system.

[4] *NEA Research Bulletin,* Vol. XXXV, February, 1957, p. 22.
[5] *Ibid.,* pp. 28 and 29.
[6] Harl R. Douglass, *Modern Administration of Secondary Schools* (New York, Ginn and Company, 1954), pp. 96–101.

Teachers in Supporting Positions. Superintendents; deputy, associate, and assistant superintendents; directors of various activities; supervisors; administrative assistants; coordinators; principals and their assistants; special secretaries; and, on occasion, receptionists are drawn from the teaching profession to serve in other than direct classroom teaching capacities.

The office of the superintendent serves in many ways as the brain and nerve center for the entire school system. The superintendent is a generalist in education and is assisted in the larger school districts by educator specialists who are given staff, i.e., advisory, and in some instances also administrative responsibilities for, e.g., elementary or secondary education, the curriculum or curricular subdivisions of the school program, budget and finance, school plant, personnel, public relations, research and records, and pupil adjustment and counselling services. Through these services, administrative coordination of the school operation is sought.

The variety of teachers for the different grades, classes, and subjects and the contrasts in their training, experience, and competency have brought about the creation of a group of employees, former teachers, who are designated as supervisors. It is their function to help teachers to improve their teaching.

The chief task of the supervisor is to help locate trouble spots, suggest ways to overcome difficulties, serve as a clearing house for the dissemination of information about promising practices, and take the part of friend and counsellor to teachers. The supervisor is greatly handicapped in carrying into effect his multi-faceted function when the administrative responsibility to rank and rate teachers is also delegated to him.

Every once in awhile a superintendent or principal discovers the need to meet a special situation by using a teacher in an elevated secretarial position. The teacher becomes in fact a sort of professional and executive secretary to the administrator and is at times designated an administrative assistant or executive secretary.

The particular value of the teacher-trained secretary with classroom experience comes from knowledge of the school system, ability to relieve the administrator of detail that can be dealt with as well without troubling him, and a nice sensibility as to what would constitute undesirable overprotection of the administrator.

A receptionist, drawn from the teacher group, to serve in a combined secretarial-receptionist capacity, capitalizes upon knowledge about the school system in general and the administrator's office in particular. This position, where warranted, justifies itself largely on the basis of consequent improved relations with the public.

Nonteacher Professional Supporting Personnel. The school district often employs some personnel who are not drawn from the teaching profession but are nevertheless professional in their own rights.

Professional groups upon which the schools often draw for specialized full or part-time services include accountants, architects, dentists, dietitians, doctors, engineers, lawyers, nurses, psychiatrists, psychologists, and social workers.

Accountants may be employed to set up, supervise, and maintain financial records as regular or as special contract employees. An independent certified public accountant is generally retained for the short-term task of reviewing or auditing the accounts kept.

Architects may be employed full-time to design buildings for the board of education or to review the designs and specifications of architects who design school buildings on contract.

Health services—via the dentist, doctor, and nurse—are generally procured as a safeguard to the pupils and result in referral to the family physician when care is needed. On occasion children from indigent families are referred to local public health services or clinical service is provided them under the auspices of the school system.

The dietitian is employed by school systems which provide food service to assure the selection, preparation, and serving of foods in accordance with sound nutritional principles.

An engineer may be a full-time employee who has responsibility for the safety of buildings, equipment, and accesses or he may be a part-time employee hired for a specific task.

Hardly ever is a school district so small that it can afford to do without the services of a lawyer. Generally it is enough to have a lawyer on retainer for such matters as may come up in the way of general legal questions, contracts, torts, and labor relations. The volume of legal work is the functional criterion as to whether a lawyer will be a full- or a part-time employee.

Psychiatrists and psychologists are sometimes employed on a full-time basis within the counselling center of the school system. In other instances they are employed by the school system on a part-time basis to help solve special problems. Their services may be direct or for referral. Social workers or teachers trained in their techniques are generally employed to provide help in correcting problems which are the cause of truancy.

Clerical Help. Depending on the size of the school district, there will be a variety of clerical help, chiefly in the central office and in part in the respective school buildings.

The help in the central office will include chiefly bookkeepers, office machine operators, secretaries, typists, and file clerks. In the respective school buildings the clerical help will be chiefly composed of secretaries who are able to do well a number of such tasks as answering the telephone, taking dictation, typing, filing, maintaining school records, and operating mimeograph or other duplicating machines.

Operational Personnel. Keeping the school in clean, comfortable, and orderly working condition is a function delegated to operating personnel. These employees are designated custodians or janitors or in the case of women, matrons. Their duties are sufficiently clear to require no further elaboration here.

Maintenance Personnel. Practices for the maintenance of school plant vary. Either maintenance is contracted by the job to nonschool affiliated individuals or organizations or, in the large school district, an extensive maintenance force composed of personnel representing a wide range of crafts is employed to do maintenance requiring such skills as those of the cabinet maker, carpenter, electrician, engineer (stationary), glazier, mason, mechanic, painter, plumber, and steam-fitter.

Other Supporting Personnel. The possible list of supporting personnel is almost inexhaustible. Chief, however, among those not mentioned up to now are the personnel who are affiliated with the school because of school-operated food, transportation, and warehousing services.

Among those involved in the school's food service program, in addition to the dietitian, are the cafeteria supervisor, the buyers of food stuffs, food handlers who prepare food for cooking or serving, cooks, scullery help.

Although regular employees, a number of the food-handling employees do not work a full-time schedule daily. The requirements for preparing, serving, and cleaning up for the one meal customarily served call for the employment of workers only a few hours daily. The full-time employment of such workers would depend on the availability of those who would want full-time employment and on the possibility of using them to meet some other part-time need within the school system.

School systems which provide transportation for their pupils sometimes do so on a contract basis in which case the personnel problem is the responsibility of the contracting agency. When, however, the school system operates buses leased or owned by it, the operation of the buses is a school responsibility and the employment of drivers, the provision of fueling and lubricating service, and the maintenance of the buses are added to the many administrative and personnel problems of the schools.

Many large school systems have found it advantageous to do their purchasing on a large quantity basis and to centralize their storage of supplies and provisions for distribution to the respective schools in accordance with developing need. Such an operation requires the employment of the necessary employees to administer the service of supplies, to maintain a continuing inventory, and to make deliveries on schedule and on short notice.

PRINCIPLES

There are a number of principles (see Chapter 1 for the full statement of each) which have close and direct bearing upon the school employee in his relationship to his job. The most pertinent are stated below in abridged form.

1. Education is the primary purpose of the schools. The goodwill and cooperation of all school employees must be secured if the optimum education is to take place.
2. The people who have instituted the schools and all employees within the school system have the same basic interest. This interest is the provision of the best education possible, . . .
3. The human factor is a variable. The variability is potentially an asset.
4. The most important single factor in getting the best that a school employee has to offer is how he feels about his work, his associates on the job, and the school system in which he is employed.
5. Esteem for the intelligence and potential of the employee group is a basic necessity and may be demonstrated by the employer group through acts of confidence.
6. Employee problems have to be dealt with in terms of the situation or the conditions at hand. . . . the continued study of the causes of personnel problems will in instances provide a clue to the circumstances under which some problems may be avoided or solved.
7. All participants in an enterprise are entitled to fair dealing.
8. The relationships among employees and between them and their employers can to large extent be summed up. . . . in written policy.

Reflective deliberation on these principles, with the school employee in relationship to his job uppermost in mind, should be productive of the insight that must precede personnel division action to improve school employee-job relationships.

JOB ATTITUDE

Attitude affects the work done by the individual and that done by his associates in like and related jobs. That is why the primary purpose of the school as an agency for learning must be uppermost in the mind of each school employee regardless of his task. Singleness of ultimate purpose welds all employees into a mutual association for achieving the recognized objective.

With as many different kinds of employment as there are in schools, it is easy for the respective groups to become unrealistically stereotyped in such a way as to impede harmonious progress toward the same ends. Thus it is too easily possible for the unitary and inclusive school personnel group to find itself divided.

Within administration there are line and staff—or, not so well-read action and better-read advisory—personnel. Supervisors often find themselves in a class by themselves, between administrators and other workers —snared betwixt the two rather than linking them together.

Among other than administrative employees, the stereotypes of teachers as impractical theorists and the semiskilled and skilled who work with their hands as practical realists exist. It is easy for each group to find refuge in a superiority assumed on the basis of selected criteria.

The making of idle comparisons generates tension and friction in place of an appropriate mutual appreciation. Realism results in recognition of the complementary nature of the different kinds of work and worker, i.e., that each has something to contribute toward reaching the objective of the school as an educational institution and that the different tasks are merely facets of the unitary job.

Every category of school employee has its justification in the importance of the work done for the functioning of the school. This importance must be fixed in the minds, understanding, and feelings of each employee in such a way as to make the work a matter of significance and pride which is fully as important as the paycheck.

A feeling of the worth of one's work and the dignity of work may be promoted in part through an appeal to reason. Probably as important as the rational approach is that of the emotions. It is important for people who are to work together to understand human behavior, its motivation, and the several means for influencing its change.

Aside from some signs of schism between the administrative and teacher groups, those who belong to the teaching profession seem on the whole to subordinate their negative feelings to the job to be done. The teacher generally loses himself so much to his teaching that he forgets his gripes completely until a moment of leisure provides opportunity to concern himself with them again.

It seems that it is in the jobs auxiliary to teaching—the health, clerical, custodial, maintenance, and other service functions of school operation—that both teachers and other workers tend to look at the job as an end rather than as a means to an end. The area of the auxiliary functions is one in which both the members of the teaching profession and all other workers must be brought to a realization of the importance of the respective jobs, particularly in the contribution that each makes to the effective operation of the education enterprise.

Whether a school employee belongs to the teaching profession or not and regardless of his actual job within the school system, each job is important in itself and for the facilitation of education. No job may be regarded merely as a means to earn a livelihood. The requirements of the school system as a social institution are such that every employee is obligated to strive for excellence in his work; none may legitimately be satisfied to do merely well enough to get by.

STATUS FACTORS

Present-day society is one in which status looms large in thought and is frankly sought through overt action. The status of the school employee is thus made important and will be examined in terms of what people think about school employment, the freedom of the employee, school pay, and the prospects of the school employee.

Consensus

School employment presents a paradox. The overwhelming sentiment of individuals and groups is without a doubt favorable to education, schools, and the employees who make school operations possible. Society places a high value on education. However the favorable sentiment and high valuation are neither reflected by nor translated into monetary terms and, in fact, the school employee seems often to be regarded with reservation if not commiseration.

Commonly quoted with approbation as apropos to the teacher is George Bernard Shaw's, "He who can, does. He who cannot, teaches." This remark has been termed "arrogance" by Sir Max Beerbohm who remarks:

Of course, it is simply untrue. Many teachers have done moving and delightful things . . . But even those who haven't—if they teach well, if they inspirit the young, they are perhaps more valuable than those who have done the moving and delightful things.[7]

Unlike Beerbohm, there seem to be many who are so captivated by the cutting pithiness of the Shaw caricature that they fail to note that his comment is merely brilliantly verbalized nonsense. In becoming the

7 S. N. Behrman, *Portrait of Max* (New York, Random House, 1960), p. 43. (Invited to address the British National Teachers Union, Shaw made his entrance to a cold, dead silence. Grinning impishly, he opened his address with: "Those who can, do: those who can think, teach." The amends, however, fail to keep pace with the repetitious use of the original statement.)

unthinking purveyors and perpetuators of this nonsense, they influence their own attitudes toward teachers and affect the attitudes of teachers toward themselves. In addition, those in school jobs with less status than that of teachers share in lowered esteem since they perform auxiliary services.

Criticism and Pressure. The schools are subjected to the pressures of criticism which have their impact chiefly upon teachers. In this respect the teaching profession is exposed as is no other. In part this is because the teacher group is convenient as a scapegoat for social ills that are generated in the home, church, and society.

If child behavior is short of parental desires, crime and juvenile delinquency are increasing, a decrease in patriotic ardor is suspected, controversial topics in the realms of politics, religion, or sex are explored, an individual case of the morals of a teacher or other school employee calls for investigation, and so on almost without end, the solution is to excoriate the school and invoke sanctions against school employees. The latter take the form of the now familiar teacher oath and a recent requirement in Montgomery County, Maryland, that all prospective school employees be fingerprinted and subjected to police check before employment.

In no other profession than teaching does the general public presume to dictate professional training, practice, and methodology. But when it comes to teaching, there is a general assumption that anyone, irrespective of background, can diagnose what is wrong and prescribe the remedy better than can the trained professional, the teacher.

No doubt the fact that teachers—much more than any other professional group—are public agents who can be reached by levelling criticism at the public institution, the school, contributes to making them an easy target. However, there is little doubt that on its rather uncertain way toward professionalism, the teacher group has vacillated greatly, torn between its functions and expertness on the one hand and an apparent need to keep segments of the population placated on the other. Having neglected the development of the rationale for meeting pressure, the teaching profession has failed to establish for itself the place it should rightfully occupy in the public esteem.

One other part of the problem of the teaching profession is that it is really not quite sure of what its task is. One segmental pole represents a stress upon the importance of an intellectual emphasis and a selected academically oriented curriculum. The opposite pole represents a stress upon the "whole" child in terms of physical, mental, and emotional well-being, personality development, and preparation for active citizenship via a comprehensive or all inclusive sort of curriculum that has little or no basis for being selective. Between the two extremes are an infinite number of intermediate individual and group positions.[8]

Job Satisfaction

If status may be assumed to determine the satisfaction a teacher gets from his job, then it would seem as if there is status in sufficient measure to maintain and even increase the teaching force. Every once in awhile a teacher reaches a period of doubt in his career. He faces the question of whether he cannot find greater satisfaction in other work rather than teaching. Encouraged by a school administrator or professor in whom they have confided, a number of such teachers have left the schools for other employment to find the answer to their questioning. Almost invariably they proved successful in terms of earnings within the first year. Nevertheless, almost without exception, they have returned to school work because they have discovered that the job satisfaction of teaching meant more to them than the satisfaction derived from an increase in income.

The observation above poses the question as to whether enough teachers have managed to get one way or another that perception of their work and its satisfactions that makes the status of their jobs in terms of their own values transcend the status accorded by others.

Teachers generally seem to think of their jobs as very important but as not being so regarded by others. Perhaps by way of compensation they underrate the esteem accorded by others and exaggerate the measure of esteem that is due the teaching profession. Rettig and Pasamanick[9] concluded from their findings that teachers particularly value their standing with the general public and that—although the standing wished for is not attained—that accorded is well above actual teacher expectation. However, teachers seem to be so unaware of this favorable position that they cannot be gratified by it.

Freedom

Many an individual holds as his ultimate goal being independent, being his own boss. This is an expression of the desire for freedom. Teachers are in a vocation in which being one's own boss must generally be limited. The teacher is part of an organization, the school system and the school. The freedom he has must be within that organization and will be expressed chiefly within the classroom. His freedom will be explored in terms of academic and personal considerations.

[8] An interesting statement of the disagreement within the profession is presented by Mortimer Smith, "Why We Disagree," *Saturday Review*, January 21, 1961, pp. 80–81 and 96–97.

[9] Salomon Rettig and Benjamin Pasamanick, "Status and Job Satisfaction of Public School Teachers," *School and Society*, 47:2149, March 14, 1959, pp. 113–116.

Academic Freedom. Often resorted to as a defense and frequently not clearly defined in the individual's thinking is academic freedom as the right of a teacher to make decisions and to express himself without restriction—subject only to the maturity of his charges—in the areas of his specific expertness and competency. To a teacher academic freedom is not merely a right. It is also a necessity. Deprived of it he cannot be effective.

Decision making is the function of those best equipped to do so. When a decision to be made involves the particular competencies of the teacher or teacher group, the decision must be made accordingly.[10] Conversely, when the expertness of teachers has no more bearing on a decision than the opinions of others, there is no reason to invoke academic freedom in an effort to gain for the faculty the right of decision making.

Academic freedom is not license. The freedom of expression facet of academic freedom stipulates a freely operating intelligence, intellectual honesty, responsibility, an open mind, and a willingness and desire to follow where the evidence leads and logic projects. This means that a teacher must be unrestricted in his studies, discussions adjusted to the maturity of the group addressed, and publication of facts and ideas. In fact, such freedom is to be encouraged within and outside the classroom.

A number of conditions have been stipulated as necessary to the operation and flourishing of academic freedom. These have been expressed in one way or another by a number of writers [11] and are synthesized below:

Conditions for Academic Freedom

1. Free intelligence exists, is treasured, is nurtured, and is actively encouraged.
   a. It is possible to conform or not, without stigma, to some accepted creed.
   b. Dissent from orthodoxy finds free expression.
   c. There is faith in the supremacy of reason to such an extent that each dares, without reluctance or fear, to state his convictions.
   d. The faculty is deliberately composed of men of diverse views.
2. Evidence is the determinant, and issues take precedence over personalities.
3. The teacher group regulates the methods and content of education and determines the objects of research, and the public is barred from encroaching upon these specifically academic preserves.

[10] For a fuller discussion of this thesis see Myron Lieberman, *Education as a Profession* (Englewood Cliffs, N.J., Prentice-Hall, Inc., 1956), p. 90, and Robert M. Hutchins, *The Higher Learning in America* (New Haven, Conn., The Yale University Press, 1936), p. 21.

[11] John S. Diekhoff, *The Domain of the Faculty* (New York, Harper and Row, 1956), pp. 82–83. H. Gordon Hullfish, in *Democracy in the Administration of Higher Education* (New York, Harper and Row, 1950), pp. 53–61. Clarence A. Schoenfeld, *The University and Its Publics* (New York, Harper and Row, 1954), p. 85. Lloyd S. Woodburne, *Faculty Personnel Policies in Higher Education* (New York, Harper and Row, 1950), Chapters 7 and 8.

4. The calling of staff meetings, extracurricular demands, the scheduling of classes, etc., take place with full and due regard for the need of the faculty members to have the uninterrupted time essential to their being truly professional.

5. Faculty members formulate and apply criteria for evaluating professional requirements and exercise the judicial function in determining violations of the professional code of ethics and in stipulating or recommending disciplinary action.

    a. Provision is made for hearings in which the faculty will, through its own representatives, determine the merits of a case brought against a member of the faculty. The determination of merit will be based on evidence whereby to gauge the fitness of the teacher to function in accord with the definition and implications of academic freedom.

6. Administrative officers, vested with authority by the Board of Education or its chief executive agent, the superintendent, nevertheless are responsible to the faculty in matters of educational policy.

The foregoing synthesis helps to bring academic freedom as an otherwise vague something into perspective as a very real concept with implications of workability. Its specificity lends additional weight and value to the concept of academic freedom. It also provides the basis for understanding the importance of realizing when the privileges and rights of academic freedom may legitimately be invoked and when their invocation has no sound foundation. And, it provides a basis for the kind of responsible action by which teachers can advance toward their aspirations and claims to professionalism.

Personal Freedom. The personal freedom of the teacher as an individual and a citizen has changed significantly during this century. The changes are due in part to the improvement in the education of the teacher, the insistence of the teacher as an individual and a member of his professional group upon his personal and civil rights, the economics of employment conditions, and the impact of these factors upon people who were at the same time influenced—by reading, discussion, radio, and television—in the direction of a liberalizing development of their outlook upon life.

The well-educated teacher finds in his competency the security which enables him to take a position and to act in accordance with his convictions. When such a teacher's actions are professionally defensible, his professional organization further reinforces his security by its readiness to support him.

The shortage of qualified teachers, particularly since the mid-1940's, has induced people in general to take stock of their positions regarding the rights of teachers to live as others do and to exercise the same kinds of privileges enjoyed by the parents of school children and other adults in the community. Thus the ban on marriage for women teachers is practically nonexistent today. The right to individual determination with respect to smoking, moderate drinking, cultural pursuits, and political and religious affiliation is with few exceptions a matter of course.

One area in which the teacher is still in a controversial situation is that of politics, especially partisan politics. This area is sometimes confused because of failure to differentiate between what is the right of the individual teacher and the proper function of the professional group. The right of the individual teacher to engage in political activity is emerging from the controversy of past decades.

Increasingly teachers are active in politics; run for municipal, county, and state offices; and campaign for their political favorites. With the general exception of board of education elections, teachers as individuals have the same obligation that all citizens have to be active in seeking public office themselves and in promoting the general welfare by working for the election of the best candidates. They ought to be encouraged in these pursuits.

For the professional teacher group to become a politically unified minority group affiliated with a partisan political group raises question as to the function of the professional group and the political, as contrasted to the educational, impact of this group upon the program of the schools instituted by the people to serve their purposes. The question posed by those outside the profession may well be whether the *public* interest or a *vested* interest is served by partisan political action of the teacher group.

Income

School employees' income will be dealt with at length in Chapter 16. However, a few words are appropriate here to provide perspective on the status and attitude of the school employee.

School employees in nonprofessional categories of work are paid on so low a scale that they make teachers' salaries look good by comparison. A discussion of teachers' salaries, therefore, will by inference shed light on the plight of school employees in general.

The median real family income for the United States was $5417.00 in 1959.[12] The average classroom teacher's salary for the United States was $4939.00 (1958–59) and $5160.00 for the 1959–60 school year.[13]

It should be noted that the higher median income is for the general

[12] "Real Family Income," *Road Maps of Industry, No. 1313* (New York, The National Industrial Conference Board, Inc., February 24, 1961). " 'Real' income: Before tax money wages and salaries, net income of any self-employed, and any other family receipts (dividends, etc.) adjusted up or down for changes in the consumer price index."

[13] Research Division, National Education Association, *Economic Status of Teachers,* Research Report 1960-R8 (Washington, The Association, May, 1960). p. 45.

population with a median education below college level. The lower-average classroom teacher salary is for a selected population with a median education at the college level. The contrast is eloquent in its implications for the esteem that has its roots in income status. There is nothing in this contrast to militate in favor of a generally high esteem for school employees; nor is there in this contrast any basis for the school employee to hold himself in high esteem. Such esteem as may be held to exist must be rooted in something other than income.

Future

There are factors which decidedly favor the future for school employees, particularly teachers.

There is an awakened consciousness and real appreciation of the value and significance of education for the individual and society. These generate a concern which must ultimately find its expression in measures to improve the staffing and equipping of schools.

Improved staffing of the schools will take place progressively and rapidly as soon as it becomes obvious to youth that school employment is so well regarded that it is assured both monetary and social recognition at least equal to what is acorded other professions that require comparable preparation, experience, and daily application. The automation of industry can contribute to making the relative vacuum of teaching so attractive that entrance into the teaching profession becomes competitive and highly selective.

Twelve-month employment of teachers—instead of a 9–10 month work period followed by a 2–3 month layoff—is a fact in a number of school districts. In these districts teachers are assigned, during the summer months, to one or more of a variety of duties including summer-school teaching; curricular study, planning, and revision; school survey activities; professional improvement via workshops, summer sessions at universities, and travel; etc. Such employment of teachers serves to better the status of the profession by reducing or eliminating the need for teachers to take on nonprofessional summer employment for one-fifth to one-quarter of the calendar year.

And, there is promise that within the schools change is in store. This change will be reflected in the functional use of television; programmed learning; and a corps of teachers of various competencies and specializations, together with clerical and other nonprofessional help. Such change is another step toward the self-esteem that is part of being professional and which finds expression through doing those tasks which make professional—as contrasted to clerical, housekeeping, baby sitting, and odds-and-ends extracurricular—demands on one's time and efforts.

PROFESSIONALISM

It has been noted (Chapter 2) that it is virtually impossible to identify any common element that makes for professionalism and distinguishes the professional from the nonprofessional activity. Nevertheless, there is a working concept of professionalism that provides teachers with a cue for attaining and re-enforcing the values that attach to being regarded as professional. Accordingly, the working criteria of professionalism, derived from Flexner,[14] adapted to the teacher group, will be discussed briefly in terms of intellectuality, scientific basis, application, communicability, self-organization, altruism, and ethics.

Intellectuality

If they are to be known as professional, teachers must take steps to operate on an intellectual and individually responsible level.

The work of teachers is intellectual, as contrasted to manual. It is in the realm of individual responsibility that teaching still falls far short of claims to professionalism. It almost seems that teachers tend to become increasingly the creatures of an organization which stipulates their conduct. Somewhat paradoxically, as school districts expand in size and employ teachers of higher qualifications, the individual responsibility of the teacher seems to become more and more subordinated to the wishes and dictates of administrators and supervisors.

Scientific Basis

Teaching and learning are rooted in psychology. This is the scientific and intellectual basis in which the teaching profession can find its satisfaction and gratification. To the extent that teachers are psychologically oriented and recognize the importance of this base for their preparation and practice, they satisfy one of the criteria for being regarded as professional.

Application

In the basic sciences there are two areas of operation, that of pure or basic research and that of applied science. For the teacher there is the area of the basic research of psychology, exploring human behavior and how to influence it, and there is the area of application of psychological principles and the theory of learning by way of classroom teaching. A

[14] Abraham Flexner, "Is Social Work a Profession?," *School and Society*, Vol. 1, June 26, 1915, p. 904.

close relationship between theory and practice favors recognition of teaching as a profession.

Communicable Technique

A practical criterion for a profession is that its techniques can be communicated to others. This criterion is met for teachers to a degree as "how to teach" is taught by way of methods courses, observation opportunities, practice teaching, and the services of helping teachers or supervisors.

Self-organization

The professional requirement that a group demonstrate a tendency toward self-organization seems to be met in the proclivity of the teaching profession to organize in one or another kind of local, state, and national association.

Altruism

In view of the general status accorded teaching to date, it is difficult to account for the able members of the profession on any other basis than that ". . . educators are dedicated to the development of children in their care." [15]

Ethics

Whereas the cue to improving the chances of being regarded professional have been mentioned; also in the realm of ethics, i.e., the standard of conduct, there seems to be room for worthwhile effort toward professionalization.

In general the teachers of the nation have a code of ethics, that formulated and revised (1952) by the National Education Association.[16] Despite the distribution of hundreds of thousands of copies, this code falls short of being effective. Teachers are generally little more than merely aware that there is a code. Relatively few are able to state the gist of the code in terms either of principle or obligations. The code is not a vital force influencing teacher conduct.

To be effective a code of ethics must be derived from the experiences

[15] Charles S. Benson, *The Economics of Public Education* (Boston, Houghton Mifflin Company, 1961), p. 59.

[16] The NEA Board of Directors approved (February, 1963) consideration of a new, unified Code of Ethics for the Education Profession by the 1963 NEA Representative Assembly.

and convictions of the group. It must come from, not be imposed upon, the group. Even when rules of conduct are the product of the life and work of the teacher, they must nevertheless be crystallized in the consciousness of teachers so that they may become effectively directional of behavior.

Should generally accepted rules of conduct seem to some teachers inconsequent to their life and work, there must be provision for disciplining those who violate the code. Throughout society laws are observed by some because of their recognized values, by others because of fear of the penalties that are invoked by infractions of the rules.

SUMMARY

The different kinds of school employees were considered as having the common objective of facilitating instruction. The work, work period, load, and status of the teacher were reviewed and the supporting roles of others than classroom teachers were noted.

In accordance with principles cited, stress was laid upon the need for the worker to regard his work as worthwhile, a means for contributing to the inspiriting of the young, and deserving of each employee's best efforts.

Teachers were found to seek greater popular esteem than they received and, conversely, to receive greater esteem than they actually expected. With improved quality in training and selection, pay, and general academic and personal freedom, teachers may be expected to free themselves of whatever sense of inferiority by which they may be plagued.

The future of teaching was regarded as promising for education, the teacher, and the gaining of regard for teaching as a profession.

SELECTED READINGS

American Association of School Administrators, *Professional Administration for America's Schools* (Washington, D.C., The Association, 1960), Chapter 11.

ARNSPIGER, V. Clyde, *Personality in Social Process* (Chicago, Follett Publishing Company, 1961), Chapter 5.

CHAMBERLAIN, Leo M., and KINDRED, Leslie W., *The Teacher and School Organization* (Englewood Cliffs, N.J., Prentice-Hall, Inc., 1958), Chapters 7, 8, 10, 23.

LIEBERMAN, Myron, *Education as a Profession* (Englewood Cliffs, N.J., Prentice-Hall, Inc., 1956), Chapters 1, 2, 4, 7, 12, 13–15.

LIEBERMAN, Myron, *The Future of Public Education* (Chicago, The University of Chicago Press, 1960), Chapters 4, 5, 8.

SCOTT, C. Winfield, and HILL, Clyde M., *Public Education under Criticism* Englewood Cliffs, N.J., Prentice-Hall, Inc., 1954), Chapters 3, 4, 9.

STOOPS, Emery, and RAFFERTY, M. L., Jr., *Practices and Trends in School Administration* (Boston, Ginn and Company, 1961), pp. 325–330, 391, and 411–422.

YEAGER, William A., *Administration and the Teacher* (New York, Harper and Row, 1954), Chapters 17, 20, 23.

YEAGER, William A., *Administration of the Noninstructional Personnel and Services* (New York, Harper and Row, 1959), Chapter 10 and Parts IV, V, VI.

.12.

Joint Control of the School Operation

LABOR-MANAGEMENT relations have grown out of conflict in which historically management sought to exploit labor and labor in turn sought to dominate management. It is only recently that it is becoming clear that

. . . employer and employee are bound together by common interests in a business undertaking, and the business undertaking can endure only by performing a worthwhile purpose in meeting human needs, (and) employers and employees must necessarily have responsibilities to each other and to those they serve.[1]

Education has thus far not actually committed itself to two such conflicting groups as those of industry. Rather, education has to date recognized the unitary principle to which industry is approaching. This unitary principle was expressed by Moehlman thus:

All executive agents and agencies must be considered as a single unit. Any person who carries out any part of the education plan is functionally a part of the executive activity.[2]

The thrust of this principle is that as members of a unitary and executive activity, the employees at the various levels and with the varying com-

---

[1] Hines H. Baker, *Labor and Management—A Common Interest and a Joint Responsibility* (Austin, Texas, The Great Issues Forum, An address, The University of Texas, October 16, 1957), p. 4.

[2] Arthur B. Moehlman, *School Administration* (Boston, Houghton Mifflin Company, 1940 and 1951), p. 142 (1940) or 73 (1951).

petencies within the unitary activity cannot logically or defensibly be in conflict within the organization.[3]

Between the schools and the community and within the schools there must exist logically, in terms of both democratic interaction and educational function, a joint control by which the will of the people, the perspective of the administrator, and the insight of teachers and other employees who are on the firing line of the school operation may be brought together to produce the best possible education for the youth of the community.

Joint control of the school operation will be explored in terms of the role of the public and the manner in which that role finds its expression, the task and authority of the administrator, and the function of the teacher and those who provide services auxiliary to teaching.

THE PUBLIC AND ITS ROLE

The concept of the public requires crystallization. In addition, a statement to clarify the logical role of the public with reference to school functioning will prove of value.

The Public

The public of the state or of the school district is the totality of its citizens. This public has common cause in its concern for conditions which foster or threaten its well-being. This common cause provides the broad basis for popular action.

The emphasis of groups of individuals upon selected satellites in the galaxy of topics that have significance for public well-being causes the emergence of subgroups which are also publics bound together by their respective common interests. These publics may be majority or minority groups; but, in either case each group—although a segment of the public in its totality—itself constitutes a public in terms of its own dominant concern.

Although education may be the kind of concern that all citizens share, the priority given it will vary in terms of the conflict of the education interest with other interests, e.g., anxiety about rising taxes, question as to whether education belongs in the domain of public or private endeavor, reservation as to what should be included in a program of education. Consequently because of diversity in emphasis, the concern or

[3] There is currently great danger that just as private enterprise approaches operation in terms of the unitary concept, education is developing the internal stresses of unenlightened and confused personnel administration which threaten it with the very alignments, e.g., administrators versus teachers and other employees, that have characterized management-labor relations in the past.

interest that can muster the support of the majority is made the basis for popular action. Meanwhile the minority groups retain the right of dissent, persuasion, and appeal while committed to conforming action as long as the majority point of view is law. Thus it is noted, for all practical purposes the public is resolved into the majority public.[4]

The Public's Role

The public in a democracy has the obligation to address itself to the task of making government of the people, by the people, and for the people a functioning reality and of providing for the perpetuation of such government.

Government of, by, and for the people is essentially a government that rests upon public opinion as to what is in the interest of the people. The success of the government so defined and motivated is contingent upon the quality of the prevailing public opinion. This the early settlers of what is now the United States recognized as they took measures (1642 and subsequently), which have been re-inforced and extended to date, to provide for the development of intelligence and the assimilation of knowledge through education. By making provision for individual development in accordance with the interests and capabilities of each, the people have laid the foundation for the informed kind of public opinion upon which self-government can rest securely.

The Area of Public Determination. Objectives and appraisal constitute the area of public determination. The area of objectives is pretty well defined by the principle (No. 2, Chapter 1) that:

The objectives of the school are functionally derived from the people who have created (and who maintain) them as institutions to meet those needs that they want fulfilled through formal education. . . .

The broad objectives—what the schools are set up to accomplish—are the distinct function primarily of the people. They are entitled to accept what leadership they wish—lay, professional, or both in some combination—in defining the objectives; however, the decision as to which to incorporate in the school program rests with the people.

The area of appraisal is a prerogative of the people. Their appraisal is properly restricted to just the consideration whether or not the objectives set up are being attained.

There is often a misunderstanding of the public's appraisal function. This becomes evident when the public follows its legitimate appraisal

---

[4] Note, however, that the majority public is constantly changing in composition, point of view, and numbers. It can become a minority public. No public can be regarded as a constant.

with an attempt to appraise the means (curriculum, teaching materials, and methods) by which the schools function. In this way the public shifts its focus from the nonspecialized area which is its proper domain to that of the specialized (professional) area in which the public cannot be expected to exercise the appraisal function with any competency.

Positive appraisal indicates public satisfaction about the functioning of the schools and provides the teachers an endorsement of their professional decisions and actions. Negative appraisal signifies public dissatisfaction with the functioning of the schools and alerts the teachers to the need to examine their decisions and practices so that they will serve better the educational objectives of the people.

How the Public Exercises Its Role

As individual appraisal takes place informally and people compare notes, the foundation is laid for more formalized individual and group conviction and action. When the individual or group is ready to take action, it is his right and obligation to make representations to the board of education as the legally constituted controlling body for the school district and to ask for consideration of those representations. Thus the initiative moves from the public to its representative agency, the board of education.

Failing to get desired action from the board of education, the public has recourse to a possibly long-term action by which it eventually gets a board of education which is representative of its point of view.

THE TASK AND AUTHORITY OF THE SCHOOL ADMINISTRATOR

The school administrator is that agent of the board of education who is employed for and charged with the execution of board policy. A corollary to execution is the role of professional advisor to the board of education, a function that the superintendent is understandably expected to assume.

In the nearly extinct one-room school of a receding era, the administrator executed board policy personally in practically all of its details. As school systems become larger, the administrator relies increasingly upon others to whom various roles in the execution of policy are delegated.

Regardless of size, the over-all task and authority of the school administrator remain functionally constant. It is only in terms of the specifics of what he does and the complexity of the organization that the job of the administrator has changed and differs from one school district to another.

As an executive agent of the board of education (the superintendent is the chief executive agent), the administrator derives his authority from state law and local board policy. He is directly responsible to the local board of education.

Administrative Obligation

The administrator has no choice except to carry out the policies of the board of education. This is what he is employed to do. Anyone who takes issue with policy or with action that is the outgrowth of policy logically addresses himself to the board of education, not its executive agent.

However, in his capacity of advisor to the board of education, as the professional charged with execution of policy, and as delegator of authority, the administrator has obligations which have particular implications for personnel administration.

Advisor. In the capacity of advisor, the administrator assumes some responsibility for all policy and chief responsibility for policies that are the direct product of his initiative. Thus, for example, the administrator —who gets the board of education to think in terms of pay increments geared to merit, or advocates that a salary increase be accompanied by an extension of the contract period, or proposes the lengthening of the school year, etc.—is rightly held responsible in a major way for board policies that are predicated upon administrative advice and leadership.

Executor. Being charged with carrying policy into operation does not make a lackey out of an administrator. He is a professional man, especially trained for his task as a school administrator and employed because of a professional competency that carries with it a large share of individual responsibility on the job.

The school administrator is obliged to take steps by which the most effective execution of policy will be assured. In general this means that he will involve those on his staff, together with outside consultants, who have the expertness to provide promising direction to policy execution.

Delegator. As one who cannot cover the entire firing line of the educational front, the administrator discharges his responsibility for executing policy by delegating tasks to personnel specifically employed for their potentialities to contribute to doing well the work of the schools.

It is the obligation of the administrator to make certain that employee potentialities are not handicapped or rendered inoperative through poor job-placement practices; inadequate facilities, equipment, and supplies; and disruptive interpersonal relations and working conditions.

If the superintendent has so much to do that he cannot attend to the job of ministering to the needs of the personnel, or if he lacks the competency to do so, he is obligated to make some other provision for enlightened school personnel administration. Failure to do so threatens the effectiveness of the school program.

It is imperative that, in the specific job of personnel administration, the superintendent or his deputy for personnel administration condition himself against using either position or authority to "push employees around."[5] Rather, it is incumbent upon the administrator to recognize that one of his greatest assets for administration is his ability to identify himself with the teacher group and to recognize that he is a member of that group both professionally and as an employee of the Board of Education.

Administrative Option

The administrator has a choice as to his decisions and actions outside the legitimate direct mandates of the board of education. Theoretically he can be as autocratic or as democratic as he wishes.

Since the 1930's there has been considerable emphasis upon democratic administration of the schools. This follows from the nature of the school as a democratically conceived social institution for the conservation, perpetuation, and improvement of the democratic society. The position taken is that the school is in a strategic position to serve as a model of democracy in action, teaching democratic concepts by its own example.

The preparation of school administrators has for the past three decades been influenced by concepts of democratic school administration. This is long enough so that evidences of democratic practices in administration should now be observable with increasing frequency.

Autocratic Option. This is an option that is now rarely advocated. It is an option that fails to hold the individual in regard and is therefore inconsistent with the nature of and developments within American society.

There are still autocrats in school administration. Their administration is characterized by programs that are devitalized because of failure to employ to good advantage the diverse talents of the staff or are ravaged by morale-disrupting discord.

[5] A former superintendent of schools, now a director of personnel in a large school district, recently replied to the query whether he was not pushing people around, "Sure I do; I have always pushed people around." This apparently was justification for a *modus operandi.*

Democratic Option. Popularly advocated, this is an option that still carries with it great confusion.

Democracy connotes regard for the individual, individual responsibility and freedom, and the protection of individual rights. It is a concept of individualism on the one hand and of social considerations on the other. Democracy may be thought of as a sort of dynamic balance between the individual and the group.

Abuse of the concept of democracy because of uncertainty or misunderstanding can generate an anarchic sort of individualism and may even find expression in an operation in which no one seems to be responsible. This is antithetical to democracy.

The implications of democratic concepts for school administration are at least initially clear.

The schools are operated by many employees of greatly diverse talents. Capitalization upon these talents is one way of demonstrating appreciation of and regard for individuals. School programs can be upgraded through increased use of the unique contributions the various employees can make.

Especially teachers are employed in terms of competency. One measure of democratic administration is the individual responsibility the teachers are permitted to exercise. This is observable in terms of the freedom with which each is allowed to work in his particular position.[6]

Democracy is not confined to the doing or manner of doing of one's task. It has implications too for the involvement or interaction of the employee and the controlling body, the board of education, in matters pertaining to his interests, e.g., working conditions, the work period, and pay. Under a democratically conceived operation, conditions for working must be arrived at by agreement, not by the coercion of serf-like employees by a feudalistically motivated type of employing body. The idea of agreements arrived at collectively by employing agencies and the employed needs much greater exploration for its development and application to the school situation.

THE FUNCTION OF THE TEACHER

The entire school operation revolves about the function of the teacher. This function, put simply, is to teach. However, teaching is an activity which takes on a large measure of complexity inasmuch as it connotes learning on the part of the one taught. It may be held that there is no teaching unless learning takes place. The work of the teacher, i.e., teaching, is the promotion of learning.

[6] It sometimes seems as if much less carefully trained and selected nonteaching employees enjoy greater freedom and individual responsibility on their auxiliary jobs than do teachers in their important and professional level tasks.

As promoter of learning, the teacher exposes youth to and involves him in experiences intended to influence his behavior to conform to what is considered socially desirable conduct. He stimulates the acquisition of knowledge and skills and calls into play individual ability to retain and recall. However, teaching does not stop here, learning involves character development and formation.

Both in the United States and in the various countries of Europe the task of the teacher is regarded as including the influencing of character and social intelligence through association, suggestion, and direction. It is fairly generally accepted that the school has both academic and social obligations to the youth that society entrusts to it.

To meet the obligations of the school, the teacher aids the pupil to acquire mastery of knowledge and skills, to develop his character potentialities and affective behavior, and to gain an insight that—although no doubt the product of himself and his experiences—is mystical in that it provides a sense of knowing without sensing or reasoning.

The nature of the work of the teacher is such that much of his task is a matter of his personal relations with the pupil(s).[7] The individuality of the child, the variation among children (even of the same age and environmental background), the differences in personality make-up of teachers, and any inclination to regard teaching as a profession and to stimulate it to merit such regard are all factors which strongly suggest that teaching is a highly personal kind of activity.

As a highly personalized activity, teaching derives much of its effectiveness from the personality of the teacher, his adaptation of technique to his personality and that of his pupils, and the freedom with which he is permitted and encouraged to assume responsibility for both the content and the method of his teaching.

Efforts to standardize the content and techniques of teaching in disregard of the individual differences of both teacher and pupils can serve to depersonalize teaching and threaten it with repressive conformity. The consequence of such depersonalization may be expected to be a decrease in teaching effectiveness. The price of lessened teaching effectiveness seems an unwarrantably high one to pay for administratively comfortable and manageable uniformity.

This examination of the function of the teacher stresses his importance to the educative process. He is a person, an individual, as well as a member of an organization.

Capitalization upon the potentialities of teachers as individuals and as members of an organization suggests the necessity to bring them and the school system into dynamic balance. This means that through interaction and agreement—as contrasted to the exercise of power politics—

---

[7] This does not preclude at all his use of such an instrument as the materials of programmed learning in the areas of his work in which the role of personal relations is either minor or limited to initiating a project.

the governing board of education and the teacher group made up of all teachers (irrespective of the professional level job they are holding) come to an understanding of and agreement about the school system and the functions of each group relative to it. This understanding and agreement provide the basis for a definition of the respective contributions that each group is expected to make to effective school operation.

THE AUXILIARY PERSONNEL

Throughout most school organizations there is a need for a variety of supporting personnel who relieve the teacher of routine tasks that must be done but which make no demands upon professional competency (See Chapter 11). The importance of these personnel lies in their facilitation of the teaching job.

In each category of the supporting personnel, some may be expected to have greater competency in terms of their jobs than any member of the board of education or the professional staff. It is just ordinary good sense to take advantage of this competency in planning and administering the school operation.

Just as in the instance of the professional personnel, so also the non-professional supporting personnel must be brought into dynamic balance within the total structure of school operation. They too must have a voice in developing understanding of and agreement about the total operation, their place in it, the contributions they can and are expected to make, and the conditions by which they and the board of education are bound.

COLLECTIVE AGREEMENT

It has been noted that the public, the administrator, the teacher, and the auxiliary personnel have individual roles in the total school operation. These roles were seen as being mutually interrelated and interdependent. Under these circumstances there would seem to exist a joint responsibility for harmonious and complementary interaction.

Where joint responsibility exists there must be corresponding authority or control. And, wherever any action in a free society involves more than one person, action must rest upon a basis of agreement—the agreement of all the parties to the operation.

If agreement is arrived at through bargaining between two power groups and in terms of the dominance or threat that can be invoked by the respective powers, the appropriate designation of the activity is collective bargaining. If, however, agreement is reached through understanding which leads to definition of individual function and is devoid of exploitative overtones, there is no collective bargaining; rather the activity is one of developing joint control through another kind of activity that is better identified as collective agreement.

The Parties to Collective Agreement

In private enterprise, management—i.e., the administration—tends to become identified with the owner. Owner and manager are jointly concerned with doing whatever can be done to maximize profits. To owner and administrator, the worker has often been someone from whom to get as much as possible for as little as possible. This was one way by which to assure maximum profits.

The worker in private enterprise has skills to employ for anyone who can use them and is willing to pay. His interest is probably more related to the opportunity to use his skills and to get paid as much as possible for so doing than to be productive of any one consumer good or service. Thus the worker can apply leverage in a competitive economy for the services he can render. He is mobile.

The parties to collective agreement in private enterprise are pretty clearly drawn with owners and management on one side and with workers on the other, each contending for as much of the profit as he can get. The analogy of private enterprise to the school scene will be explored with the purpose of identifying the parties to collective agreement in the school situation.

The School Scene. The school scene includes four major groups: 1) the board of education, 2) the administrators, 3) the teachers, and 4) the nonprofessional auxiliary personnel.

At first glance the school scene seems very like that of private enterprise. The same interests seem represented. Instead of owners there are the people. The board of education has been likened by some to the board of directors of a corporation. There are administrative employees with the superintendent of schools cast in the role of the chief executive (top management) agent of the board of education. And, there are nonadministrative employees, professional and nonprofessional.

The board of education represents the state and the people of the school district. It has the responsibility to provide and develop the legislative (policy) framework for school functioning. In addition it has the obligation to appraise the outcomes of its legislative (policy making) activities as a basis for correlative action. And, finally, it is incumbent upon the board of education to make provision for the execution of its policies.

In no way, however, does the profit motive enter into board of education considerations or, for that matter, the school scene. In this respect the entire school operation differs basically from private enterprise in a way that affects fundamentally the relationships of all employees to each other and to the employing agency, the board of education. There are no profits for which to compete.

The first step taken by the board of education to provide for the execution of its policies is the employment of one who will be its chief executive agent, the superintendent of schools. He is first of all a teacher and is given the title and job of administrator only because the size and complexity of the school system demand specialization. The superintendent of schools is an employee of the board of education but, since there is no profit motive or substitute for it, there is no reason or him to ally himself with the board of education to exploit anyone.

The administrators in the school situation are naturally and functionally allied to the total employee group. Administrators, just as other school employees, are employed for the contribution they can make to executing board policy. It is for this reason that Moehlman speaks of all school personnel as part of the executive activity.[8]

All teachers who are not in specialized administrative tasks are also members of the executive branch of school operation. They are distinguished from workers in general in that their professional services are on the one hand not generally marketable except to the schools and on the other by the professional type of dedication that ordinarily either induces one to become a teacher or overcomes him once he engages in teaching.

The dedication of teachers differentiates them from the great body of workers by reason of the motivation with which they address themselves to their tasks. Once in the classroom, the teacher subordinates other issues to the task at hand, teaching. The teacher finds his gratification in doing well a nonspectacular job which he regards as having prime importance to the individual and society.[9]

The nature of teaching requires the teacher to retain his individuality and freedom of operation. He must be encouraged to try out ideas, to exercise initiative, and to assume personal responsibility. It is his obligation—one he must be given freedom to meet—to do what he can to better himself as a teacher, to improve his teaching, and to promote the effectiveness of the education enterprise with which he is associated.

The teacher, then, is the natural partner of the administrator and cannot logically be placed in conflict with him. Teachers and administrators belong to the same professional group, have identical professional interests and motivation, and differ only in the places they occupy within organization and the specializations they have developed.

[8] Arthur B. Moehlman, *School Administration* (Boston, Houghton Mifflin Company, 1951), p. 207.
[9] The teacher does not have the competitive leverage of workers in general. Nevertheless, many have left teaching and have become economically successful in other ventures. However, a large number of such return to teaching because of the feeling of worthwhileness that accompanies teaching and which they failed to find in the more lucrative ventures outside teaching.

Teachers are aided in doing their jobs by a considerable number and variety of employees who do not belong to the teaching profession. These clerical, custodial, maintenance, and other service personnel bear a closer analogy to workers in private enterprise than do administrators or teachers. Their skills and services could be utilized about as well in private as in the public employ. For some reason—pay, convenience, hours, independence on the job, job availability, etc.—they are school rather than private enterprise employees.

The position of the auxiliary personnel is, however, unlike that of workers in general in that they are engaged in a nonprofit enterprise and that their work finds its justification in the contribution it makes to the nonprofit job of education. Thus, these workers too are clearly aligned with teachers who, in turn, are part of the executive family of the school administration.

Conclusion. The two chief parties to possible collective agreement or joint action relative to school operation are the employer and the employee, i.e., the board of education on the one hand and the employed executive agents (all employees) on the other.

In view of the essential unity of the executive group in the school situation, the role of the administrator is logically that of chief advocate for his executive family in terms of the needs voiced by its members.

In view of its representative and public nature, the board of education must regard all representations of the total employee group in the light of the public interest in education. This will not have to be overly difficult in all probability except where money is at stake. Financial considerations are subject to such limitations as the wealth of the school district and the authority of the board of education to tap that wealth.

Issues Subject to Joint Action

Most of the issues for collective agreement within private enterprise pertain also to the school situation. These are:

apprenticeships	pay
arbitration	probation
conditions of employment	scope of joint control
day-to-day relationships	seniority
employee services	suspension
grievance machinery	training
holidays	vacations
hours	work assignment
joint control machinery	work conditions
leaves	health
legal formalities	safety
overtime	work period

This list of issues is important for helping to recognize the problems that do arise and that can be jointly studied and resolved to the advantage of the board of education, the employees, and the school system. The list could be extended almost infinitely to include virtually every problem of school personnel administration.

In addition to the foregoing list, there is a very important area of joint control that identifies education with the manner of operating of other professionally oriented organizations.

Both the what (curriculum) and how (method of instruction) of school operation are matters which make demand on professional competence gained by training and experience and resolved into their derivative, professional judgment. It is incumbent upon the board of education that it recognize, define, and observe the legitimate area of operation of the people and of itself as the lay representatives of the people. It is further incumbent upon the board of education that it recognize, define, and observe the legitimate area of operation of the teaching profession. Arriving at these respective legitimate areas of operation may well be a function of joint exploratory action.

It might be expected that exploratory action as to the lay and professional areas of operation would be resolved in terms of the competency of the lay versus the professional group to make a determination and whether a decision to be made requires or does not require special competency.

Another area of distinct activity on the part of the profession, the board of education, and the people of the school district is that of appraisal, judgment as to the functioning of the school program. Appraisal is the prerogative of everyone and every group interested in education. It is not the sole prerogative of any. It lends itself to joint action by those who engage therein. Appraisal may become effective, moving out of the arena of criticism into that of potential action, when the various appraisers compare their findings.

Means to Secure Collective Agreement

The collective agreement that leads to joint action or control implies an extension of democratic principles from the field of government to the field of work.[10] Collective bargaining is a "persuasive process through which representatives of employer and employee attempt to reach a tenable agreement."[11] The hope is that the resolution of conflict "will

[10] Peter Henle, "A Union Viewpoint," *Labor Relations Policy in an Expanding Economy, The Annals* of the American Academy of Political and Social Science, Vol. 333, January, 1961, p. 7.
[11] William G. Caples, "A Management Viewpoint," *Ibid.,* p. 18.

come through reasoning and persuasion rather than through a test of economic strength."[12]

The term collective bargaining or the process through which collective agreement takes place in industry connotes effort to negotiate a contract with all industries employing members of the representing organization or union. This discussion of collective agreement in education includes both such action and the action that may involve merely the employing agency, its agents, and its employee groups without reference to an employee organization outside the school system.

Board Policy. A major step toward providing for joint agreement is for the board of education to set up in policy broad and general rules to govern the conditions under which school employees will work and to stipulate that the details pertaining to these conditions be worked out cooperatively by the administration and its executive family. It is assumed that most personnel problems can be worked out, without reference to the board of education, between the administration and other school employees.

Board policy may well empower the superintendent to negotiate and sign contracts with employee organizations within limits that are carefully defined so as not to threaten the public welfare and the official responsibility of the board of education.[13]

[12] David L. Cole, "Government in the Bargaining Process: The Role of Mediation," *Ibid.*, p. 49.

[13] These rules may follow those approved by President John F. Kennedy in accordance with the report of his task force on employee-management cooperation in the Federal service. This would mean that board policy might, for example, agree that:

1. Employees have the right to join employee organizations but not to strike.

2. Employees have the right to refuse to join employee organizations and that the school system will not tolerate either the union- or closed-shop.

3. Salaries and other conditions are fixed by Board policy, these are not subject to negotiation except as appeal is made to alter Board policy.

4. All agreements must be consistent with sound and long-term principles of school and public administration.

5. No union will be recognized that engages in corrupt practices or discriminates against members because of race, creed or color, or advocates the overthrow of Government.

6. Specific areas for consultation and collective negotiation include the work environment, supervisor-employee relations, work shifts and tours of duty, grievance procedures, career development policies, and the implementation of policies related to rates of pay and job classification.

The President's action of December 4, 1961, and the recommendations of the Task Force headed by Labor Secretary Arthur J. Goldberg are reported by Staff Reporter Carroll Kilpatrick in *The Washington Post and Times Herald*, December 5, 1961, pp. 1, 8.

Consultation. When the administration and other employees do not see eye to eye on some matter, consultation between them and possibly involving an employee organization serves to reduce or eliminate misunderstanding, clarify issues, and lay the foundation for a reasonable solution that is acceptable to all around.

Joint Committees or Councils. It is possible to meet many needs on a continuing basis so that no crisis of even a minor nature arises. This may be done through the establishment and use of joint councils that have the function of noting the problems in their embryonic stage so that they may be solved before they mature to critical proportions.

The role of the joint committee will most likely be advisory, alerting as needed and serving the function of preventing situations that would interfere with the effective operation of the schools.

Negotiation. When a difference exists, there is usually something to be said for each side of the controversy. Experience demonstrates that life often calls for a give and take that proves enlightening and makes consequences reasonably agreeable. Hence, the parties to a dispute enter into a conference with the purpose of exploring all the facets of the issue at stake and of finding common ground for immediate agreement and, in the remaining areas of conflict, acceptable compromises. This exploratory conferring in search of agreement is negotiation.

The product of negotiation may serve as an advisory instrument which, by reason of its impartiality and reasonableness, appeals to all parties to the issue—board of education, administration, employees, and/or employees' representative organization—and therefore elicits the support and action desired. Or, the product of negotiation may take the form of a written agreement which is in the nature of a contract.

Contractual Agreements. Within limits provided by the board of education, the administration may consummate contracts with the other school employees or their representative associations. Beyond the limits of administrative latitude, the contractual agreement may be entered upon between the board of education and its employees or their representatives subject to one limitation. The board may not enter into an agreement that would require it to surrender or permit to be circumvented, compromised, supplanted, or superseded the authority and power conferred upon it by the people and through law.

As a legislative body, the board of education may develop and adopt those policies, within its area of determination, which will make possible a contractual agreement. In the area outside its jurisdiction, the board of education would have to refer suppliants to the appropriate legislative (usually the state) body for its official consideration and action.

Conciliation. Sometimes feelings are so strong that there is no mood for negotiation. This calls for an initial effort toward conciliation. It is possible that one of the parties to the conflict will take action to win over the other, perhaps completely or to the point at which negotiation can take place. However, should both parties be intransigent, the offices of one who serves as conciliator may well be provided as an avenue for restoring the communication necessary to break the stalemate.

In practice the conciliator generally limits his activities to serving the conflicting parties as a go-between. He transmits points of view and overtures from each group to the other until a truce is called, negotiations are begun, or the attempt is considered a failure. In the last event a firmed up form of conciliation may be initiated under what is termed mediation.

Mediation. A mediator is a go-between. However, whereas in practice the conciliator usually restricts himself to so serving, the mediator goes one step farther. In dealing with the opposed factions, he gains a perspective that stimulates him to consider possible solutions. He interposes his ideas about how to resolve the dilemma in an active effort to promote and accelerate a reconcilement of the opponents to each other.

Arbitration. When conflict threatens the effective operation of the schools because of the uncompromising positions of the opposing groups, it may be necessary to break the deadlock through a final resort type of action, i.e., arbitration.

Arbitration is termed a final resort, with some negative connotation, because the issue is not resolved harmoniously and on the basis of reasonableness and understanding by the parties affected. Rather, it represents a giving up, an admission that reason cannot prevail. Then, since the deadlock must be broken in the interests of the school system and the conflicting parties, the issue is turned over to an arbiter.

An arbiter differs from a conciliator or mediator in that he assumes a judicial role. He examines the facts, conducts hearings, and when he believes he has the necessary perspective renders a decision. Although an arbiter (individual or group) is expected to render a decision, the parties to the controversy may or may not be bound thereby.

Arbitration is engaged in with the prior understanding as to what function the decision is to serve. If the function is to provide for an offsetting of biases by the neutral arbiter, the decision provides the foundation for the resumption of a reasonable attempt to move from a power struggle toward a joint effort to solve the problem that is at the root of the conflict. If the decision is intended to be binding upon the affected parties, each is left no alternative but to yield to the condition stipulated and to abide by the decision of an umpire-type arbiter.

The arbiter may be any person or group of persons stipulated by policy or law or agreed upon by the affected parties. Ordinarily a requisite for serving as an arbiter would be a general and comprehensive understanding of the problems of a school system. A neighboring school system, the state or national association representing school employees, the state department of public instruction, and a public or quasi-public university are potential resources from which to draw an arbiter or an arbitration committee.

Where the demand for arbitration services warrants it, the state department of public instruction, the university, and the school employee association would do well to make special provision on their respective staffs for someone who has the competency to serve as arbiter.

Cooling-off Period. At any stage of settling conflict it may be desirable to make some provision for a cooling-off period during which the status quo is maintained and preparations are made to engage in positive efforts to settle the problem. The heat of emotionalization is not conducive to the rational consideration by which issues can be analyzed and resolved.

Employee Organization. It has become obvious that the weakness of one agency does not enhance the strength of another. Rather, the board of education will find it advantageous to provide for and encourage a truly strong, voluntary employee organization which is independent of it. Such an organization tends to promote the feeling of solidarity and comradeship that is basic to employee group morale. The encouragement of such an organization generates confidence on the part of employees in the board of education.

The chief functions of the employee organization will be 1) serving the people of the school district through improvement of the school operation, 2) promoting the welfare of its membership in every way— e.g., economic, social, working conditions—consistent with advancing the education activity, and 3) supplying means and stimuli to help every member to become more proficient as a school employee.[14]

Communications. Many of the problems of school administration, school personnel administration, and employer-employee relations would be simplified if communications—vertically and laterally—were provided for and used.

It is easy to raise the question as to how to get the employees to cross the threshold when the administrator has sincerely set up and announced an "open door" policy. It is almost impossible to answer the question.

---

14 Arthur B. Moehlman and James A. van Zwoll, *School Public Relations* (New York, Appleton-Century-Crofts, 1957), pp. 130, 131.

Yet, it is important that every effort be exerted to make the open door policy work. It will work if confidence in the administration has been generated.

Confidence is the product of long-term and continuous effort on the part of the administrator and experience on the part of the employee group. There is no short-cut to a confidence build-up. The key to gaining confidence is a functioning system of communications.

Conclusion. Capitalization upon the competencies of school employees, decision making on the basis of the competencies required to do so, and the appeal to reason through the use of the instruments for collective agreement described in the foregoing pages can produce a responsible sort of collective agreement which will function as joint action or joint control. The result is expected to be decreased tension and increased effectiveness in school operation.

SUMMARY

A differentiation between private enterprise and the public school situation was noted as stemming to considerable degree from the profit motive in the one and the lack of it in the other. This difference was augmented by the lesser mobility, the specialized competency, and the dedication attributed to the majority of school employees.

The concern of the public in and its role relative to education were recognized. The concern is 1) the setting up of objectives, providing the basis for board of education action, and 2) appraisal. Concern as represented by these two activities is an area in which professional expertness or competency is not requisite.

Administration was regarded as an extension of the classroom activity, part of the unitary activity encompassing all employees of the board of education. Thus the superintendent is visualized as an employee of the board of education and allied to the other employees, professional and auxiliary, all functioning to carry into effect the policies of the board of education.

All personnel find the justification for their employment by the board of education in the specific competencies by which they are able to facilitate instruction. The recognition of and capitalization upon these competencies calls for a sort of joint action by which school operation may be expected to be improved.

Within the over-all organization problems arise between the employing agency and the employed, and also among the categories of the employees. These problems can conceivably be resolved to large extent, if not altogether, through collective agreement.

Collective agreement is a joint sort of action and results in a form of joint control of the school system; a joint control in which the public, the board of education, the administration, school employees, and an organization representing school employees may participate.

Collective agreement connotes less of a power struggle than is implied by "collective bargaining." Its instruments, however, are largely the same as those commonly identified with collective bargaining, i.e., 1) provision of enabling board policy, 2) consultation, 3) joint councils, 4) negotiation, 5) contracts, 6) conciliation, 7) mediation, 8) arbitration, 9) cooling-off period, 10) employee organization, and 11) communications.

It is concluded that an inclination toward joint action can be successfully implemented to decrease stresses and to promote the effective functioning of the school system.

SELECTED READINGS

DIMOCK, Marshall Edward and Gladys Ogden, and KOENIG, Louis W., *Public Administration* (New York, Holt, Rinehart, and Winston, 1958), Chapters 25, 26.

DUBIN, Robert, *Human Relations in Administration* (Englewood Cliffs, N.J., Prentice-Hall, Inc., 1951), pp. 312–318.

DURAND, Robert Y., *Business* (Englewood Cliffs, N.J., Prentice-Hall, Inc., 1958), Chapters 13, 14.

Labor Relations Policy in an Expanding Economy, The Annals (of the American Academy of Political and Social Science), Vol. 333, January, 1961, pp. 1–152.

Labor Study Group, *The Public Interest in National Labor Policy* (New York, Committee for Economic Development, 1962).

MERIAM, Lewis, *Public Personnel Problems* (Washington, D.C., The Brookings Institution, 1938), Chapter 10.

MOSHER, William E., and KINGSLEY, J. Donald, *Public Personnel Administration* (New York, Harper and Row, 1941), Chapter 25.

NIGRO, Felix A., *Public Administration Readings and Documents* (New York, Holt, Rinehart, and Winston, 1951), Chapter 7.

PRERAU, Sydney (Editor), *J. K. Lasser's Business Management Handbook* (New York, McGraw-Hill Book Company, Inc., 1960), pp. 352–359.

STAHL, O. Glenn, *Public Personnel Administration* (New York, Harper and Row, 1956), Chapter 12.

TEAD, Ordway, and METCALF, Henry C., *Personnel Administration* (New York, McGraw-Hill Book Company, Inc., 1933), Chapters 27–34.

WAITE, William W., *Personnel Administration* (New York, The Ronald Press Company, 1952), Chapters 22–25.

YODER, Dale, *Personnel Principles and Policies* (Englewood Cliffs, N.J., Prentice-Hall, Inc., 1959), Chapters 6–10.

.13.

The Principal and Supervisor

SCHOOL PERSONNEL administration is the complex of specific activities distinctly engaged in by school authorities and their agents to make pointed effort to secure the greatest possible worker effectiveness consistent with the objectives of the school system.

Personnel administration as an activity concerned with the functioning of the school system is the responsibility of the superintendent and, in the larger districts, the personnel division organized and staffed to provide him specialized assistance.

Even in the relatively centralized activities of many an industry, the personnel division is aided in its task by others throughout the plant, probably most of all by the foreman. The school system is organized generally to operate under conditions of considerable decentralization. Although the board of education offices are the administrative nerve and control center for the school system, the schools where the job of teaching and learning takes place are dispersed throughout school districts that encompass many square miles.[1]

Under conditions of decentralized operation, all the principles of personnel administration[2] by which the superintendent is governed apply also to the agent who functions for him in each school, i.e., the principal and the supervisor. As a matter of fact, the principal and supervisor are the ones who are sufficiently close to the educational opera-

[1] Areas of several hundred square miles per school district are common in states where the county is the school district.

[2] The reader is referred to the full statement of these principles as they appear in Chapter 1. Consideration of each for its specific implications for principals and supervisors should prove rewarding.

tion to engage in and maintain the personal kind of relations that are necessary to make the principles operative.

Books have been written about each, the principal and the supervisor. In this chapter these two functionaries are discussed with the purpose of noting chiefly and particularly their roles in school personnel administration.

THE PRINCIPAL

The principal is to the individual school what the superintendent is to the school system. Just as in the small school system the superintendent has little or no staff, the principal of the small school is likely to have little more than clerical help, and that on a part-time basis. With an increase in the size of the school district, the superintendent gains assistants in his administrative family; so also in the large school, the principal is aided by vice- and assistant-principals, assistants to the principal, coordinators, supervisors assigned to the school, and department heads, as well as a full-time clerical staff.

Among many statements regarding the job of the principal, there is great stress upon the decentralization that accords to the classroom teacher "the actual and psychological importance essential to a truly functional teaching institution."[3] The principal is regarded as "the chief executive officer of the faculty, . . ."[4] and "not only an office manager but also an educational statesman."[5]

It has become common to designate leadership as the primary function of the principal. This concept of the role of the principal has developed progressively since 1918.[6] The consensus about and emphasis upon the leadership role, together with a zealousness to apply the leadership label, are relatively new—a product of the late 1950's and early to mid-1960's. In any event, the focussing of attention upon the principal's leadership role does highlight the personnel administration facet of individual school administration.

Current literature dealing with the elementary and secondary school principalships reveals an appreciation of a number of personnel administration factors that are considered the concern of the principal. Outstanding among these is the one that asserts that it is a major function

[3] Arthur B. Moehlman, *School Administration* (Boston, Houghton Mifflin Company, 1940 (p. 539) or 1951 (p. 275). Note also the specific plans outlined for developing and assuring faculty responsibility in the accompanying pages.

[4] Edgar L. Morphet, Roe L. Johns, and Theodore L. Reller, *Educational Administration* (Englewood Cliffs, N.J., Prentice-Hall, Inc., 1959), p. 288.

[5] Will French, J. Dan Hull, and B. L. Dodds, *American High School Administration* (New York, Holt, Rinehart, and Winston, 1957), p. 120.

[6] Arthur B. Moehlman, *School Administration* (Boston, Houghton Mifflin Company, 1940), p. 530.

of the principal to provide for 1) the identification of the potentialities of the personnel in his school and 2) the outlets, opportunities, and conditions by which the educational operation may capitalize upon or profit from the various talents of the respective teaching and nonteaching employees.

Other personnel factors that appear regularly in the literature and are important because of their implications for the school operation have to large extent been reviewed in detail in the preceding chapters in terms of the general problems and functioning of personnel administration. These will be considered briefly in the context of the principal as personnel administrator on the local scene.

Staff Potential

Staff potential sets the ceiling of effectiveness that a school may reach. Therefore the discovery of potential, provision for growth and progress, establishment of a system of communication, and other influences having bearing upon potential; all merit consideration.

Discovery. The principal may try and even be moderately successful in personally discovering and identifying the potential of employees in his school. However, the chances of doing a better job of bringing to light the particular talents of each employee are generally improved when there are numerous opportunities to observe the employee under different circumstances and to have him express himself 1) in conference and discussion, 2) through experimentation and innovation, and 3) by the assumption of responsibilities that are in accord with his ability, interest, willingness, and the authority delegated for the occasion.

Growth and Progress. Sometimes growth and progress are the products of group effort. At other times the group activity supplies a stimulus to further individual exploration and effort. It is also possible that an individual will work at his best if he is free to exercise his particular genius independently of the group. Limiting opportunities for advancement of the educational process to group effort is indefensible. The principal who regards function rather than form will avoid giving his blessing directly or by implication to either, group or individual effort, at the expense of the other; he will keep clear for himself and his coworkers in the school that the focal point is an ever more effective program of instruction.

Communication. Whether advances come from the group or the individual, it is necessary that there be a system of communication which will let others understand and make the most of new ideas and techniques.

The principal is the agent through whose endeavors provision is made to keep others on the staff abreast of developments.

Subsidiary Influences. Staff potential is influenced by a number of subsidiary factors, some very definitely outside the immediate control of the principal, others as decidedly subject to his control, and then a number which are only partially controllable by the principal.

Not Subject to Principal's Control. In general salaries conform to a schedule that is set up in and administered from the central office. To the extent that such salary is the source of misunderstanding and discontent, the principal has a responsibility for clarifying matters with the expectation that as understanding is promoted a major step will have been taken toward removing the basis for discontent. Of course there are questions of salary that are subject to the principal's control. In some instances a salary increment may be withheld upon the recommendation of the principal. In this case the principal is well advised to have the school employee cognizant of his action and the basis therefor, and, if possible, acquiescent thereto.

Tenure is a matter of vital concern to every school employee. This again is a matter set by board of education policy, probably long before many a current employee has been hired. Again, it is the responsibility of the principal, as the central administration's administrative agent on the spot, to provide for understanding on the part of every employee. In this instance too, should tenure status be threatened by some action of the principal, he owes it to the employee concerned to let him know the circumstances and the steps that may be effective to remove the threat.

To some extent school program and organization are determined by board of education policy. To the extent that such determination might be improved through ideas from the front-line experience of employees in the respective schools, the principal has the opportunity and the obligation to promote localized activity, call the attention of the superintendent of schools to ideas and practices in the field, and secure for school employees both administrative and board of education recognition of their place in policy making.

Subject to Principal's Control. The principal has theoretical and functional control of his school staff. This begins with his insistence upon the right of participating with the central office administration in the selection of employees for his school, and continues with the approval of appointment to a position in that school. Next it is the obligation of the principal to assign the new employee to the specific kind of work for which he has competency and was employed.

To the extent that an employee needs help in becoming oriented to his situation—a continuing and never ending process—it is primarily the responsibility of the principal to take the measures necessary to generate the atmosphere of general helpfulness to one another that is essential to becoming and remaining effective in the constantly evolving school situation.

Among the means to get and keep employees oriented to the school operation is an on-going program for involving personnel in accord with their ability, interest, and willingness in policy making, program development, organizational change, and evaluation in each of these areas. This involvement is possible on the individual school level within the framework of central policy and administration and requires only the inclination of the principal to work in this way to become truly effective.

Aside from the evaluation of the total school operation, employees may well be involved in self-evaluation, not an evaluation for a report to the principal but rather a thoroughgoing introspective self-appraisal with the purpose of assessing personal strength and weakness in order to capitalize as much as possible on the former and to offset as much as possible the latter through corrective effort.

In addition to self-evaluation for purposes of improvement, administrative appraisal may be warranted by symptoms for which the administrator must be on the alert. From the point of view of sound personnel administration, an employee hired by way of the rigorous process characteristic of good personnel administration practice ought generally to be salvable to the advantage of the school system if initial efforts at placing him in accord with his qualifications are not productive of the desired results.

The principal of the school generally has the first opportunity to note whether an employee shows promise on the job. He may discuss with the director of school personnel those who fail to come up to expectation. Between the director of personnel and the principal, a transfer within the school or from the school to another spot within the school system may be decided upon and then discussed with the employee. The principal who understands this way of operation will be careful not to threaten to fire an employee or recommend that he be dismissed from school employment.

When an employee is assigned to a school, the principal does well if he sets up for him, as for each employee in the school, a personnel folder containing as complete information about him as possible. This record will stand him in good stead when problems arise. Understanding of the problem and the basis for solving it may be provided in some facet of the employee's background. This record should be supplemented from time to time with pertinent information which will provide the foundation for favorable or adverse recommendations or actions by the principal.

The matter of status in the community or neighborhood served by the school is important to every school employee. Status for school employees begins with the attitude of the principal to them. They have status immediately to the extent that they are regarded as individuals of worth. There is something contagious about such status. Recognition by one generates recognition by others. Particularly teachers, among school employees, seem to require reenforcement of their status. This they should get initially from the principal and from each other. Next it will be forthcoming from their nonteaching colleagues, especially if the recognition of individual worth is extended to them by the teaching personnel. It is only a step further, perhaps by way of the P.T.A., to gain for school employees the recognition of the people whose children attend the school.

One way in which the principal can command for school employees the esteem they value is to provide them warranted support every chance he gets, regardless of who or what else may be involved or what the expedient action at the time may be.

Like the superintendent, principals are often invited to be speakers for special groups and on special occasions. The implication seems to be that if one gets the superintendent or the principal to serve as speaker, competency to deal with the topic assigned is assured. Of course, as a matter of fact, many a time greater competency to deal with some specialized topic might be found among selected teachers. It is for this reason, as well as to accord the teacher the status to which he is entitled, that it is held that:[7]

One of the best ways of increasing popular confidence in the teaching profession is to bring both teachers and principals forward so that their abilities may be displayed through speaking and other personal demonstrations. . . . Focussing the spotlight on other school personnel not only relieves the already burdened superintendent (or principal); it also signifies to the community that their educational plan rests on the cooperative efforts of many persons, each an able and accomplished individual in his own area of operation. Bringing forward and building up the teaching personnel in terms of their competencies are a powerful means for creating within the community the greater respect and confidence due the profession.

This same means for gaining warranted respect for and confidence in the teaching profession may be utilized for other school employees, e.g., the school doctor, dentist, nurse, counselling personnel, nutritionist, as they are utilized in accordance with the occasion and their talents therefor. School employees can hardly expect greater esteem outside the school than they enjoy inside it. The place to begin is to have proper self-esteem and esteem for fellow-workers within the institution.

Every administrator is concerned to some degree with the main-

[7] Arthur B. Moehlman and James A. van Zwoll, *School Public Relations* (New York, Appleton-Century-Crofts, 1957), p. 266, part in parenthesis added.

tenance and improvement of employee competencies. As change takes place, knowledge is expanded, and innovation takes place, school personnel can maintain and extend their competency only as they keep abreast of developments in theory, substantiation of evidence, and new tools or instruments and techniques for doing their jobs. When this process of keeping abreast takes place on the job or as a concurrent activity, it is referred to as inservice training.

Inservice training has been discussed [8] in terms of informal and formal activities. The informal are generally reflective of personal interest, are hard to evaluate, and could easily be among the most important of inservice growth activities. To stimulate informal inservice training effectively ought to be the objective of every school administrator. This he may do through the provision of a professional library in the faculty room and through the encouragement of discussion when the opportunity presents itself. The nonstructured luncheon group, ready to explore anything that strikes its fancy at the moment, provides a too little-used opportunity for principal and teacher to establish rapport regarding some issue.

Formal inservice training activities within the school system are probably necessary. The workshop as a medium of great freedom 1) for expression and 2) from pressure offers an excellent opportunity for personnel to become conversant with a variety of points of view. This is probably its great strength. The establishment of a formalized program of inservice training for teachers is often rather sterile, doing more for the self-concept of the one administering it and for the personal aggrandizement of those employed in it than it does for those who are supposed to benefit from it.

The principal who finds it necessary to engage in a formalized program of inservice training has the primary responsibility to make certain that the program is dynamic, geared to and stimulative of interest, responsive to a feeling of need, as free as possible of barren formality (form without substance), and able to withstand the test of being noncoercive (truly voluntary) without prejudice to those who do not participate.

As a matter of fact, much that has preceded this section, dealing with the various activities in which to involve personnel and the means for gaining for them the status they are due, provides an active program in which inservice training and growth take place as byproducts of working for other objectives all of which are pointed toward making instruction more effective.

Freedom for the individual is implied in keeping coerciveness in personnel relations to a minimum. Some people may require at times the assurance that what they are doing is in accord with the ideas of the principal. Perhaps during a formative period of maturation these indi-

[8] See Chapter 5.

viduals need someone upon whom to lean heavily and to prevent them from feeling lost, without chart or compass. Eventually, it is to be hoped, they will be helped to develop the self-confidence, the sense of direction, and the personal and individual responsibility that are the marks of the professional. Some have the competence and confidence to be self-directive practically from their first day on the job. The principal has the responsibility to distinguish between these two types of personnel and to give the former a needed helping hand and the latter full freedom to do his work without administrative harassment, interference, or interruption.

Ideas, improvement, and growth are the logical concomitants to individual freedom. They are inhibited by unnecessary restraints.

Partially Subject to Control by the Principal. At times the central school administration is adversely criticized by the personnel in a school. Such criticism may be warranted in which case control by the principal is very limited indeed. He may be able to do little more than transmit the criticism to the central administration in the hope that an enlightened administration would want to be informed so that it could take such measures as seemed warranted. However, when the criticism is unwarranted the principal may well examine his own actions to discover whether he has made the central administration the remote scapegoat for his own actions or whether there is some misconception about the position of the central administration. In either case the principal has the task of rectifying the situation; in the first instance by assuming responsibility for his own actions and in the second by advancing the legitimate case for the central administration so that there will be no further misunderstanding.

The work-load of school personnel is to some extent determined by the number of employees allowed for a school of a certain size. The question of work-load is not a simple one. Its complexities have been explored earlier.[9] The total work-load-to-employee ratio is presumably determined at the central office. If the number of employees is below necessity, it is the duty of the principal to make a case for increased staffing for consideration by the administration and the board of education or for the elimination of the less important tasks for the time being. However, within his total work-load-to-employee ratio, the principal has latitude to apportion work. He is constantly faced with the question as to whether he is dealing with the work-load problem fairly or whether he is playing favorites with some at the expense of others. Probably most important is the confidence of the school employees in the principal. If the employees have confidence in the principal, they will have that important feeling that he is being as fair as it is possible to be.

Crowdedness is a complaint heard from teachers. Upon hearing that a situation is crowded, the principal may first check to discover whether

[9] See Chapter 11.

space available is utilized in the most defensible manner. Assigning large classes to large rooms and small ones to small rooms may in some instances eliminate complaints of overcrowdedness. In other instances, it may be necessary to make a careful analysis of available space and the use to which it is put. If a utilization study reveals underutilization of space, the principal may well re-examine the school schedule to discover whether it is possible to reschedule classes and activities to alleviate the feeling of overcrowdedness through a more efficient use of available space.

If available space is inadequate, the principal is faced with the problem of presenting the shortage to the central administration together with suggestions and recommendations as to how to meet the problem. The suggestion could be that adjustments be made internally for the current year and that an expansion of the building be projected for the following year; it might be recommended that pupils be transported to a neighboring school that has space to spare; or it might be recommended that temporary or mobile facilities be provided to provide the needed space immediately.

THE SUPERVISOR

In industry the supervisor is often referred to as a key individual and his function as one of the most important in improving productivity. In order to avoid confusion, it is necessary that school personnel realize that the supervision generally spoken of for schools is very different from the supervision spoken of for industry. Whereas school supervision is generally thought of as a staff, i.e., advisory and noncoercive activity, industrial supervision has reference to individuals

having authority . . . to hire, transfer, suspend, layoff, recall, promote, discharge, assign, reward, or discipline other employees, or responsibility to direct them, or to adjust their grievances, or effectively to recommend such action, if in connection with the foregoing the exercise of such authority . . . requires the use of independent judgment.[10]

In industry the job of supervisor is obviously identified with all levels of administration. One of the most important supervisors, because he is so close to the worker, is the foreman. If there is an analogy between industry and education, the foreman would be more like the school principal than the school supervisor. In fact, the administrative-supervisory relationship of the principal to the nonprofessional workers is indistinguishable from that of the foreman in industry.[11]

In industry a distinction may be and often is made between a job

10 *U.S. Statutes at Large* (1947), Vol. 61, Part 1 (Washington, D.C., U.S. Government Printing Office, 1948), pp. 136–138.

11 William H. Roe, *School Business Management* (New York, McGraw-Hill Book Company, Inc., 1961), pp. 47–52.

in which the major characteristic is the responsibility that it entails as contrasted to a job in which one just does work assigned,[12] work that is often far removed from the employee's ability to identify himself significantly with the end-product. The foreman supervisor's job carries with it responsibility for an efficient operation whereas the workers in his department simply do their work-tasks. Here again is seen the inapplicability of the industrial concept to the school operation. It is true that the principal, not the supervisor, has over-all responsibility for the effective operation of the school. However, the nature of the teacher's work is identical to that of the principal except that the scope of his responsibility is centered within the classroom rather than in the school premises.

As a member of a profession, the teacher is not just another worker doing a narrowly specialized task; he is a responsible individual who must have perspective with reference to the implications of his work for the ultimate behavior of his pupils within society. The teacher is continuously involved in and reminded of the end-product of his efforts. The teacher must have freedom and latitude to make independent decisions within the classroom, without reference to the principal's office, to gear instructional activities to the ability and achievement levels of those in the class.

With responsibility for the over-all school operation allocated to the principal, the responsibility of the supervisor must logically be well defined and carefully limited. Failure to do so results, as does happen in some schools, in teacher confusion and frustration as to which of two masters to serve, and when.

The limitation upon and definition of the function of the supervisor has moved progressively during the period of the late 1920's in the direction of having him serve as confidante, friend, and advisor to the teacher. Earlier aspects of inspection, routine and surprise, formal visitations, directives intended to produce conformity, coerciveness, and implied or actual threat have, since the early 1930's, gradually given way to the idea that the objective of the supervisor is to help the teacher in order that instruction might be improved. It has come to be recognized that help can be given most effectively when the teacher realizes that he needs it and that there is one to whom he can turn without fear of adverse consequences. Thus, the role of the supervisor has come to be largely that of consultant; one who considers with the teacher both the problem and the possible ways of meeting it.

Mutual confidence between the teacher and the supervisor is at the heart of a promising professional relationship. It is easier to speak of developing confidence than to do so. The development of confidence grows

[12] Charles R. Allen, *The Foreman and His Job* (Philadelphia, 1922), p. 11.

out of experience, is a never ending task, and is subject to sharp reverses upon slight provocation until confidence has been proved over a long period of time and under trying circumstances. Today, there is still considerable suspicion engendered by a past or passing era in supervision and the hold-overs in administration and supervision who adhere to the past. However, there are now many signs indicating that supervision is finding its place and that the new supervisors are a new professional breed.

The young man who was present at all faculty meetings and mixed freely with teachers on numerous occasions in one of the larger Montgomery County, Maryland, schools was asked after several weeks how it was possible for him to spend as much time as he seemed to spend in the school's faculty room. He replied that he was a supervisor attached to the school.

It developed that during those initial several weeks he had visited no rooms, called no teachers in for conference, and issued no directives. Rather he had become acquainted with teachers and had casually discussed with them their problems in the informality of the faculty room during such hours as teachers were there. He had been working on the development of the personal relationships that are basic to the confidence necessary for professional relationships. He now let it be known that he was available for consultation and was willing, if the teacher desired it, to visit classrooms.

In this discussion of the supervisor there is an almost imperceptible undercurrent that has very real implications for the climate of supervision and its potential effectiveness. If the supervisor is to work with the teacher on a voluntary and invitational, noncoercive, helpful basis in an aura of mutual confidence, then there can be no requirement that a supervisor participates in a rating that has implications for teacher tenure, promotion or transfer, or salary.

Evaluation

A supervisor cannot do his work without evaluating teaching methods and effectiveness. However, there is a great difference between evaluation done in order to determine a teacher's employment and pay status and evaluation done in order to help a teacher overcome difficulties.

Employment and Pay Status. As long as there is the thought that employment and pay status may be adversely affected by the action of the supervisor, the teacher may be expected to invite the supervisor to visit classes during those periods when there are no problems and no improvement can be expected from the visit. In fact, the entire period may be staged with the children cautioned to be on their best behavior at least for that period. The period or class for which the teacher needs help will be kept secret. Improvement in the problem situation, in teacher growth, and in supervisory effectiveness will be delayed unnecessarily as the teacher continues to work on his own problems by trial and error or resort to fellow teachers while the supervisor remains in ignorance of the problem situation.

Improvement. Once convinced that he can call upon the supervisor for counsel and aid in meeting problems without fear of adverse consequences, the teacher will generally avoid asking the supervisor to visit the classroom during periods which present no problems. Instead, he will confide in the supervisor about problems that he has tried but failed to solve to his satisfaction. The class or period in which these problems arise is the one he will invite the supervisor to observe and consult on. As a result, the teacher is encouraged under such circumstances to identify and admit problems because they can then be attacked systematically, with supervisory assistance, until resolved. Not only is the problem situation improved, but also the teacher and probably the supervisor have also added to their resources for meeting problems in the future.

Personnel Implications

If the necessary climate for effective supervision for improvement requires the supervisor to treat teacher problems confidentially, then how can personnel administration benefit from the teacher-supervisor relationships?

Most importantly, the supervisor may make excellent use of his experiences with teachers to call to the attention of the administration—including the personnel division—those matters in the way of problems, issues, grievances, injustices, and needed competencies of which they must be informed in order to take the necessary administrative action to improve the working situation. This may be done without betraying confidences as long as no individual is identified in fact or by implication.

In some instances, in order, for example, to correct an injustice, the supervisor may counsel the teacher to make his case known to the administration in order that proper action may ensue. In this case he may serve as intermediary to support the teacher and give him an ally before the administration. Taking action with the knowledge and consent of the teacher will not be a violation of a confidence. It is then up to the administration to demonstrate its good faith by dealing justly, and without defensiveness for having a matter of injustice, oversight, or grievance laid at its door.

The Personnel Record. When issues and problems have been resolved and the teacher has gained in experience, insight, and resourcefulness, the supervisor may well be held responsible for entering upon the teacher's personnel record a statement reflecting the growth that has taken place. It is advisable for the supervisor to initiate such an entry only when it is favorable. This will further encourage teachers to call upon the supervisor in time of need.

No doubt there will be times when supervisory efforts are not successful in solving problems or helping teachers to do so. Under these circumstances, the role of the supervisor must nevertheless be a strictly positive one. He must exert every effort to be helpful and failure to make progress must be kept confidential between him and the teacher. No negative report must be initiated by or subscribed to by the supervisor as long as the teacher is in the school employ. Whether the supervisor should be required to make a warranted negative report after the teacher has been dismissed from service is open to some debate. It would seem preferable if even this were neither required nor considered desirable.

Dismissal of Teachers. Despite the best efforts of the administrator, supervisors, fellow teachers, and himself, a teacher on occasion has simply gotten into the wrong occupation. This is not always easy to admit and for some it may be impossible to do so. In this situation, the school must nevertheless be protected from the ineffective teacher's threat to instruction.

In practice, it is not uncommon to find that the principal and supervisor move from an initial position of collaboration to help the teacher to a secondary position—when their efforts are unproductive of improvement—of collaboration to make a case against the teacher. In this instance the supervisor has left the role of helpfulness and alliance with the teacher to one of developing and prosecuting a case against the teacher. The supervisor has become a threat to rather than a trusted friend of the teacher. This may not matter greatly to the teacher who is beyond hope, except that psychologically he has lost one more source of support. What does matter greatly is that such action by the supervisor will affect grievously the confidence he can engender among the remaining teachers who need help but are unwilling to take a chance on the helper turning into an adversary.

The supervisor's position will be strengthened if he can be kept completely free from the dismissal action to which the principal will then have to address himself through his own efforts and the assistance of others who are not in the vulnerable position of having their major function negated by acts that make the teacher feel threatened.

In all of this, the informed educator will see an analogy between the evolving teacher-supervisor relationships and the developments in pupil-counsellor relationships. In both instances the relationships began with disciplinary overtones and in both it has been found that effective functioning for improvment on the part of the teacher on the one hand and the pupil on the other required the elimination of these overtones and the substitution of clinical type diagnosis and treatment in place of disciplinary threat or action. Both supervisor and counsellor are clinicians, not disciplinarians.

Objectives of Supervision

The major objective of supervision is to provide needed assistance to teachers. This has been amply indicated in the foregoing passages. There are two major areas in which the objective of helpfulness find their expression, that of the novices to teaching and that of the experienced teacher. In addition, there is an objective upon which the administrator and the supervisor ought to keep their focus, i.e., the reduction to a minimum of the supervisory activity.

Novices. Those who are new to teaching and those who are new to the school or school system may find their adaptation to their new circumstances eased and the period thereof shortened as a result of help given to them during their first few weeks or months in their new situation.

Although assistance in adaptation and orientation is the professional responsibility of all employees to each other, their preoccupation with their own duties and problems limits the amount of time and effort they can contribute. The supervisor is therefore a logical supplementary agent to provide needed assistance.

However, provided the personnel procedure for procuring personnel has been what it ought to be, it may be expected that the new employees are basically people who have the necessary qualifications for the job to which they are assigned. In that event, it may also be expected that the help they are getting will enable them relatively soon to help themselves and to require supervisory assistance with decreasing frequency.

Experienced Personnel. Without a doubt the supervisor has been employed as an inservice training agent whose employment is considered necessary to offset the incompetency of teachers who were employed although their qualifications were below par. The supervisor was then expected to help these teachers come up to par.

In this instance too, it may be expected that if the experienced teachers who lacked some qualification for the job to which they were assigned are helped to develop the necessary competencies, their need for supervisory assistance will become rare.

It may be assumed that any personnel, new or experienced, may at some time be confronted by a need for help to meet some urgent and unusual problem that is beyond his immediate experience. Supervisory, i.e., consultative and advisory, service for such occasions should always be available from some source within the school or school system.

Reduction of Supervision. In the case of both neophytes and experienced teachers who lack some qualification, the objective of the supervisor is to help teachers develop the ability to help themselves. To the extent that the personnel division improves its total personnel procurement and assignment procedure and the supervisor succeeds in getting people to help themselves, the supervisor will in a way be working himself out of a job. This will be not quite true for there will probably always be need for some supervisors.

It is quite conceivable that the corps of supervisors for the future need not be nearly as large as it is today, that the major share of supervisor time will be apportioned to new teachers, that the consultative services will decrease in demand because of the increase in teacher competency, and that such supervisors as are needed will find it increasingly necessary to address themselves to becoming resource people with respect to innovations that appear on the educational frontiers—and even this last may not be so compelling a factor as it may now seem if professionalism produces the interest which stimulates teachers to keep abreast of developments.

If supervisors now on the job adopt the professional attitude that will cut down to a minimum the number of supervisory jobs for the future, they can provide for the time being a very much needed service without fear that their own jobs will be jeopardized. To the extent that they are successful in decreasing the need for continued supervision, natural attrition by way of transfers, retirements, separations, and deaths will deplete numbers sufficiently and will no doubt require the training of some replacements on a continuing basis.

MORALE

Intangible and elusive, yet obtruding itself as real and of major importance, morale has been discussed at some length.[13] The discussion of the principal and the supervisor in their impact upon the implications of their activities for personnel administration is replete with overtones suggestive of morale implications.

The perspective that the principal and supervisor have with reference to their respective jobs, their understanding of their functions, the extent to which the conditions under which they are permitted to operate are favorable, and what they do and how under this complex of circumstances will unquestionably influence the self-confidence, personal and group discipline, and contentment that spell employee morale.

[13] See Chapter 10.

SUMMARY

The principal in particular and the supervisor in part are reminded that their functions are basically like those of the superintendent. The major difference lies in scope rather than essence. Therefore, especially in the area of personnel administration, all principles developed with reference to the superintendent's office apply also to the principal and supervisor. Each is enjoined to apply these principles to the solution of personnel problems.

The evolution of the principalship has led from autocratic to democratic concepts of administration in which the leadership function has come progressively into its own since 1918.

As a leader and with respect to personnel administration in his school, the principal faces problems of identifying, providing outlets for, and exploiting means for discovering the potentialities of his staff. He is concerned with stimulating growth through individual and group effort and providing for the sharing of ideas and techniques.

On occasion the principal is confronted by questions of:

salary	education program
tenure	school organization
control of staff via	personnel record keeping
selection	employee status
appointment	employee competency
assignment	individual freedom
orientation	criticism of the administration
involvement	work load
evaluation	physical working conditions

Supervision in industry was contrasted to that of the schools as was the industrial worker to the classroom teacher. The contrast, together with recognition of the principal's responsibility, laid the foundation for limiting and defining the function of the supervisor relative to issues of school personnel administration.

The role of supervisor was seen as a constructive, consultative, and helpful one which is operable only on a basis of mutual confidence and freedom from suspicion. Supervisory evaluation was considered in terms of its use with respect to employment and pay status and as an instrumentality for improvement.

The confidential nature of the professional teacher-supervisor relationship was stressed as was the need for the supervisor to be kept free from activities pertaining to employee dismissal.

Supervision was seen as meaningful for novices, the unqualified, contingencies, and for decreasing the need for supervisors. Decreases were envisioned as not jeopardizing anyone holding a supervisory job because progress in this direction would be accompanied by routine attrition.

All of the professional activities of the principal and supervisor discussed were seen as having implications for morale among school employees.

SELECTED READINGS

Austin, David B., French, Will, and Hull, J. Dan, *American High School Administration* (New York, Holt, Rinehart and Winston, Inc., 1958), Chapter 6.

Burr, James B., Coffield, William H., Jenson, Theodore J., and Neagley, Ross L., *Elementary School Administration* (Boston, Allyn and Bacon, Inc., 1963), Chapters 1, 2, 5, 8–12, and 14.

Burton, William H., and Brueckner, Leo J., *Supervision* (New York, Appleton-Century-Crofts, 1955), Chapters 1, 4, 6, 7, 15, 18.

Corbally, John E., Jenson, T. J., and Staub, W. Frederick, *Educational Administration: The Secondary School* (Boston, Allyn and Bacon, 1961), Chapters 3, 6.

Dimock, Marshall Edward and Gladys Ogden, and Koenig, Louis W., *Public Administration* (New York, Holt, Rinehart and Winston, 1958), Chapters 24, 26, 27.

Durand, Robert Y., *Business: Its Organization, Management and Responsibilities* (Englewood Cliffs, N.J., Prentice-Hall, Inc., 1958), Chapters 5, 9.

Elsbree, Willard S., and McNally, Harold J., *Elementary School Administration and Supervision* (New York, American Book Company, 1951), Chapters 2, 7, 26–29.

Gwynn, J. Minor, *Theory and Practice of Supervision* (New York, Dodd, Mead & Company, Inc., 1960), Chapters 1, 2.

Hansford, Byron W., *Guidebook for School Principals* (New York, The Ronald Press Company, 1961), Parts I, II.

Jacobson, Paul B., Reavis, William C., and Logsdon, James D., *The Effective School Principal* (Englewood Cliffs, N.J., Prentice-Hall, Inc., 1963), Chapters 1, 2, 5, 16, 20, 22.

Morphet, Edgar L., Johns, Roe, L., and Reller, Theodore L., *Educational Administration* (Englewood Cliffs, N.J., Prentice-Hall, Inc., 1959), Chapters 4, 13, 16.

Spain, Charles R., Drummond, Harold D., and Goodlad, John I., *Educational Leadership and the Elementary School Principal* (New York, Holt, Rinehart, and Winston, 1956), Chapters 1, 4–6, 13.

Yoder, Dale, *Personnel Principles and Policies* (Englewood Cliffs, N.J., Prentice-Hall, Inc., 1959), Chapters 18, 19.

.14.

Merit Rating and Pay

A MUCH DISCUSSED topic and one that has cyclical ups and downs and whose shadow is ever present, the merit rating issue cannot be summarily dismissed any more than it can be resolved simply by endorsing a merit system.

THE NEED FOR DEFINITION

A first consideration is getting those who are concerned with the issue of merit rating to mean the same thing. Support of or opposition to merit considerations without understanding and agreement as to what is meant by them means little more than that a label, merit, appeals to some and revolts others. The personal reaction is in terms of the connotation that merit has for the individual. It is quite possible that agreement is possible or disagreement either less sharp than it is made to seem or unnecessary.

To some merit connotes a measure of effectiveness that is to be gauged and recognized; to others it is analogous to or identified with a civil service sort of classification system; and to still others it represents constancy on the job, seniority, with career status and longevity pay implications.

The three concepts mentioned do not have to be mutually exclusive of each other. Throughout the various connotations of merit there runs a common thread. The first emphasizes effectiveness on the job as something to be measured and rewarded. The second has its basis in the assumption that effectiveness is predicated upon a classification system in which employment results from the establishment of the qualifications that are requisite to effectiveness. And, the third has been supported on the basis of the proposition that experience is the best teacher. Therefore, effectiveness improves with experience; hence career recognition and an automatic pay schedule geared to length of service. All three of the approaches to merit rating and pay truly relate to effectiveness, i.e., educational productivity on the job.

It may be stipulated that the concern of educators, as well as that of the general public, has centered on the question of employee effectiveness. This concern has been expressed by attempts to establish qualification requirements for employment, to provide bases for recognizing and rewarding effectiveness by measurement and rating techniques, and to encourage the improvement that comes from experience by career recognition and longevity or automatic pay increments.

On the whole, the question of merit—as it deals with the qualifications of the worker for the job he is employed to do or with job tenure, i.e., making a career of his job—is virtually noncontroversial. Employee qualification and stability are generally supported as desirable attributes to the functioning of the organization, in this instance the school system.

What is controversial is the concept of a merit system in which ranking or the relative rating of employees takes place. It is this concept which rouses a furor of controversy and to which major attention is given in this chapter.

The Definition

Merit rating is the measurement of educational productivity or effectiveness through which employees are ranked. Ranking establishes relative merit, i.e., one's merit or level of effectiveness in relationship to or comparison with that of those who are more, less, or equally productive. Merit pay is the rewarding of employees in accord with their places along the scale of educational productivity or effectiveness. This is the concept of merit rating and pay that incites heated controversy and that must be scrutinized with reflective thoughtfulness.

PRINCIPLES

In one way or another each of the principles of personnel administration apply to the issue of merit rating and pay. However six have been selected for their particular application.[1] These are presented together with a brief statement to illustrate the pertinence of the principle to the merit question.

The Best Education

The people who have instituted the schools and all employees within the school system have the same basic interest . . . the provision of the best educa-

[1] See Chapter 1, particularly principles 3, 4, 7–9, and 11.

tion possible, consistent with the clearness of the people's mandate and the means made available for doing the job.

There is no doubt that educational productivity on the part of school employees varies and that one way to assure a high level of educational productivity is to make certain that the means, personnel in this instance, are of the quality or qualification needed. The possibility of realizing a superior educational activity is in part proportionate to the competency of school personnel. There is here an implication that merit may, at least in part, be related to qualification and that qualification must be bought at a price. Among the means for providing the best education is the money with which to secure top personnel and with which to supply and equip them so that they can work at a high efficiency level.

Selection and Coordination

Maximum effectiveness . . . requires the best possible selection and coodination of all elements. . . . It is the job of personnel administration to assure the optimum in the selection, assignment in terms of job, physical placement, and equipment of personnel.

A first step toward establishing the high level of competency, without which high educational productivity is impossible, is the selection of personnel on the basis of actual needs and carefully developed job descriptions and specifications. This is an activity that deserves much more attention than it has received in even the best-organized school districts.

A second step is to coordinate the well-selected personnel with the job and working conditions that will give them the opportunity to be effective. Excellent selection of personnel can be largely negated by poor job or work-place assignment or inadequate material for doing the job. In many an instance a low level of educational productivity is the result of handicaps imposed by the administration or, conversely, the key to improved educational productivity is an enlightened and functioning school personnel administration.

The measure of school functioning depends to large extent on how well the job of staffing the school and of coordinating personnel, job, and working conditions has been done.[2]

Variability and Conformity

The human factor is a variable. The variability is potentially an asset. It is also the cause for many of the most complex and perplexing problems in personnel administration. Temptations to make concessions to the administrative

[2] See also Chapters 6 and 7.

expediency of promoting conformity must be shunned in favor of recognizing and promoting the unique individuality and consequent possible personal development of each within the school system.

In both the professional and nonprofessional facets of school operation there is possibility for latitude, for differences in ideas to operate, and for individual experimentation with variants in practice and consequent preparation of the way for innovation. Latitude is necessary to create the climate for progress at the level of each job and supplements, without in any way impairing, the possibility of making progress through administrative leadership or even fiat. In fact, the provision of latitude for individual variation is an act of administrative leadership.

The encouragement of individual initiative and variation, together with a premium on ideas and careful experimentation as the forerunners to improved practice, potentially raises the ceiling on individual and school functioning.

Morale

The most important single factor in getting the best that an employee has to offer is how he feels about his work, his associates on the job, and the school system in which he is employed.

The importance that the school administration attaches to each job is made manifest by its care in selecting personnel and coordinating all matters pertaining to them. Careful selection and coordination set the stage for high level individual and school functioning. They are beacons by which the employee is made aware of the importance attached to him, his colleagues, and the school function. The recognized importance of one's employment is a powerful morale factor, potentially stimulative of the kind of effort that promotes effectiveness.

Demoralizing is the conviction that one's selection was haphazard, assignment and job unimportant, and colleagues of like lack of consequence. The circumstances leading to such conviction cannot legitimately be expected to promote efficiency in school operation.

Intelligence and Potential

Esteem for the intelligence and potential of the employee group is a basic necessity and may be demonstrated by the employer group through acts of confidence.

Industry has for some time recognized that improvements in production can often come from those who are on the production line. Maintenance, custodial, clerical, and professional employees of the school are on the educational production line. Each is in a position to assess how he may improve his facet of school functioning. His suggestions are important for himself, the recognition they bring him, and the potential they have for improving school functioning.

One of the most promising acts of confidence the administration can make is that of recognizing its carefully selected and placed teachers as professionals. This means that they will be expected, not merely permitted, to demonstrate individual responsibility on the job with a minimum of administrative supervision. The theory here is that sound selection, placement, and equipment of personnel prepares the way for the progress that can be made best under conditions of freedom for the individual.

Fair Dealing

All participants in an enterprise are entitled to fair dealing. . . . Fairness has implications for monetary rewards, work load, the working period, various conditions that are concomitant or auxiliary to the job, and virtually every other element making up the total working situation.

Fairness would suggest that pay be commensurate with the work done. However, in this connection it has been said that, "Since salaries and wages in our society are not generally based on considerations of equity, this (the case for merit salary) is probably a very weak argument."[3] Fairness would suggest also that the employee should be rewarded for the productivity that can be credited to him and that he shall not be penalized for a lack of productivity which is the fault of circumstances imposed upon him and beyond his control. Some of the complexities of the merit pay issue are sharply implied here.

PURPOSES OF MERIT RATING AND PAY

Consideration of merit is stimulated by one or a combination of a number of motives or objectives. Expression of these objectives is generally associated in some way with equitability, i.e., the fairness of paying the best teachers the most, average teachers an average, and the still acceptable teacher who is low on the totem pole the least.

In at least some instances there is little doubt that the theme of reward geared to productivity is advanced to camouflage objectives which have little or no concern either with equity or the advancement of education. Seven of the more obvious reasons for advocating merit pay will be mentioned briefly.

1. *Equity.* One of the purposes often advanced for a merit system is to reward each employee in accord with his just deserts.

[3] Charles S. Benson, *The Economics of Public Education* (Boston, Houghton Mifflin Company, 1961), p. 430.

2. *Classification.* Job analysis and classification—from which categories of jobs may be arranged in terms of such factors as training and experience required, duties, and responsibilities—theoretically make it possible to set up levels of positions and of correlative pay. Here the merit consideration lies not in the personal effectiveness of the job holder but in the nature of his position and in his possession of the qualifications called for. Similar to the job classification approach is that of ranking as it is practiced in colleges and universities and in the military establishment. The hierarchy of ranks is presumably related to variations in accomplishments, duties, and responsibilities.

3. *Improvement.* It is maintained by some advocates of merit rating and pay that these serve as stimuli toward improved effort and results. The employee is supposedly encouraged to try to do a superior job because his pay will be favorably affected in recognition of improved productivity. The sum total of everyone's efforts is expected to be better schools and improved instruction.

4. *Screening.* Closely related to the improvement goal is that of using rating not only to vary pay but also to give preferential treatment to employees considered superior and to discharge unsatisfactory employees. This screening is expected to shift the norm of employee competency and productivity upwards.

5. *Raise in Pay.* On occasion the conviction that attempts to get a salary schedule revised upwards cannot succeed prompts resort to the advocacy of increments in pay to be awarded on a merit basis.

Because of the plausibility of the merit concept, an increase in pay on the merit basis is considered a means for making a breakthrough for the moment. The pay increments are expected to be given to virtually all, with perhaps a withholding of the increment from a token few who have distinguished themselves by an apparently low productivity. Interest lies in securing a pay increase rather than in the merit concept and little consideration is given to the problems conjured up by the introduction of at best a rough characterization of the merit idea.

6. *Prevention of Pay Increases.* Merit pay is also the concession by which upward revision of the pay scale is deliberately blocked. This is done to keep costs down and is rationalized by calling attention to the possibility that there are relatively ineffective teachers who ought not to benefit from pay increases. Pay increases are thought of as reserved to a presumably small elite group.

7. *Politics.* The board of education or the school administration, either assessing public opinion regarding the school or desiring to distract public attention from some other school issue, on occasion makes use of the merit issue as a diversionary tactic, not primarily to improve instruction but rather to gain for itself a generally favorable and supporting public opinion.

CLAMOR FOR MERIT PAY

Merit pay plans are often accompanied by a popular clamor. Emerging from this clamor are four kinds of publics or groups. One of these is concerned with morality, the morality of right or the amorality of expediency. Another is the group that confuses the merit label of governmental civil service with the merit proposed for school systems. A third is primarily concerned with the quality of education and its improvement. And, the fourth is responsive to pressures, either internal or external.

Moral Issues

The common ingredient called into play regardless of the real purpose in advocating merit pay is the idea of equity, pay in accord with educational productivity. There is something attractive in the simple justice of paying the worker what he deserves and, there is genuine justice in this concept. This objective of the merit pay issue is a highly moral one that, by itself, demands popular support.

Less moral, if not positively amoral, are the objectives of those who use the merit label as a device either to gain or to block a salary increase. However, the general appeal of merit is re-enforced by those who flaunt the banner of merit in order to disguise their true objectives of favoring or opposing an increase in the pay scale.

Confusion

Some support of a merit system for schools is the result of confusion. The civil service merit system—predominantly a classification system— of government agencies is confused with the idea of merit as directly related to effectiveness on the job. A segment of the public lends support to a merit label that does not describe the contents of the merit package at issue in the school system. Again, irrespective of issues or understandings, voices are added to the support of merit pay considerations.

Educational Concern

Education has for long been a genuine concern of many, particularly those whose children will benefit or suffer from the school program.[4] The concerned tend to favor merit systems for the stimulus toward improve-

4 John F. Kennedy in the section of Education in his State of the Union Message to the Congress on January 11, 1962, as reported in *U.S. News & World Report*, Vol. LII, No. 4, January 22, 1962, p. 92, reflected the concern about education as follows: "Equally important to our strength is the quality of our education. . . . I shall . . . recommend bills to improve educational quality, . . . excellence in education must begin at the elementary level."

ment they are assumed to provide and for the possibilities they seem to present for screening out the inadequate teacher.

Public Pressure

Within the board of education and the school administration there is an awareness of public pressures. The merit issue may receive support in recognition of the general and particular appeals it has among various groups or it may be seized upon because of the strength of its appeal as a means for diverting pressure from other areas of policy making or administration. The focussing of attention upon so controversial an issue as merit pay can serve effectively to distract attention from otherwise unsound administration, curricular weakness, a padded budget, a new school building that early reveals lack of educational design, change for the sake of change and without the supporting evidence of research, maintenance of the status quo without the encouragement of the experimentation that is an initial step toward desirable innovation, etc.

Summary

On one basis or another—and even because of capitalization upon many purposes that are in some instances diametrically opposed to each other—merit pay has undeniable appeal and widespread support. It brings into common cause and unites under the merit banner many different groups whose interests may be basically unlike.[5]

WARRANTABILITY OF MERIT PAY

Considered apart from the general operations of the society and its government and economy, the theory of pay in accord with merit seems unassailable. Controversy about it stems from two elements that cannot be ignored. One is the apparent general absence and frequent denial in practice of the merit pay concept, as proposed for education, within both government and private enterprise. The other is the problem of developing a reliable yardstick by which truly to measure the merit that is identified with educational productivity.

The Government Scene

Government employment falls into two major categories; that which is subject to the controls of the Civil Service Commission and that which is not subject to such controls.

[5] Arthur B. Moehlman and James A. van Zwoll, *School Public Relations* (New York, Appleton-Century-Crofts, 1957), pp. 70–75.

Civil Service. The Civil Service Act of 1883 was the beginning of effective formal action to move from a spoils system of political patronage towards employment on the basis of competency. This act introduced a civil service that is often referred to as a merit system. The merit is that of job classification and employee selection on the basis of qualification.

Governmental civil service has supplemented its classification-qualification type merit system by a performance rating. The performance rating has been done on the basis of satisfactory versus unsatisfactory service until employee dissatisfaction forced the introduction of an outstanding rating. In 1959, it was reported that "less than two per cent (of employees) are given unsatisfactory and outstanding performance ratings."[6] Recognition of the ineffectiveness of its rating system has produced repeated proposals to circumvent the issue by leaving it to each department to develop its own evaluative instruments. In fact, in 1958 the Civil Service Commission formally recommended repeal of the Performance Rating Act because of its inadequacies.

On the whole efforts to evaluate performance in government service are still frustrated as "The barriers in the way of an adequate solution of the problem of employee rating are prodigious, owing both to its complexities and to technical difficulties involved."[7] That frustrations of merit rating have not been overcome is indicated by the statement that, "Once regarded as something of a panacea for many ills, more recently rating systems have been de-emphasized in many jurisdictions because, unless properly applied, the work they involve is not justified by the results."[8] The foolproof way of rating performance has not yet been developed in the government service. Attention seems to have been transferred to providing for the supervision by which government employees can be trained on the job to work more effectively.

Government Employment Outside Civil Service. There is still a large body of top level and other jobs in government that are noncompetitive, filled by appointment, and not subject to the Civil Service Act. In these there are a number of considerations any one of which may be the major determinant for appointment. Bases, other than competency, for putting individuals on the public payroll become particularly evident with the initiation of a new administration. Among the bases are:

1. Color or race—when the major concern is to cater to or gain support from an interest group.

[6] Jerry Kluttz, "Federal Diary," *Washington Post and Times Herald*, July 25, 1959.

[7] William E. Mosher and J. Donald Kingsley, *Public Personnel Administration* (New York, Harper and Row, 1941), p. 480.

[8] Marshall E. and Gladys O. Dimock and Louis W. Koenig, *Public Administration* (New York, Holt, Rinehart and Winston, 1958), p. 317.

2. Competency—when the prime concern is with outstanding capability to do what is required for the job.

3. Influence with political or economic interests (including labor)—when the reason for employment subordinates capability to the fact of interest group membership.

4. Leadership in the "right" political party—when the dominant factor is reward of loyalty through serving as national chairman of the political party, national committee woman, or leader within the opposing party to support the successful candidate.

5. Relationship to those in a position to appoint or influence appointment —when nepotism is practiced, sometimes on the self-serving basis of providing jobs for wife or husband, son, daughter, or other relative.

6. Sex—when the issue is maleness or femaleness rather than competency, probably with the object of gaining the support of the favored group.

7. Wealth—when favors of the past are to be rewarded or favors for the future anticipated, prestige positions are awarded primarily on the basis of wealth.

The large role played by considerations other than competency in securing for the favored appointments to $50-per-day consultantships, cabinet posts, federal judiciary posts, ambassadorships, and the Civil Service Commission indicates that the merit consideration is in fact not typical of a way of life in the United States.

Private Enterprise

The major two elements within the field of private enterprise operation are on the one hand capital and management and on the other labor.

Capital and Management. Chairmanship of the board of directors for an enterprise is often determined by the number of shares of stock held rather than some other criterion, such as competency. Also, within the managerial organization, competency as a criterion for a management post is rivalled by influence and blood relationship.[9]

Labor. With the exception of a few industries in which piecework is traditional, labor has bargained for contracts in terms of seniority job rights, hourly wage rates, a limitation upon the length of the regular work week (for example, the electrical workers of New York received in 1962 a contract for a 25-hour work week), and, currently, an annual wage subject to periodic renegotiation and unrelated to either, how

[9] It will be an interesting exercise for the reader to think of a few of the great private enterprises of our time—e.g., The E. I. duPont de Nemours, Ford Motors, International Business Machines, Kaiser Industries and Steel, and Sun Oil companies— to note the coincidence of managerial position with both stock ownership and blood relationship.

much of the year there was employment or how productive the individual worker was. (In fact, in October, 1961, the Railroad Telegraphers Union obtained an agreement not only for a guaranteed annual wage but also lifetime employment for all employees.)[10]

It is generally contended that crediting the individual worker with the measure of his productivity is impossible, first because it is not possible to assign to any one in the production process his particular and indisputable contribution to the final product and second because even the product or output defies measurement because of variations in the kinds and qualities of goods and services.[11]

The School Scene

Employment for service in the schools generally takes place in terms chiefly of two factors; first, qualification for the job, and second, availability. For at least three decades, school employment on the primary basis of such factors as nepotism, influence, wealth, race, religion, politics, sex, etc. has been rare. When a basis other than competence or availability obtruded itself in rare instances, it has generally been as a part of a receding scene, a past era, or it was subordinated to competency and availability.

Qualification. Both in teaching and nonteaching jobs, the schools have for long sought to employ those who were qualified for the vacancies to be filled.

In the teaching jobs competency was equated with extent of training and ability to meet state certification requirements. Within the past 30 years, this meant an increase in training requirements for elementary school teachers from 6 weeks normal training beyond high school to the currently prevalent 4-year college and bachelor degree training program and an occasional 5-year program. For high school teaching, it is becoming common to require a master's degree.

The relatively low pay that teachers get, as compared to others with equivalent training and experience, has undoubtedly served as a deterrent that has caused the ablest youth for the most part to prepare for more remunerative vocations. This has left teaching as a field for the dedicated able and for a nonselective group of undistinguished ability.

Many of the nonteaching jobs also were so poorly paid that those with the desired competencies could accept school employment only under unusual personal circumstances.

10 "Next for Workers in U.S.: Lifetime Jobs?" *U.S. News & World Report,* Nov. 13, 1961, pp. 117, 118, 120, 122.

11 "Can Wages Be Tied to Productivity?", *Engineering News-Record,* April 2, 1959, pp. 21, 22.

Availability. Upon the advent of World War II, the schools found themselves in a particularly difficult position. Many teachers left the schools to serve in the armed forces or to work in better paying jobs directly related to the immediate defense effort. By the end of World War II this situation was further aggravated by the great increase in the number of children of school age.

Faced with an appalling shortage of teachers, school districts and state departments of education lowered training and experience requirements and provided for emergency certification in an effort to staff classrooms. Thus many were employed because they were available, not because they were competent.[12]

The high level of employment in the American economy and the continued low level of economic return for school employment has also perpetuated the hiring of workers for the nonprofessional jobs on the basis of availability, not of competency.

Level of Educational Productivity. The level of the school system's productivity is not known, nor is it possible in terms of today's knowledge to measure it. No doubt low pay in all school positions, professional and nonprofessional, have decreased the selectivity of the schools as employing agencies. This lack of selectivity carries with it implications of over-all mediocrity or worse. These implications impair confidence in the schools and result in the criticism of personnel and program which has stimulated consideration of merit rating.

Educational Efforts. From the inception of the emergency certification and employing activities, school districts have urged or required the uncertified teachers to qualify themselves for the jobs they held. Teacher-training institutions cooperated by providing late afternoon, evening, and summer teacher-training programs geared to aid in qualifying uncertified teachers. State departments of education encouraged activities to improve the professional status of emergency teachers and have set up time limits within which certification requirements must be met or the uncertifiable eliminated.

Salaries have improved in the larger or wealthier school districts narrowing the gap between starting salaries in education and other employment requiring comparable training. The period for reaching the maximum on the salary scale has in numerous instances been shortened at the same time that the maximums have been increased.

Certification requirements have been stiffened, with increased em-

---

[12] The decision of the educators is in sharp contrast to that of the New York City Engineers which resolved that "The shortage of engineers will not be solved by reducing or waiving educational and/or experience standards." See "Brookings Institution Does Study on NYC Engineers," *American Engineer*, February, 1962, p. 22.

phasis on the area of academic (as contrasted to professional) preparation. All teachers are required to come up to the new certification standards. Monetary incentive is in instances given through increments paid upon completion of an advanced degree or the equivalent of an additional year of graduate work.

And, while a number of positive steps are being taken to correct and improve a situation which is deep seated because of the long-term low economic position of school employees and the subsequent employment of nonqualified personnel, there are also attempts at shortcuts. During this century[13] attempts have been made to improve school operation by means of a merit pay plan of one kind or another. The attempt to employ the shortcut toward efficiency has been made so far without adequate exploration as to whether there actually was a shortcut and whether the means employed would facilitate the attainment of school-community educational objectives.

Merit Rating Research. A great deal of research has gone into various facets of merit rating. However, it seems that much of the research has taken place without reference to an agreed upon design for research.[14] The result is a large number of research studies, each of which stands by itself without relationship to others. Thus the studies done do little if anything to advance knowledge in regard to merit rating. Some of the spottiness of the findings can be observed from the following research conclusions between 1917 and 1959:[15]

[13] Currently there are school districts, such as Canton, Connecticut, and Montgomery County, Maryland, that have recently introduced merit pay plans and received publicity stating that the introduction of the merit principle is an innovation. As a matter of fact, the Newton, Massachusetts, School Committee adopted a merit plan in 1908. A number of plans has been put into operation during the twentieth century, but the mortality rate of such plans is extraordinarily high.

[14] The result is much the same as that achieved if a number of individuals, given copies of the same picture to cut into pieces for jigsaw puzzles, haphazardly contributed a number of their cutouts made without prior design to make up one puzzle. Putting the pieces together would be impossible except as a modern art composition to be interpreted by each in terms of his perceptions.

[15] 1) G. E. Bird, "Pupil Estimates of Teachers," *Journal of Educational Psychology*, 1917, 8:35–40; Frank W. Hart, *Teachers and Teaching* (New York, The Macmillan Company, 1934); Arthur T. Jersild, "Characteristics of Teachers Who Are Liked Best and Least," *Journal of Experimental Education*, December, 1940, 9:139–151; and Paul A. Witty, "Evaluation by Students of the Characteristics of Efficient Teaching," *AERA Bulletin*, 1948, pp. 198–204. 2) W. B. Bliss, "How Much Mental Ability Does a Teacher Need?" *Journal of Educational Research*, June, 1922, 6:33–41. 3) George Payne, "Scholarship and Success in Teaching," *Journal of Educational Psychology*, 1927, 2:217–219. 4) A. S. Barr and L. M. Emans, "What Qualities Are Prerequisite to Success in Teaching?" *The Nation's Schools*, September, 1930, 6:60–64. 5) H. J. Anderson, "Correlation between Academic Achievement and Teaching Success," *Elementary School Journal*, September, 1931, 32:22–29. 6) Elizabeth Breckinridge, "A Study of the Relationship of Preparatory School Records and Interest Tests Relative to Teaching Success," *Educational Administration and Supervision*, September, 1931, 17:649–660. 7) R. K. Bent, "Relationship between Qualifying Factors and

1. The well-liked teacher is kind, fair, sociable, humorous, good-tempered, neat, patient, prepared, clear, and maintains discipline. The inference is that the good teacher will have or develop the implied traits and be both effective and well liked. (1917, 1934, 1940, and 1948).

2. The greater the mental ability of the teacher, the better is the chance that he is successful and effective. (1922).

3. Scholarship has only a slight relation to being a successful teacher. (1927).

4. Analysis of 209 rating scales containing 6000 items indicate that the profession emphasizes more social and human traits than any others. (1930).

5. The academic achievement of the teacher is only moderately related to his success as a teacher. (1931).

6. Intelligence correlates with academic achievement but neither has significance for teaching success. Personality factors (initiative, perserverance, and interest) are closely related to teaching success. (1931).

7. The more preparation—academic and professional—a person has, the more effective he may be expected to be as a teacher. (1937).

8. The majority of a group of teachers who were rated superior as teachers were also superior in scholarship. (1937).

9. Student ratings of teachers do not generally agree with those of administrators, supervisors, or colleagues. (1940).

10. Close personal ties between teacher and pupil produce less learning of subject matter and higher rating for the teacher, indicating halo effect. (1945).

11. At least average intelligence is needed by elementary school teachers.

Student Teaching Performance at the University of Minnesota," *Journal of Experimental Education*, March 1937, 5:251–255. 8) Dewey Stuit, "Scholarship as a Factor in Teaching Success," *School and Society*, September 1937, 46:382–384. 9) Wilbur B. Brookover, "Person to Person Interaction," *Journal of Educational Research*, December, 1940, 34:272–287. 10) Wilbur B. Brookover, "The Relation of Social Factors to Teaching Ability," *Journal of Experimental Education*, June, 1945, 13:191–205. 11) Mary V. Seagoe, "Pre-Training Selection of Teachers," *Journal of Educational Research*, May 1943, 36:678–693 and "Prognostic Tests and Teaching Results," *Journal of Educational Research*, May, 1945, 38:685–690. 12) Floyd B. Bolton, "Evaluating Teacher Effectiveness through the Use of Scores on Achievement Tests," *Journal of Educational Research*, May, 1945, 38:691–696. 13) C. V. LaDuke, "The Measurement of Teaching Ability," *Journal of Experimental Education*, September, 1945, 14:75–100. 14) K. P. Riesch, "A Study of Some Factors in Pupil Growth," *Journal of Experimental Education*. September, 1945, 18:31–55. 15) L. E. Rostker, "Measurement of Teaching Ability, No. One," *Journal of Experimental Education*, September, 1945, 14:6–51. 16) J. F. Rolfe, "Measurement of Teaching Ability, No. Two," *Journal of Experimental Education*, September, 1945, 14:52–74. 17) L. C. Kemp, "The Prediction of Teaching Success," *The Forum of Education*, August, 1947, 6:14–15. 18) T. E. Lanke, "Personality and Teaching Success," *Journal of Experimental Education*, December, 1951, 20:217–259. 19) Arthur C. Hearn, "Case Studies of Successful Teachers," *Educational Administration and Supervision*, October, 1952, 38:376–379. 20) W. I. Ackerman, "Teaching Competency and Pupil Change," *Harvard Educational Review*, 1954, 24:273–289. 21) Harold W. Montross, "Temperament and Teaching Success," *Journal of Experimental Education*, September, 1954, 23:73–97. 22) G. C. Burgess, J. E. Morsch, and P. N. Smith, "Student Achievement as a Measurement of Teaching Efficiency," *Journal of Educational Psychology*, February, 1956, 47:79–88. 23) D. M. Medley and H. E. Mitzel, "Defining and Measuring Teacher Behavior," *Journal of Educational Psychology*, December, 1959, 50:239–246.

However, intelligence and scholarship do not play an important role in the success of the elementary school teacher. (1943 and 1945).

12. Academic achievement testing is possible if controls are carefully established and statistical procedures are employed with precision, integrity, and sophistication. (1945).

13. Intelligence and professional knowledge relate significantly to teacher effectiveness. (1945).

14. Administrative ratings of teachers do not correlate significantly with pupil growth as measured by mental maturity, achievement, and social adjustment tests. (1945).

15. The most important significant factor conditioning teacher ability is intelligence. Social attitudes, attitudes toward teaching, and knowledge of subject—but not personality—are significantly correlated to teaching ability. However, supervisory ratings do not correlate to data on pupil gains. (1945).

16. Personality, but not intelligence, correlates highly to effective teaching. (1945).

17. The better teachers know something about the psychology of learning and motivation and the principles of teaching. At the extremes, the very worst teachers are more intelligent than the very best. (1947).

18. Good teachers are good for a variety of reasons and poor teachers are poor for a variety of reasons. Thus teaching success is possibly an interrelated balance of the teacher's total personality traits and characteristics. (1951).

19. The human relations characteristics of teachers, more than anything else, are important to a teacher's success. (1952).

20. Personality and training—rather than age, experience, or professional knowledge—are significantly related to pupil gain. (1954).

21. There is no relationship between personality and effective teaching; however, good teachers can associate things, concentrate, and drive better than can weaker teachers. (1954).

22. Student gain can be measured by testing procedures; however, such gain does not correlate to supervisory ratings. (1956).

23. Supervisors tend to rate high teachers who establish and work in a friendly atmosphere; however, their ratings have not been established as measures of actual teacher effectiveness. (1959).

The research into merit rating has consisted of opinion surveys, attempts at evaluation of and prediction about pre-service performance, measurement of pupil change (achievement or gains), the development of scoring techniques to accompany observations of teacher characteristics and performance, and the development and use of tests.

Strangely, without having defined just what constitutes teaching, individual raters tend to rate with considerable consistency although different raters will vary in their rating in accord with their own perceptions and biases. This consistency leads the rating administrators and supervisors to have faith in the reliability of their ratings.

Even if the reliability of rating could be stipulated in general, this would be meaningful only if it were known just what it was that the reliable or consistent rating measured. At present, with the possible exception of the measurement of pupil change as a criterion of teacher efficiency, the emphasis has been on supervisory evaluations as criteria of teacher efficiency. There is no evidence to suggest that supervisory evaluations do in fact measure teacher effectiveness. Hence the validity of supervisory ratings has to date not been established.

Devices for Rating. Criteria, rating methods, evidence, and formulas or scales are the descriptive terms that abound in proposals and plans for rating teachers.

Those who are willing to use achievement gain as the criterion for rating teachers are in a theoretically somewhat defensible position. Their position is predicated upon the equating of scholastic achievement with effective teaching. However, their position is less simple than it seems. First, there is evidence that some of the highest rated scientists and engineers come from the lower academic levels of their college classes and from schools which are not top-rated.[16] Next, there is the problem of how to credit any one individual with pupil gains that have been made under a complex of individual and social influencing factors. And, third, there is the problem of just what allowances to make for differences in the abilities of pupils. Presumably, if achievement gains are to provide a measure of teacher effectiveness, a graduated scale of pupil achievement gain expectations in accord with the ability levels of pupils must be drawn up to provide the basis for rating.

The complications that seem to attend the relatively simple criterion of pupil gain become compounded when criteria include also a consideration of personality and social development. Some indication of the compounding and resulting confusion is found in the nonspecific language that is used in an attempt to describe the effective teacher, language that may be superficially reassuring to the unsophisticated but which actually means that each rater with all his own biases and idiosyncrasies becomes the yardstick by which teachers are rated. Thus, ratings vary with the yardsticks used and are neither comparable to nor definitive of any species of teacher effectiveness.

A review of a number of criteria[17] suggests that rating, i.e., the measurement of teacher effectiveness, is defined as: effectiveness in a number of things, such as classroom management, pupil and community relationships, use of counselling materials, and participation in nonformal school

16 "Good Scholars Are Not Always Best" (based on a 1948 study for the National Advisory Committee for Aeronautics and a 1956 study by Robert A. Martin and James Pachares of Hughes Aircraft Company engineers), *Business Week*, February 24, 1962, pp. 77, 78.

17 Gilroy and Monterey, California; Canton, Connecticut; Barrington and Glencoe, Illinois; Montgomery County, Maryland; Newton, Massachusetts; University City, Missouri; Summit, New Jersey; Ithaca, Niskayuna, and Seneca Falls, New York; Cleveland Heights, Ohio; and Abington, Pennsylvania.

activities. In other words, teacher effectiveness is effectiveness in a number of itemized activities. This kind of criterion development fails to solve any problems while it violates the basic rules of definition. Likewise, there is indication of the sterility in developing criteria that is unavoidable when there is no identified basis for rating. Claims to originality and innovation, under the circumstances, must be limited and of dubious credit to the claimant.

Administrative self-concern is suggested by frequent inclusion in rating factors of such a protective item as one or a combination of: 1) acceptance and use of suggestions, 2) adherence to the course of study, 3) attitude toward administrative policies, 4) compliance with rules and regulations, 5) effective execution of assigned duties, 6) loyalty, 7) performance of duties [playground, noon hour, bus, homeroom, record keeping and reporting being specified], and 8) teamwork. Although all of these may be considered as contributory to administrative comfort, a number of these items either do not lend themselves to measurement or pose the question whether conformity is to be equated with excellence.

The techniques used for rating were one or a combination of the following: 1) identification of major categories and their subclassifications of characteristics to be judged, 2) weighting of characteristics in terms of number scores or letter grades, 3) scaled interpretations of activities and qualities, 4) letters of application by the individual to be rated in which he sets forth his outstanding contributions and plans for further professional improvement, 5) self-evaluation, 6) comparisons with other successful teachers, and 7) placement above a designated percentile of the Commons Battery of the National Teacher Examinations.

Rating is done by one or more individuals and must in all instances be accompanied by the recommendation of the superintendent for action by the board of education. Those designated as having lone or joint parts in rating are the superintendent, assistant superintendent, supervisor, principal, department head, teacher (self-evaluation), and committee of teachers.

Rating procedure varies greatly. There are attempts to introduce a degree of reliability by having evaluation take place in terms of a consideration of the same kinds of factors and with the same scales for numerical or letter rating. There are also instances in which the evaluation takes place merely on the basis of the evaluator's comparison of a teacher with his images of the different levels of teacher competence. Practices vary between such extremes. Even at best, the allocation of number scores or letter grades is subjective and therefore a summing up of numbers allocated does not provide an objective measure.

Much is sometimes made of the degree to which teachers have taken part in the formulation of the rating plan and have agreed upon and participated in its use. These factors may have some implication for morale. They make no contribution to the validity of the rating that will result. Even with the most meticulously developed scale and a consistency in rating by those who use the scale, there is no assurance that what is being measured is teacher effectiveness or superior teaching.

What is lacking to date is the knowledge of just what is meant by effective or superior teaching and the evidence by which such teaching may be measured. A first step forward would be identification of or agreement upon the essence of effective teaching. Thereafter progress may be made in the direction of programmed research into the identification of the factors which contribute to effectiveness or superiority in teaching.

SUMMARY

It is necessary at least to agree as to what the concept of merit rating connotes; qualification for a job, seniority status, or a measure of quality of performance. Merit considerations are implied by the principles of school personnel administration in terms of quality education, qualifications for employment, capitalization upon human variability and employee potential, morale, and fairness.

The purposes of merit rating are devious, including the provision of equity, job classification, employee improvement, screening of employees for differential treatment, and promotion or prevention of increase in pay.

Merit pay receives ready popular support on moral bases, as the result of confused thinking, because of concern about education, and in response to pressure. Its warrantability is difficult to sustain in terms of current public or private enterprise employment practices in the United States.

The shortages of personnel for school jobs have resulted in an emphasis upon availability rather than on qualification for the job. This further complicates the difficulty of measuring the contribution that the schools make to the social and economic well-being of the nation.

Merit rating research has not aided greatly in evaluating educational productivity. The research done in regard to merit rating has been spotty, largely unrelated, and on occasion contradictory in its findings. Practices in rating have to date been expediential, subjective, and nondefinitive of what constitutes effective teaching. When effective teaching has been defined, it is necessary to program research in order that the factors that contribute to such teaching may be productively explored and identified in measurable fashion.

SELECTED READINGS

ALEXANDER, William M., *Are You a Good Teacher?* (New York, Holt, Rinehart, and Winston, 1959), pp. vi plus 57.

American Association of School Administrators, *Who's A Good Teacher?* (Washington, D.C., The Association in cooperation with the Department of Classroom Teachers of the NEA and the National School Boards Association, 1961), pp. x plus 54.

BARR, A. S. and Associates, *The Measurement and Prediction of Teacher Effectiveness* (Madison, Wisconsin, Dembar Publications, 1961), pp. 156.

HALSEY, George D., *Handbook of Personnel Management* (New York, Harper and Row, 1947), Chapters 13, 17.

"Merit Salary Schedules for Teachers," *The Journal of Teacher Education,* VIII:2, June, 1957, pp. 114–197.

STAHL, O. Glenn, *Public Personnel Administration* (New York, Harper and Row, 1956), Chapters 2, 3, 9, 13.

STOOPS, Emery, and RAFFERTY, M. L., *Practices and Trends in School Administration* (Boston, Ginn and Company, 1961), Chapter 23.

Symposium, "Merit Rating and Pay," *Phi Delta Kappan,* XLII:4, January, 1961, pp. 137–163.

TULIN, T. G. (Editor), *Latest Thinking on Appraisal and Improvement of Teacher Performance* (New York, Barrington and Company, Inc., 1961), pp. 118.

VANDER WERF, Lester S., *How to Evaluate Teachers and Teaching* (New York, Holt, Rinehart, and Winston, 1958), pp. vi plus 58.

WEBER, Clarence A., *Personnel Problems of School Administrators* (New York, McGraw-Hill Book Company, Inc.. 1954), Chapter 6.

YEAGER, William A., *Administration and the Teacher* (New York, Harper and Row, 1954), Chapter 14.

YEAGER, William A., *Administration of the Noninstructional Personnel and Services* (New York, Harper and Row, 1959), Chapter 5.

YODER, Dale, *Personnel Principles and Policies* (Englewood Cliffs, N.J., Prentice-Hall, Inc., 1959), Chapter 18.

.15.

Change in Employment Status

CHANGE IN position takes place in a number of ways and for a variety of reasons. The common ways in which change of position takes place are promotion, transfer, suspension, demotion, and dismissal. Reasons for change are often phrased in terms of recognition and reward, desire better to match worker qualification and job, and discipline. All of these resolve themselves into the one of improving the functioning of the organization, in this instance, the school system.

PRINCIPLES

Change in position calls into play a number of the principles of personnel administration.[1]

That *working must be a gratifying social experience as well as a means for a livelihood* has great implications for every change in position whether upwards, laterally, or downwards. The administrator must prognosticate as to whether the employee being considered for a change of position would find his new status a source predominantly of gratification, worry, or resentment. The prognosis is based upon an estimate of the objectives of the individual and his potential.

That *the maximum effectiveness of the schools requires the best possible selection and coordination of personnel and job* has implications initially for selection and placement and continuously for reappraisal of placement in terms of changes in the nature of the job or in the qualifications of the employee. Adjustments in placement in order to make the

[1] See Chapter 1, principles numbers 1, 4, 11, and 12.

best use of the capabilities of the employee are one means of improving the effectiveness of school operation by correcting placement errors and by capitalizing upon employee growth.

That *every school employee is entitled to fair dealing* is axiomatic. The occasions for being or for being thought fair or unfair are particularly manifest in the area of the various kinds of changes that affect job status. Every change of job status demands the highest integrity, and awareness of such integrity, on the part of everyone involved in any way. The provision of an appeal mechanism is one demonstration of intent to act with justice.

That *consistency of action, the promotion of feelings of security, and avoidance of expediential action are advanced and safeguarded by written policy* is generally recognized. In the change of position area of personnel administration there is particular opportunity for the misinterpretation, jealousy, caprice, shortsightedness, and introduction of the personal element through favoritism or spitefulness by which effective school operation is jeopardized. The public interest in an effective school system, the institutional interest in morale conducive to effective functioning, and employee interest in finding satisfaction in the working situation are furthered by the written policies which clearly chart the conditions governing changes in job status.

The four principles discussed are implicit to every personnel action that produces a change in position whether that be by way of promotion, transfer, suspension, demotion, or dismissal and regardless of whether the stimulus to the action be recognition, personal adjustment, organizational accommodation, or a resort to disciplinary measures.

PROMOTION

The conditions which make promotions possible are new positions resulting from school system growth and vacancies created by deaths, retirements, transfers, and demotions.

Promotions in the schools are somewhat anomalous in view of the fact that classroom teaching is the single most important activity within the school operation. Nevertheless, since teachers are the large majority group of school employees, promotion means, for them, leaving the classroom for some other job.

Promotion Defined

Promotion—at once a reward for past confidence-inspiring performance and the expression of an estimate of the employee's ability and potential—is advancement to a job that is regarded as better because of one or a combination of such factors as broader or greater responsibility, higher status, and a corollary increase in pay.

Policy

Promotions can take place in terms of carefully developed and well-defined and promulgated ground rules, called promotional policies. Or, promotions can take place in a fashion that is unplanned, personal, subject to pressure, political, and expedientially haphazard.

A systematic promotion policy establishes bases for advancing personnel from within the organization and makes provision for such promotions to take place by way of procedures set up to make them defensibly possible. It creates a career situation for employees, enhancing the morale of those eligible for promotion as well as those, either ineligible or not interested, whose confidence in administration is strengthened by every display of equity. The advantages of a systematic promotional policy are negated by expediential and capricious filling of vacancies.

Bases for Promotion

Schools, like private enterprises and other governmental organizations, are plagued by a number of considerations in the filling of vacancies that offer promotional opportunities. These find repeated expression in internal pressure to promote in terms of seniority or some other established and acceptable procedure and, of course, from within.

School systems, like other enterprises, have developed the rationale of employing the best qualified personnel for a job whether from within or outside the system. This rational position is one with which reasonable employees, convinced of the fairness of procedures set up, cannot quarrel. It makes the filling of jobs competitive on the basis of competency.

When qualifications become the issue, it is necessary that jobs be accurately described and the job specifications scrupulously met. The qualifications of the candidate must match the requirements for the job.

Promotion Procedures

The matching of job and candidate is so important that it is essential to use a number of safeguarding approaches to the task.

All candidates may be required to take a battery of tests suited to the job under consideration. Appropriate tests may be given to test for aptitude, attitude, interest, knowledge and abilities expected of teachers (e.g., the National Teacher Examinations), mental ability (e.g., I.Q. tests), personality, clerical knowledge and skills, mechanical comprehension, level of knowledge and skill in some trade.[2]

Tests administered have the function of serving as a check on other procedures. They are not suitable as a sole measure for selection or promotion. They are valuable as an aid for recognizing and neutralizing in part the halo effects of personal appraisals and recommendations. Provisions for including appropriate tests and examinations improve measures for filling job vacancies by promotion or otherwise.

Test results and training and experience information must be available for every prospect for a job whether from within or outside the organization. Sound personnel procedures make regular provision for much test, performance, personality, and developmental information to be entered in the personnel record of each employee. In addition, provision may be made for involvement in training programs (university, cooperative university-school district, and on-the-job) to groom interested individuals for advancement.

The making and recording of comparisons in employee performance on the job and in training programs provides some basis for promotion. Also, extended experience with an employee will yield some estimate as to two very important factors, his ability as demonstrated to date and his potential as projected.

The number of weighty factors that favor promotion from within are supplemented by another, the relative ease with which an employee may be given opportunity to prove himself by either a formal or informal on-the-job trial, e.g., by way of "acting" status.

In spite of the factors weighing to the advantage of promotion from within, there are administrators who prefer filling vacancies with promotional implications from the outside. They believe this avoids problems of favoritism and of resentment among those who would have liked the job. Their preference for selecting from outside the organization is bolstered by an argument that has merit when it is not mere rationalization, the value of bringing in "new blood" and avoiding the inbreeding of ideas and practices.

All other factors being equal, preference may best be given to an employee from within the system. One who adds to the other attributes seniority should be in an incontestable position. However, seniority cannot be substituted for competency, and competency outweighs all other considerations.

The posting of vacancies is important so that the personnel division may be assisted in reviewing its records by expressions of employee interest in being considered. The recommendations for filling vacancies

[2] See Chapter 6, and also "Educational and Psychological Testing," *Review of Educational Research* (Washington, D.C., The American Educational Research Association, N.E.A., Vol. XXXII, No. 1, February, 1962), pp. 114.

by promotion from within or application from outside the system should come from the personnel division. Selection should take place by the administrator, subject to action by the board of education.

Cautions. In the schools teachers who were considered good or even superior have been rewarded by promotion to principalships. Experience has shown that too often the good-superior teacher may be a mediocre-poor administrator. Similarly, principals who have performed satisfactorily in the principalship do not necessarily have the qualifications to be satisfactory superintendents. Promotion must be in terms of ability, not for the current job but for the prospective one.

The school situation lends itself to having too many teachers who think of themselves as prospective administrators. It should be emphasized that the most important job is the one in the classroom, that there are relatively few administrative and supervisory jobs in the school system, and that selection for administrative and supervisory jobs must be in accord with the especial attributes required for the jobs and possessed by those to be considered.

Whether a candidate is from outside, from within the school system, has seniority, has local roots, is looked upon as successful in his present position, is favorably regarded in the school and the community, and all other factors are functionally subordinate to and transcended by the one consideration—that he is the best of the qualified candidates available. Nothing may be permitted to becloud the selection and promotional criterion of excellence and competency.

TRANSFER

Technically a transfer could cover any kind of a move of personnel, vertical or lateral. Since the movement upward has been discussed under promotions, a transfer is differentiated by implication from promotions. It is likewise differentiated from suspensions, demotions, and dismissals.

Transfer Defined

A transfer is the shift of an employee to a job of generally equal responsibility, status, and pay in another department or school within the school system. It is a lateral, as contrasted to a vertical shift.

Policy

Transfers, like promotions, can take place haphazardly or systematically. Haphazardness rests upon unplanned attempts at adjustment through a trial and error approach. Systematic transfer rests upon a carefully developed and continuously modified plan provided for through policy.

The policy governing transfers should include:

1. grounds for and preferences that are to affect transfers
2. provisions for getting a transfer action started
3. use of job classifications (establishing comparability)
4. reference to job analysis, description, and specification information
5. review of selection and placement considerations and actions
6. examination of the personnel record for diagnostic purposes
7. a statement of the role of the personnel division in effecting a transfer
8. designation of how transfers are authorized

Bases for Transfer

The improved operation of the education function is the overriding reason for any transfer within the school system. Corrollary to it is the desire to place the employee where he can realize best his own objectives.

Defensible personnel actions preparatory to employing and at the time of placement reduce the occasion for transfers. However, adjustments may nevertheless be required to make up for errors in judgment, for contingencies, for virtually unforseeable personality conflicts or inabilities to adapt to some working condition peculiar to the assignment made, and on rare occasions for disciplinary reasons. In addition, either the expansion or contraction of a school system creates transfer conditions.

The expanding school system has new posts to be filled. Customarily a number of them are filled by transferring to new schools personnel who are already oriented to the school system. This begins a possible chain reaction of transfers throughout the school system, providing an excellent opportunity to make desirable readjustments of personnel and jobs.

The contracting school district is faced with the problem of attempting to maintain balance between a decreasing need for personnel and those personnel who are already on the payroll and desirous of remaining there. In anticipation of having to make transfers, the administrator may encourage employees to whom it is important to remain to qualify themselves for a variety of assignments so that they may be functionally transferrable as the working force is depleted by attrition.

Transfer Procedures

School administrators at any level ought seldom, if ever, to serve notice of dismissal until the case has been referred to the personnel division and its recommendations have been received. It is wholly possible that, where selection procedures are sound, a transfer will turn an employee liability into an asset, making dismissal unnecessary. Line officers should inform the personnel division of the fact that an employee is unsatisfactory and may request his transfer to another jurisdiction.

Requests for transfer may also be initiated by the employee. When this occurs, the personnel division has a distinct obligation to investigate in order to discover whether the request is caused by a remediable situation. Remedial action, where possible, may decrease subsequent transfer requests. The personnel division is a listening post where complaints and requests for adjustments may be registered freely and without fear of prejudice.

When a transfer seems to offer the solution to a problem, the personnel division has the responsibility to put into operation within the organization the same sound selection and placement practices which apply to new employees.

Serving as a clearing house for the personnel problems of the school district, the personnel division is in a strategic position to make recommendations to resolve problems by transfer or other remedial action.

Transfers within a school, involving no change of jurisdiction, may take place with or without reference to the personnel division, depending on the significance attached to the transfer by either or both of the parties to the transfer and the implications of the transfer for the personnel record of the employee. However, transfers from one school to another, involving a change of jurisdiction, calls for referral to the personnel division and authorization of the recommended transfer by the superintendent of schools.

Cautions

Transfers sometimes disrupt a way of life that has become familiar. Disturbance of the familiar introduces the fear of the unknown and consequent feelings of insecurity. Transfers also lend themselves to various interpretations, positive and negative. In order that the affected employee may find himself in the most unassailable position possible, he must be made to understand fully the reasons for the transfer and the benefits that are expected to accrue to him and to the school consequently.

SUSPENSION

Whereas promotions and transfers, as already dealt with, are nonpunitive, suspensions are or frequently have connotations of penalties.

Suspension Defined

A suspension is a temporary deprivation of such worker rights and privileges as duties, responsibilities, and, generally, pay. A suspension is a layoff and is properly limited to a stated period of time. Without a terminal limit, a suspension could amount to dismissal without the certainty of the latter.

Policy

The kinds of circumstances under which suspension may be resorted to, limits upon the duration of suspension, the individuals who have the power to suspend, the conditions under which pay will be awarded or withheld for the suspension period, and the bases (e.g., legitimacy of the action as contrasted to the duration of the suspension) and provisions for appealing a suspension order ought all to be covered by policy.

Policy might also well include not only the provision for suspension but also and unmistakably the intent to use this provision only when there are no comparably promising alternatives.

Bases for Suspension

Suspension takes place for a number of reasons. The most common are punitive, investigatory, and organizational.

Punishment. Unsatisfactory service, failure to follow instructions legitimately given, and interfering with or undermining the effective operation of the school might in extreme instances be causes for suspension.

Investigation. Suspension may be necessary to provide time for investigation, hearings, and corollary decision and action when a school employee has been charged with impropriety or crime—thus raising serious question about his effectiveness, his influence upon the immature, and the impact of the charge upon school-community relations. The employee is suspended until the charges are dismissed or he is found guilty. The suspension serves as a protection to the public.

Organization. When suspensions take place because of reorganization within or of the school system or as a result of contraction in the school operation, the intent is to recall suspended personnel either in accordance with the progress of the reorganization or as rapidly as attrition through such causes as dismissal of nontenure personnel, resignations, retirements, and deaths allows.

Suspension Procedures

Suspension is so extreme a measure that it ought to be ordered only from the central office. Some case might be made, particularly where discipline is at issue, for principals of schools to have the power to suspend employees under their immediate jurisdiction. However, if the central office makes possible quick action to suspend upon the supported recommendation of the principal, the reason for decentralized suspension authority is largely dissipated.

No suspension should take place without the laying of an honestly straightforward foundation for the action, neither should suspension be the expression of whim or personal pique.

The legality of suspension should be open to appeal. An appeal board may be set up outside or within the school organization, the board of education may serve as the appeal board, or, in some instances, resort may be had to court action. However, as suspensions should be in accord with policies governing them, the duration of the suspension would ordinarily be a matter for administrative determination.

Suspensions that are the result of charges of improper or criminal action take place in accordance with policy. Pay under such circumstances would also generally be withheld pending the outcome of the investigation. Pay would ordinarily be withheld in instances in which charges were proved and appropriate subsequent action would also be decided upon. When charges are dismissed, reinstatement to both job and pay status, together with back pay for the period of suspension would generally be in order.

When suspensions are resorted to in order to gain time during a reorganization, the reason for the suspension should be made clear and the duration indicated in terms of the time schedule for realizing the steps in the reorganization program. Suspensions resulting from a reduction in force also should be explained fully to affected employees together with an indication as to what their expectations for reinstatement to active employment are.

Cautions

If a suspension is disciplinary, the affected employee must understand thoroughly the reason for the action, must be convinced that the action is merited, must be inconvenienced by the action, and must be made to see the action as one by which he is given an opportunity to return to active status without prejudice provided his conduct is in accord with school policy and conducive to improved school operation. Every possible action should be taken to prevent the development of unjustified resentment that is the byproduct of lack of understanding.

Suspensions that are ordered pending investigations of charges against an employee are protective of the public interest. There should be general understanding among the public and within the organization that, whereas substantiation of charges justifies the withholding of pay, failure to substantiate charges requires the public to pay for the protection it has received through back pay for the period of suspension.

To the extent possible, suspensions ordered for the convenience or out of the necessity of the board of education should be accompanied by pay status. To the extent that that is impossible, particularly for financial reasons, every effort is in order to keep the period of suspension at a minimum and understanding at a maximum lest resentment build up as hardships mount.

DEMOTION

In common parlance and as a matter of semantics, demotion is the direct opposite of promotion. However, there are variables that cloud the demotion scene.

Demotion Defined

Ordinarily a demotion is the selection or marking of an individual for a reduction in one or a combination of: pay, rank, authority or responsibility of position, desirability of locale, and job status or prestige because of failure to meet established job standards.

Policy

Because demotion can take place for any of a variety of reasons, it is desirable that general conditions for demoting personnel be carefully developed out of past experience, continually reviewed, modified as necessary, and contained in written policy to serve as reference and guide to employer and employee and to administrator and administered. Some idea as to what may be covered by policy will be suggested under the heading of procedures.

Bases for Demotion

Actually the soundest basis for demotion is the matching of employee competency to his work assignment. If this were done perfectly initially, the major reason for demotion should be eliminated, barring a decrease in employee capability.

On occasion the basis for a demotion is a promotion that took place without sufficient grounds. It is often stated that a good teacher does not necessarily make a good principal. Withdrawal of a promotion from one who does not come up to job standards at the higher level is a demotion.

In addition, there are found under the bases for transfer and suspension a number of bases that apply also to demotions. Change in school organization, contraction of the school system, discipline, and time needed for investigation are among possible reasons for demotion.

Discipline. A demotion for disciplinary reasons, i.e., exclusive of failure to meet job standards, is defensible only to the extent that the action is constructive. When the demotion, even if it is termed a transfer, is used as a penalty with no other constructive aspect than to subordinate employees and to emphasize the power of the administrator, demotion cannot be expected to serve the best interests of the school district.

Investigation. If time is needed to investigate charges in order to determine action to be taken, it may be possible to use the employee in a nonsensitive position within the school system. When this is possible, such an assignment will probably be warranted only on a temporary basis and is, according to the definition employed, a demotion only if any one of the factors connoting demotion is involved. It is possible that temporary reassignment involves no demotion at all.

Demotion Procedures

An obligation of all who exercise the power of demotion is to comply first of all with the spirit of the policies governing demotions.

Demotion ought normally to take place only after sincere and sufficiently long-term efforts have been exerted to adjust the employee to the job level for which he was selected. Only after failure to secure acceptable adjustment should demotion take place, and then on the basis of documented facts and such other evidence as can be adduced. The keeping of a case record is strongly advocated. The employee must be made to see the demotion as a matching of worker qualifications and job requirements.

Cautions

Demotion must take place as a well-considered action based on evidence, not caprice. To be constructive it must not be regarded as irrevocable. Should the worker improve or augment his qualifications, he must be assured a sincere reconsideration of his job status.

On the rare occasions when demotion is disciplinary, the possibility of regaining lost status and becoming eligible for further advancement must be open to the employee if he is to continue as an asset to the school system. Demotion must never be used as a device for maneuvering an employee into a position which virtually forces him to leave the employ of the school system.

A demotion must be thoroughly understood by the employee. To the extent possible, the reasons for demotion must be accepted by him as just. To insure a degree of understanding and to provide for fairness, a demotion must be subject to appeal by the employee affected. The appeal body must be sufficiently removed from the responsible administrator's jurisdiction to assure genuine impartiality of review and judgment. The appeal procedure must never be allowed to degenerate into a formality.

DISMISSAL

Dismissal of a school employee means that for whatever reason and regardless of who has initiated the action, the school system loses both an employee and whatever investment it has in that employee. Sometimes the liquidation of an investment, the taking of consequent losses, and a new investment intended to regain losses are the part of wisdom. The need to take a personnel loss occasionally reflects the humanness of judgment. The need to take personnel losses frequently reflects unsatisfactory personnel administration. It is a major role of personnel administration to improve school functioning by reducing and keeping personnel losses to a minimum.

Dismissal Defined

Dismissal of an employee is the severing of the employee from the organization, terminating his employment. There is a finality to dismissal regardless of whether it takes place with or without prejudice to the employee.

Layoff. A layoff of limited duration has been dealt with as a suspension. Sometimes a layoff is regarded as a separation without likelihood of reemployment. This is a permanent layoff, a dismissal, and a form of discharge. Such a discharge is generally the result of change to which the employee cannot be expected to adjust, e.g., a reduction in force or the need for different competencies.

The discharge that is no reflection on the worker and results from organizational or operational change is sometimes termed a permanent layoff rather than a discharge. It is without prejudice to the worker.

Discharge. When the reason for separation from employment is disciplinary, the term discharge is used and is attended by connotations of prejudice to the employee. The school system would expect either not to reemploy the discharged professional or nonprofessional worker at all or to reemploy him only on the basis of strong evidence of the warrantability of giving him another chance, and then only under clearly understood probationary conditions.

Policy

Whether with or without prejudice to the employee, dismissals usually may be expected to affect the economic status of the dismissed employee, the morale status of his fellows, and/or the operational effectiveness of the school system. Hence it is necessary that dismissals take place in accord with clearly stated policies that are the product of careful consideration.

The policies governing dismissals will have to indicate the official attitude to be taken toward resort to dismissal action, the kinds of situations for which dismissal actions are to be considered warranted, the conditions to be met before dismissal takes place, provisions for hearings when dismissals are disciplinary, who may recommend dismissal and to whom, and who exercises the actual power of dismissal.

Bases for Dismissal

Not exhaustive, the following is a list of the more common bases for removing an employee from school employment. Inspection will indicate that in most instances there are implications for discharge with prejudice to the employee. Several of the bases for dismissal do not or do not necessarily have implications for prejudice to the dismissed employee.

The More Common Reasons for Dismissal

Age—advanced, compulsory retirement
Conduct—misconduct, unbecoming a teacher, unprofessional
Contract—breach of
Contraction—school system, abolishment of job
Crime—conviction of
Cruelty—demonstrated and proved
Disloyalty—as proved
Duty—neglect of
Health—physical or mental disability
Immorality—as proved
Inability—as substantiated
Incompetence—as substantiated
Inefficiency—as substantiated
Insubordination—as proved
Intemperance—as proved
Law—failure to abide by school law or board policy and regulation
Oath—refusal to take

Qualifications—lack of competency or legal certification requirements
Reputation—loss of
Striking—engaging in school strike
Subversion—as substantiated
Testifying—refusal to testify at congressional, legislative, or grand jury hearings on constitutional or other grounds
X-Y-Z—other good and just cause

Dismissal Procedures

The procedures for dismissal will be largely specified by policy. Among the procedures, in addition to those that are implicit in policy, are: the documentation of the steps that have been taken in an effort to avert invocation of dismissal procedures, the presentation of a written notice of dismissal in which the reasons for the action are clearly and fully stated, and a reminder of the conditions that pertain to a hearing.

Cautions

Since dismissal of an employee is accompanied by a loss of all that has gone into that employee by way of application and selection procedure, orientation, supervision, and the experience he has gained in the employ and at the expense of the school system, every reasonable effort should be extended to remedy the causes for dissatisfaction with him before dismissal is considered.

The grounds for dismissing an employee from school employment must ordinarily have genuine relationship to his fitness to do the work expected of him. Charges placed must be themselves substantial and subject to proof by overwhelming evidence. The employee who is dismissed and his colleagues must be convinced, whether they like it or not, that the action taken is just.

Dismissal lends itself a bit too conveniently to the rationalization that the educational interests of the community and the welfare of the children are protected by the action taken. Such rationalization could cause or serve as a cover for injustice, something to be assiduously avoided.

SUMMARY

Promotion, transfer, suspension, demotion, and dismissal are changes in employment status. Underlying such changes are principles that relate to institutional effectiveness, job satisfaction, coordination of worker and job, fairness, and the charting of appropriate courses of action through written policy.

Promotion constitutes advancement and connotes appreciative recognition. Transfer is a lateral change of position. Suspension is a layoff that is temporary and is terminated either by reinstatement to active employment or dismissal. Demotions constitute downgrading of some kind and connote failure to meet established job standards. Dismissal is the discharging of an employee with or without prejudice to him.

Each of the major kinds of position change is thought of as being governed by specific and pertinent written policy. Each is rooted in grounds peculiar to the action. For each, the procedures that grow out of policy are conceptually equally protective of the welfare of the school system and the rights of the employee. In each instance precaution must be taken to take the most defensible and constructive action, not necessarily the easiest or simplest. Such action is predicated on a high regard for each employee as an individual, on whatever stake the school system has developed relative to the employee, and on the over-all implications of actions that engender feelings of injustice.

SELECTED READINGS

CASTETTER, William B., *Administering the School Personnel Program* (New York, the Macmillan Company, 1962), pp. 288–298.

DIMOCK, Marshall Edward and Gladys Ogden, and KOENIG, Louis W., *Public Administration* (New York, Holt, Rinehart and Winston, 1958), pp. 317–336.

DURAND, Robert Y., *Business* (Englewood Cliffs, N.J., Prentice-Hall, Inc., 1958), pp. 125–130.

GARBER, Lee O., *The Yearbook of School Law 1962* (Danville, Illinois, The Interstate Printers and Publishers, Inc., 1962), pp. 130–145.

GENTRY, Dwight L., and TAFF, Charles A., *Elements of Business Administration* (New York, The Ronald Press Company, 1961), pp. 261–263.

KEARNEY, Nolan C., *A Teacher's Professional Guide* (Englewood Cliffs, N.J., Prentice-Hall, Inc., 1958), pp. 252–257.

NIGRO, Felix A., *Public Personnel Administration* (New York, Holt, Rinehart, and Winston, 1959), pp. 322–334 and 344–356.

PRERAU, Sydney (Editor), *J. K. Lasser's Business Management Handbook* (New York, McGraw-Hill Book Company, Inc., 1960), pp. 326–333.

SPRIEGEL, William R., and DAVIES, Ernest C., *Principles of Business Organization and Operation* (Englewood Cliffs, N.J., Prentice-Hall, Inc., 1960), pp. 351–353.

STAHL, Oscar Glenn, *Public Personnel Administration* (New York, Harper and Row, 1956), pp. 154–163 and 451–453.

WEBER, Clarence A., *Personnel Problems of School Administrators* (New York, McGraw-Hill Book Company, Inc., 1954), pp. 180–191.

YODER, Dale, *Personnel Principles and Policies* (Englewood Cliffs, N.J., Prentice-Hall, Inc., 1959), pp. 299–307.

.16.

The Salary Schedule

ONE OF THE MOST important things to every employee who is not financially independent is his salary or wage.

In private enterprise one's pay is the product of the bargaining power of the worker. This bargaining power is created by competition for his services, a supply-demand consideration, and by the strength of the organization to which he belongs and which speaks for him. The bargaining power is affected, and at some point limited, by the demand for what he produces.

School employment has not proved to be competitive for workers except during severe economic depressions. The school employee organizations have generally been considered ineligible to use the power techniques available to other worker organizations. And, although much has been said to indicate that education is highly prized in the United States, the implied high demand for education is not matched by a corresponding readiness to pay. Thus it is clear that school employees lack the usual leverages through which pay is normally determined for other occupations.

As pay is important in a society in which social status is to considerable degree influenced by economic considerations, the pay of school employees is examined in terms of principles, policies, problems, pay plans, methods of paying, and measures of the adequacy of the salary schedule.

PRINCIPLES

Among the principles of school personnel administration[1] five relate particularly to the pay of school employees.

[1] See Chapter 1, principles 1, 4, 8, 10, and 11.

1. An optimum education is in part produced when *employee good will and cooperation are the byproducts of employment in which working is both a gratifying social experience and a means for making a livelihood.*

2. Maximum effectiveness of the schools *requires the best possible selection and coordination of all elements comprising those means.* Employees constitute one of the elements.

3. *The most important single factor in getting the best that a school employee has to offer is how he feels about his work, his associates on the job, and the school system in which he is employed. Everyone has the need to regard his work as worthwhile and to take pride in it if he is to work at his best.*

4. *The continued study of the causes of personnel problems will in instances provide a clue to the circumstances under which some problems may be avoided or solved.*

5. *All participants in an enterprise are entitled to fair dealing. Fairness has implications for monetary rewards.*

Teaching is generally a gratifying social experience to those who teach. However the edge of gratification is blunted, for a considerable number of those who have dependents, by pay scales that are marginal.

The low salaries paid by school systems have the effects of 1) inducing those in teaching, or prepared therefor, to engage in other more remunerative occupations, 2) causing teachers to discourage interested youth from preparing themselves to teach, and 3) deterring realistic young people from considering so poorly rewarded a vocation. These consequences are conducive to something less than top quality staffing and maximum school effectiveness.

How an employee feels about his work is conditioned in part by evidence of the value that others place upon it. If he is forced to conclude, from the evidence of low pay and the consequent employment of personnel who tend to downgrade the total staff, that his work is not regarded as worthwhile, he can hardly feel pleased about the school system, his associates, or his work. The pride necessary to excellent performance is sadly undermined when the economic recognition of the transcendent value of education as an investment in people is neglected.

The entire problem of economic recognition is of such importance that continued efforts to study and resolve it are among the major tasks of the school administration and its personnel division. It is the key to the improvement of staffing that can come only under conditions of greater selectivity, conditions promoted by attractive pay conditions, and of comparability in economic rewards between education and other industries.

It is important for school personnel, as for everyone, to see themselves as dealt with fairly. The element of fairness is not merely internal to the school system. School personnel must be able to make favorable comparisons between their pay status and that of other school and community workers of comparable qualification and responsibility.

The lack of adequate salaries affects school effectiveness adversely in terms of morale, a decrease in personnel selectivity, and the danger that the employee will come to place upon his job a value corollary to the level of his income. In order to enhance its effectiveness the school system must take positive economic measures to protect its interests and improve its growth potential through well-placed investments in its educational enterprise. The school employee's pay envelope is a promising place to make a beginning.

POLICY

In the past, lacking a carefully and defensibly developed policy to govern pay, boards of education have found themselves virtually forced into the position of preventing or tempering pay increases. The employees, conversely, found themselves in the position of regarding each position attained as a beach head for a new campaign for further pay increases. This way of operation, without a sound basis and placing in opposition forces that functionally work in the same direction, becomes a sort of inadequate policy which does come to govern the scheduling of pay.

That there must be some better way of settling the pay issue than the tug-of-war approach that is so common is readily conceded among rational men. The arrival at the better way is a problem to be solved jointly by the school employee group(s) and the school authorities.

The solution to the pay issue must be a plan which will compensate for the school employees' lack of bargaining leverage and provide flexibility for adjustment to change. This plan must be: incorporated in the pay section of board of education policy, accompanied by provisions for its implementation, and made known and available to every school employee and the public.

Once decided upon and adopted, the policy must be subjected to continuous scrutiny to make certain that it is accomplishing its purpose and will be progressively improved through modificaton or amendment.

PROBLEMS

There will be many problems that relate to the scheduling of pay. Among them are five that seem to be major problems: 1) determining an equitable salary and wage plan, 2) readjusting thinking—board of education, or other legislative body,[2] employee, and public—from the traditional set to any departure, 3) promoting the general understanding which is essential as the basis for intelligent public acceptance and support of the plan, 4) recognizing the limitations upon the full operation of the plan, and 5) exercising the judgment that is necessary to make desirable or necessary modifications in the plan.

The Basis for an Equitable Plan

The first problem, that of determining an equitable salary and wage plan is complicated by the intangibility and to a considerable degree immeasurability of the school's product, the learning that has taken place.

It is generally recognized or accepted that education has an impact upon social development and economic productivity. However, no instrument has been devised to measure the contribution of education to either one or to provide some basis for putting a price label on the education provided through the schools.

Readjustment of Thinking

Having developed salary schedules and wage plans without a point of reference outside the school system and without any real rationale, the school system, its personnel, and the public have became accustomed to live with the pay situation that has evolved. There is a tendency to accept what has become customary as also right and defensible. A departure from the usual will be accompanied by wrenches that will cause mental discomfort to school personnel and the public.

Any proposed plan must find acceptance with all concerned on the basis of a rationale that cannot be gainsaid, a rationale that has so much logical appeal to reasonable men that it outweighs the traditional way of looking at and thinking about pay for both professional and non-professional school employees.

Public Relations for the Plan

A matter of such importance to the school personnel, the school system, and the public as a salary plan that will undoubtedly make added demands upon the financial resources of the people must be so sound that it can endure the most exacting examination by the public.

Any plan that has implications for the improvement of education

2 To the extent that there are national, state, county, and municipal as well as school district implications in projected change, the appropriate legislative bodies will be involved.

has the psychological advantage of the emotional response of parents. However, the proposed plan should be such that it can be promulgated defensibly on a strictly rational basis. Combining emotional and rational defensibility, the plan and its advocates have all to gain and nothing to fear from having the people fully informed.

The understanding that the people have of the pay plan is the only sound basis for the support which they will be required to provide in order to finance the plan. This underscores the need that the school's public relations activity justify itself by being in the best sense educational.

Limitations

Regardless of the wealth of a community, state, or nation, there is a ceiling to the financial ability of the people. There is therefore the problem of developing a pay plan which takes into account practicability. The pay plan must be realizable in terms of the financial resources that can be brought to bear upon it.

Transition. Changes of a minor nature can probably be taken in stride. However, should a proposed plan call for drastic change, it will be necessary to plan the steps and the timetable by which to advance toward the full attainment of the plan.

Modification

The perfect plan has probably yet to be devised, and if devised will probably not be recognized as such. Any pay plan will very likely have to be appraised for miscalculations and oversights that necessitate adjustments of various kinds, including upward or downward scaling. Both, school personnel and the public must be psychologically prepared at the outset of the plan to make adjustments, aware of the fact that those adjustments may not appeal to one or another of the groups affected. The criteria for acceptance of adjustments are fairness and educational advantage, criteria that need never be in conflict.

PAY PLANS

Pay plans originated with bargaining between the individual school employee and the community. This prevailed until the early 1900's and then diminished until today this basis for paying is the rare exception, existing only in a few small school districts.

Some kind of a salary schedule has been adopted by school districts progressively since the early 1900's.[3] Currently the existence of a salary schedule is common to virtually all school districts in the United States.

The salary schedule of the years since the turn of the century pretty much set the stage for all subsequent schedules. They took into consideration one or more of the following:

training	the stimulation of
experience	professional improvement
cost of living	educational improvement
need for recognition	minimums and maximums

the desirability of a single salary schedule
the need that the salary schedule be of simple structure and flexible

The salary schedules of today will be reviewed in terms of the state, bases, characteristics, promotional rationale, method employed, and the factor of security.

The State

The role of the state with reference to the pay of school employees is one of protecting and advancing education, a state function, of furnishing leadership, and of providing encouragement. This role is met in most states through the provision of some kind of minimum salary scale.

The state minimum pay scale is ordinarily made effective by making state-aid payments conditional upon compliance with this facet of state law or regulation. In addition, the local school districts are free and are further encouraged through state leadership and permissive legislation to exceed state minimums in accord with the value they place upon education and their willingness and ability to support a program of quality education.

The oft stated fear that minimums tend to become maximums seems not to apply to the salaries of school employees. It seems that there is sufficient difference in the emphasis and value placed upon education, and that the competition among school districts for qualified teachers is so great, that it would be exceptional not to exceed the state minimum.

Bases for Salary Scheduling

School districts generally incorporate in their pay plans one or more of the following considerations which constitute the basis for the schedule:

preparation	position
experience	sex
merit	dependency

[3] See Arthur B. Moehlman, *Public School Finance* (Chicago, Rand McNally & Company, 1927), Chapter 9.

Preparation. It is common to find that salaries for teachers are classified by some such preparation designators as:

Less than Bachelor's degree
Bachelor's degree
Master's degree or 30 semester hours advanced work beyond the Bachelor's
Master's degree plus 30 hours (or other designated semester hours beyond the Bachelor's)
Doctor's degree

Preparation, that is academic training, is seldom the sole basis for determining salary. It is most frequently accompanied by an experience factor.

Experience. Increments averaging from $129 to $319 for each year of experience for a period of time ranging from 7 years to 18 years seem to characterize the salary schedules for teachers.[4] In combination with preparation, the preparation-experience schedule classifies the teacher in terms of his preparation and then further categorizes him in terms of his experience.

In some instances allowances are made for experiences other than teaching, such as travel and other employment experience, when these have implications for teaching competency. Military service, particularly when it has interrupted teaching employment, is often accepted for pay purposes as equivalent to teaching experience.

Merit. As indicated in the chapter on rating,[5] there are a number of ways in which merit considerations may be called into play. The employment of teachers in terms of their having the qualifications for the job in question conforms to the civil service type merit in terms of classification. Pay in accord with level of training and experience is predicated on the improvement that is considered implicit in training and experience. These, however, have just been covered under the headings of *Preparation* and *Experience*.

In addition to preparation and experience as merit pay considerations, extra pay is awarded for the acceptance and carrying out of added duties or responsibilities, for participation in school and professional organizations, for authorship and publication, for suggestions that in some way improve school operations, and for experimentation. All of these are sometimes subsumed under and provide the justification for what is termed merit pay.

Merit pay also appears within the salary structure in the form of an attempt to appraise performance. In this instance, at some point along the

[4] *NEA Research Bulletin*, 39:4, December, 1961, p. 122.
[5] See Chapter 14.

preparation-experience schedule, the teacher becomes eligible for a merit increment. The technique for camouflaging the lack of an instrument to measure performance can become very elaborate but generally condenses to a sort of averaging of the judgments of a number of individuals, including one's peers, supervisors, and administrators.

The merit pay in terms of performance carries with it so many negative side effects that it either is eliminated or resolved into a more defensibly administered career recognition plan.[6] This often merely puts a premium upon a combination of longevity and generally satisfactory work. Thus, teachers whose work is considered satisfactory receive an increment at some key points in service, e.g., 15, 20, or 30 years of service, serving as an added inducement to making a career of school employment.

Position. At one time a distinction was made in salary schedules between elementary and secondary school employment. In recognition of the relatively equal importance of each level of instruction and of the fact that whereas one teacher is at his best at one level of organization and another at some other level, generally no distinction is now made on the basis of position alone. To the extent that in some instances, the elementary school teacher is required to have a minimum of a bachelor's degree whereas the secondary school teacher is required to have a minimum of a master's degree, the differential is truly one of preparation rather than of position.

Sex. The single salary schedule which does not differentiate with respect to organizational level today applies also in general to the sexes. No differentiation is ordinarily made on the basis of sex. This too is a product of the evolution that has taken place progressively since the early 1900's.

In principle, the single salary schedule which rewards competency and has its basis in the job rather than in either position or sex has become firmly entrenched. There are two occasions when departure from the general principle seems warranted. If the job entails duties that are assigned when a man fills the vacancy and which are not assigned when a woman fills the vacancy, then all other factors being equal, the pay for the man ought to be the greater. The greater salary for the man is not paid on the basis of sex, however, but because of the difference in job requirements. Also, if it is necessary to induce members of one sex to enter the profession in order to arrive at a desired balance, e.g., 50 per cent of each sex, then it may be necessary temporarily to increase the pay for the minority sex group of employees as an inducement to bring

6 "Call It Anything, but Don't Say Merit Pay," *School Management,* 4:1, January, 1960. pp. 34–38, 77.

employee balance and pay up to par. The use of increments based on sex imply a pay scale that is too low.

Dependency. In some school districts the pay scale is adjusted in terms of the number of dependents the employee, usually a teacher, has. There is no justification for dependency allotments in a system in which pay is intended to be compensation for work done. Resort to dependency allotments is tacit admission that the pay scale is too low and that supplementation by some means and on some basis at least remedies to some extent the inadequacies of the pay schedule.

If there is any justification for dependency allotments it lies in the degree that it is used as a means for providing added pay for the most needy, and then only as an intermediate step toward arriving at a salary schedule of such adequacy that dependency allotments can be discontinued.

Salary Schedule Characteristics

Salary schedules for school employees have been characterized by a range from the minimum to the maximum. The median for this range has with considerable consistency been just about at the median for all wage earners. And the range has, with a few exceptions, been limited to a maximum which did not quite double the minimum. The period of years to move from the minimum to the maximum varies from school district to school district but has for long been from approximately 10 to 20 years. Only during recent years has there been indication of forces moving strongly to make the maximum more than double the minimum [7] and decreasing the period for arriving at the maximum to something less, e.g., 5 to 12 years.

Rationale for Promoting Pay Increases

Virtually every effort to gain an increase in pay for school employees has its rational basis in terms of the importance of education and the deprivation with which children and the society are threatened if the economic lot of school employees is not improved.

Selectivity. The arguments for improved pay conditions are generally accompanied by some reference to the tradition of poor pay for so important an activity and the long suffering dedication of teachers. It is usually pointed out too that the pay aspects of school employment deter many able young people from entering the profession of teaching. It is

[7] Eric Rhodes, "How to Plan Better Salary Schedules," *NEA Journal,* December, 1958, 47:9, pp. 605–606.

assumed that improvement of the economic conditions for teachers would make possible the higher selectivity upon which improvement of education in general is to considerable degree dependent.

Special Increments. As temporary and tentative steps to make some headway toward better pay, groups of school employees have promoted increments for men or/and those who have dependents. This is to induce more men to enter teaching. Such plausible grounds for less than full-scale measures to bring teacher and other school employee pay to a defensible level are expected to be initially acceptable to the board of education and the community and are thought of as first steps to over-all improvement of pay conditions.

Price Index. For those already on the school payroll, every upward turn of the consumer price index is cited as grounds for an increase that will at least maintain the economic status quo. Failure to keep abreast of cost of living increases is regarded as equivalent to a salary cut. Price index increments do no more than to maintain the status quo.

Comparisons with Other Professions. Comparisons have often been resorted to, generally comparisons with other professions whose economic lot is envied. The medical and legal professions are the ones with which comparisons seem most often to be made. Comparisons with the nursing profession are conspicuous by their absence. Understandably, if not wholly wisely, the teacher group sets its sights upon the professions that are most favorably rewarded. Rather inexplicably, comparisons with engineering are rare although this profession most closely approximates the teaching profession with its academic preparation of four to five years.

Comparisons with All Wage Earners. There have also been comparisons with wage earners in general. Not only does this comparison not aid the cause of teachers since the median of their earnings is generally close to that of all wage earners, but also teachers see themselves as distinct from the educationally heterogeneous all-wage-earners group. Particularly as teachers tend increasingly to be 4- and 5-year college graduates with the bachelor's and often the master's degree, they regard themselves as more educationally favored than the all-wage-earner group and consequently eligible for correspondingly preferential pay.

An Index Related to Unskilled Labor. Moehlman [8] developed what he called a "rough index" which was based on the earning power of unskilled labor. This was used because of the premise that the pay for

---

8 Arthur B. Moehlman, *Public School Finance* (Chicago, Rand McNally & Company, 1927), Chapter 9.

unskilled labor was reflective of minimum economic need and was therefore also highly sensitive to changes in the economy. In 1922 the index range for a teacher who had graduated from a 4-year college training program was from a minimum of 175 to a maximum of 300.

The 1922 index was supplemented in 1945 with increases in the index as an adjustment to the changed scene following the depression of the 1930's and end of World War II.[9] Thus for teachers with 5 years of preparation the index provided a range of 180 to 310 and for teachers with 6 years of preparation a range of 200 to 330. In addition these latter two groups of teachers became eligible for flat sum annual "merit" increments on two levels. The merit increments were respectively approximately 5 and 12 per cent of the maximum that had been reached. It was thought that in terms of the teachers considered, probably 65 per cent would qualify for the merit increments. This approach to pay would provide today, with the federally imposed minimum wage of $1.25 per hour and a 40-hour week, the following schedule:

TABLE 16-1
Unskilled Labor Index Applied
to Teacher Salaries
(Pay per Month) *

Years of Preparation	Minimum	Maximum Automatic	MERIT	
			First Step	Second Step
4	$380	$650	—	—
5	390	670	$700	$785
6	430	715	750	840

* This would be affected by any change from a 40-hour week.

The application of the Moehlman index would obviously increase salaries in many school districts; in others it has already been surpassed. The index has one major weakness which is common to status studies. It has been derived from the range of practice in the payment of unskilled, skilled, and teacher employees. This imposes upon the teacher salary index the arbitrary ceiling of past questionable pay practices.

Attention was also given on similar basis to the wages of nonteaching employees.[10] These are noteworthy chiefly because they demonstrate

9 Arthur B. Moehlman, Personnel Policies and Procedures for the Glencoe, Illinois, Public Schools (Glencoe, Illinois, The Board of Education, September, 1945, a mimeographed report), p. 19.

10 As a matter of interest the school administrator or one preparing for such a position may apply the indices provided by the two Moehlman references, *Public School Finance* (Chapter 10) and the Glencoe, Illinois, Personnel Policies and Procedures (pp. 26, 27, and 30) in order to arrive at one basis for appraising local school district pay rates.

concern for school employees other than teachers. The bases used appear in Table 16-2.

TABLE 16-2
Unskilled Labor Index Applied
to Nonteaching Employee Salaries

Employee	INDICES		PAY PER MONTH	
Classification	Minimum	Maximum	Minimum	Maximum
Superintendent's secretary	150	200	$325	$433
Chief building clerk-secretary	120	180	260	390
General clerk	110	160	238	346
Maintenance personnel *	—	—	—	—
Engineers (stationary)	180	226	390	560
Custodians **	100	150	217	325

* Prevailing rates in the community for comparable skill level in the respective trades.
** An arbitrary increment that amounted to a decreasing percentage of 17 to 5 per cent of custodial wages for those on the same level of the scale. The scale had 10 steps.

Comparable Pay for Comparable Qualifications. Largely since the latter 1950's, there has been an awakening to the fact that implicit in all the bases employed to date is a basis that is common to them all. The implications of all the approaches has really been that there is a relationship between school jobs and jobs outside the school service.

It was in subconscious search of just what the relationship was that all of the bases enumerated were adduced to the problem of teacher and other school employee pay. Much of the searching was a relatively blind groping in a dark unknown that was nevertheless pierced occasionally by a glimmering of light, a glimmering that was at the time too slight to permit comprehension of what was momentarily revealed.

As early as 1927, Moehlman [11] stated that, "The requirements for school engineer and janitor parallel similar service in private commercial and manufacturing activity in contrast to the teacher, who has no such parallel." Later, in 1945, he applied this principle to school maintenance personnel (See footnote to Table 16-2).

Perhaps during the early days of teaching, when professional requirements were appallingly low, the application to teaching of the principle of equal pay under similar working conditions could not be seen because teachers were not comparable to other groups. It seems strange, however, that the principle was not early applied to school secretarial and clerical employees who had their match-mates in industry and government.

Today the scene has changed. Teacher preparation has its counterparts in the preparation required for many jobs in both private enter-

[11] Moehlman, *Public School Finance,* p. 156.

prise and government. The number and kinds of positions that require graduation from a four-year college program have multiplied greatly. Among the more common kinds of jobholders for whom a college education at some level (often beyond 4 years) is a prerequisite, or virtually so, are:

accountants	management personnel
the clergy	nurses
dentists	pharmacists
doctors (medical)	salesmen
engineers	scientists
journalists	social workers
lawyers	statisticians
librarians	teachers

Under this changed scene, it may be perceived that although the actual work done by teachers is unique to teaching and distinct from such other occupations as those listed, nevertheless a consideration of major importance to all jobs in which college training is required or preferred is an academic training that is recognized as equivalent.[12] The period of preparation is a common requirement and a possible economic equalizer.

During 1961, the Arlington Education Association entered into a contract with the Bureau of the Census of the U.S. Department of Commerce to get its sampling of the earnings of persons 25 years old and over who completed 4 years or more of college education, and who worked 40 weeks or more in 1959, by age, for Arlington County, Virginia. This action by the Education Association reflects due recognition of the equating importance of the length of academic preparation for pay status. The preliminary data thus procured are cited in Table 16-3.

The finding in Arlington was that the median incomes of teachers were approximately $3,000 less per year than those of all others in the community who also had a college level education. This finding is not wholly surprising. Apart from the difference in the length of the school year, it is noted that all those with four or more years of college education were included. It might be suspected that the proximity of Arlington to Washington, D.C., has influenced a large number of men with well above the 4-year college preparation to reside in Arlington.

A more defensible position for teachers would be one in which the college graduates had been classified by number of years of academic

---

12 The baccalaureate is generally conferred upon the completion of a four-year approved program and is regarded as equivalent irrespective of the discipline involved. Similarly, the master's and doctor's degrees normally involve programs of one and three years of fulltime graduate study respectively irrespective of the discipline, although in the latter instance the time factor is somewhat complicated by research requirements and other evidences of competency that do on occasion extend the time period.

TABLE 16-3
Earnings in 1959 of Persons 25 Years Old and Over Who Completed
Four Years or More of College Education, And Who Worked 40 Weeks
or More in 1959, by Age, for Arlington County, Virginia; 1960

Total Money Earnings		Age (years)			
	Total	25–34	35–44	45–54	55 and over
Total with earnings	100.0	100.0	100.0	100.0	100.0
$15,000 and over	7.2	1.4	7.8	10.8	11.2
10,000 to $14,999	30.0	5.0	36.2	45.9	36.7
9,000 to 9,999	8.2	5.3	10.5	7.5	10.6
8,000 to 8,999	9.8	8.5	13.4	8.0	7.8
7,000 to 7,999	9.8	12.7	10.3	7.5	6.8
6,000 to 6,999	10.7	19.4	7.1	7.1	7.6
5,000 to 5,999	9.7	18.1	6.4	5.8	7.0
4,000 to 4,999	7.3	16.7	3.7	3.2	3.4
1 to 3,999	7.4	12.9	4.7	4.1	8.7
Median earnings	$8,520	$6,119	$9,419	$10,741	$9,821

Source: 1960 Census of Population. These are preliminary data prepared by the Population Division, Bureau of the Census, U.S. Department of Commerce. The figures are subject to sampling variability as well as to errors of response and nonreporting. The data appear here by courtesy of Richard G. Neal, Executive Secretary of the Arlington Education Association.

preparation as well as by an age or experience classification. This would have permitted the comparison of teacher incomes with those of other professions which had comparable academic preparation and experience. Such refinements may be expected as the principle of comparisons on the basis of like qualifications becomes more firmly established.

The principle of comparisons on the basis of like academic preparation is illustrated to a degree by the "Campus Story of '62."[13] In this story of the typical ranges of pay offered to newly graduated college students, the range of pay varied for each job classification, sometimes little and sometimes greatly. The graduates reported on were accountants, engineers, journalists, lawyers, librarians, management trainees, mathematics majors, medical interns (including living allowances), salesmen, scientists (biological), social workers, statisticians, and teachers. The over-all range in beginning pay offered was from $210 to $650 per month. The midpoint for the pay for each job classification ranged from $345 to $575 with teachers at $418 per month.

Relatively, the beginning pay of teachers does, in the economically

[13] The "Campus Story of '62—Jobs Waiting at Higher Pay" was based on reports of the College Placement Council, Inc., and appeared in *U.S. News & World Report,* LII:21, May 21, 1962, pp. 76–78. The midpoints of the ranges were derived from the table in the article cited.

favored school districts of the country, approach that of comparably prepared employees for other occupations. Actually, the low median salary of teachers, comparing most nearly to all wage earners rather than to a cross section of comparably trained professional level workers, suggests that the real problem area in even the economically favored school districts is the pay at levels subsequent to initial employment, e.g., for 5-year periods from initial employment to a peak and then to retirement.

Method of Securing Pay Increases

The method of gaining support for pay increases is implied by the rationale employed. An appeal is made to the public, by way of the board of education, to demonstrate an appreciation of the value of education, the worth of school employees, the plight of school employees as consumer prices mount, and comparisons with other wage earning and professional groups.

Although in instances each of the kinds of appeals used is effective to a degree, probably the real talking point is reached when a neighboring school district adopts a pay scale that is superior. This puts that school district in the position of being selective in its employment activities, leaving those whom it would not employ to seek employment in the less favored school districts. It also provides the situation by which teachers from neighboring school districts are induced to leave their current employment in favor of the better paid neighboring school district. Thus the less well paid school districts are doubly threatened. The threat applies the leverage for pay increases.[14]

Emerging seems to be the possibility of a method that, providing for adjustments to regional and local conditions, places the income of teachers and other school employees on a schedule that conforms to what those of comparable academic preparation, training, or skill are paid initially and progressively as they gain in experience.[15]

The emerging method for establishing teacher and other school employees' pay has the value of integrating the economics of school employees' pay with the economics of the community, school district, or region. Such integration constitutes one unquestionable facet of the axiomatic integrality of the educational system with the community.

[14] It is no expression of altruism when the teachers of one district rejoice at pay increases in a neighboring district. Realistically, they recognize that such increases improve greatly the likelihood of a like, if not even greater, raise for themselves.

[15] See Committee on Tax Education and School Finance, *Financing Professional Salaries for Professional Teachers* (Washington, D.C., The National Education Association, September 1958), pp. 3–22; and, Maryland Congress of Parents and Teachers and the Maryland State Teachers Association, *Investing in Our Future through Quality Education* (Baltimore, Maryland State Teachers Association, January, 1960), pp. 1–12.

The workability of the emergent method is abetted by progressive refinements in Department of Commerce and Bureau of Labor Statistics procedures which make possible a sensitivity and adjustment to economic conditions that were not possible in the pre-data processing equipment era.

The Security Factor

Undoubtedly school employees, like other governmental employees, have a job security that exceeds that of employees in private enterprise. The demand for education, as for any government service, is continuous.

It is wholly conceivable that the advantages of job security must be paid for in some way. The individual who risks greatly stands to gain or to lose greatly. He who risks little stands to gain or lose little. This may be expected to apply also to the pay scene. The worker in private enterprise lacks the security of those who work in the public employ. His gains may consequently be expected to fluctuate more widely than those of his public employee counterpart.

There is a real probability that the school employee, even under the assumed emergent approach to pay scheduling, will find his pay fluctuating close to the medians for his private enterprise counterpart. He cannot expect to match the peaks any more than he cares to match the valleys of remuneration. Security has its price, and part of that price is a lower individual pay ceiling.

METHODS OF PAYING

The chief methods of paying involve the total pay period, i.e., the length of the school year; the pay periods throughout the school year; special pay provisions for additional duties; adjusting for change in pay schedule; pay for sabbatical or other leaves, and pay advances.

The Total Pay Period

The school year has been traditionally one of 9 school months, approximately 180 school days, for which teachers were paid during the 10 calendar months of September to June. There has been some tendency to lengthen the school year to 185–195 school days, to require teachers to report some days in advance of the opening of school to the children, and to require teachers to remain on duty for some days after the children's school year has ended.

In some instances the lengthening of the period that the teacher has been required to be on duty has been accompanied by a pro-rated increase in salary, a practice that is eminently fair. In other instances, teachers have been required to be on duty for the extended duty period with no adjustment in their pay, an eminently unfair and exploitative practice resented by teachers and a reproach to those who use their power to the disadvantage of the profession.

In addition to 9- and 10-month school years, there are school districts that have 12-month employment for all employees. In this instance the prevailing practice seems to be the employment of teachers for a 52-week year, a one-month paid vacation in addition to regular school holidays, assignment to classroom teaching duties during the regular school year, and assignment during the summer months to approved activities.

Usually August is set aside as the month for vacations. The extra duty assignments are for the months of June and July. The duties include one or more of the following:

Classroom teaching for acceleration, enrichment, or remedial purposes.
Outdoor education, by way of camps and farms.
Enriching experiences in the arts, crafts, and sciences.
Recreation.
Special opportunities for the gifted, normal, and retarded.
Curriculum, school plant, school-community studies and reports.
Professional inservice training workshops.
Summer school advanced academic work.
Travel, as approved for its pertinence to educational improvement.

The pay implications of 12-month plans are that teachers are on a full year's pay status, adding proportionately (usually 2, possibly 3 months' pay) to their former annual pay. Teachers are no longer subject to a 2- to 3-month unpaid layoff annually. Exploitation of teachers through the extension of the employment period, without commensurate pay, is made more difficult.

Pay Intervals

Pay day for school employees may follow any of a number of patterns, among which the more familiar are monthly, first and fifteenth of the month, and biweekly. These pay days are spread either throughout the work period or the calendar year.

The Pay Pattern. The specific interval—whether a month, a half-month, 2 weeks, or some other—at which pay checks are made available probably is not of major significance unless there is strong sentiment on the matter among the employees. Generally, whatever employees are accustomed to and to whatever they have become adjusted is at the moment preferred by them and ought not to be disturbed except for overridingly excellent reasons that are then made wholly clear.[16] There is something to be said for being paid more often than once a month. Personal budgeting may be facilitated for those who might otherwise face a lean end of the month.

Work-Period Payment. School employees are comprised of those who are on 12-month duty and those who are on something less than 12-month, e.g., the 9- or 10-month school year, duty. The 12-month professional and nonprofessional employees present no special payroll problem. A problem has been introduced with respect to the less than 12-month employees.

Generally teachers and others employed for the duration of the school year are paid for their services during the months of the work period. However, there has been much debate about the value of having the school year pay issued in equal installments throughout the calendar, not the school, year.

The advantage of distributing 9- or 10-month pay over a 12-month period is that the board of education, through such payments, takes a hand in the personal budgeting of its employees. Employees may expect under such a system that each pay day of the calendar year the individual or family finances will be bolstered until the next pay day by the allotment due. There is no protracted period of weeks or months for which the individual has to plan and budget in advance. For those who are unable to manage their own financing, the 12-month distribution of the 9- or 10-month pay is undoubtedly helpful.

There are disadvantages to the 12-month distribution of 9- or 10-month pay. The money earned is not available at the will of the earner. It cannot be saved or invested to earn interest or dividends. Individual control over finances is weakened. In addition, a public relations problem is intensified.

The public thinks of teachers and other employees who work during the school year as having a long vacation. In a way it is sensed vaguely that teachers are not paid for this vacation; however, this knowledge is submerged. For any other industry, an annual involuntary and unpaid vacation of two or more months would be regarded as a disadvantage of employment in that industry and would be called a layoff. The stretchout of pay to cover 12 months rather than the actual period of employment lends itself to the public's understandable interpretation that teachers and other like employees have a 2- to 3-month paid vacation.

[16] Departure from a well-accepted monthly pay period to one of greater frequency on the basis, for example, of its being more economical is at least on the surface an affront to the intelligence of the employee. Even though the unit cost per check issued by means of a punch card machine operation is reduced, the employee will wonder about the true total cost in terms of more checks, more power consumed, more clerical time employed in the payroll office and at the distribution centers, more time consumed by employees in getting their checks, and more time spent in bank line-ups.

Although paid vacations are part of the economic scene in the United States, a paid vacation exceeding one month's duration would be rather uncommon. A pay plan that provides the semblance of a 2- to 3-month paid vacation, in addition to the regular school holidays, would play squarely into the hands of economy minded critics of the school operation.[17]

Debates about the advantages and dangers of 12-month pay plans for less than 12-month work periods could go on without end and would probably have to be determined by arbitrary decision. However, in view of the advantages and disadvantages of the pay stretchout, it would probably be desirable to institute two kinds of payrolls (one for 12 months and one for the actual work period) and to give the less than 12-month employee the option annually to be on the one or the other.

Pay for Additional Duties

Extra pay for extra work sounds like a fair proposition. It is eminently more defensible than the exploitative addition of "duties" which come to be regarded as a part of the job. Nevertheless, when provided, extra pay artificially inflates teacher pay to make it look better than it deserves to look. Consequently extra pay for extra work can actually serve as an obstacle to seeing the pay situation as it truly is and to gaining for the teacher a defensibly adequate income.

In addition to beclouding the pay issue, extra pay for extra work puts a premium value upon the extra work. This premium value can too readily result in encroachment upon and deterioration of the primary instructional job of the teacher.[18]

Far better than extra pay for extra work would be the more careful definition of what actually are the professional requirements to be met by the teacher and the limitation of demands made upon the teacher to these requirements. It is neither logically nor economically defensible to utilize the teacher's work time for "duties" that make no demand on his professional preparation and competency. Tasks that do not require professional competency may better be performed by nonprofessionals employed for the purpose.

17 Along the same line of argument is one that is real to those who experienced the depression of the 1930's when emotion ran high and reason was either brushed aside or subordinated through rationalizations. In times like those, pay during non-work periods would constitute an invitation to cut income for those months. Explanations that the paychecks were merely deferred payments of earnings during the 9- or 10-month working period would carry little if any weight.

18 "Extra-Pay Provisions in 1959–60 Salary Schedules," *Educational Research Service Circular*, No. 4 (Washington, D.C., Research Division, National Education Association, May, 1960), pp. 1–32.

Adjustment to a New Pay Schedule

A sharp increase in pay, necessitated by the neglect of many years, may require a period of some years for its implementation.[19] Care has to be exercised throughout such an adjustment period to avoid placing new employees in a preferential pay bracket as contrasted to that of those who have comparable education, training, and experience and who are already in the employ of the school system.

Sabbatical or Other Leaves

Leaves will be discussed subsequently (See Chapter 19). However, among leaves are those which have full or partial pay status for the employee concerned. Under conditions of paid leave, the employee is generally kept on the regular payroll and payments for the amounts due are made at the regular pay intervals.

Pay Advances

There are occasions when contingencies can be met when an advance on pay is possible. Sometimes the knowledge of such a possibility provides a feeling of well-being and security even when there is no occasion to apply for an advance in pay.

Provision for an advance in pay gives the administration an excellent opportunity to demonstrate the interest it has in, concern it has for, and value it places upon the individual employee. The demonstrated regard of the board of education and the administration affects the employee's feeling about his job, his colleagues, and the school system—the most important single factor in getting the best possible service of which an employee is capable.

It may be argued that the sophisticated will prepare for eventualities, that there are ways of meeting them other than through advances, that advances are disruptive of efficient business office operation, and that the public interest must be protected through refusal of advances.

The principles, objectives, and functions of personnel administration are no doubt so well understood at this juncture that it is unnecessary to meet any of the objections to pay advances, except the one involving the public interest.

It is necessary to deal scrupulously in matters of public concern. To a degree this need not interfere with pay advances. Certainly any advance

[19] The 1962 Kennedy Administration proposed pay schedule for federal employees was planned to take effect progressively over a 3-year period. See *U.S. News and World Report,* February 5, 1962, p. 42.

that has been earned at the time of request is merely advance payment for services already performed and does not threaten in any way the public interest. Pay advances that are limited to what has been earned at the time the advance is made are easily and wholly defensible.

Needs beyond earnings are most defensibly met only through the special provision by either the board of education or an employee association (possibly a credit union) of a loan fund upon which employees may draw in accordance with loan policies.

MEASURES OF SALARY SCHEDULE ADEQUACY

The objective of school personnel administration has been summed up as:

. . . to do whatever is necessary to make certain that all school employees have the competencies needed for their respective jobs, the will to use their competencies in optimum fashion, and the working conditions under which each can exercise and improve his competency in such a way that the educational job of the schools will be done with utmost effectiveness.[20]

The objective of school personnel administration has been reflected in the principles of school personnel administration, particularly the five mentioned in this chapter. The combination of objective and principle provide the basis for the criteria to measure the adequacy of the salary schedule.

Affirmative answers to the following questions are indicative of an adequate pay scale; negative answers of an inadequate pay scale:

1. Are school employees in the various categories able, on the basis of their regular school pay, to have a standard of living comparable to that of others outside the schools who have like skills or a comparable level of education required for the job?

2. Does the pay scale for school employees place the school system in a favorably competitive position to attract to its employ its share of the more able youth?

3. Is the pay scale such that the employee has economic evidence that his work is regarded as truly worthwhile?

4. Are pay scales reviewed and modified in terms of the findings of studies, conducted continuously, pertaining to issues that have or may have bearing on pay issues?

5. Are school employees, particularly the newer ones, more fully reliant upon their school employment income as their sole means for earning, i.e., is moonlighting on the wane?

6. In summary, do pay scales compare equitably with those for jobs that are at least roughly equivalent throughout the economy?

[20] See Chapter 1.

SUMMARY

The implications for improving the functioning of the schools and the quality of education through adjustment of the pay scale for school employees are found in five of the principles of school personnel administration.

Adjustment of pay scales has taken place traditionally without a basis in defensible policy. There is need to provide a basis in a policy that compensates for school employee lack of bargaining leverage and that provides for adjustments to change. Departure from the familiar ways of getting salary adjustments poses all the usual problems of breaking with tradition, making the transition to the new, and assuring necessary modification progressively.

Implicit in virtually every salary schedule are factors that have been introduced over the years, many of them present during the period of the 1920's. Pay increases were rationalized or justified for the personnel selectivity theoretically made possible, special increments to favor men, increases in the consumer price index, comparisons with pay in other professions or occupations, and an index related to the wage of unskilled workers. Somewhat new, crystallizing during the latter 1950's, is the basing of school employee pay on that of others in private or government employ who are required to have comparable education, training, skill, and experience.

The job security of school employees is seen as a factor that limits extremes of pay fluctuations from the median pay of comparable workers in public and private enterprise. The avoidance of the valleys and inaccessibility of the peaks of economic reward are at once the compensation for and the price of public school employment.

The usual school year, some tendencies to extend it, and 12-month plans have implications for the pay of school employees. Pay intervals, particularly for employees who are on school duty only during the school year, introduce questions of advantages versus disadvantages. Generally, the employee regards as advantageous the system with which he is familiar and to which he is adjusted.

Pay for additional duties is regarded as a handicap toward attaining an adequate pay scale and a threat to the professional effectiveness of the teacher. Adjustments to a radically increased pay scale call for a nonpreferential time schedule for the attainment of the schedule over a period of years. Leave pay is generally on the same schedule of payments as is that of active duty pay. Requested advances in pay, when not threatening the public interest, are advocated as consistent with the principles of school personnel administration.

The criteria for the adequacy of school employee pay are derived from the objective and principles of school personnel administration and are formulated as six questions to which an affirmative answer is indicative of adequacy; a negative answer is indicative of a problem area in the adequacy of the pay scale.

SELECTED READINGS

CASTETTER, William B., *Administering the School Personnel Program* (New York, The Macmillan Company, 1962), Chapter 6.

CORBALLY, John E., *School Finance* (Boston, Allyn and Bacon, 1962), Chapter 16.

ELSBREE, Willard S., and REUTTER, E. Edmund, *Staff Personnel in the Public Schools* (Englewood Cliffs, N.J., Prentice-Hall, Inc., 1954), Chapter 6.

KEARNEY, Nolan C., *A Teacher's Professional Guide* (Englewood Cliffs, N.J., Prentice-Hall, Inc., 1958), Chapter 9.

KNEZEVICH, Stephen J., and FOWLKES, John Guy, *Business Management of Local School Systems* (New York, Harper and Row, 1960), Chapter 6.

JOHNS, Roe L., and MORPHET, Edgar L., *Financing the Public Schools* (Englewood Cliffs, N.J., Prentice-Hall, Inc., 1960), pp. 423–437.

MOORE, Harold E., and WALTERS, Newell B., *Personnel Administration in Education* (New York, Harper and Row, 1955), pp. 244–269.

NEA Research Division, *Economic Status of Teachers in 1959–60*, Research Report 1960–R8 (Washington, D.C., The National Education Association, May, 1960), 50 pages.

National Industrial Conference Board, *The Economic Almanac 1962* (New York, The Conference Board in Cooperation with Newsweek, 1962), pp. 136–137.

OVSIEW, Leon, and CASTETTER, William B., *Budgeting for Better Schools* (Englewood Cliffs, N.J., Prentice-Hall, Inc., 1960), pp. 262–266.

STOOPS, Emery, and RAFFERTY, M. L., *Practices and Trends in School Administration* (Boston, Ginn and Company, 1961), Chapter 21.

WEBER, Clarence A., *Personnel Problems of School Administrators* (New York, McGraw-Hill Book Company, Inc., 1954), Chapter 15.

YEAGER, William A., *Administration and the Teacher* (New York, Harper and Row, 1954), Chapter 16.

YEAGER, William A., *Administration of the Noninstructional Personnel and Services* (New York, Harper and Row, 1959), pp. 111–117.

.17.

Tenure and Job Stability

WITH IMPLICATIONS for each other and of importance to a school system, tenure and job stability are interrelated facets of the school personnel scene. Tenure provisions are an instrument of personnel administration to improve educational efforts by endowing employees with a warranted sense of job security. An objective of tenure provisions is to bring about the stabilization of job holding that permits the school system to capitalize upon the competencies, enhanced by experience, of its employees. Tenure and job stability, regarded as closely related and mutually complementary topics, constitute the two major subdivisions and topics of this chapter.

TENURE

Once the exception and now the rule, tenure must be fought for, in order to attain it, in relatively few instances. However, wherever tenure has been attained there must be continuous effort and even struggle to retain the tenure privilege, improve and justify it, and render it less vulnerable to attack and the threat of its revocation.

Tenure will be reviewed in terms of definition, principle, objective, corollary, law, extent, and effect.

Definition

Since the very early 1900's when tenure was first introduced on the state-level scene in the field of education (The District of Columbia, 1906), it has gained for itself the connotation that identifies it with and defines it as *security in holding office or of having the right to employment status under prescribed conditions*. The security referred to in the definition is that of continuous or permanent employment subject to conditions specified in the tenure provisions.

Principles

Tenure provisions rest upon or are derived in terms of principles that govern school personnel administration. The exploration of the tenure question and issue has its reference base or point of departure in those principles. The principles that are particularly pertinent to tenure are:[1]

1. . . . The goodwill and cooperation of all school employees must be secured if the optimum education is to take place. Such goodwill and cooperation are the byproducts of employment in which working is a gratifying social experience as well as a means for making a livelihood.

One aspect of the "gratifying social experience" is the reasonable assurance of job security that tenure laws and policies provide.

2. The people who have instituted the schools and all employees within the school system have the same basic interest. This interest is the provision of the best education possible, consistent with . . . the means made available for doing the job.

The means for securing to the school system the continued services of its personnel makes it possible for the school system to capitalize upon the experience assets of its employees as well as upon their increasing familiarity with the school and the school district. Tenure provisions create the conditions for such capitalization.

3. . . . all the personal considerations of the (school) employee are part of the problem of personnel administration to the extent that they have implications for the work he does.

A major concern of everyone who earns his living is the security of his job. A threat to that security is an invitation to the anxieties that undermine worker efficiency and is a stimulus to him to engage in such activities as putting out leads for another job in order to compensate for insecurity. Tenure provisions ease unwarranted anxieties and thus permit full attention to the requirements of the job.

4. The human factor is a variable. . . . It is also the cause for many of the most complex and perplexing problems in personnel administration. Temptations to make concessions to the administrative expediency of promoting conformity must be shunned in favor of recognizing and promoting the unique individuality and consequent possible personal development of each within the school system.

The easy way to administer is to eliminate nonconformists and to surround oneself with conformists. There are administrators who follow

[1] See Chapter 1, Principles 1, 3, 5, 7, 11, 12.

the easy way at the expense of the job security of competent school employees. Not only do the school employees face the threat of job loss, but also the school system suffers the loss of competent personnel. Tenure provisions secure to the school system the assets of variability and protect it from the liabilities of conformity.

5. All participants in an enterprise are entitled to fair dealing. Unfairness and the appearance of injustice are causes of rankling resentment which is a threat to worker effectiveness. . . .

Increasingly in our society a premium value is placed upon security. As the yeast of security permeates the society, unwarranted violations of security or insecurity for the competent are consonant with unfairness. The resentment of unfairness is not limited to the employee who suffers its consequences; it is a source of disquiet among all of the other employees who see themselves threatened in like manner. Tenure provisions are a means for setting up rules of fair play.

6. The relationships among employees and between them and their employers can to large extent be summed up. The summing up should be expressed in written policy. Written policy is a means for assuring consistency, promoting a feeling of security, and avoiding pitfalls of expediency.

The principles that are addressed to the avoidance of expediency and conformity, the promotion of variability, the consistency that spells fairness, and the security that benefits first of all the school district and incidentally also the school employee produce optimum results in terms of their implementation and their morale potential when they lend themselves to ready communication to the citizenry, administration, and school employee. The written policy statement is the means for ready communication.

The six principles presented serve as reference points for the further consideration of tenure provisions for school employees.

The Objectives of Tenure

To considerable extent the principles governing tenure pretty much indicate also the objective of tenure. Tenure provisions have truly but one objective; that is the furthering of the well-being of the educative function. This is an objective to which all who appreciate the importance of education agree and it is, therefore, in terms of this objective that tenure provisions have become generally accepted as desirable and necessary to the scene of teacher employment.

There are, however, other objectives that are sought through tenure, objectives that improve the well-being of the teaching profession. These objectives are subordinate to the one objective and are corollary to it in terms of either the public or the professional interest—possibly both.

When the interests of the profession actually or seemingly subordinate the public interest, the profession and the schools become vulnerable to suspicion, criticism, and even attack as a skeptical public takes defensive measures against what appear to be the self-serving interests of the profession.

The language used to promote and support tenure provisions can be a source of confusion to the general public when the same language that gained the support of the beneficiaries, the teachers, is used without variation to gain the support of the public. What may be the right language to gain employee support may prove the wrong language to gain employer support.

The interests of the school employee and of the public do converge at a common point, the point at which each is concerned about the effectiveness of the school operation. At this point school employees and the public may be expected to be in harmony about support measures that promise improved school operation. From this point, however, interests diverge in terms of the perspectives and particular interests of each. Whereas the interests of school employees understandably gravitate about the benefits that tenure provisions confer upon them, the public's interest in the welfare of school employees is distinctly limited to its comprehension of the implications of that welfare for education.

School employees may be expected to support tenure on the dual basis of its contribution to the effectiveness of the schools and to employee welfare. The public may be expected to support tenure on the single basis of its contribution to the effectiveness of the schools and may even be expected to regard with some suspicion any mention of or stress upon employee welfare.

The objectives of tenure provisions may be summarized as being:[2]

1. A means to improve the teaching-learning situation in the schools by providing for the continuity of service which makes possible capitalization upon experience and increasing familiarity with the school and community served.

2. The provision of a gratifying social experience, one that is conducive to professional growth and freedom from unwarranted anxieties about job security.

3. The assurance of protection against possibly capricious administrative behavior by which those who display independence or originality are threatened.

4. A safeguard to protect and capitalize upon employee variability demon-

---

2 For other statements of objectives, see any of the following: *Annual Report of the Committee on Tenure and Academic Freedom* (Washington, The National Education Association, 1954), p. 5.

Leo M. Chamberlain and Leslie W. Kindred, *The Teacher and School Organization* (Englewood Cliffs, N.J., Prentice-Hall, Inc., 1958), pp. 178, 179.

B. J. Chandler and Paul V. Petty, *Personnel Management in School Administration* (Yonkers-on-Hudson, N.Y., World Book Company, 1955), pp. 342, 343.

William B. Castetter, *Administering the School Personnel Program* (New York, The Macmillan Company, 1962), pp. 341, 342.

strated by responsible independent action, the exercise of ingenuity, and the experimentation that is the forerunner to innovation and progress.

5. The institution of fair employment practices which protect employees from possible pressures either internal or external to the school system. Learning can take place effectively only in an atmosphere of freedom to seek and extend knowledge.

6. The incorporation of tenure provisions in a statement of policy that is easily communicable and readily accessible to all who are subject to its provisions.

A Corollary to Tenure

Without tenure the employee is subject to whatever action the administration may deem desirable for whatever cause. Under these circumstances there is one advantage that may accrue to the schools. It is easy to dismiss employees of low competency.

The introduction of tenure provisions provides such a protective cover for school employees that there is danger that the incompetent will benefit to the detriment of the teaching-learning situation and contrary to the intent of tenure policy.

In order to offset the potential danger of tenure to the school system, a corollary to tenure provisions has been made necessary. This corollary provides the school system with protection against the retention of incompetent employees by setting up procedures by which the incompetent may be dismissed from service without any weakening of tenure provisions for the competent and without impairment of the principle of fairness and justice which underlies and permeates all of personnel administration. As tenure is concerned with job holding, any provision for ridding the school system of incompetent personnel is corollary to but not an objective of tenure provisions.

Tenure Laws

Tenure is provided for under law in two distinct ways. These two ways of endorsing tenure are not always clearly understood either within the school system or by the public. Weber has given a clear statement in this regard, stating that:[3]

Two types of tenure laws have been developed, the first being the contract-type tenure law and the second being a policy-stating tenure law. . . . The first type of tenure law creates contracts of a continuing nature between teachers and school districts or between teachers and the state. The second type of law does not create a contractual relation but merely states legislative policy which may be changed by subsequent legislative enactments.

[3] By permission, from Clarence A. Weber, *Personnel Problems of School Administrators* (New York, McGraw-Hill Book Company, Inc., 1954), p. 144.

Thus if a teacher has "tenure" under the first type of law, which is contractual in relationship, the Constitution of the United States prevents its change in spite of subsequent legislative enactment since the Supreme Court of the United States has established sacredness of contractual relationship as one of the basic guarantees of American democracy. However, if a teacher has "tenure" under the second type of law, . . . where the law merely sets forth policy, . . . (he) can lose all tenure benefits by subsequent legislative action because the same courts have held that in matters of policy one legislature cannot tie the hands of a future legislature.

Tenure that is provided by way of a contractual agreement provides greater security to the competent employee than does tenure that is only an expression of policy.

Tenure legislation that does no more than establish legislative policy has value for the intent it displays and is undoubtedly pretty generally accepted as a firm legal basis for tenure, indistinguishable on the surface from tenure by contract. However, tenure based on legislative policy is vulnerable to change and even cancellation, leaving those who felt secure under supposed tenure provisions without job security.

Tenure legislation that establishes tenure as a part of a contractual agreement provides all who are employed subject to that legislation with job security that cannot be legitimately undermined as long as the conditions of employment and of tenure are met. Nevertheless, it is within the power of the legislature or its successor body to change and even cancel legislation that provides for tenure by contract. However, should that occur, those who are under contract are protected thereby and the changed tenure provisions affect only those employed subsequent to the change in tenure legislation. These latter are subject to the new conditions created by amendment or revocation of the law.[4]

In some states the tenure laws clearly identify tenure with contractual status. In these states the problem of interpretation of the law seems minimal. However, in a number of states the wording of the tenure law is such as to leave in doubt the legislative intent, whether to make tenure a matter of contract or merely to set forth a statement of policy. In the latter states the only recourses of those who are interested are 1) to secure clarifying amendments, 2) to subject the legislation to the opinion of the state's attorney general, and 3) to submit a test case for court decision. Recourse to the legislature or to the courts is accompanied by a degree of certainty and reliability that cannot attend the opinion of the state's attorney general.

4 See NEA Research Division, *Trends in Teacher Tenure through Legislation and Court Decision* (Washington, National Education Association, May, 1957); also Willard S. Elsbree and E. Edmund Reutter, *Staff Personnel in the Public Schools* (Englewood Cliffs, N.J., Prentice-Hall, Inc., 1954), p. 200.

Extent of Tenure Provisions

In the overwhelming majority of states there is some kind of provision for tenure of school employees, particularly teachers. The state tenure scene is one of flux with a trend toward increasing statewide tenure provisions. In 1960 there were tenure provisions in 38 of the 51 state-level jurisdictions (50 states and the District of Columbia). Of these 38, 25 had tenure laws that were statewide; 7 made provision for tenure but allowed the exception or exclusion of some and/or the exercise of local option in other school districts; and in 6 there was provision for tenure for designated city, county, or other school districts. And then there remained 13 states which had no tenure laws. Practices in these 13 were about evenly divided in their dependence on term contracts and statewide continuing contracts that make use of spring notifications if an employee is not to be re-employed.[5]

The extension of tenure from its early beginnings [6] in the District of Columbia (1906) and in New Jersey (1909) to its present day proportions is phenomenal when regarded in isolation from the general employment scene in the United States. When viewed within the context of developing employment practices in both government and private enterprise, the extension of tenure for school employees is seen as a part of a continuously evolving socio-economic scene, and a somewhat lagging part at that.[7]

The extent of tenure provisions may also be considered in terms of the types of employees covered by tenure. Ordinarily tenure provisions are for those who belong to the teaching profession. More specifically, generally tenure actually applies to classroom teaching jobs and is extended to those in administrative and supervisory personnel only in terms of their teacher qualification rather than their nonteaching job status. Thus administrative and supervisory personnel ordinarily have tenure as teachers, not as administrators or supervisors. This situation becomes clouded and controversial where tenure provisions specify that demotion or decrease in pay violate the tenure interest.

School employees other than those who belong to the teaching profession are generally not covered by tenure provisions except as they may

[5] For specific state information see: Research Division of the NEA, *Research Bulletin*, 38:3, October, 1960. pp. 81–85 and *State-by-State Abstracts of Tenure Laws*, Research Memo 1960–32 (Washington, The National Education Association, October 1960); also
William B. Castetter, *Administering the School Personnel Program* (New York, The Macmillan Company, 1962), pp. 344, 345.

[6] See Willard S. Elsbree, *The American Teacher* (New York, The American Book Company, 1939), p. 477.

[7] Labor Week, "Next for Workers in U.S.: Lifetime Jobs?" *U.S. News & World Report*, November 13, 1961, pp. 117–120.

be employed as classified civil servants by a municipal or county school system that has a civil service type organization for the administration of these employees. There is also the possibility of tenure provisions, either on the contractual or the policy basis, by local board action for any board of education employee, professional or nonprofessional. In this latter instance all that has been said about job security applies equally to the state and to the local scene.

Since all employees of the board of education are in fact and in principle executive agents to facilitate the school function, there is really no legitimate reason for differentiating between employees as to their professional status in providing for tenure. The thesis is that tenure is advanced and justified by the beneficial effects it is expected to confer upon the educational system. The professional organization would be well advised to assist the nonprofessional employees to attain tenure status.

Effects of Tenure Provisions

The effects sought by way of tenure provisions are implicit in the statement of tenure objectives. To what extent those objectives have been attained is somewhat conjectural. Evidence as to the extent to which the teaching-learning situation in the schools is enhanced by tenure is not available.

Some evidence was accumulated early in the history of tenure indicating that the totals of teacher turnover seemed generally unaffected by tenure provisions.[8] There was, however, some evidence of change of pattern in that the central tendency of the distribution of dismissals or separations became skewed in the direction of those employed during the initial or probationary period and the turnover of experienced teachers lessened somewhat.

Several studies indicated that, contrary to expressed fears, teacher tenure laws did not cause teachers to lose interest in improving their professional competency. Holmstedt [9] found that teachers on tenure made as great effort to improve themselves as those not on tenure; it was found too [10] that summer school attendance at selected universities was not adversely affected by the job security provided through tenure provisions;

---

8 Willard S. Elsbree, *Teacher Turnover in the Cities and Villages of New York State*, Teachers College Contributions to Education, No. 300 (New York, Bureau of Publications, Teachers College, Columbia University, 1928); and Raleigh W. Holmstedt, *A Study of the Effects of the Teacher Tenure Law in New Jersey*, Teachers College Contributions to Education, No. 526 (New York, Bureau of Publications, Teachers College, Columbia University, 1932), pp. 100–102.

9 *Ibid.*

10 Committee on Tenure, *The Effect of Tenure upon Professional Growth* (Washington, The National Education Association, 1940), p. 12; also, W. S. Monroe, Ed., *The Encyclopedia of Educational Research* (New York, The Macmillan Company, 1950), p. 1438.

Weber [11] found that the ratio of schools employing teacher growth procedures in tenure states as compared with those in nontenure states was 12.4 to 1; and the proportion of teachers having master's or higher degrees was considerably greater for states having tenure than for those lacking tenure provisions for teachers.[12]

With reference to the second objective, it is self-evident and therefore not necessary to adduce proof that tenure does in fact set those covered thereby free from one source of anxiety, to that extent making school employment that much more gratifying.

The already mentioned decrease in the transiency of experienced teachers, together with the setting up of machinery for notifying a teacher of impending dismissal action, developing the case, providing for a hearing and, when desired, an appeal, is evidence that teachers are protected from capricious administrative behavior and indefensible administrative personnel action. Unfortunately, incidents occur too often for mental comfort indicating that the problems of developing and pressing a case against an incompetent employee is so harrowing an experience that the administrator shrinks from his responsibility and retains personnel to the detriment of the school system. Such irresponsible administration presents a threat to both education and tenure.

Evidence that tenure actually has promoted capitalization upon individual variability resulting in innovation is not available. As a matter of fact, it is often observed that such innovations as are made are often by administrative fiat rather than through the efforts of classroom teachers, the ones in the field and on the firing line.

On the whole the school scene is relatively free from outside political and other pressure groups. It has not become as free to make educational determinations as seems warranted, i.e., in areas wherein decisions call for expertness, the educator (teacher and administrator) often finds his views subordinated to those of the general and lay public. However, in general, public pressures are rarely brought to bear upon individual employees and when they are, the tenure policy provides the administration an effective means for resisting pressure and putting into operation the procedures pertinent to the case.

With progress in clarifying and extending tenure provisions, it has been recognized that potentialities for improving education are the justification for tenure and that side effects that threaten educational functioning are foreign to the tenure objective and must be offset through corollary provisions. The result of these two considerations has been the

[11] Clarence A. Weber, "Techniques Employed in a Selected Group of Secondary Schools of the North Central Association for Educating Teachers in Service," Ph.D. dissertation, Evanston, Illinois, Northwestern University, 1943, Appendix C.; also reported in his book, *Personnel Problems of School Administrators, op. cit.*, pp. 149, 150.

[12] The Council of State Governments, *The Forty-Eight State School Systems* (Chicago, The Council, 1949), Derived from Table 29, p. 202.

development of policies which set forth the conditions under which employees are protected by tenure and those under and by which they forfeit tenure privileges or rights.

Both the evidential and the *a priori* effects of tenure are apparently sufficient to justify tenure for school employees. However, in addition, the direction of socio-economic forces and of consequent employer-employee relations is such that even without the effects summarized, tenure is a product of the times. The question is no longer whether there should or should not be tenure. It is how tenure provisions may be developed to serve best their basic purpose, the furthering of the well-being of the education function. At the same time, it may be expected that appeals against dismissal and the invocation of tenure rights or privileges will be subject in part to the position of the appeal board membership with respect to a double standard of conduct, one for teachers and one for all other generally respectable members of a community.[13]

JOB STABILITY

Job stability is the term used to designate the measure of turnover among school employees. There are *a priori* reasons for concern among school personnel. These reasons will be brought into perspective by first considering the concern shown in both private enterprise and government with respect to labor turnover.

Private Enterprise

In private enterprise there has been concern since before the turn of the century with the implications and the problems of labor turnover. This concern has found expression in developments particularly since 1918 and has been accentuated by the cyclical fluctuations of the economy.

Personnel administration is primarily concerned with the achievement of organizational objectives. Labor turnover has implications for the objectives of organization as it:

1. interrupts productivity
2. calls into operation intensive activities on the part of the personnel division, activities that increase unit costs per employee in direct ratio to the rate of turnover
3. requires a break-in, training, or orientation period during which productivity is low and corresponding production costs are high
4. results in at least temporary less-than-full use of productive facilities
5. produces a threat to employee morale

13 Gilbert Geis and Robley Huston, "Trends in the Dismissal of Tenure Teachers," in Lee O. Garber, *1962 Yearbook of School Law* (Danville, Illinois, The Interstate Printers & Publishers, Inc., 1962), pp. 199–209.

    6. is accompanied by the ill-will of those who leave the employment of the organization

    7. creates problems of community relations

    8. affects adversely the quality of job applicants

The several by-products of labor turnover in one way or another menace the production and profit objectives of the industry. Therefore private enterprise has shown great interest in improving employment stability or decreasing labor turnover.

    In dealing with labor turnover virtually every reference on personnel administration or management takes the position that an unusually high turnover rate is symptomatic of something wrong, something to be uncovered and identified, and something to be remedied.

    A high labor turnover is generally considered cause for demoralizing unrest among employees, nevertheless, it has been stated, "Far more important than as a *cause* of demoralization among workers is the turnover as a *symptom* of demoralization which exists for other reasons." [14] Slichter's statement brings into focus the possible use of turnover data for diagnostic purposes, to probe into the causes for turnover and to provide the basis for modification of practices in selecting, administering, and paying personnel in order to reduce to a minimum all avoidable turnover.

Government

    By the late 1920's and since then the concern of the federal government with employee turnover found its expression in the literature [15] and practices of public personnel administration. The reasons for concern were very much the same as those expressed with reference to private enterprise except that the profit motive was absent.

    Government is possibly troubled more than is private enterprise by the turnover of its executive personnel. The problems, issues, and work situations that accentuate the importance of executive turnover in government are dealt with by Bernstein.[16] Turnover is regarded as a sticky problem, one to be solved.

    In addition, it is necessary only to read the daily newspapers and the weekly magazines that concern themselves with news of national import to sense the governmental concern with national employment stability.

    [14] Sumner H. Slichter, *The Turnover of Factory Labor* (New York, Appleton-Century-Crofts, 1921), p. 158.

    [15] Paul F. Brissenden, "Labor Turnover in the Federal Service," *Report of Wage and Personnel Survey* by the Personnel Classification Board (Washington, 70th Congress, 2nd session, House document No. 602, 1929), p. 320; and Lewis Meriam, *Public Personnel Problems* (Washington, The Brookings Institution, 1938), pp. 111–112 and 332–336.

    [16] Marver H. Bernstein, *The Job of the Federal Executive* (Washington, The Brookings Institution, 1958), Chapter 7.

Maximum employment conditions are promoted, unemployment elicits criticism and expressions of fear about the health of the economy, and the economic welfare of the nation is identified with a productivity that is affected by both, the employment rate and job stability.

The Schools

On the school scene there has been an interest in improving employment stability analogous to that on the private enterprise and government scenes. The *a priori* or common-sense reasons for seeking to promote greater job stability and decreased turnover follow in general the kinds of reasons listed for private enterprise and subscribed to also for government employment. The actual effects of increased job stability for school employees, especially in the way of gains in the facilitation of instruction, are assumptive rather than evidential.

A too-high turnover among school employees is considered undesirable because:

1. Continuity in service is regarded as facilitative of instruction.
2. Turnover is thought of as both disruptive of instruction and costly in terms of the activities engendered to fill vacancies.
3. The teacher is viewed as handicapped in effectiveness until he has become truly oriented to the school and community and fully aware of the resources available to him and how to make use of them in his teaching.
4. The unwarranted and on occasion the warranted turnover of personnel is believed to be demoralizing to the remaining school employees.
5. Unnecessary, i.e. avoidable, turnover of personnel carries with it the danger of the resentment of the affected employee, a matter of concern as long as he remains in the community and thereafter to the extent that the public has become involved.
6. There is fear that a high turnover will call attention to the causes therefor, with the consequence that otherwise prospective candidates will be discouraged from applying.

The attention of educators to the problems of teacher turnover was aroused early and found expression in an address before The National Education Association in 1907.[17]

Reasons for Teacher Turnover. The reasons for teacher turnover on the national scale are to considerable extent the product of the times. Earlier in this century, for example, marriage voided the contract of a woman teacher. She was not permitted ordinarily to continue teaching after marriage. During the years 1940 to 1944, the defense production and military service requirements of the United States caused many teachers

---

[17] National Education Association, *Journal of Proceedings and Addresses, 1907* (Winona, Minn., the Association, 1907), p. 371, as also reported in NEA Research Division, *NEA Research Memo 1960–24, Some Whys and Wherefores of Teacher Turnover* (Washington, The National Education Association, August, 1960), p. 3.

to leave school employment. After 1944, the schools found themselves in a losing competition for manpower with those who were eager to gear the nation's economy to meet the wants of a people who had for years been deprived of their consumer needs. This competition was heightened by a continued high level national defense effort with all its implications for staffing. The result for the schools was not only difficulty in recruiting to teaching but also a loss of personnel to private enterprise and government, both of which paid better.

At this time, with some levelling off of production, some increases in teacher pay, the promises and threats of automation in industry, and the fears of unemployment, the present reasons for turnover are sometimes summed up as "the four M's" of Marriage, Maternity, Money, and Moving. There is something to be said for this. Almost any listing of statistics dealing with turnover indicates that a very high percentage of the reasons come under these four headings.[18]

There is danger in complacently attributing turnover to the 4-M's. They seem so unavoidable that the personnel division may be lulled into disregarding the remaining causes for turnover, causes about which something can be done, causes which may be used diagnostically to correct disadvantageous working situations.

Added to the danger of complacently attributing turnover to unavoidable causes is the fact that both in industry and government, as well as in some school districts, it is recognized that the reason for leaving given at the time of separation is often a superficial, not the true, reason. It is therefore advocated that each separation be accompanied by an "exit interview." Even then it is recognized that the exit interview will be subject to considerable emotional overtones to such a degree that it is considered desirable to use either a post-exit interview or a questionnaire (or both) at some time after the employee has been firmly established in a new job. The purpose of the follow-up is strictly the enlightenment of the personnel division so that remediable causes for the loss of competent personnel may be identified and removed.[19]

Extent of Turnover. At its most favorable, teacher turnover on the national level seems to be at a rate of a little over 10 per cent. At the local levels the turnover rate will vary considerably above and below the

18 In a Maryland study it was found that about 68 per cent of separations fell under the 4-M's. See Office of Educational Research and Planning, Baltimore County Teacher Recruitment, Teacher Retention, Teacher Turnover, Needed Action—a mimeographed report (Towson, Maryland, Board of Education of Baltimore County, 1957), pp. 22–26. See also NEA Research Memo 1960–24, *op. cit.*, pp. 1–25 and Ward S. Mason and Robert K. Bain, *Teacher Turnover in the Public Schools, 1957–58*, Office of Education, U.S. Department of Health, Education, and Welfare, Circular 608 (Washington, Superintendent of Documents, Government Printing Office, 1959).

19 Kenneth Dunn, "Do You Know Why Your Teachers Resign?" *Overview* 2:6, June, 1961, p. 32; also Sydney Prerau (Ed.), *J. K. Lasser's Business Management Handbook* (New York, McGraw-Hill Book Company, Inc., 1960), pp. 327–328.

national figure. A turnover rate of 20 to 25 per cent is not at all rare in even some of the better paid urban areas of the nation.[20] This compares to a rate of labor turnover in manufacturing of 3.6 per cent for 1958 and 3.3 per cent for 1961. In fact the turnover of labor in manufacturing between 1930 and 1961 was in the range of 2.9 to 8.3 per cent. During 23 of these 32 years the rate of turnover in manufacturing was within a 3.0 to 4.4 per cent bracket.[21]

Computation of Turnover. Turnover for any employee group is the rate at which employees move into and out of employment. Usually turnover is expressed as the number of accessions or separations per 100 employees.

There are a number of ways by which to compute turnover. It is possible to devise computation formulas to suit one's purpose, e.g., either to minimize or exaggerate the rate, or to focus attention upon some one facet of turnover, such as avoidable vs. unavoidable turnover.

Since conditions vary with school districts and in time, it seems that uniformity and comparability of data may be introduced through the use of one of two differentiating formulas. The one formula would be for a contracting and the other for an expanding school district. Either of these might be used for a district in which the number of employees under consideration has been stabilized.

A school district in which the number of employees is being decreased will achieve some reduction in force through attrition, the deliberate and planned failure to replace personnel lost. In such a situation the turnover figures that are important are those reflected by accessions, new employees, rather than by the number of separations. The turnover formula for a contracting school district will then be for any group of employees:

$$TR = \frac{Ac \times 100}{Em}$$

TR = Turnover Rate per 100 employees
AC = Accessions or new employees
Em = The average number of employees
     on the payroll for the time
     period under consideration

[20] In 1958 the following turnover figures were obtained from the administrative, personnel, or statistical offices of school districts in the Washington, D.C., metropolitan area: the District of Columbia, 13.4 per cent; Maryland: Montgomery County, 19.3 per cent; Prince Georges County, 17–20 per cent; and Virginia: Alexandria, 15.6 per cent; Arlington, 25 per cent; Fairfax, 18 per cent; and Falls Church, 25 per cent. See also the 16 per cent rate estimated for 1960 on the national basis by Frank Lindenfeld, "Teacher Turnover in the Public Schools, 1959–60," *School Life,* 44:4, February, 1960, pp. 11, 12.
[21] National Industrial Conference Board, *The Economic Almanac 1962* (New York, The Conference Board in cooperation with *Newsweek,* 1962), p. 54.

On the other hand is the school district in which the number of employees is expanding so that it would be necessary to add employees even if there were no loss of personnel. In this expanding school situation, the accessions reflect a combination of turnover and growth factors. The turnover figures that are important are those reflected by separations. Under such circumstances the turnover formula for the expanding school district will then be for any group of employees:

$$TR = \frac{Sep \times 100}{Em}$$

TR = Turnover Rate per 100 employees
Sep = Separations
Em = The average number of employees
    on the payroll for the time
    period under consideration

Either of these formulas will apply to the stable situation because separations will equal accessions.

The Stable Force. It is sometimes maintained that concentration on turnover distracts attention from the positive factor, the part of the organization or that group of employees which does provide for continuity of service, growth in and utilization of experience, knowledge of and interrelationship with the school-community, and capitalization upon school and community resources to heighten the effectiveness of teaching. The formula for computing the stable force is:

$$SF = \frac{NSep \times 100}{Em}$$

SF   = The Stable Force in percentages
NSep = The number not separated from
    service for the time under
    consideration
Em   = The average number of employees
    on the payroll for the time
    period under consideration

It is sometimes stated that stability may be so great as to connote stagnation, that some turnover is desirable in order to introduce other ideas and ways of looking at matters. It would seem that for the forseeable future this need not be a concern for the schools. Past experience, the continuing rate of teacher turnover, and an expanding national population combine to suggest that education will have the benefits as well as the problems of an influx of new personnel. It would also seem at this juncture that teacher turnover is of such magnitude that school personnel administrators face the problem, not of creating, but rather of decreasing turnover.

Unavoidable Turnover. On the whole consideration of turnover or of its other facet the stable employee force has taken place with an eye toward the elimination of the problems, or the betterment of the work conditions, that cause turnover. This emphasis neglects the fact that some turnover is not preventable.

Among the chief causes for unavoidable turnover on the school scene are: death, family conditions, illness, old age, transfers within the school system, and the transfer of a teacher's spouse by his employer. There are no alternatives to unavoidable turnover.

SUMMARY

Tenure and job stability through the reduction of turnover have implications for the stabilization of job holding. This stabilization is sought to benefit instruction through the continuity in service of school personnel. Stabilization is provided through tenure and such improvement of working conditions that the number of school employees leaving the schools will be drastically reduced.

Tenure or job security has become so much a part of the socio-economic scene that it has become the rule both in school and non-school employment. In the schools tenure remains sensitive because of the public nature of the schools. It is consequently incumbent upon all who are concerned with the well-being of education to reduce the vulnerability of tenure provisions in the schools first of all by supporting or engaging in sound practices of personnel administration and second by setting up safeguards against possible abuses of tenure provisions. In no instance is it the intent that tenure should provide security to the incompetent.

Values that accrue to the schools by reason of tenure have been identified both through *a priori* reasoning and evidence. Tenure provisions constitute one facet of job stabilization. Another facet of job stabilization is the reduction to a minimum of the unnecessary separation from employment of competent school employees.

By comparison with an annual labor turnover of about 4 per cent in manufacturing, the annual turnover of teachers at a rate of 10 to 15 per cent and often ranging from 15 to 25 per cent shows up as a matter of grave concern for education. Any preventable turnover in which needed and competent personnel are lost to the schools is too great a turnover regardless of what the rate is.

Concern about turnover was found to prevail in private enterprise, government, and education. In each instance this concern relates to the primary function of organization, the promotion of conditions for optimum productivity. Corollary to the productivity factor is that of costs. Turnover was in all instances regarded as having implications for increased costs without correspondingly increased productivity.

Reasons for turnover fall into two major categories, the unavoidable and the unnecessary. The unavoidable leave no alternatives; the unnecessary are accompanied by the alternatives of identifying causes and changing working conditions to make them conducive to retaining competent personnel for continued school service.

Tenure and job stability serve together to further the cause of education and the effectiveness of the instructional activity to the extent that they retain in school service all competent personnel, professional and nonprofessional.

SELECTED READINGS

CHAMBERLAIN, Leo M., and KINDRED, Leslie W., *The Teacher and School Organization* (Englewood Cliffs, N.J., Prentice-Hall, Inc., 1958), pp. 171–181.

HUGGETT, Albert J., and STINNETT, T. M., *Professional Problems of Teachers* (New York, The Macmillan Company, 1956), pp. 17–19 and Chapter 8.

KEARNEY, Nolan C., *A Teacher's Professional Guide* (Englewood Cliffs, N.J., Prentice-Hall, Inc., 1958), pp. 182–187.

MOSHER, William E., and KINGSLEY, J. Donald, *Public Personnel Administration* (New York, Harper and Row, 1941), Chapter 16.

PIGORS, Paul, and MYERS, Charles A., *Personnel Administration* (New York, McGraw-Hill Book Company, Inc., 1951), Chapter 9.

TEAD, Ordway, and METCALF, Henry C., *Personnel Administration* (New York, McGraw-Hill Book Company, Inc., 1933), Chapter 19.

WAITE, William W., *Personnel Administration* (New York, The Ronald Press Company, 1952), Chapters 19, 20.

YEAGER, William A., *Administration and the Teacher* (New York, Harper and Row, 1954), Chapter 21.

YEAGER, William A., *Administration of the Noninstructional Personnel and Services* (New York, Harper and Row, 1959), pp. 87–90.

YODER, Dale, *Personnel Management and Industrial Relations* (Englewood Cliffs, N.J., Prentice-Hall, Inc., 1948), pp. 455–461 and 576–579.

NEA Research Division, current publications (Washington, The National Education Association).

State Education Associations. Among those that have made studies of teacher turnover are: Arkansas, California, Connecticut, Idaho, Illinois, Iowa, Minnesota, Montana, Nebraska, New Jersey, New York, Oregon, Pennsylvania, Utah, Virginia, and West Virginia.

U.S. Department of Health, Education, and Welfare, The Office of Education, current publications (Washington, Superintendent of Documents, Government Printing Office.)

.18.

Employee Welfare on the Job

THERE ARE many factors that pertain to the welfare of school employees. In a sense all that has been said up to this point and all that is to follow in this book pertains to employee welfare.

Employee welfare is an administrative concern because it is basic to efficient production or, in the schools, the facilitation of instruction. Therefore, this chapter will concentrate on four aspects of employee welfare that merit greater consideration than their passing mention in earlier chapters. Employee welfare will be discussed in terms of health, safety, physical plant, and work load.

HEALTH

Health is a physical, mental, and emotional state of great importance to both the individual and those with whom he associates. Often one kind of health, e.g., physical, is affected by other states of being such as mental and emotional. The probable interrelationships of these three states of health are such that no attempt will be made here to deal with each separately. Rather, attention will be given to the over-all problem of health.

There are a number of ways by which the health of school employees may be given consideration. The following of the more common health considerations will be discussed in this section: applicant's statements, medical or physical examination, tests of mental-emotional state, services provided, sick leaves, health insurance, social and recreational programs, and physical plant conditions.

Applicant's Statement

Ordinarily the application blank requires the applicant to indicate physical defects and the general state of his health. This is subject to at least a partial if somewhat superficial check when the prospective employee is observed at work and subsequently during the interview.

Medical Examination

Medical examinations fall into two categories, the pre-employment and the post-employment periodic examinations.

Pre-employment Examination. One of the usual conditions for school employment is a medical or physical examination. It is imperative that this examination be undertaken seriously. The welfare of all involved and the interests of the public virtually demand that a doctor, other than the applicant's or the employee's personal or family physician, approved and paid by the board of education conduct the examination and submit his findings directly to the board of education.

Screening out poor health risks protects the children, other school employees, and the community from possibly avoidable consequences. These consequences have particular reference to an absenteeism for health reasons that has serious implications for the functioning of the school system.

Post-employment Examination. Examinations subsequent to employment are advisable in order to induce personnel to maintain their health, detect conditions requiring attention, and bring about the appropriate remedial action. The maintenance of sound health among the school personnel is one of the essential steps toward establishing and maintaining an effective instructional situation.

The post-employment examination, taken periodically, perhaps every 3 or 4 years, differs from the examination that is a condition of employment in that its purpose is not to screen out or dismiss employees but to provide the basis for corrective action during the earlier stages of health deficiency. The school system has such a stake in the periodic medical examination of its employees that it ought to insist upon the examination taking place under its auspices just as at the time of initial employment. Also, the medical examiner's report should be forwarded directly to the board of education.

Mental-Emotional Tests

Under this heading are included all provisions for testing such aspects of mental health as attitudes, emotional maturity or stability, and personality. A considerable number of tests with implications for adult mental, emotional, and personality behavior are available.[1] Some tests are situational, i.e., the subject is placed in a complex, lifelike situation and then observed for his behavior under the circumstances. Other tests are projective, i.e., the subject is given an ambiguous stimulus (the inkblot, or Rorschach, test is among the more familiar of this type) to which he is required to react. His reactions are the clues to his state. This latter type of test is known as a Thematic Projective Test. A somewhat related test is the Thematic Apperception Test in which the subject is required to develop a story from a picture. The story told is considered indicative of the mental-emotional-personality state of the subject.[2]

Under conditions in which tests are available, diagnosis can be made, and treatment can be undertaken, there is no more reason to tolerate remediable mental illness or disturbance than there is to forego medical treatment for physical ailments. The school system has reason to be greatly concerned about the capitalization upon its investment in a carefully selected and experienced personnel, and the salvaging of such personnel whether their problems are physical or mental.

Services Provided

Aside from the physical examinations provided, chiefly at the time of employment, the school system ordinarily provides virtually no health services to its employees. This is the more remarkable because among the employees of many of the larger school systems there are doctors, dentists, psychologists, psychiatrists, and nurses.

The various healing arts personnel include part- and full-time employees who contribute to the maintenance of the mental and physical health of the school children. Their responsibilities and activities have generally been so defined that:

They usually act in the capacity of diagnosticians who aid in the detection of conditions demanding attention, advise parents to refer the child to competent practitioners in the areas of physical, mental, or emotional disorders, and give

1 Among the tests available are the following published by the:
Psychological Corporation—Edwards Personal Preference Schedule, Minnesota Counselling Inventory, Minnesota Multiphasic Personality Inventory, Minnesota Personality Scale, Mooney Problem Check Lists, and the Wittenborn Psychiatric Rating Scales
Consulting Psychological Press—Bell Adjustment Inventory
California Test Bureau—California Test of Personality
World Book Company—Gordon Personal Profile and Gordon Personal Inventory
Western Psychological Services—Guilford-Zimmerman Temperament Survey
Science Research Associates—Thurstone Personality Schedule
2 Henry A. Murray, *et al., Explorations in Personality* (New York, Oxford University Press, 1938).

clinical assistance under very limited conditions, largely in emergency and indigent cases.[3]

It would conceivably take but little to extend to school personnel at least the same services rendered the pupils. This would protect community interests, be a step toward salvaging personnel in whom the school system has a considerable investment, and thus protect and enhance the instructional program of the schools. As a matter of fact, a still further extension of actual clinical services, although radical on the school scene, would be in accord with practices in many industrial plants under private enterprise management where pre-employment and subsequent physical examinations are supplemented by consultations, treatment, provisions of technical medical services (blood tests, X-rays, etc.), and even complete medical care for employees and, in instances, for their dependents.[4]

Sick Leave

Sick leave is a sort of insurance that the employee receives to set him at ease about contingencies caused by illness and permit him to use his financial resources to meet other needs.

School systems commonly provide sick leave. Through this provision, school boards make it possible for the employee to absent himself from his work without anxiety about his job in order to hasten the recovery of his health and his return as an efficient worker. Shortening the period of illness decreases the period of reduced efficiency resulting from illness, protects all with whom the employee has contact from possible contagion, and consequently affects favorably the functioning of the school(s).

Sick-leave policies vary greatly. Ordinarily sick-leave allowances increase with service in a school system, are not transferrable from one school district to another, are cumulative to some maximum, and have assumed the proportions of a right as well as a privilege.

It matters little whether sick leave is regarded as a right or a privilege as long as it is used for the purpose intended and is not abused. There is little sense to the occasional proposal that a pro-rated per diem be paid for unused sick leave at the time that an employee leaves the service of the school system. Any practice that serves as an incentive to an ill person not to use sick leave legitimately is antithetical to the *raison d'etre* for sick leave.

Sick leave is not earned time-off or vacation. It may not legitimately or ethically be used for any purpose other than that intended. The use

---

[3] Arthur B. Moehlman and James A. van Zwoll, *School Public Relations* (New York, Appleton-Century-Crofts, 1957), p. 328.

[4] William W. Waite, *Personnel Administration* (New York, The Ronald Press Company, 1952), pp. 421–428.

of sick leave for personal reasons not covered by the sick-leave policy is the kind of abuse which endangers leave provisions, calls into being controls that are onerous to the school administration as well as to those who are ill, and handicaps efforts to liberalize or improve sick-leave provisions.

Conceptually, where there is no abuse of sick-leave, a progressive sick-leave accumulation without a ceiling would make sense for the school system and the employees. Such a policy would have to be accompanied by continuous education of all personnel to the values of sick-leave and accumulation privileges.[5]

Health Insurance

Group hospitalization, surgical benefits, and medical care are often provided singly or in some combination under the auspices of the school system. Such services may be provided under Blue Cross and Blue Shield or other group insurance plans.

On the whole, the idea of having health insurance paid for wholly or in part by the school district is catching on with boards of education rather slowly. An estimate that 25 per cent of those school districts that have some form of health insurance contribute to the payment of the premiums would probably be liberal.

School practice contrasts sharply with the federal government contributory plan for nearly two million employees and their dependents (a total of over four million potential beneficiaries) and with full or partial financing of group health plans by private firms in 78 to 90 per cent of the many that subscribe to group health insurance for their employees.[6]

An emerging area of health insurance is that intended specifically for major medical expense. The incidence of cancer and heart ailments involving expensive long-term treatment by specialists and often under costly controlled conditions has alerted the individual and the insuring agencies to the advantages offered by relatively low-cost major medical or catastrophe insurance.

The schools, their personnel, and the organizations in which school

5 One federal government employee, having used 4 days of sick leave during 22 years of government service accumulated 225 days of unused sick leave. Upon his retirement, he sent government officials a letter of appreciation for the feeling of security that he was able to enjoy progressively for 22 years as he had sick leave to fall back upon should this be necessary. In this letter, he "turned back" the unused leave with an expression of particular pleasure that he had had no occasion to use it. See Jerry Kluttz, *The Washington Post,* July 30, 1962.

6 For a clearly stated synthesis of National Education Association, National Industrial Conference Board, and other sources of information in this regard see, Jack H. Kleinmann, *Fringe Benefits for Public School Personnel* (New York, Bureau of Publications, Teachers College, Columbia University, 1962), Chapter 3.

personnel have membership have an obligation at least to keep abreast of the times in seeking to serve and protect school personnel, in the interests of better education, by improvements in the over-all working situation.

Social and Recreational Programs

Both in government and in private enterprise, attention is given to the social and recreational programs which have implications for mental health, social adjustment, physical fitness, and *esprit de corps*. School systems also make some provisions along these lines.

There is some question as to the necessity for an elaborate program of social and recreational activities for school personnel. The small school district does not generally need such a program because the school employee is quickly included in the life of the community. The larger school districts have available such a range of cultural, recreational, and social activities and opportunities that it would seem ordinarily unnecessary for the school system to organize such programs.

Nevertheless, it would seem advisable for the school administration and its personnel division to organize and make available such programs as can be adequately supported for those who wish to participate in them and at all costs to avoid setting up coercive programs that the school employees would regard as oppressive and demanding of time that they would prefer to use in ways deemed more advantageous.

Physical Plant Conditions

The school plant has for long been recognized as having implications for the health of its occupants; hence the care in providing cubage where forced draft ventilation is not furnished, large window areas before the improvements in artificial lighting, and heating where temperatures drop to the point of discomfort.

Today health considerations have promoted refinements in temperature (heating and cooling), humidity, ventilation, and lighting controls; acoustical treatments; color schemes; equipment; safety features; aesthetic touches that are as conducive to the mental and physical health of school employees as to that of the pupils; and greatly improved sanitary facilities and conditions.

Some strange inconsistencies become evident as educators forget to subordinate architectural design to educational function. Thus classrooms are sometimes unnecessarily made windowless,[7] apparently in

[7] Recently some American military personnel just released from a prison camp in Laos recounted the horror treatment to which they had been subjected in "black" rooms, windowless rooms that were painted black.

answer to the architect's search for something different from classrooms with window walls. Also some areas are treated acoustically to combat distracting noise. At the same time "team teaching" rooms are designed with the premise that distractions result from visual not auditory causes. It has even been suggested that such rooms be provided a built-in super-imposed sound just a little louder than the normal sounds of regular instructional activities. Actually the idea of such superimposed sound is not something new. Univent heating-ventilating systems have provided such superimposition to the regret of teachers for many years.

Those (lay and professional people) who have misgivings about windowless classrooms wonder about their psychological and mental health implications. Teachers have found that increases in noise level place them under greater tension and require of them added effort, thus several vocal groups within the same room, the operation of the univent, and any noise that is foreign to the acts of teaching and learning handi-cap instruction and put a strain upon mental health.

In some manner unknown, many teachers have come to think in terms of "the bigger the classroom, the better the teaching situation." This thesis is supported by several authors in the school plant field. How-ever, experimentation at the University of Maryland has indicated that too much classroom area tends to create some of the same problems—and some additional—as too little classroom area. These problems have implications for the mental health and personality development of the room's occupants, pupils and teachers.

There are school districts that plan faculty lounge, rest, and dining facilities. These provide for that break in the day that all workers, and particularly those whose work is with people, need in order to regroup their resources for the balance of the day. There are also many schools in which such faculty facilities are not provided and in which teachers are not given a lunch period away from their charges.[8]

Many of the problems of teacher health lend themselves to some relief through school plant design that is oriented always and first of all to the educational program and those considerations through which the educational program is enhanced and facilitated.

[8] In California, Illinoins, Massachusetts, Minnesota, and Ohio, it was necessary to pass state "right to eat" laws for teachers, laws that it would not have been necessary to pass if the administration of school personnel were only a little enlightened. *NEA Research Bulletin*, 30:4 (Washington, The National Education Association, December, 1960), pp. 105, 106.

In Denmark, Norway, and Sweden, school buildings are designed with faculty lounges and kitchens. There are, in addition to the lunch periods, coffee breaks in midmorning and afternoon. The faculty room is considered so necessary that it is not violated even if crowded conditions and double sessions develop. As a result, there is a tendency for many teachers to unwind at the end of the day by spending some time in social intercourse in the faculty lounge room. In addition, this room is a place where teachers can work during a free period, meet for professional purposes, and hold their social events.

SAFETY

The physical safety of all school personnel is a matter of genuine concern to them and an obligation of the school system. Some aspects of safety, those pertaining to the health of school personnel, have been covered. There are other aspects that pertain to the safety of the personnel and these are the concern of this section.

In general the safety of school personnel is protected through care in the design and maintenance of buildings, selection and maintenance of equipment, and planning and maintenance of grounds and their facilities.

Buildings

The National Council on Schoolhouse Construction, organized in 1921, has devoted an entire chapter of its *Guide* for planning school plants to the problems of school plant safety.[9] What the Council has developed as the responsibility of school officials to their communities applies as well to the school employees.

It has been noted that one of the chief factors in employee morale is the feeling of each, supported by evidence, that his welfare is a matter of concern, "an expression of the value placed upon the work and consideration for the worker."[10]

The safety of the school building will be dealt with under the same headings as those used by the Council, i.e., structural safety, fire resistance, fire protection, circulation safety and convenience, modernization and rehabilitation for safety, disaster shelters, and miscellaneous safety factors.[11]

Structural Safety. The structural safety of a school building should be assured through the design and inspection services of a competent structural engineer who has full responsibility for the structural safety of the building in terms of design and construction. The structural engineer demonstrates his responsibility through design, inspection, and a written statement vouching for the building's safety.

Should a building be or become unsafe, it is one of the functions of personnel administration to take steps that will result in a correction of the inadequacy. In this way the personnel administrator serves that

---

[9] National Council on Schoolhouse Construction, *Guide*—for planning school plants (Nashville, Tennessee, Peabody College, The Council, 1958) Chapter 6.

[10] See Chapter 10, the section on environment.

[11] For a full statement of the conclusions and recommendations of the National Council on Schoolhouse Construction, see its *Guide, op. cit.*, Chapter 6. Most of this section is derived from this source, as are also the quotations accompanied by page references.

part of his function that is concerned with the coordination of personnel and materiel for the efficient operation of the educative enterprise.

Fire Resistance. The safety of school personnel is assured to a degree by the resistivity of the building to fire. Thus,

One-story buildings may be constructed of any type of suitable materials if adequate exit facilities are available and "hot spots" like furnace rooms are sufficiently isolated.

Two-story buildings may provide acceptable . . . protection against fire hazards if they have fire resistive exterior walls, corridors, and stairs, and adequate exit facilities.

Buildings of three or more stories should be fire resistive throughout except that wood may be used for floor coverings and trim (p. 155).

Fire Protection. The obligation of school officials to safeguard life by providing and maintaining fire-safe conditions is a responsibility to school personnel as well as to others.

In school plant planning, fire safety involves . . . fire-safe construction, adequate exits and rapid evacuation facilities, fire stops, facilities for fire extinguishment, and the insulation of hot spot areas. Every feasible precaution should be taken to prevent the development of panic-creating conditions (p. 155).

Of particular concern are furnace and fuel-storage areas which should be designed and constructed for resistance to and containment of fire and the protection of the engineering or custodial employees who have duties in these areas.

Electrical services are accompanied by fire hazards resulting from the over-loading of circuits, failure to shield hazardous motors, and heat transfer and build-up from high wattage spots, arc lights, and dimmer banks that are not shielded from nearby combustibles. Compliance with the Underwriters Code is an initial step toward fire safety from electrical causes.

Fire alarms should be designed for operation from a number of convenient locations and "from areas having unusual fire hazards such as shops, kitchens, and boiler rooms. . . ." The alarm should be such as to be heard above other noises in the building, should not be panic producing, and should be manual or, if electrical, on segregated and protected circuits.

Fire-control equipment should consist of appropriate extinguishers located at such points that there is an extinguisher well within 100 feet of any place in the corridor and in each area having unusual fire hazards. Where possible, "fire hydrant facilities should be conveniently accessible to school property" and where complete sprinkler systems are not feasible, consideration should be given to partial installations in hot spot areas.

Miscellaneous fire-protection precautions include the treatment of stage scenery to make it fire resistive, installation of automatic drop fire-resistive curtains at stage fronts, and exits from dressing rooms, away from the stage; use of fire-retarding roof surface materials; reduction of all trash-catching areas to a minimum, keeping them clean, and provision of fireproof storage for all inflammables, such as oils and paints; adequate isolation or insulation of heat producing or conduction units or conduits; and the grounding against lightning of those parts of the building that project above neighboring structures and trees.

Circulation Safety and Convenience. The operation of a public building requires attention to public safety as well as to that of the employees who serve the public function. Safe and convenient circulation requires planning for:

a. Safe facilities under all conditions for mass or emergency evacuation

b. Minimum travel distances for all building occupants in accomplishing the day's work

c. Minimizing traffic congestion and interference

d. Reduction of disturbance of class work because of student traffic

e. Ease of supervision of student traffic

f. Desirable segregation of student groups

g. Easy circulation between building and contemplated future extensions (p. 158).

A number of these planning considerations focus attention upon the convenience of reduced and facilitated traffic. This has implications for convenience and also for the orderliness, decrease in distance covered, and lessening of congestion which contribute to safety.

"Corridors, doors, lobbies, stairs, ramps, elevators, walks and driveways provide the means for circulation." Corridors should be sufficiently wide for the traffic to be carried and should be open, i.e., it should be possible to see an exit or a stairway from any place in any corridor. Doors that separate corridors from stair enclosures should be self-closing, swing with the exit travel, and meet the requirements of their location to resist the spread of fire or to check the spreading of smoke and heat to other parts of the building. Corners in corridors should be rounded or coved and be of fire-resistive construction in multi-story buildings.

Buildings of more than one story should have at least two stairways that are remote from each other and unconnected, located in fire-resistive wells at right angles to the corridor, constructed of fire-resistive materials, convenient to building exits, of standard riser and tread design with nonslip tread surfacing, adequately lighted, and equipped with handrails.

All school buildings should have more than one exit, each of adequate size, opening outwards, and equipped with anti-panic hardware, checks, stops, and closers. Classroom doors should open outward from the room and be so constructed that they at no time encroach upon corridor area. Classroom and exit doors should be fitted with hardware that cannot be locked against egress.

Signs. Readily legible exit signs should be located at appropriate points throughout the building and, if electrically operated, should be operable independently of the ordinary power source and circuits.

Modernization and Rehabilitation for Safety. Buildings that are still generally structurally and educationally sound, but built during an era when present-day construction materials and techniques had not yet been so fully developed, can often be made more safe through structural reinforcements where needed, removal of corridor obstructions, relocation or replacement of stairways and their reconstruction in terms of present-day knowledge and materials, equipment with smoke screen and fire doors, installation of anti-panic hardware at all exits, rehanging of doors to make them swing outward, renovation of boiler and fuel-storage rooms to conform to current standards for new construction, and the installation of fire alarm, escape, extinguishing, and sprinkler equipment or facilities.

Disaster Shelters. Where public opinion and financial ability are sufficient to support the construction of disaster shelters for protection against the elements of nature or the effects of nuclear fission, the personnel of the school, together with the pupils and a considerable number of the residents of the community, are to be accommodated. Although not nearly enough is known about the designing of such shelters, indications are that they require meticulous design and construction in accordance with specifications that are still in an emergent stage. Independent ventilation, lighting, sanitation, water, food storage and preparation facilities, communication with the outside, and egress provisions are among the special design problems that accompany those of hardening the shelter against even direct nuclear hits.

Miscellaneous Safety Factors. French doors, glass panels in doors, and particularly those glass panels along classroom and corridor walls that extend below a height of four feet from the floor should be glazed with wired or laminated safety glass.

Glazed doors and windows located in or *en route* to stair wells or in other areas where fire or heat retardation is essential . . . should be fitted with approved wired safety glass.

Electric switches and fuse boxes should be of the front type where feasible. Each fuse box panel should be marked to indicate the maximum fuse amperage that may be used. Corridor or other public space panel boxes should be kept locked.

Floor surfaces should be of a nonslipping type. This is particularly important for stair treads, in shower and locker rooms, and in shops (pp. 168, 169).

Nonslip floor surfaces are also particularly important in corridors where a nonslip floor wax may be used if waxing is necessary, on ramps, and in areas of the kitchen such as in front of sinks, dishwashers, and cooking ranges where either water or cooking greases may splatter to make walking surfaces dangerous to the worker.

Hot-water temperatures in lavatories and showers should be kept at safe levels to prevent accident. Also, whenever hot water or steam piping comes within ready reach it ought to be insulated against or screened from contact by the unwary.

Equipment

Probably the areas where extraordinary care in the selection, spacing, placement, and installation of equipment has particular implications for the safety of employees and others are those in which the more specialized kinds of equipment are necessary. These specialized areas include those for:

arts and crafts	homemaking
audio-visual instruction	instruction for the handicapped
auditorium	science
business machines instruction	shops
food preparation and service	special education (retarded)
game rooms	stage
gymnasiums, physical education	swimming instruction

In all rooms, the more general as well as the above-mentioned specialized, safety is very definitely promoted by an efficient and serious program for the repair or replacement of equipment that endangers safety and by the use, in appropriate places, of standardized color-coded hazard indicators.

Grounds

Usual safety considerations pertaining to the site are ordinarily focussed primarily upon child safety. In this section the focal point is the safety of school employees.

Walks. All street frontages of a school site should be provided with walks that are maintained in good conditions and free from obstructions or the hazards of winter conditions. In addition, similarly maintained access walks should be provided from the street(s) and joining the various school facilities, including parking lots, along the lines of most convenient use. Walks ought to be crossed by driveways as little as possible.

Driveways. There will be need for driveways to facilitate entry for deliveries, school-bus loading and unloading, and employee and other parking.

Service driveways should be separate from others, as short as possible, and coordinated with a building design that has taken into account the need for cafeteria, stage, homemaking classes, shop, school instructional supply, and fuel deliveries. Through a grouping of facilities requiring delivery services, it is possible to provide for efficient planning and use of a service driveway. The separate service drive, segregating commercial delivery type vehicles from other school traffic, reduces the chance of traffic accidents.

Driveways for access to employee and public parking lots should be sufficiently wide to accommodate two-way traffic with safety and should terminate in the parking lot. The same driveways may be used when possible to provide access to bus loading platforms that are kept apart from other vehicular traffic. A turning loop should be made available for buses so that no backing will be necessary for loading or unloading passengers.

The U-shaped driveway in front of the building should be discouraged; no driveway should encircle the building; and all intersections of drives and walks should be avoided if possible.[12]

Parking Lots. Employee parking lots should be as near and as accessible to their place of work as possible.

Reduction of travel for the staff should have consideration. Teachers' lounge rooms, work rooms, and professional libraries should be easily accessible. The provision of elevator service may be necessary in multistory buildings.[13]

In buildings that require elevators, other than service, the parking lot should be readily accessible to the entrance(s) nearest the elevator(s). Elevators in multistory buildings provide an added safety feature for employees who ought not to use stairs.

Other parking lots should provide ready access to the auditorium,

[12] National Council, *Guide. Ibid.*, p. 33.
[13] National Council, *Guide. Ibid.*, p. 164.

play fields, gymnasium, and entrances to facilities most used by the public.

Playground Equipment. The selection, spacing, placement, installation, and regulations as to use of playground equipment, together with the maintenance or replacement thereof, are activities conducive to the safety both of the users of the equipment and of the personnel who are held responsible for supervising its use.

Landscaping. The location of shrubbery and trees should be such as to beautify the school setting without, however, interfering with the visibility necessary to vehicular and pedestrian safety. Also, the selection and existence of shrubbery and trees entails care not only to enhance their beauty but also to prevent them from becoming hazardous through, e.g., unfortunate selection of thorny or otherwise potentially injurious plants, growth that blocks visibility or traffic, and possible falling limbs or trees.

PHYSICAL PLANT

The implications of physical plant for employee health and safety have been dealt with. There are other plant factors that underlie those already covered and that are a primary concern of school personnel and the public, the concern that the school plant be such as to facilitate, not merely accommodate or *not handicap,* instruction.

Actually, the best conditions for instruction may be expected to provide also the side-effects of healthful and safe working conditions for employees. There is a need on the part of school personnel to feel that their work is considered of such importance that effort is put forward to provide plant—site, buildings, and equipment—and plant conditions that make it possible for each to do his job more easily and better.

Among the physical plant factors that especially concern the effective functioning of the schools and their personnel are educational design, equipment, operation, and safety factors.

Educational Design

A school plant is the product of two kinds of design, architectural and educational. Architectural design is commonly comprehended in a general sort of way. Architectural design is the task of experts in architecture assisted by experts in structural engineering. Architectural design depends on the competency of the architect. However, just what educational design is is not commonly understood. Even many an educator seems to lack understanding of educational design.

Educational design is the product of that aspect of school plant planning that is primarily concerned with the facilitation of instruction. This aspect of planning is primarily the task of those who are expert in the field of education. Just how good an educational design for a school plant is depends on the competency of the educator(s) who do the educational designing. Educational designing ought no more to be left to architects or others not expert in the field of education than architectural planning ought to be left to educators or others not expert in the field of architecture.

The educational design is the initial point of departure for the architect to begin the development of the architectural design. The architect who, for lack of an educational design, forges educational specifications on the basis of his experience and ingenuity operates outside the area of his competency. What he does can only be makeshift. He cannot be expected to turn out an educational design that has the earmarks of expertness. Any need for the architect to engage in makeshift educational designing is a reflection upon a school administration that falls short of its obligations in school plant planning.

However, whether or not there has been sound educational designing to begin with, any review of plans by educators reflects some of the essence of educational designing. Plans are approved or change of plans is ordered on the basis of the educational expert's judgment as to how well instruction will be facilitated by the proposed plant plans.

The most suitable physical conditions for effective teaching may be expected if the basis for the architectural design is a thorough and defensible educational design. The educational design may be expected to be at its best if those who are most familiar with the use of the respective facilities are consulted for their recommendations.

Consultation contributes to a building planned to facilitate the work of the respective kinds of employees because the design is in part the product of those who face the front line problems in the auditoriums, boiler rooms, classrooms, corridors, food preparation and service facilities, garages and service stations, gymnasiums and physical education facilities, laboratories, offices, shops, and warehouses in which school employees work.

Consultation of employees may be expected to result in functional buildings by which the work of the schools can be facilitated, an improved morale that derives from the availability of suitable physical plant and the involvement of the employees in planning, and a personal interest in utilizing plant effectively as evidence of the soundness of the recommendations elicited through employee participation in planning.

Adaptability. No matter how well a school building is planned for an existing or projected program, it is rendered somewhat less functional with changes that come with progress and innovation. It is for this reason that school building planners have advocated such internal structural flexibility and external expansibility of plant that it may be adapted to those several new developments that may be expected to take place in the course of the life of the building.

Equipment

Part of the educational plant is the equipment with which it is furnished so that it may best serve its function. School equipment includes office, conference, and classroom furniture; apparatus for the teaching of science; machines for office, business education, and shops; appliances, machines, and furnishings for home economics instruction and food services; building operation apparatus; auditorium and stage furnishings; lockers; athletic and physical education apparatus and gear; warehouse storage and inventory facilities; and school passenger and delivery vehicles. In each instance the justification for equipment provided is that it is needed to facilitate work essential to effective school functioning and that it serves its purpose in the best way possible under existing circumstances.

Selection of equipment through the involvement of those who will use it may be expected to contribute to a better choice, a feeling of self-consequence that is morale boosting, and a use expressive of desire to justify the judgment exercised.

Operation

The operation of the school plant involves cleaning, humidity control, lighting, temperature control, and ventilation. All of these factors in operation are important to ease teaching by the provision of optimum conditions for learning, to protect the health of employees and others who occupy the building, and to reinforce teaching by providing a continuous institutional demonstration of the importance of such matters in all day-to-day living.

Safety

Safety devices and regulations on the grounds, in corridors, gymnasiums, auditoriums, shops, and laboratories, and wherever there are hazards to safety are protective both of employees and all others who enter the school plant. In addition they serve as a means to reinforce the teaching of safety and demonstrate administrative regard for the individual, including all employees.

EMPLOYEE WORK LOAD

The work load of all school employees is the concern of the school administration and the particular concern of the personnel division. It is essential that the work load of all personnel who do not belong to the teaching profession, as well as of all that do, be reasonable and fair.

For personnel other than teachers it is relatively easy to develop work load standards. Cleaning areas by type can be worked out and assigned to custodial personnel; school bus driving regulations, routes, and time schedules limit the demands upon bus drivers; the hours of employment, as well as the limits of competency, tend to protect the clerical employee; and so it is, to varying degree and subject to administrative or employee aberration, with respect to all school employees except the key group, the teachers. Teachers have no built-in provisions to protect them from exploitation.

Some of the best examples of the use of recently developed equipment to decrease load and increase productivity are found in the nonteaching aspects of school operation. Electric and electronic office machines, photocopying and other reproduction equipment, new chemical detergents, automatic air conditioning controls and floor and wall cleaning equipment are to be found in many schools. Productivity per man is improved by an investment in cost- and labor-saving devices.

Since some aspects of work load have been touched upon progressively in preceding chapters,[14] this section will be largely devoted to a succinct presentation of the problem of teacher load and some prospects for solving it. The major topics will be class size, teacher duties, work period, and means for resolving the problems of teacher load.

Class Size

For years much has been said about the preference of teachers for a class size that will permit them to be more effective. Teacher conviction that a class generally approximating 25 pupils will be conducive to improved teaching is in accord with the concept of individualization of instruction and is supported by the findings of the Institute of Administrative Research of Teachers College, Columbia University, over a 15-year period.[15]

Class sizes today are generally well above 30 and often above 40.

[14] See the subheadings designated: Chapter 3, Job Description, Job Classification, and Job Rating; Chapter 7, The Contract; Chapter 8, Orientation Practices, and Making Orientation Effective; Chapter 10, Work Load; and Chapter 11, The Teacher and Teaching.

[15] Bernard H. McKenna, "What Research Says about Greater Learning in Smaller Classes," *NEA Journal,* 46:7, October, 1957, pp. 437, 438.

These conditions, Hollister has indicated, compound geometrically the number of possible personal interactions within the classroom from 45 such interactions for 10 pupils to 190 for 20, 435 for 30, and 780 for 40 children.[16] The compounding of possible interactions affects load by compounding teaching problems.

Teacher Duties

At one time the teacher's job was well defined. An academic emphasis limited his duties to the school day plus such additional time as was needed for preparation and the grading of papers.

A broadening concept of the school's task has resulted in the imposition upon teachers of many added duties, the extension of his work period, a failure to adjust pay to the altered situation, and a blurring of the concept as to just what the teacher's job really is.

Currently teachers' duties may be divided into three categories, of which one is that of teaching and those activities that are immediately related thereto; another is that of activities that are not teaching and that are at best very remotely related to the teaching duties; and the third is one that falls between the other two, a virtual no-man's land of duties of which some are sometimes considered curricular to a degree. Under some circumstances a good case could be made to include some of these activities under the teaching category, in other instances it is virtually impossible to make such a case.

The Teaching Category. The list of specific duties that fall under the teaching category is a short one and includes:

> the preparation of instructional materials
> individual work with pupils
> grading nonobjective tests
> reporting progress

The Nonteaching Category. The list of duties that is at best remotely related to teaching includes:

> bus duty
> chaperoning school social events
> classroom housekeeping
> corridor and washroom duty
> lunchroom or cafeteria supervision
> money collection and accounts
> PTA attendance
> other school collections and drives, e.g., paper
> school grounds supervision
> supervision of magazine subscription projects
> supervision of safety patrols

16 "Class Size and Human Relations," *NEA Journal,* 46:7, October, 1957, p. 442.

The Intermediate Duties Category. It might be better to label these the indeterminate duties since it takes analysis in each instance to determine whether it ought to be classified as a teaching or a non-teaching duty. The following are included:

> administrative assignments
> coaching
> conferences
> counselling
> disciplinary action
> faculty and departmental meetings
> field trips
> grading objective tests
> home room administration and supervision
> in-service workshops
> monitoring the study hall
> personal study and planning
> pupil records; academic, personal, health
> sponsorship of pupil organizations and activities
> teacher-association activities

None of the foregoing lists is exhaustive. They are indicative of a breakdown of activities that have become very time consuming. The current importance of the types of activities listed derives from the complexity brought about by increased size and other change. Change is accompanied by problems with personnel implications, particularly those of acquiring personnel of the needed competencies and then using them in efficiently optimum fashion and without exploitation.

Work Period

The work period falls into the two distinct classifications of the school year and the school and work day.

The School Year. The length of the school year varies among school districts and states. The state average school year in the United States is within the range of 170.0 to 182.1, with an average of 177.6, school days per year.[17] The range is likely to shift upwards with a like but more gradual shifting of the average.

During the earlier years of smaller school districts and less complex educational operations, the teacher's work year consisted of the number of school days. Today, it is not uncommon for the teachers to be required to report for duty before and to remain on duty after the school session for increasingly long periods. The fore and aft extension of the school year represents a formalization of tasks that teachers used to do

[17] NEA Research Division, *Research Bulletin*, 40:1 (Washington, The National Education Association, February, 1962), p. 12.

on their own time at or away from school. The formalization, it is feared, results in a loss of functionality and introduces feelings of coerciveness and oppression.

A variation of the ordinary school year is the bonafide 12-month employment of teachers with pro-rated increases in salary, assured vacations of one month in addition to all school holidays, and with prescribed or approved assignments for those of the summer weeks that have been added to the contract period. The 12-month employment of teachers promotes some spreading of load, doing research, engaging in creative activities, providing for professional improvement, and placing a limit upon the exploitative extension of the annual working period without pro-rated compensation.

The School and Work Day. The length of the school day for pupils varies among school districts. Recent medians were 6 hours and 29 minutes in Grade 1, 6 hours and 50 minutes in Grade 8, and 6 hours and 58 minutes in senior high school.[18] The teacher's *day at school* was about one hour longer than that of the pupils.[19] In addition, teachers spent a median of about 2 hours more per day on school duties each school week.[20] Thus the teacher's work day consists of 7.5 to 8 hours at school plus at least 2 more hours of work per day, a 9.5 to 10-hour work day or a 47.5 to 50-hour work week.

The teacher's work week contrasts markedly with the commonly achieved 40-hour week of industry and government and the provision of overtime pay or compensatory time-off for work above 40 hours.

A tendency to increase the teacher work period is contrary to the trend of several decades in other occupations. Revived currently is the urge of the 1930's for a further reduction in the length of the work week. New York electricians have achieved a 30-hour work week contract. Big labor unions seek a 35-hour week and double time pay for overtime. Unions covering federal employees are backing a drive for a 35-hour work week.[21]

Noting developments in the work week in other occupations, teachers disclaim the desire to fare likewise and seem to identify professionalism with the martyrdom of long and unpaid-for hours of work. In this they distinguish themselves from all other professions which do not

[18] NEA Research Division, "How Long Is a School Day?" *Research Bulletin,* 39:1 (Washington, The National Education Association, February, 1961), pp. 8–10.

[19] Fred Guggenheim, "Nonteaching Activities of Teachers in a Staff Utilization Study," *Journal of Educational Research,* 54:9, May 1961, p. 325; also NEA Research Division, *Research Bulletin. Ibid.,* p. 9.

[20] NEA Research Division, *Research Bulletin,* 35:1 (Washington, The National Education Association, February, 1957), p. 30.

[21] "If Industry Had a 35-Hour Week. . .", *U.S. News & World Report,* 53:9, August 27, 1962, pp. 91, 92, 96, 100; "Why Labor Is Pushing the 35-Hour Week," *Business Week,* No. 1721, August 25, 1962, p. 116; Jerry Kluttz, "Federal Unions to Back Drive for 35-Hour Week," *Washington Post,* August 24, 1962, p. D-1; and "Steamfitters Shrink Workweek," *Engineering News-Record,* 169:2, July 12, 1962, p. 15.

hesitate to demand fees for services rendered and which have made great progress in curtailing the length of their work week. Thus education has the questionable distinction of exploiting its agents to provide added public services, extending such services without compensation, and regarding the exploitation of the teacher as a symbol of professionalism and particularly high ethical conduct.

Means for Resolving Work Load

There is no panacea for the conditions that have been described. However, the conditions are such that it is incumbent upon the school administration and the entire profession to reserve judgment on suggestions put forward, explore possible means for relieving load, experiment, and venture into the innovation of promising practices which will of course depart from traditional ways of doing the job.

Among the means that are apparent today, that have been tested to varying degrees, about which there is still much reservation, that are looked at askance, and that are often condemned without benefit of trial or even careful investigation are: audio-visual aids, television, teacher aides, team teaching, and automated teaching through programed instruction. These merit understanding, consideration, and trial. Open-mindedness and the experimental approach to new or different ideas will no doubt produce still other alternatives in the way of innovations for the relief of teacher load and the improvement of educational productivity. Each of these means will be briefly presented and discussed.

Audio-Visual Aids. These are probably the best known, most accepted, and least controversial aids to facilitate the instructional task of the teacher. They connote properly but too narrowly the use of slides, film, and projectors. A truer connotation of audio-visual aids would include all visual and auditory means to convey meaning and reenforce learning. The following ought to be included in any list of audio-visual aids:

blueprints, charts, graphs, posters	displays
books; text, reference, and others	filmstrip
duplicated materials	globes
on-the-spot illustration; e.g., using chalkboard,	maps
overhead projector, etc.	models
periodicals; newspapers, magazines	movies
pictures, etchings, paintings, photo-	music
graphs, sketches	puppets
recordings; disk and tape	statuary
samples of animal, plant, soil and	television
industrial materials or products	radio
sound systems; public address, etc.	slides

The teacher's problem is to envision what audio-visual aids to use, to use them at the right time, and to avoid using any that are not pertinent to the teaching task. Some teachers can benefit from developments by which slides, motion pictures, film strips, overhead projectors, tape and public address systems, and closed circuit television may be integrated and made to facilitate instruction automatically from a control panel convenient to the teacher. This automated and integrated system has been termed "telemation."[22]

Television. As an audio-visual means of communication, television has implications for education. At first there were those who saw in television a potential panacea for a good many of the problems of education, notably those of unit or per-pupil costs and classroom and teacher shortages.

In a number of instances the initial use of commercial and educational television for purposes of instruction was so disillusioning as to result in the abandonment of televised programs. However, toward the middle to latter 1950's there was an initially heartening turn toward experimentation in the use of television for instruction.[23]

There is some question as to the degree to which the promise of the experimental approach was realized. It is difficult for experimenters to remain personally detached from their experiments. An experimenter who becomes personally involved becomes a promoter rather than a scientist.

Despite problems, everyday experience with television at home and in school suggests that television can serve the purposes of education. It may be expected to serve well in large group lecture-type instruction and it is clearly advantageous in many situations in which demonstrations are a desirable part of instruction, e.g., in many instances of home economics, health, science, and shop instruction. No doubt other areas of instructional usefulness will become apparent.

It is the concern of the personnel division that the teacher have television available where it is advantageous to facilitate instruction and that he be protected from pressure to use television where its use is not advantageous to instruction.

Teacher Aides. Contrasting with supply and equipment aids to instruction, teacher aides are people who serve in designated capacities so that

---

[22] "Multiple Sight and Sound," *Overview*, 2:7, July, 1961, pp. 40, 41; and John Moldstad and Harvey Frye, "A Complete Materials Center," *Overview*, 2:5, May, 1961, pp. 48, 49.

[23] A few examples are cited: Pittsburgh, 1955–56; St. Louis, 1956: Washington County, Maryland, 1956–61; and in 1959 The Midwest Council on Airborne Television Instruction announced plans for the launching in 1960 of a flying classroom to beam instruction to students in six states within a 200-mile radius from Montpelier, Indiana.

teachers may be freed from nonprofessional tasks to devote more time to duties that require their professional competency. The teacher aide would be to the teacher what the dental assistant is to the dentist, the secretary-receptionist and the nurse to the doctor, and the legal secretary to the lawyer.

As in the case of the other professions, the aide enters the work scene when the work load becomes too great for one person. The professional faces the alternatives of lightening his over-all load by 1) delegating nonprofessional duties to an aide or 2) securing on some basis the assistance of a professional colleague. The efficient utilization of competencies favors the use of the first alternative whenever possible.

The combination of teacher shortages and pupil increases sparked a 5-year trial of an experiment with teacher aides in Bay City, Michigan, from 1952 to 1957.[24] The use of teacher aides is not new. It was implicit in the Lancasterian movement of the late 1700's. Today many school districts make use of some kind of teacher-aide plan.[25]

The teacher-aide plan has unquestionable promise; its concept of efficient utilization of staff is fundamentally sound. However, it is no more a panacea than any other proposal for improving instruction. It is necessary to explore carefully the advantages of using teacher aides and to set up safeguards against its potential or real disadvantages.

There seems in the instance of teacher-aides, as with reference to other innovations in teaching, to be a reluctance attributable to fear of change and feelings of personal insecurity on the part of the teaching profession. These find expression in concern about class size and the relative pay of professionals and their aides.

Team Teaching. A relatively new and not precisely defined term for a variety of teaching activities of which many are virtually as old as teaching, team teaching is a departure from the teacher and teacher-aide concept and in some instances a refinement of it. Whereas team teaching has in the past been characterized by informal and voluntary cooperation, its advocacy currently is identified with a formalized and organized system for cooperation.

[24] See the Symposium by the director of the experiment and a curriculum specialist, school administrator, child psychologist, administrator of a teacher-education institution, educational experimentalist, classroom teacher, and editor of an educational journal, *Journal of Teacher Education,* 7:2, June, 1956, pp. 100–153.

[25] Among school districts that have experimented with some form of a teacher-aide plan in recent years are: California—Palo Alto and Salinas; District of Columbia—Washington; Illinois—Beecher Community Unit School District; Kentucky—Louisville; Massachusetts—Newton; Michigan—41 school districts; Minnesota—Mound and Rockville; New York—22 central school districts in the Chenango, Delaware, and Otsego County area of the Catskill Mountains; Ohio—Ashland and Columbus; Tennessee—six school districts in Davidson County; and Virginia—Richmond.

The advantages of team teaching stem from its capitalization upon the special competencies of personnel and emphasis upon specialization.[26] The personnel envisioned as comprising the team include teacher specialists (presumably career teachers), general teachers (presumably novices and noncareer teachers), instruction assistants, clerks, general aides, community consultants, and staff specialists.[27]

Proponents of team teaching stress its promise.[28] The specific advantage held out is the improvement of instruction through:

> employing personnel that are not overqualified for the job in question
> but have the competencies needed
> improved utilization of employee competencies
> economically sounder personnel assignment, use, and pay
> decreased teacher load
> increased time for teacher creativity and reflection

Reservations about team teaching result from concern that 1) particularly in the elementary school, no one teacher really gets to know the child or vice versa and 2) on all levels using large group instructional procedures, the pupils become little more than listeners as teachers present materials for which they have done research, generalized findings, put information to use, and asked questions, giving pupils no chance to raise their questions at the time they come to mind.[29]

There is an appeal to team teaching that has caused it to be tried in many school districts,[30] reflecting the feeling of need to do something, sometimes even an urgency to do anything different, in an effort to improve education.

[26] The team-teaching concept is that the teacher is a specialist. This contrasts to a long-favored concept that the teacher on the elementary school level is and on the secondary school level would most desirably be a generalist.

[27] J. Lloyd Trump, *Images of the Future* (Urbana, Illinois, the Commission on the Experimental Study of the Utilization of the Staff in the Secondary School, 1959), pp. 15–22.

[28] Robert H. Anderson, "Team Teaching," *NEA Journal,* 50:3, March, 1961, pp. 52–54.

[29] Anne Hoppock, "Team Teaching: Form without Substance?" *NEA Journal,* 50:4, April, 1961, pp. 47, 48; and Harold D. Drummond, "Team Teaching: An Assessment," *Educational Leadership,* 19:3, December, 1961, pp. 160–165.

[30] Many of the schools using teaching aides could as well be listed as using team teaching. In addition, among school districts in which some form of team teaching has been tried are:
California—the Chaffey and Citrus Union High School; Claremont City; Fullerton Joint Union High School and Junior College; Covina Valley, Montebello, and Palm Springs Unified; Ontario Elementary; and Riverside City school districts; Colorado—Jefferson County, School District R-1; Connecticut—Norwalk; Illinois—Evanston Township; Maryland—Montgomery County; Massachusetts—Lexington; Minnesota—Roseville; Texas—Snyder; West Virginia—Richwood; and Wisconsin—Janesville, Madison, and West Bend.

Programed Instruction. Somewhat popularized by references to teaching machines or mechanical tutors, programed instruction in its currently most popular form is chiefly the product of B. F. Skinner's efforts dating back to 1954 and reaching fruition since 1960. Nevertheless, the theories underlying programed instruction are old.

The material to be learned through the programing of instruction is broken down into minute components arranged in a sequence that is logical from the learner's point of view. This method of instruction was used by Socrates (469–399 B.C.) about 2400 years ago.

Programed instruction is a system for capitalizing upon stimulus-response associations. Stimulus-response, as related to learning, was implied by the *associationalism* of David Hartley (1705–1757), the *conditional reflex* and *reinforcement* findings of Ivan Pavlov (1849–1936), and the nervous system *connectionism* of Edward L. Thorndike (1874–1949).

Through the use of the programed instruction approach to learning, such familiar teaching objectives as the following are brought closer to realization:

1. the organization of subject matter to provide logically sequential learning with provision for reinforcement along the way.

2. the reduction of student anxiety through the diminution of conditions of frustration.

3. the recognition of the theory of individual differences through a procedure that permits students to progress independently and at their own rates.

4. the involvement of students in the learning process so that learning by doing will take place.

5. the requirement that the student understand what is basically involved before he can supply an answer.

6. the elimination of regrettable lag between student action and knowledge of the results through immediate confirmation as to the adequacy of his answers.

7. the reduction of student boredom by rewarding his efforts by the knowledge and feelings of success.

8. the freeing of the teacher from the things that make little or no demand upon his professional competency to do those things for which he is professionally prepared.

As in other instances, the teaching profession seems to be characterized by an insecurity that inhibits open-mindedness to different ideas and experimentation with an eye to innovation. There is some feeling, that prevails also in industry, that the machine will take the place of the worker. Under present day conditions of teacher shortages and burgeoning school memberships, no teacher is threatened by a loss of job because of automation or mechanization. Rather, as expressed by Hilgard, "If much of the *science* of teaching is taken over by the machine, the *art* of teaching will again come into its own, residing where it should, in the teacher as a person."[31]

SUMMARY

Health, safety, plant, and work load have implications for the welfare and efficiency of school employees in general and teachers in particular.

Health includes physical, mental, and emotional well-being. The school's concern with employee health is demonstrated by way of the initial application form, examinations and tests, health services and sick leaves, insurance provisions, and social and recreational programs. In addition, physical plant conditions of temperature, ventilation, humidity, light, noise, color, social and sanitary facilities, and room size have implications for one or more aspects of employee health.

The structural, fire resistance and protection, traffic circulation, exit, renovation, and disaster shelter factors relative to the school building have implications for employee safety. In addition, the safety of employees is affected by equipment and grounds, including walks, drives, parking lots, playgrounds, and landscaping.

The school plant is a means for facilitating instruction. As such it is the product of two very different but essentially complementary activities, educational and architectural designing. Educational design is the function of the expert in education whereas architectural design is the function of the expert in architecture. All classifications of school employees ought to be involved in both the planning of and equipment selection for the school building.

The operation and the safety of the school plant have implications for both the employee and the reinforcement of instruction pertaining to cleanliness, health, and safety for everyday living.

Whereas the work load of all employees is a matter of concern, that of the teacher presents the greatest problem. An overview of work load includes considerations of class size, teacher duties, and the length of the work period. Audio-visual aids, television, teacher aides, team teaching, and programed instruction are among the means by which teacher load can be alleviated.

Each means for lightening teacher load has potential for facilitating instruction and increasing efficiency in utilizing employee competencies. There is, however, need to experiment sufficiently to provide an evidential basis for change and to avoid substituting promotionalism for

[31] Ernest R. Hilgard, "What Support from the Psychology of Learning?" in a special journal feature—Teaching Machines and Programed Learning in the NEA *Journal*, 50:8, November, 1961, p. 21 and pp. 15–30. See also Finley Carpenter, "How Will Automated Teaching Affect Education?" The University of Michigan *School of Education Bulletin*, 31:1, October, 1959, pp. 8–12.

experimentation. Unwarranted haste to effect change can jeopardize the most promising of innovations. Worthwhile change can await the progressive training of personnel to make it effective.

Resistance to change is the product of inertia, resentment of the implication that a new and relatively untried means should be considered superior to the techniques produced by training and experience, and fear that jobs will be eliminated or made less significant by innovation.

There is need for open-mindedness to ideas, innovation in practice, and ascertainment as to what means to use most advantageously under what circumstances. No one of the means discussed can be considered to be the sole answer to the many and complex problems of education in today's world.

SELECTED READINGS

BERGER, Wilhelm, *Schulbau von Heute fur Morgen* (Gottingen, Germany, Musterschmidt-Verlag, 1960), pp. 7–184.

COULSON, John E. (Editor), *Programmed Learning and Computer Based Instruction* (New York, John Wiley & Sons, Inc., 1962), 291 pp.

Ford Foundation and Fund for the Advancement of Education, *Teaching by Television* (New York, the Foundation, January, 1961), 87 pp.

HOLLAND, James G., and SKINNER, B. F. *The Analysis of Behavior* (New York, McGraw-Hill Book Company, Inc., 1961).

LUMSDAINE, Arthur A., and GLASER, Robert (Editors), *Teaching Machines and Programmed Learning* (Washington, Department of Audio-Visual Instruction, The National Education Association, 1960).

MARGULIES, Stuart, and EIGEN, Lewis D. (Editors), *Applied Programmed Instruction* (New York, John Wiley & Sons, Inc., 1962), 291 pp.

MINOR, (Ed.), *Simplified Techniques for Preparing Visual Materials* (New York, McGraw-Hill Book Company, Inc., 1962), 136 pp.

National Council on Schoolhouse Construction, *Guide for Planning School Plants* (Nashville, Tennessee, Peabody College, The Council, 1958), Chapters 2 and 4–8.

RINGNESS, Thomas A., KLAUSMEIER, Herbert J., and SINGER, Arthur J., *Psychology in Theory and Practice* (Boston, Houghton Mifflin Company, 1959), Chapters 5–8, 10, 13.

SMITH, Mary Howard (Editor), *Using Television in the Classroom* (New York, McGraw-Hill Book Company, Inc., 1961).

"The Teacher and The Machine," *The Journal of Educational Research*, 55:9, June-July, 1962, pp. 405–531.

THOMAS, R. Murray, and SWARTOUT, Sherwin G., *Integrated Teaching Materials* (New York, Longmans, Green & Co., 1960).

THORPE, Louis P., *The Psychology of Mental Health* (New York, The Ronald Press Company, 1960).

TRUMP, J. Lloyd, *Images of the Future* (Urbana, Illinois, The Commission on the Experimental Study of the Utilization of the Staff in the Secondary School, 1959).

.19.

Fringe Benefits

THE SCHOOLS are in competition with each other and other employing agencies to tap manpower resources so as to align for themselves the competencies needed to make possible the realization of the school function. The schools improve their competitive position to gain and retain employees by using various means, commonly referred to as fringe benefits, to make school employment particularly attractive. Industry has increased fringe benefits from $10.5-billion (11 per cent of payroll) in 1947 to $44.4-billion (27 per cent of payroll) in 1962.[1]

Fringe benefits that will be discussed include food service, housing, library, publications, consultative services, social-recreational services, insurances, leaves, and retirement.

FOOD SERVICE

Probably one of the greatest needs of the teacher is to have a break in his day. The break in teaching duties provided by the lunch period is not in itself sufficient. It must be supplemented by relief from child associations.

On all school levels, most notably the elementary, it is necessary for teachers to have adult associations. The lunch period provides an opportunity for fellowship, conversation, and discussion of topics of current interest. The noncoercive and informal involvement in a lunch period session can provide the occasion for some very effective inservice personal and professional growth.

The lunch-period break calls for consideration of dining facilities and food.

[1] "Wages: Going Up; 'Fringes': Going Up Faster," *U.S. News & World Report* 57:3, August 13, 1962, pp. 79–81.

Dining Facilities

Possibly the very small schools of 1–4 teachers can *make shift* with the use of a small office space or a vacant classroom for the lunch period. For larger schools, a sufficiently large room to accommodate all teachers who would have their lunch period at the same time should be provided.

The faculty dining room should be located in a quiet part of the building, facing a pleasingly landscaped nonplay area. Its decor should be in quietly cheerful good taste. If the school provides food preparation and service facilities for the pupils, the faculty dining room should be located so as to utilize those facilities efficiently.

The minimum equipment for the faculty dining room should include furniture that is comfortable, functional, and pleasing to the eye, a refrigerator, and adequate facilities to prepare coffee, tea, and the like.

Food

Schools that provide food service for their employees do only what is commonly done in industrial and federal governmental establishments.[2] The provision of food service is justified in terms of its implications for the personal welfare, morale, and effectiveness of the personnel.

Some underwriting of the costs of food service by the employing agency is justified by the implications of this service for employee productivity. Food services constitute an investment by the employing agency upon which it anticipates a return. However, since food services are not properly part of the employee's pay for work done, he ought to be expected to pay for them.

A middle ground that seems reasonable is one in which the schools provide all the physical facilities—rooms, furnishings, and equipment—and that daily operation costs of food and the personnel involved in its procurement, preparation, and serving be incorporated in the price to the consumers. This combines the elements of investment and nonprofit operation.

HOUSING

The problem of providing for housing varies greatly with the times and location. For many years there have been school districts of the one-room-school variety that provided a house adjacent to the school for the teacher. This house was known as a teacherage. The reason for such a

[2] Dale Yoder, H. G. Heneman, John G. Turnbull, and C. Harold Stone, *Handbook of Personnel Management and Labor Relations* (New York, McGraw-Hill Book Company, Inc., 1958), section 21, pp. 23–27.

house under those circumstances was the general unavailability of housing conveniently located, the frequent impassability of roads, the low salaries paid, and the need to provide housing or suffer the consequence of having a school but no teacher.

During several years following World War II, the general shortage of housing in the United States was such that even city school districts found it necessary to supplement improved teacher salaries with apartments or other housing in order to get teachers.

During any time of severe housing shortage, the school district or any employing agency that wishes to attract to its employ nonresidents will have to take cognizance of the housing situation by doing something about it. However, ordinarily, when housing is readily available, the most that the school district is expected to do is to help the new employee to locate housing. It may do this through direct efforts or through liaison with real estate firms.

LIBRARY

It is not uncommon for business to establish library services for its employees, through its own facilities, arrangements with libraries, and interlibrary exchanges, in order that employees may 1) become better informed about matters pertinent to their employment and 2) gain a pleasurable and worthwhile personal diversion through reading.

Improvement of Personnel

Direct and vicarious experiences are means by which personnel learn to become more efficient in their work. Reading is a vicarious experience, a shortcut to having to learn entirely from one's own experience.

Office, operational, and maintenance personnel can all benefit from readily available guides—how-to-do-it books—pertinent to their respective jobs. Similarly, the professional personnel can benefit from sources and reference materials that are pertinent to their work and ready at hand.

The library can provide all employees who belong to the teaching profession with the book and periodical references that help to keep them abreast of developments in the theory of learning, teaching techniques, curriculum, their own teaching or other educational specialties, and related areas pertaining to the organization and administration of schools.

A promising practice is the maintenance in the school professional library or in the faculty room of a rack containing the current issues of periodicals dealing with professional and socio-politico-economic affairs. Another service of potential merit is the selection and review of books that have particular value, the prominent posting of a well-written review on a bulletin board reserved for this purpose, the placement of the reviewed books on a specially provided shelf for recent books of exceptional merit, and provisions for freedom to use the book within the room and ease in checking it out.

Personal Diversion

Itself a visual aid, the written word of the book and periodical still provides advantages, over more recent means of communication, for precise wording and a beautifully meaningful turn of the phrase. The educated individual today is also well-read. The potential of all workers in the school system is enhanced if they add to their initial competencies for their jobs the broadening of perspective that comes from reading.

Also, whereas personnel administration concerns itself with the welfare of the employee, the relaxation, temporary escape from personal concerns, and enjoyment of reading have fully as great implication for the mental health of the employee as many another activity sponsored by the employing agency. It is the recognition of the general values of reading that has prompted many an enterprise to include in its library some purely recreational reading for its employees.

PUBLICATIONS

Establishing and maintaining contact among school employees throughout the school system, the employee publication is a substitute for and a supplement to personal contact. It aids in developing group morale and solidarity, serves as a medium of communication, and provides a stimulus to growth.

A stimulus to the crystallization and expression of employee points of view, the publication provides an excellent opportunity to provide for personal recognition, the sparking of interest and discussion, getting to know others via the references to them, their sentiments, and their activities.

The renaming of Baltimore's *Superintendent's Newsletter* to *Staff Newsletter* in 1952 had sound psychological implications. In addition, shortening the issue from 16 to four pages increased the likelihood of its being read in its entirety. The supplementation of administrative editorial control by an editorial committee representing the major interest groups among the employees can effect a decentralization of control and a co-operation that are conducive to the improved functioning of the employee publication.

As to content, there are no hard and fast rules. What is of interest and value to the school and its employees is appropriate for inclusion. So far as teachers are concerned Stevenson's finding in 1932 probably still holds generally.

. . . Stevenson found that five items ranked highest in teachers' favorable reactions to house organs: educational news and teaching information, official calendar and news, articles by teachers, editorials, and financial information.[3]

Particularly in the larger schools or school systems, consideration should be given to including items of interest to the nonteaching employees, possibly in a page set aside for this purpose. A separate publication for nonteaching employees is considered inadvisable in view of the unit concept of school functioning and staffing.

CONSULTATIVE SERVICES

Much of personnel administration is akin to counselling, an activity with which school personnel are well acquainted.

Counselling in the schools impinges upon such areas of pupil life and development as pupil physical and mental state, educational program and problems, vocational objectives and aptitudes, and social-recreational activities. The counsellor considers every pupil problem, personal or otherwise, that affects pupil behavior to be within his realm and he encourages the development of such pupil confidence that problems will be brought to his attention. The counsellor's concern for the pupil relates to the realization of the institutional objectives of the school and of the individual objectives or potentialities of each pupil.

An extension of the principles of school counselling, as already practiced with reference to the pupils, to help employees with their problems is defensible because of the implications for the improved efficiency of the employee who has been helped. Such an extension, operating through existing school administrative and supervisory personnel and additional personnel in the personnel division, would parallel the services that are frequently provided in industry.[4]

The kinds of problems on which counsel might be requested and given would constitute a virtually endless list. In order to expose somewhat the diversity of problems to be met, each of the following will be

3 Fred G. Stevenson, The House Organ in City School Administration, unpublished doctor's dissertation (Ann Arbor, University of Michigan, 1932) as reported by Arthur B. Moehlman and James A. van Zwoll, *School Public Relations* (New York, Appleton-Century-Crofts, 1957), p. 499. See also p. 498.

4 As early as 1914 the Ford Motor Company instituted a program to help employees with all phases of living. See Samuel M. Levin, "Ford Profit Sharing," *Personnel Journal*, 6:2, 1927, pp. 75–86 as also reported in William W. Waite, *Personnel Administration* (New York, The Ronald Press Company, 1952), p. 571.

dealt with briefly: the job-related, social, health, legal, financial, and retirement problems.

Job-Related Problems

Included among these are problems of orientation to the job, training for the job, and possible transfer. Or, in the event of unemployment for whatever reason, there is the problem of helping the employee with information about the unemployment, disability, and workmen's compensation benefits that apply.

Adjustments that improve the coordination of worker competencies with job requirements contribute to improved efficiency on the job. Aid given to those who become unemployed not only helps them but also is evidence to those still on the payroll of the concern of the employing agency for its personnel and their well-being. The help given promotes good will for the employing agency within the community. Thus is morale heightened and public relations improved.

Social Problems

Especially the newcomer to the school district has social problems of meeting and getting acquainted with people and discovering the cultural and recreational opportunities available. In addition, family, religious, and welfare problems are a common occurrence within today's society. It would be strange indeed if school employees did not experience social problems just about as much as does the population as a whole.

To some extent school districts, especially the larger and wealthier ones, can provide services to aid their employees to solve their problems. In areas in which some school districts cannot or do not have the specialized personnel or other resources to provide needed counsel, they have the obligation to be fully informed about community agencies that do provide specialized services with reference to family, welfare, religious, and other problems. The full knowledge of community resources for counselling and helping makes it possible for the school district to supplement its own counselling service by referring those in need to the appropriate community agency.

Health Problems

The school district is in a strategic position, because of such services already provided to pupils, to extend to its employees medical, psychological, and psychiatric consultative, clinical, and referral services to bring about and hasten recovery that will salvage to the school system's advantage its investment in personnel. Good over-all health is prerequisite to the effectiveness of all school employees.

Health problems are met by means appropriate to each problem. The means include, in addition to those already mentioned, examination, testing, health education, the provision of nutritional supplements, the provision of occupational and nonoccupational disability benefits, and participation in group hospitalization, medical, and surgical insurance plans. The extension of health services to the dependents of employees, as well as to the employee, seems to be gaining acceptance in industry and in some school districts.

Legal Problems

Many employees, sophisticated in their own fields, are completely at a loss in matters requiring the exercise of what might seem ordinary business sense. Any employing agency that can do so will build for itself a reservoir of goodwill by helping its employees in such legal matters as making a will, drawing up and understanding a contract (e.g., for the purchase of a home or a car), and understanding one's rights and recourses in civil and criminal proceedings.

The school district that cannot provide legal consultative services can do the next best thing, provide reliable information about where to go for the help needed.

A wholesome development in an era of easy suits for damages is the school's assumption of the obligation to provide legal defense for its employees when they become involved in suits consequent to the performance of their duties.

Financial Problems

As fortunate as he is exceptional is the employee who never needs help with his financial problems. The provision of a loan fund, where possible, enables the counsellor to back his words of wisdom with the substance needed on occasion. Where school district loan funds are not available, there are at least two other possibilities when there is need for money; the one is an advance in pay and the other is referral to reputable loan agencies within the community, agencies that are not extortionate in their interest charges.

In some instances, more important than money is advice about the management of money. Either within the school system or the community, there ought to be available someone who has a special knowledge of the management of personal and family finance to whom school employees can be directed.

Credit Unions and Preferential Purchasing. The school administrator who is truly interested in preventing financial problems as well as in assisting in their solution, may well consider the possibilities for organizing an employee credit union [5] and establishing preferential purchasing agreements.

To assure success the credit union usually requires a minimum initial membership of 100. Preferential purchasing agreements with local retailers and wholesalers become realizable when the employee group is large enough to give promise of volume sales to offset reductions in profits. In both instances there is dependency upon school district size and the number of employees.

Small school districts can benefit from credit union and preferential purchasing agreements through participation in such plans in cooperation with other school districts or under the auspices of county or state education (teacher) associations. The administrator is in a position to assist teachers by advice, information, and encouragement.

The credit union helps to stretch the income dollar by making available to members reasonable and nonextortionate loans and a savings plan that encourages thrift by providing added income by way of dividends. At the same time the purchasing power of the school employee's dollar is extended through reduced-cost buying under preferential (discount) purchase plans.

Retirement Problems

For some the toughest problem in retirement is to find something to do that keeps life interesting and worthwhile. Whereas geriatric study has resulted in increased longevity and improved health, gerontological studies have been addressed to providing a basis for favorable attitudes toward and treatment of the elderly. Between geriatrics and gerontology, the elderly may find that the years added to their span of life can be truly worth living, enriching and contributing to society and personal enjoyment. It is generally conceded that the best preparation for retirement requires adjustment to the conditions that antecede retirement age. Another problem of retirement is that of not overlooking benefits that are probably important to one at that stage of life when earnings from employment come to an end.

The school personnel division, having in its records detailed information about the employee, is in a strategic position to aid him to take the right steps both, to prepare himself for retirement and to secure his due

[5] For information about the rapid growth of teacher credit unions, see "Teachers Help Themselves through Credit Unions," *NEA Research Bulletin*, 38:3, October, 1960, pp. 78–80. The NEA has a Committee on Credit Unions that provides no-charge help to members.

from pension, retirement, social security, veteran's, and other benefits, and to confer with him on questions that may arise with respect to any one of the benefits.

SOCIAL-RECREATIONAL SERVICES

Where it becomes evident that there is need for a program of social-recreational activities for school employees, the school district that takes steps to meet the need does what is commonly done by governmental and business establishments which spend from $5.00 to $10.00 a year per employee on social-recreational programs.[6]

School district concern for meeting the social and recreational needs of school employees stems from the implications of activities to meet those needs for employee health, happiness, and consequent effectiveness on the job.

The school district's first step toward meeting the social-recreational needs of its employees may well be the investigation of community resources, such as municipal recreation departments and cultural centers. It may be that the needs of school employees may be met through already existing organizations and their programs and facilities. To the extent that existing provisions do not meet the needs of school employees, the school district may follow corporate lead by having within its personnel division someone qualified and employed to help employees organize those social and recreational activities in which they are interested.

INSURANCES

Particularly in the insurance area of fringe benefits the schools are far behind private enterprise and government. There are reasons for this.

All employing agencies share the desire to do what is necessary to improve employee productivity and organizational efficiency. The insurances are justifiable because of their contribution to improved functioning.

In addition to the common incentive, private enterprise has been abetted in the development and expansion of its insurance programs by 1) wage-stabilization programs that did not apply to insurances, 2) excess-profits taxes that largely offset the cost of the programs, and 3) the income tax break provided by a lowered tax bracket, resulting from allowing insurance costs as a legitimate business expense, in effect paying in part for insurances provided.

6 Dale Yoder, *et al.*, *Handbook of Personnel Management, op. cit.*, section 21, pp. 15–21; and William R. Spriegel, *Principles of Business Organization and Operation* (Englewood Cliffs, N.J., Prentice-Hall, Inc., 1960), pp. 339–342.

Governments lack the added incentives of business. Consequently those units of government most remote from the people or least subject to their control are in the best position to provide insurances. The units of government closest to the people and subject to the public will are at a disadvantage. The school district is the unit of government that is held most directly accountable to and subject to control by the people.

The disadvantage of the school district is probably not the product of opposition to insurances for school employees. More likely, the disadvantage results from a tax structure that puts the burden of school support upon local real property with insufficient aid from state and federal resources regardless of how heavy the burden may be. The taxpayer's resistance to any increase in school costs is his response to real property taxes that resemble rent rather than tax figures. His reaction is that this at least is one tax that he can do something about, hence his criticisms of and opposition to programs proposed for the schools, including employee insurances.

Despite the handicaps to be overcome before school employees receive insurance benefits to an extent comparable to that of employees in private enterprise and other units of government, an appreciation of the value of education compels facing up to the problem of making and keeping the schools competitive in the recruitment and retention of employees.

Emphasis here is upon insurances provided by the employing agency as a fringe benefit. Should the employing agency impair its competitiveness by failing to provide insurances for its employees, the employees do have recourse to other avenues to obtain for themselves the protection afforded by insurance. Employees may band together to form a group with a minimum to conform to state regulations (ranging from 5 to 25) and then contract with one or a combination of insurance underwriters to provide what they want. The local, state, and national school employees associations are possible second choice alternatives to school district group insurance plans.

Among the chief insurances currently provided in industy and government, and in some school districts, are life, disability, income, and health insurance. Each of these will be discussed briefly to bring it somewhat into perspective relative to the school scene.

Life Insurance

The greatest life insurance benefit for the least cost may be provided through *group term* life insurance. Since the term plan serves the company's objectives and protects the employee most economically, nearly all plans are of the term type. Generally the employer pays all or most of the premium. One study indicated that 89 per cent of factory and 92 per cent of office workers are covered by life insurance plans to which the employer and employee contribute.[7] Life insurance policies are written either in an amount related to annual income, a graduated amount; or unrelated to annual income, a flat amount. The graduated amount has some implication, lacking in the flat amount policy, for the standard of living attained. Flat and graduated amount policies vary greatly in their liberality. An example of one actual graduated policy is shown (Table 19-1).

TABLE 19-1
Sample Insurance Benefits*

Income	Life and Disability Insurances	Sickness and Accident Weekly Benefit
Less than $ 3,000	$ 4,000	$30.00
$ 3,000 – 4,499	5,000	40.00
4,500 – 5,999	7,500	55.00
6,000 – 7,499	10,000	70.00
7,500 – 9,999	15,000	70.00
10,000 – 19,999	20,000	70.00

* The disability insurance is for total and permanent disability. Derived from the "Schedule of Benefits for Salaried Employees," *Group Insurance Plan*, United Aircraft Corporation (in effect in 1962).

Whereas some school districts provide group life insurance for their employees just as do government and industry, others make a somewhat comparable provision through a death benefit rider to the retirement system. Maryland contains the following statement in its retirement system handbook:

Upon the death of a member in active service all contributions paid by him with interest, are returned to his designated beneficiary or to his estate; and if a member has had one or more years of creditable service, a benefit of fifty per cent of his "average final compensation" is also made to his designated beneficiary or to his estate, in a lump sum payment.[8]

Disability Insurance

Employees may be incapacitated for work by one or more of a number of causes. Included in these causes for which some kind of in-

[7] Otto Hollberg and Alexander Jarrell, "Supplementary Wage Benefits in Metropolitan Areas, 1959-60," *Monthly Labor Review*, No. 84, April, 1961, pp. 379–387. Note that employees generally contribute to an over-all insurance plan for life, disability, sickness and accident, and a combination of health insurances so that the contribution to the life insurance premium may be as low as 10 cents a month per $1000 policy.

[8] Board of Trustees, *Handbook of Information Explaining the Teachers' Retirement System of the State of Maryland* (Baltimore, Teachers' Retirement System, June 1961), p. 12.

surance benefit is provided are permanent and total disability and temporary disability.

Permanent and Total Disability. The insurance covering complete disability is corollary to life insurance. It ordinarily provides protection in amounts equal to that of the life insurance provided. For an example of a plan providing such insurance see Table 19-1.

Teachers may find that their retirement system complements the employing school district in efforts to make employment attractive by providing for disability retirement. Thus, in Maryland, a member of the retirement system who qualifies for disability retirement receives benefits that consist of:

(1) An annuity which shall be the actuarial equivalent of his accumulated contributions at the time of retirement; and

(2) A pension which, together with his annuity, shall provide a total retirement allowance equal to one-seventieth of his average final compensation multiplied by the number of years of his creditable service, if such retirement allowance exceeds one quarter of his average final compensation; otherwise a pension which, together with his annuity, shall provide a total retirement allowance equal to one-quarter of his average final compensation, provided, however, that no such allowance shall exceed one-seventieth of his average final compensation multiplied by the number of years which would be creditable to him were his service to continue until the attainment of age 60.[9]

Temporary Disability. Disabilities resulting from illness and job-related accidents are the chief objects of temporary-disability insurances. Among these insurances is one that provides a weekly income during the period of incapacity due to sickness or accident. For an example of benefits provided under such a plan see Table 19-1. In addition there are workmen's compensation and group health insurances.

Workmen's Compensation. Initiated in 1908 by the federal government to cover its civil employees, workmen's compensation laws have now been passed in all the states. The workmen's compensation laws are, in effect, employers' liability laws.

Under workmen's compensation provisions, those covered are eligible for such benefits as: compensation for job-related disabilities; immediate medical, surgical, and hospital care as needed; cash benefits, generally in some ratio to earnings; and temporary total disability payments for a specified period of time and/or up to a designated maximum amount. These benefits are financed through premiums paid into private insurance companies or state or self-insurance funds set up for the purpose.

Schools have for some time had their nonteaching employees covered by workmen's compensation. An extension of coverage to include teachers

9 *Ibid.,* p. 12.

is inexpensive in view of the low accident risk of teaching. Such extension has taken place in some school districts and states.[10]

Group Health Insurance. Under group health insurance are subsumed hospitalization, surgical, medical, maternity, and major medical benefits. Each of these may be provided through insurance companies or the nonprofit Blue Cross and Blue Shield type plans operating throughout the United States and Canada.

The insurance companies are likely to issue an indemnity benefit plan under which payments are made to the individual in fixed amounts, sometimes on a deductible or co-insurance basis, in accord with a schedule that is part of the insurance policy. Nonprofit plans, such as those of the Blue Cross and Blue Shield, are likely to be of the service type under which payments for specified services are made to the hospital or the doctor in accord with a schedule of fees for hospital, surgical, medical, and maternity services. Below a stated level of the insured's income and subject to the conditions laid down for the plan, the fee allowed under the plan is accepted as payment in full. Above the stated level, the insured is required to pay the difference between the usual fee and the amount allowed under the insurance plan.

Major Medical Insurance. An insurance benefit that has gained general acceptance since 1951, major medical insurance generally features:[11]

1. A broad scope of coverage, including just about all types of physicians' charges and other necessary medical expenses, whether the individual is in the hospital or not.

2. A high maximum, such as $5,000 to $15,000, for benefits.

3. Dependent coverage.

4. Safeguards designed to keep costs (and therefore premiums) within reasonable bounds:

    a. A cash deductible amount (e.g., $100.00–$500.00).

    b. A co-insurance percentage (e.g., 20% payable by the insured).

    c. Two special limits on covered expenses; a maximum on private room and board in the hospital and a limit on charges for out-of-hospital psychiatric care.

5. A benefit period after which a cash deductible amount must again be paid to establish a new benefit service.

6. A reinstatement provision which permits one who has used a substantial amount of his maximum to restore the original maximum benefit amount, e.g., by providing satisfactory evidence of insurability.

[10] The Maryland General Assembly passed legislation in 1954 to include all teachers under Workmen's Compensation. This protection is provided through the purchase of insurance by Boards of Education. Payments are made for permanent total disability, temporary total disability, permanent partial disability, temporary partial disability, and death. For a full statement of benefits see the current issue of the Maryland State Teachers' Association, *Handbook for Maryland Teachers* (Baltimore, The Association), an annual publication.

[11] Derived from, Teachers Insurance and Annuity Association, *TIAA Group Insurance for Major Medical Expenses* (New York, The Association, 1959), pp. 11, 12.

Group major medical insurance can be contracted for separately or it may be integrated with other health insurance plans. The newness of major medical insurance and the lag of school systems in contributing to the underwriting of health insurance in general provide an opportunity for the school districts to improve their competitive standing among all enterprises by underwriting an integrated health and major medical insurance plan. Such action would bring school districts into line with the many enterprises that now underwrite group health insurance plans for their employees and would put them in advance of those that have not yet adopted major medical insurance plans.[12]

LEAVES OF ABSENCE

Leaves have come to be accepted to cover a number of situations. Ordinarily they are administered on a purely local school district basis. Conceptually, however, the transfer of leaves as the employee changes his place of employment to another school district is possible. In practice, transfer of leave would be expected to be unusual. If provided for at all, the transfer of leave would be most feasible within states—not from one state to another—in which schools are operated virtually as parts of a centralized state school system.

Among the kinds of leaves of absence possible, those to be discussed include sick, maternity, military, personal, professional, and sabbatical leaves.

Sick Leave

Generally accepted in government, private enterprise, and school districts, the provision of sick leave is scarcely an issue today. However, the conditions under which sick leave is administered vary greatly. Thus there is no uniformity in the amount of sick leave allowed, how soon after employment it is available, whether or to what degree it may accumulate, and whether pay during the allowed leave is to be in part or full.

Practices. Within the plan in which a specified number of days is allowed for sick leave, one major difference is that of allowing, e.g., one or two

12 Blue Cross and Blue Shield type benefits, including maternity, and Major Medical expense benefits at 75 per cent of covered expenses and to a maximum of $5,000 are part of the United Aircraft Corporation group insurance package. All the health insurance benefits are for both the employees and their eligible dependents. The total semi-monthly contribution by the employee toward the entire Life, Disability, Weekly Benefit, and Health insurance package ranges from $2.30 for the lowest paid single employee to $7.32 for the family plan of the highest paid employee. See citation, Table 19-1, United Aircraft Corporation, *Group Insurance Plan, op. cit.*

days per month as contrasted to making the full school year's leave available immediately upon employment.[13] There is also great difference in policies relative to the accumulation of sick leave. The major difference is between limiting the accumulation and not limiting it. Where limits are imposed, 120 days is a commonly found maximum. With respect to pay, the tendency is to provide for a period of fully paid sick leave for the allowable time. In some instances, partial pay is provided in terms of the difference between the cost of substitute service and the pay of the absent teacher, either during the allowable sick leave period or during a subsequent extension of the sick leave.

Recommendation. The sick leave policy should be clearly stated and called to the attention of and understood by all employees. As a policy statement, it should chart the course of administrative action relative to sick leave while leaving the administrator latitude for taking into consideration special circumstances. Policies provide a frame of reference, not a substitute, for administrative judgment.

Provision should be made, on the basis of past experience, for financing sick leave. The provision of a liberal sick leave allowance may be expected to work to the advantage of the school system in terms of employee morale and the use of leave in such a way as to promote the over-all effectiveness of the employee.

Accompanied by such protective measures as the provision for submitting a physician's certificate, e.g., for absences exceeding a minimum number of days designated or upon request by the administrator, the provision of insurances to provide compensation during periods of disability, and the education of school employees to the values and the ethics pertaining to sick leave should make it possible to institute unlimited sick leave with full pay for an initial portion of it and partial pay in terms of provisions made therefor for the remainder of the leave.[14]

Maternity Leave

The necessity and desire to encourage married women of child bearing age to enter and remain active in the teaching profession require the provision of maternity leave.

Ordinarily maternity leave is a leave without pay, except as compensation may be provided through partial disability insurance. The

[13] In Racine, Wisconsin, the annual permissible sick leave of ten days is available the first month and is cumulative to 100 days. In the large (county) school districts of Maryland, state law provides for 10 days of sick leave annually at full pay; there is considerable variety in the provisions for accumulating unused sick leave.

[14] It is recommended that the reader turn back to the section on sick leave in Chapter 18 to supplement the above discussion.

benefit conferred by maternity leave is not a direct monetary one; it is rather one of assuring the employee that she has a job upon the expiration of the leave.

Practices regarding maternity leave vary. One practice is that of requiring the employee to take maternity leave at some designated stage of pregnancy, e.g., by the end of the first five months.

Military Leave

The national welfare has for long required employers to grant reservists and members of the National Guard time off for active duty. This requirement was considerably strengthened during World War II with the assurance that employees could return to their jobs upon return from military service. The continuance of uneasy world conditions since World War II has resulted in an extension of the war-time policy to protect the job rights of those who entered military service on a temporary, i.e., noncareer, basis. The military leave is without pay, for extended service, sometimes with pay for limited reserve duty of less than 31 days.

Personal Reasons Leave

The area of leave for personal reasons is probably the one in which the administrator will have to exercise judgment to considerable extent. It includes leave for family illness, paternity, bereavement, civic duty, religious holidays, incompetency, and emergencies that should be given consideration. The leave may be with or without pay.

Leave with pay for family illness and paternity are undoubtedly expressive of humaneness. They are also economically and functionally questionable. Economically and functionally, it would be sounder to provide additional compensation to pay for limited nurse, practical nurse, or housekeeper services that would usually meet the exigencies of the time better than most men could and at a cost per day substantially below that of the teacher's pay.

Paid leave for bereavement is another expression of humaneness. Generally such leave is provided for a limited time in connection with the death of a member of the employee's immediate family. Policy ought to spell out who is specifically regarded as in the immediate family and allow latitude for interpretation in unusual circumstances.

Civic duty leave might be expected to be for pay, possibly on the basis of the difference between the employee's pay and that received for the duty performed when the duty is short term as, e.g., jury duty or serving as a witness in a court action.

Increasingly the issue arises whether school employees should be prohibited from or encouraged to enter the field of politics. If the question is resolved affirmatively, the question of leave to perform the duties of elected office, e.g., a 90-day session of the state legislature, arises. The encouragement of teachers to serve in civic matters suggests the provision of unpaid leave during extended periods of such paid service.

Leave for religious holidays is a protection of the religious freedom of the individual. A liberal policy would allow pay for such leave. Lack of pay provisions would, however, not seem unjust. The holding of beliefs and convictions may be expected to exact a price, such as the loss of pay for the days that school is in session but the employee provides no service. Justice is served by the safeguarding of the employee's job during his religious holiday leave.

Incompetency is a sound basis for leave. Compensation would be dependent upon provisions for temporary and permanent disability. The leave makes provision for the employee to return to employment in the school district when he is again able to perform his duties reliably and effectively.

There may be emergencies not covered by specific leave provisions mentioned in this section. It is desirable that policy be specific about the personal reasons for leaves in as much as that is possible. However, it would be regrettable if the stated policy would exclude other reasons. To what extent other reasons can be accepted is a matter for careful and conscientious judgment on the part of the administrator.

Professional Leave

Limited professional leave is given without sacrifice of pay and, on occasion, with provision of expenses for attendance at and participation in professional conferences, conventions and like activities. Less formal and perhaps not calling for an invocation of leave policy, is the provision for personnel to improve themselves for school service by visiting other classrooms and other schools.

Extended professional leave without pay is sometimes given for a year or more for study or for special service to a state or national educational organization (State Department of Education, U.S. Office of Education, state or national education association, etc.) The benefit conferred by this leave is the guarantee of a job upon the termination of the leave.

Sabbatical Leave

Derived from the Sabbath, the seventh day of the week, a day of rest or repose, or the sabbatical year during which fields were required to remain untilled, the sabbatical leave is a recurring period of release. The period of work before eligibility for a sabbatical leave varies from the original concept of six time units of work followed by one of rest. Currently sabbaticals are granted in industry and education on the basis of such varying periods as 5, 6, 7, 10, or 11 years of work to establish eligibility for a sabbatical leave that is generally less than a year in duration.

Conditions. Theoretically the concept of a period of rest implies that the sabbatical should be free from work requirements. Some case might be made for a restriction upon the acceptance of other gainful employment during the sabbatical.

In practice, however, sabbaticals are often subject to approval of a program submitted and to be followed by the eligible applicant. In the field of education, a program of: 1) full-time professional study or research, possibly leading to an advanced academic degree, 2) travel with implications for one's teaching field, 3) writing for publication in an area that has implications for one's teaching field, 4) rest as needed for rehabilitation, or 5) "other reasons" are the required or accepted bases for approving applications for sabbatical leave.[15] A further condition in practice is the requirement that the employee return to his school district for a stated period of service, e.g., two years, or repay the school district the money received by him during his sabbatical leave.

Leave Pay. Among school districts, sabbatical leave pay varies greatly. Variations from full pay include:

1. Full pay for a semester or half pay for a school year.
2. The difference between the employee's pay level and that of his substitute during the leave. (Substitutes are secured on the lowest pay level possible.)
3. A flat sum.
4. A stated fraction of salary, sometimes limited to some maximum amount allowable.

Duration of Leave. In private enterprise, where the sabbatical leave is a recent innovation, the leaves range from 2 weeks to 10 months. In the field of education, where sabbaticals have for long been commonly accepted in nearly all of the states, the leave is thought of as being for one school year.

However, the sabbatical of one school year's duration is sometimes shortened to a half year as a result of leave pay policies that so curtail

15 In "Sabbaticals for Businessmen," *Harpers Magazine,* May, 1962, pp. 39–42, Richard B. McAdoo describes Bell Telephone, A.T. and T., and Aspen Institute sabbatical leaves and proposes full salary and complete freedom of action during the leave.

the employee's income that he cannot meet his financial obligations if he avails himself of the full school year's sabbatical leave privilege.

Sabbatical Dividends. The sabbatical leave is justified by the promise of dividends to the school system. These dividends come from professional improvement, contributions to the field of knowledge in education, the rehabilitation of the employee, employee opportunity to engage freely in pursuits that broaden perspective, and the encouragement—provided by freedom from job pressures—to become engrossed in reflective thought. These are dividends that accrue to both the individual and the school district that is the beneficiary of his improved competence.

Recommendation. The sabbatical leave should follow 6 years of fulltime employment, be unrestricted except possibly with respect to gainful employment elsewhere, command full pay, be of one year's duration.[16]

Annual Leave

Because of the summer vacation of as much as 13 weeks for the children, a period when teachers undergo an unpaid seasonal layoff, the issue of annual leave or a formal paid vacation for teachers has been generally neglected. Cognizance of the unpaid and layoff nature of the teachers' "summer vacation," together with extensions of the school year and the 12-month employment of teachers, makes continued avoidance of the issue of paid annual leave or vacation for teachers impossible.

The principle of paid vacations for teachers is already met to a degree in two kinds of programs. Under one kind of program, teachers are placed on a 10-month contract but are required to be on duty from 9 to $9\frac{1}{2}$ months. This is sometimes a specific and sometimes a tacit provision for paid vacation. When tacit, this provision lends itself to ready violation by exploitative administrators who lack understanding or appreciation of the principles of personnel administration.

Where teachers are on a bona fide 12-month contract, a number of school districts make specific provision for teachers to have one month's paid vacation in addition to the regular school holidays.

The principle of paid vacations for school employees is also already met in two other areas. The professional and the nonprofessional full-time employees who are on 12-month contract are generally given paid vacations ranging from 2 weeks to a month in duration.

Working as they do with children, teachers are placed under considerable stress. They need a vacation and they need pay during their

---

16 If the work year is a calendar year, the sabbatical should be a calendar year; if the work year is a school year of less than a calendar year, the sabbatical should be a corresponding school year.

vacations fully as much as does any other worker. In a society in which the paid vacation is generally accepted in government and private enterprise, depriving teachers of a paid vacation is indefensible discrimination. A carefully formulated and clearly stated policy covering paid vacations for all school employees is necessary and desirable.

RETIREMENT

Some kind of plan to provide retirees with some income has existed for centuries. A benevolent sort of pension plan, often informally voluntary on the part of the employer and dependent upon his means and generosity, was the means by which faithful retainers were cared for when they became unable to work efficiently. Informal plans were followed by formal ones that de-emphasized the paternalistic and welfare implications of pensions and provided bases for retirement payments as earned rights.

The employer-supported pension provided at will and in amounts determined by the employer, although it may have been earned in fact, had the dominant aspect of a gratuity. The employer-supported pension provided as a scheduled payment, made in accord with specified conditions on the parts of the employer and employee, has the dominant aspect of a delayed payment of earnings. And, the retirement plan that is jointly supported by employer and employee in accordance with the needs of an agreed-upon retirement compensation plan has the aspect of a combined earned pension and an employee savings plan.

Private Industry and Retirement

In private nonmanufacturing industries, 6.1 per cent of the payroll in 1959 was paid into pension plans. In 1960, private pension and welfare supplements to the payroll came to 8.45-billion dollars and covered approximately 21-million employees.[17]

With the passage of the Social Security Act in 1935 (becoming effective January 1, 1937), industry was in the position to make one of three adjustments to its retirement provisions. The employing agency could 1) discontinue its retirement plan, 2) modify its plan so as to have it become complementary to Social Security payments, or 3) develop or retain its plan independently to provide a retirement income wholly supplementary to Social Security payments. Of the three possible adjustments, the third has proved to be by far the most common.[18]

[17] The figures quoted here are from: The National Industrial Conference Board, *The Economic Almanac 1962* (New York, The Board in cooperation with *Newsweek,* 1962), pp. 78, 69, and 164 respectively.

[18] Walter Dill Scott, Robert C. Clothier, Stanley B. Mathewson, and William R. Spriegel, *Personnel Management* (New York, McGraw-Hill Book Company, Inc., 1941), p. 457.

The Federal Government and Retirement

The federal retirement system was established in 1920 and has been subsequently amended a number of times. Civil service employees of the federal government come under the federal retirement plan which is joint-contributory, the government and the employee sharing equally in payments that at present total 13 per cent of annual salary. In contrast to the supplementation of Social Security by independent retirement plans in industry, as employees of the federal government those under civil service are excluded from coverage under social security.[19]

The Schools and Retirement

Some provision for the retirement of teachers was made through the mutual association of teachers in New York in 1869. Later (in 1894), the New York legislature made provision for a limited pension under specified conditions for incapacitated teachers. New Jersey seems to have been the first state to provide a state-wide and state-administered plan (from 1896), geared to the employee's salary, for teacher retirement. Since these early beginnings, state-wide retirement systems for teachers have been instituted in every one of the United States.[20]

In almost all instances, teacher retirement plans are joint contributory and, increasingly, attention is being given to making and keeping the plan actuarial. There seems to be a sort of average provision to approximate 50 per cent of the average annual pay for the final five or ten years of employment (*final* is sometimes defined as the *best consecutive*).

In some states the retirement plan is such that an individual account is set up for each employee with the contributions made by him and the employer credited to his retirement account. In others, the amount contributed by the employee is credited to his account while a legislative appropriation, made available upon the employee's retirement, complements the annuity built up to make up the retirement payment made.[21]

There is generally a provision to return to the employee his contributions, sometimes with interest, if he terminates his employment before he is eligible for retirement benefits. In other instances there is provision

---

19 John M. Pfiffner and Robert V. Presthus, *Public Administration* (New York, The Ronald Press Company, 1960), pp. 325–329.

20 Paul Studensky, *Teachers' Pension Systems in the United States* (New York, Appleton-Century-Crofts, 1920). See also Willard S. Elsbree and E. Edmund Reutter, *Staff Personnel in the Public Schools* (Englewood Cliffs, N.J., Prentice-Hall, Inc., 1954), pp. 332, 333.

21 New York is an example of the first instance and Maryland of the second. In Maryland the legislative appropriation is such as to complement the annuity built up so as to provide an annual retirement income of 1/70 of average final compensation for each year of service credited.

to reactivate retirement privileges after termination of employment in the state by meeting conditions of subsequent employment and repayment of contributions withdrawn.

Influence of Social Security Act on Teacher Retirement. There was fear and division of opinion about the value of the provisions of the Social Security Act for teachers who were already members of a state or municipal retirement system. The primary advantage sought by teachers was that of survivor benefits for the employee who had not yet retired, benefits not generally conferred under state retirement provisions. The primary fear was that coverage under the provisions of the Social Security Act might eliminate or weaken the existing retirement system.

In fact, the experience of the schools paralleled that of industry as the schools faced the same alternatives. By 1961 teachers in over 75 per cent of the states were contributing to both Social Security and their state or local retirement plans. Yet, in no instance was the existing retirement system abolished following admission to Social Security coverage. In about one-third of the state or local systems some downward adjustments were made in the rate of contributions paid into the state or local retirement fund. In the majority of cases, the rate of payment either remained as it was or was increased to further strengthen the existing retirement plan.

Social Security, aside from having no great negative impact upon existing retirement plans—total benefits being in no instance decreased—has provided, in addition to survival benefits, the benefit of coverage irrespective of geographical location. It has made it possible for school employees to move without penalty with respect to that part of their retirement programs covered by Social Security.

There are a number of arguments intended to show that even greater benefits than those conferred by Social Security could have been provided had the same deductions been added to already existing retirement systems.[22] These arguments generally tend to disregard the fact that coming under the coverage of the Social Security Act had leverage values that were not operative and seemed difficult, if not impossible, to invoke for the improvement of existing retirement plans.

Limitations of Retirement Plans. Outside the retirement provided under Social Security, state and local retirement systems generally do not provide for reciprocity in the transfer of retirement credits if an employee accepts school employment in another state. State and local school employees retirement systems generally operate on a joint contributory

[22] For an excellent summation of such arguments see: Jack H. Kleinmann, *Fringe Benefits for Public School Personnel* (New York, Bureau of Publications, Teachers College, Columbia University, 1962), pp. 101–117.

basis with about equal contributions by the employer and employee. The amount of retirement approximates one-half average final annual salary after a long period of service. Provisions for retiring earlier are limited and carry with them the penalty of heavy reductions in retirement income.

Reciprocity. The differences among the retirement plans of the states and a number of independent municipalities are such that the development of a system of reciprocity is virtually impossible in terms of current organization. However, serious question may be raised as to whether the benefits of reciprocity may not be approached without actual reciprocity.

If the retirement system is set up on an actuarial basis, it seems logical that all contributions credited to a member's account (both his and the employer's) should serve as the basis for annuity payments. The annuities would increase with the growth of the account, e.g., every $100 in the account would purchase an annuity of a specified amount determined by the age of the employee at the time of his retirement.

An employee who remained in the schools of one state would simply accumulate annuity values in the one system. One who moved from state to state would accumulate varying annuity values in the respective states, putting in his claims and collecting proportionately from the respective states upon his retirement. He would be slightly penalized as his premium payments increase each time he accepts employment in another state. However, he would at least conserve retirement benefits earned in each instance.

Contributory basis. The theory of a sound retirement system is that it should be joint contributory; the employer and the employee each having a direct stake in it. Prior to World War II this theory was practiced in private as well as in public enterprise. However, with excess profits regulations and the admission of deductions for retirement plans as business expense for income tax purposes, private enterprise gained advantages in its competition for the manpower market by shifting toward retirement plans to which the employer made the greater, if not the entire, contribution.

Public agencies, including school systems—being nonprofit, income tax exempt, and dependent upon public largess—are at a disadvantage with private enterprise and under pressure to continue in accord with the joint contributory theory which private enterprise has compromised or abandoned. Thus the schools are confronted with one more handicap in the competition for talented employees. For jobs paying the same, the take-home pay of the school employee will generally be less than that of the employee in private enterprise because of his greater contribution to the retirement fund.

As the social scene changes, the school as an institution that is integral to society cannot afford to lag greatly behind social change if it is to be in a position to compete effectively for the manpower it needs in order to be functional. In this connotation this means that the school systems must make themselves competitive with other agencies by increasing their share of the contributions to retirement funds in accordance with the practices prevailing in private enterprise in the state.

Retirement income. Retirement income from school employees retirement systems provides an annuity of roughly one-half average final annual pay, i.e., if the employee has served long enough, e.g., 35 years. His annuity will be greater if he serves longer. However, 35 years is a long time to establish eligibility for retirement on half pay, and half pay after so long a period is far from a generous allowance. In addition, whereas a compulsory retirement age of 70 has been common, progress toward lowering the permissive retirement age has pretty much stopped at age 60. A teacher who begins teaching at age 22 can have served 38 years by age 60.

It would seem reasonable that he could, if he chose, retire earlier at a decreased annuity based on actuarial tables of life expectancy. The retirement conditions with respect to amount, length of service, and retirement age representative of general practices in the state must be matched by the schools to keep them functionally competitive.

SUMMARY

The chief fringe benefits extended in the competition for employees are food services, housing, library, publications, consultative services, social-recreational services, insurance, leaves, and retirement.

Food services include the need to provide a lunch period free from school duties, dining facilities segregated from those serving the pupils, and food provided on a nonprofit basis. The responsibility of the school district in helping employees to find housing increases inversely with the availability of housing. Library services promote the personal and professional improvement of personnel and have implications for their mental health. Staff publications serve as mediums of expression and communication for all school employees.

Consultative services are an expression of the counselling function of personnel administration. The responsibility of the school district to provide social-recreational services to its employees is considered to be in inverse ratio to community social and recreational resources. The school district has an obligation to take an interest in providing or supporting life, disability, workmen's compensation, group health, and major medical insurance to protect its employees so as to enhance their effectiveness.

Commonly or increasingly provided leaves of absence include those for illness, maternity, military duty, personal reasons, and professional service or improvement. Some leaves are with full or partial pay; others are without pay. A leave requiring greater consideration is the annual leave for teachers who are on a 9–10 month contract. Teachers are in fully as great need of a paid vacation as any other worker.

Retirement has progressed philosophically from the status of a benevolent gratuity to that of a deferred payment of earnings. The schools have generally supplemented their retirement systems with Social Security as has private enterprise. They lack provisions for reciprocity and lag behind private enterprise in their contributory systems, amount of annuity, and permissive retirement age.

In all matters pertaining to fringe benefits, as also with respect to salaries and wages, it is incumbent upon school systems to adapt to social change, making their personnel policies and practices conform to or surpass those of private enterprise within the state. Only thus can the schools hope to become competitive for the quality personnel necessary to school functioning in a democratically oriented society.

SELECTED READINGS

California Teachers Association, "Non-Wage Benefits for Teachers," *Research Bulletin 132,* May, 1960, 69 pp.

CASTETTER, William B., *Administering the School Personnel Program* (New York, The Macmillan Company, 1962), pp. 303–324 and 354–377.

ELSBREE, Willard S., and REUTTER, E. Edmund, *Staff Personnel in the Public Schools* (Englewood Cliffs, N.J., Prentice-Hall, Inc., 1954), Chapters 7, 13.

KEARNEY, Nolan C., *A Teacher's Professional Guide* (Englewood Cliffs, N.J., Prentice-Hall, Inc., 1958), Chapters 12, 13.

KLEINMANN, Jack H., *Fringe Benefits for Public School Personnel* (New York, Bureau of Publications, Teachers College, Columbia University, 1962), 178 pp.

N.E.A. Research Division, "Sabbatical Leave Practices of Representative Educational Agencies," *Research Memo 1960–22,* July, 1960, 53 pp.

N.E.A. Research Division, "School Districts that Pay Part of the Premiums for Certain Insurance Programs Covering School Employees," *Research Memo 1961–23,* June, 1961, 13 pp.

N.E.A. Research Division, "Statistics of Retirement Systems to Which Teachers Belong," *Research Report 1961–R16,* October, 1961, 60 pp.

WATKINS, Gordon S., DODD, Paul A., McNAUGHTON, Wayne L., and PRASOW, Paul, *The Management of Personnel and Labor Relations* (New York, McGraw-Hill Book Company, Inc., 1950), Chapters 23–25, 29, 30.

YODER, Dale, HENEMAN, H. G., TURNBULL, John G., and STONE, C. Harold, *Handbook of Personnel Management and Labor Relations* (New York, McGraw-Hill Book Company, Inc., 1958), Sections 9, 13, 14, 17, 18, 21.

.20.

Forms, Records, Reports, and Research

FORMS, records, and reports are to an extent overlapping in their meaning. Forms may be thought of as vehicles for gathering information. Records carry with them the implication of at least relative permanence. And, reports cover a wide range of activities from the individual reporting that takes place as a form is filled out to the consolidation of selected items of information to provide group perspective and the recounting of research findings that pertain to personnel administration. Each of these will be dealt with briefly.

PERSONNEL FORMS

A number of forms have been devised in order to facilitate the functioning of the personnel division. The forms are designed to provide for the recording of information in the systematic fashion that lays the foundation for analyses, comparisons, correlations, reports, research, and decisions that are all part of personnel administration.

Some idea of the kinds of forms used in personnel administration in private enterprise,[1] where the personnel activity is often developed to a more sophisticated degree than in the field of education, may serve the

[1] Discussions of personnel forms, records, and reports may be found in: George D. Halsey, *Handbook of Personnel Management* (New York, Harper and Row, 1947), Chapter 5, 13; Gordon S. Watkins, Paul A. Dodd, Wayne L. McNaughton, and Paul Prasow, *The Management of Personnel and Labor Relations* (New York, McGraw-Hill Book Company, Inc., 1950), Chapter 11; Dale Yoder, H. G. Heneman, John G. Turnbull, and C. Harold Stone, *Handbook of Personnel Management and Labor Relations* (New York, McGraw-Hill Book Company, Inc., 1958), Section 22.

school administrator as a check against his practices and his needs. A fairly comprehensive, but not exhaustive, list of the forms used in private enterprise personnel administration follows.

Forms Used in Private Enterprise

Job analysis, description, and specification
Personnel inventory
Internal recruitment inquiry
Preliminary application
Application
Checks on education, training, experience, and references
Tests: intelligence, aptitude, attitude, interest, human relations, judgment, etc.
Physical and psychological examination request
Physical and psychological rating
Diagnostic interviewer's guide
Interviewer's rating
Qualification card
Employment notification and contract
Payroll authorization
Service record
Induction (orientation and probation)
Performance rating
Absenteeism and punctuality
Accidents
Transfers, promotions, and demotions
Authorization for payroll and personnel record change
Work load
Suggestions
Discipline
Warning notice
Separation notice
Exit interview guide
Exit interview record
Turnover or employee stability
Association (union) membership
Financial report and unit costs

The specific personnel forms to use and the items provided for in them may be expected to vary from one organization to another in terms of what is expected of the personnel division, the size and complexity of the organization, the recognized problems of the organization, the research capability and orientation of the personnel division, and the money available for a truly functional operation of the personnel division.

Forms for the administration of school personnel have been developed in the personnel division of the Detroit, Michigan, Board of Education Offices since the introduction of such a division prior to

World War I (circa 1914).[2] The forms in use during the 1962–63 school year include:

Forms for Teaching Positions

Application (1)
Grade point average (1)
Supplementary information and eligibility (1)
Verification of professional experience (1)
Interview sheet (1)
Medical director's report (1)
Speech and hearing report (1)
Psychological report, applicant's self-analysis (1)
Credential sheet (1)
Notice and record of personnel action (1)
Emergency substitute teaching service approval and release (1)
Report on quality of emergency substitute teacher service (2)
Principal's recommendation concerning substitute teacher (1)
Request for personnel action (3)
Recommendation for permanent certificate (2)
Authority for salary differential for graduate degrees (1)
Request for additional salary for 30 credit hours above the master's
     degree (3)
Request for approval for special employment situations (3)
Request for leave of absence or extension of leave (2)
Progress report on satisfactory probationary teachers (4)
Special (i.e., unsatisfactory) report on services of a certificated employee (5)
Record of satisfactory service, administrative and supervisory personnel (4)
Principal's recommendation concerning a resigned teacher (1)

Forms for Nonteaching Positions

Preliminary application (1)
Application (1)
Referral to police department for fingerprinting and check by Subversive
     Detail of Criminal Information Bureau (1)
Notice and record of personnel action (same as above) (1)
Oath of allegiance and fidelity (1)
Report on probationary employee (2)
Report on quality of emergency substitute service (2)
Rating form for candidates for promotion to clerical assistant (1)
Special service report (3)
Rating—temporary or seasonal employee (2)

2 A copy of each of the Detroit personnel forms was provided through the courtesy of the Detroit Superintendent of Public Schools, Dr. Samuel Miller Brownell; the Director of Personnel, Dr. Albert Schiff; and Miss Adelaine Callery, Personnel Assistant for Records and Certification. The copies appear in the Appendix and are reproduced by permission. The numbers in parentheses indicate the number of copies required. The reproductions in the Appendix include the legend as to where each copy goes.

What forms are to be used by any one school district, what their content provisions are, and the number of copies to be made are variables that depend on the problems, needs, and organization and capabilities of the school district, and the uses to which the information is to be put.

PERSONNEL RECORDS

When completed, the personnel form generally becomes either a part of the personnel record or the source of information for setting up the personnel record. Thus, compiled from forms and reports, personnel records are and serve as enduring summaries of information considered important for the realization of organizational (i.e., school) objectives through personnel administration.

Purposes of Personnel Records

The chief purpose served by the keeping of personnel records, aside from the overriding one of furthering organizational objectives, includes the provision of the information needed for research, for meeting legal requirements, for managing fiscal matters, and for arriving at administrative decisions regarding matters pertaining to personnel.

Keeping the Personnel Record

The personnel record will be discussed in terms of where it is kept, who sets it up and keeps it up to date, when entries are made, what the mechanics of maintaining and using it are, and what safeguards to employ.

The "Where" of Record Keeping. The central office location of the personnel division is the place where the personnel record should be kept. It is here that the information recorded is readily at hand for the summarization or review that logically precedes final administrative decision making and action.

The central office locale for personnel records does not preclude each principal's having in his office a complete file of copies of information sent to the central office and of further supplementary information that is awaiting decision as to whether or not it should be made a matter of record. Every principal is well advised to maintain a file on each employee in the school for which he is responsible.

The "Who" of Record Keeping. Upon the filing of an application for employment and subsequently through every act of providing information, e.g., about change of address, interests, health, competency, the employee involves himself in the setting up and keeping of his personnel record. Often, the completed application blank becomes a part of the personnel record upon employment of the applicant.

The immediate supervisor—the principal, a department head, or both—submits information for the personnel record periodically and upon special occasions that call for an entry.

Finally, the actual setting up and keeping of the personnel record is the function of the central personnel office to which all pertinent information is channeled. The actual entering of information upon the record is clerical work and will be delegated to clerical employees in all but the very smallest school districts.

The "When" of Personnel Records. The value of personnel records lies in their being current. This means a minimum lag in submitting information and making entries. The keeping of personnel records is a continuous activity which is subject to periodic review.

The "How" of Record Keeping. A number of forms, when completed, become part of the personnel record. Such forms may be filed in individual folders or jackets for each employee. Folders and jackets containing completed personnel forms lend themselves best to blind filing, i.e., filing in standard filing cabinets with the necessity of opening the drawer and finding the desired folder either to make an entry or to check on information already entered.

A master card may be drawn up so as to contain in standardized form information that is considered of major importance. Such a master card form may serve as a summary that is included in the blind file. On the other hand, summarization of information on a single card suggests the possibility of visible filing. Visible index equipment provides for virtually instantaneous location of the card desired, ready reference, and ease in making entries.

The problem of alphabetical or numerical filing of all employees versus that of filing by some classification, department, or school may be solved by the use of a cross-reference file. Thus, e.g., if individual personnel records are filed in accord with some convenient category, a cross-reference file set up alphabetically serves as the ready reference for quickly identifying the category under which to look for the desired record. A rotary file for as many as 6500 employees can be accommodated by a wheel of 21-inch diameter [3] and is one convenient means for cross-referencing.

The increase in the size of school districts, the complexity of large school system organization and operation, and the increased understand-

[3] Stanley M. Brown (Editor), *Business Executive's Handbook* (Englewood Cliffs, N.J., Prentice-Hall, Inc., 1953), p. 397.

ing about the variety of uses to which electronic data processing equipment and techniques lend themselves for all manner of school records, including those for personnel administration, leave no choice but to consider the use of punched or mark-sense cards.

Electronic data processing permits easy and fast recording, sorting, and tabulating of data. Further, it makes possible the seeking out and computing of interrelationships. Thus is electronic data processing a means for gaining a quick and accurate analysis of mass data to provide the basis for making policy and administrative decisions. It serves also as the basis upon which to make reports to the board of education, interest groups, and the general public.

School districts that are too small to buy or lease electronic data processing equipment have the alternative of joining with neighboring school districts, municipalities, or businesses in the use of equipment that is made available to each through a pooling of resources and cooperation.

One other alternative is possible for those who cannot make independent or cooperative use of electronic data processing equipment. The small school district will find it possible to make good use of the key-sort technique of recording information for more than usual facility in analyzing, tabulating, and interrelating information.

The punch card used in electronic data processing (in which the mark-sense card can be used in similar fashion) and in the use of the key-sort technique is a great aid to keeping records in condensed and highly usable form, making reports, and engaging in research.

The Safeguarding of Records. Personnel records are so important to both the organization (school system) and the employee that it is essential that they be safeguarded. The records must be kept safe against the wear and tear of use; hazards, such as fire; and tampering.

The quality of the stock used for the record should be determined by the planned use of the record. The right quality of stock, determined by use, assures serviceability and economy.

Fire-resistive filing facilities provide protection against damage by fire. Records that are irreplaceable and sufficiently valuable to warrant doing so should be placed in a fire-resistive vault which, in a large organization, would be of the walk-in type.

Tampering by an employee, or someone acting for him, can be guarded against to some degree by securing the rooms in which files are kept, locking filing cabinets, and having the walk-in or other vault as burglar proof as possible. A further protection against tampering is the use of multiple copies of the more important forms in all instances in which copies also serve to facilitate personnel administration under the combination of central and decentralized operation characteristic of school systems.

PERSONNEL REPORTS

There are basically two kinds of personnel reports; reports to the employees and reports to the administration. Both kinds of reports may combine information from other report sources and be used as the basis for further reports, e.g., to the board of education and the public.

Sources of Reports

The sources of information for reports may be some kind of primary report, e.g., sick leave forms; or, they may be individual or group records in which primary report information has been entered, e.g., the individual personnel record or the annual (or biennial) reports of state departments of education (public instruction) and of local school districts.

The General Nature of Reports

Reports are generally descriptive of what has been or is. They may provide comparison of 1) past and present, 2) an actual situation with a forecast or prediction made in anticipation thereof, and 3) one school system with another or others. Many reports are statistical in the sense that they are compilations of data, sometimes accompanied by one or more kinds of computation, e.g., totals, means, and medians.

Some statistical reports are in fact group archival-type records having the purpose to preserve information in conveniently available form. The annual or biennial reports of state departments of education and of local school districts, aside from the popularized annual reports that supplement them, generally fall into the archival-record category of reports.

Purposes Served by Reports

The archival-record type of report serves the purpose of preserving information for future reference. Some reports by those in the school system have the primary purpose to serve as public-relations instruments. They contribute to the understanding essential to gaining public confidence and generating public support for warranted objectives, including those pertaining to school personnel administration.

The specific personnel purposes of reports are covered by the two headings, communication and morale. Both of these headings have direct implications for the understandings essential to promoting the employee efficiency that underlies the effectiveness of the organization, the school system.

Reports to the administration serve the dual purposes of supervision and control. They provide in organized form the information that is necessary as a basis for improvement and change.

Topics for Reports

The topic on which a report is to be made will vary with the need of the organization or school system. There is no virtue to reporting without other purpose than that of reporting. Every report must be drawn up in response to a problem so pressing as to give it priority over other problems for doing what is necessary to produce the needed report.

To prepare a complete list of all possible topics for reporting is impossible. However, in the preceding chapters there have been many cues to issues that do at one time or another, or one place or another, serve as report topics. A partial list of such topics follows.

Report Topics

Demand for and supply of school employees (by category)
Recruitment
Applications
Tests
Selection
Competence and assignment
Load and work period
Rating (as permitted by criteria)
Performance (by field workers, e.g., supervisors)
Education and training
Attitudes and morale
Complaints and grievances
Suggestions
Experimentation
Innovation
Gains or improvements

Employer-employee joint relations, and action
Transfers (including promotions)
Leaves of absence (by reason)
Compensation
Fringe benefits
Ethics
Working conditions
Aids (materiel and personnel)
Freedom (academic and personal)
Absenteeism and punctuality
Accidents, health, illness
Job security and tenure
Separations (by reason)
Fairness or justice
Unit costs
Public relations

Miscellaneous, including: age, sex, experience, certification status, school department or division, school or other place of work, place of residence, telephone number, personal or family physician, hospital preference, etc.

The topics for the foregoing reports are derived from information reported by the individual, made available from personnel records, and submitted by the unit of school organization in which the employee works. In addition, there will no doubt be reports based upon research activities that go well beyond the mere summation and compilation of report information. The real hope for the immediate improvement of school personnel administration and the ultimate improvement of the school operation has its basis in research activities and reports that are the grounds and justification for ensuing action.

RESEARCH FOR PERSONNEL ADMINISTRATION

Personnel administration shares with many other fields of endeavor the need for and a growing appreciation of research. As "the complex of specific activities distinctly engaged in by the employing agency to make pointed effort to secure the greatest possible worker effectiveness consistent with the agency's objectives,"[4] personnel administration virtually connotes research; research to discover what activities to maintain, discard, or strengthen, what the defensible criteria for appraisal are and how to apply them, how to attain high worker effectiveness, why worker effectiveness is affected positively or negatively by varying situations or working conditions, and how the varying concerns and activities of the personnel division relate to the objectives and functioning of the agency, the school system.

Research Defined

A normal and necessary function of personnel administration, the research activity has distinctive characteristics that contribute to a working definition. Research is a systematic and intensive means for getting and analyzing facts in order to: answer questions pertaining to cause and effect relationships (ascertaining the *how* and *why* of what *is*), add to the fund of knowledge, bring what is known into clearer perspective, develop principles as guides to defensible practice, and provide the basis for prediction and projection.

The Nature of Research

Research may be sporadic or continuous. Since the extension of knowledge is important for survival and improvement, and such extension is contingent upon research, research ought to be continuous.

Basic Research. Research for the sake of knowing, understanding, and being able to predict and project is basic or pure research. Basic research is an adventure into and an exploration of the unknown. Basic research could conceivably be self-serving, providing those engaged in it the gratification and feeling of fulfillment that come with each step beyond the known and with every addition to their own knowledge. Basic research could also be an expression of an urgency to extend knowledge and to make these extensions available to society.

[4] See Chapter 1.

Applied Research. Research that has as its object capitalization upon the product of basic research by seeking ways for putting it to use is applied research.

The practitioner, the school administrator, has the findings of research as the chart and compass by which to set his course. Without the resource of research findings, the administrator is adrift, without direction and without a secure basis for action. Reviewing the findings of research, he finds the evidence upon which meaningful action can and should be taken and explores it in order to discover the practical uses to which he can put it.

The Importance of Research

Some of the importance of research is unmistakably implied by the statements defining and characterizing it. It is held that basic research is as useful to and holds as great promise for personnel administration as for such sciences as chemistry and physics.[5]

Of three functions basic to a personnel office operation, research was regarded as second in importance by Appley.[6] Research was listed second among five functions and emphasized as one of the two most important functions of a state department of education by Weber.[7] In addition, time and again throughout this book it has become evident that worker efficiency is the product of a number of such factors as ability, aptitude, assignment, attitude, fairness, incentive, morale, motivation, orientation, participation, personal relationships, recognition, security, training, well-being, etc. These factors and the specific parts they play in contributing to the improved functioning of the school system are prime subjects for the research that is conducive to improving the effectiveness of the school operation.

Personnel Research Objectives

The transcendent objective of personnel research is to obtain answers to questions as to how to influence behavior, account for changes in behavior, and predict behavioral responses to stimuli provided so that the organization, the school system, may function in optimum fashion.

---

[5] See Michael J. Jucius, *Personnel Management* (Chicago, Richard D. Irwin, Inc., 1948), p. 653; and Dale Yoder, *Personnel Management and Industrial Relations* (Englewood Cliffs, N.J., Prentice-Hall, Inc., 1948), p. 832.

[6] The three functions are 1) developing influence with operating officials, 2) performing research relative to personnel administration, and 3) administering routines, e.g., examinations, recruitment, classification, certification, rating, etc. See Lawrence Appley, "Organizing for Personnel Administration," *Public Personnel Review*, 3:2, April, 1942, pp. 100–106; also reported in Felix A. Nigro, *Public Personnel Administration* (New York, Holt, Rinehart, and Winston, 1959), p. 32.

[7] Clarence A. Weber, *Personnel Problems of School Administrators* (New York, McGraw-Hill Book Company, Inc., 1954), p. 88.

Subordinate to the over-all objective of personnel research are the four purposes to:

1. Derive and formulate statements of principle to serve as bases for planning and as guides to decision making and action
2. Develop methods for improved personnel policies and procedures in order to improve school operation
3. Crystallize criteria by which to appraise conditions and evaluate efforts to improve and facilitate the teaching-learning situation in the schools
4. Promote the proper functioning of each department within the school organization so as to coordinate human resources with materiel for the maximum utilization of each in the performance of the tasks that the schools are instituted to do

To the degree that the transcendent and subordinate objectives of personnel research are realized, one or a combination of the following results should become manifest:

1. Improvement 1) in early recruitment and training to prepare for school employment and 2) in selecting, assigning, orienting, supervising, providing for training in service, appraising, and rewarding school employees
2. Progressive solution of problems pertaining to employee effectiveness, turnover, morale, values, involvement, grievances, justice, and unit costs
3. Compilation of facts, tabulation of data, establishment of interrelationships (cause and effect), and interpretations
4. Identification and provision of working conditions conducive to effective work, a pay formula that is defensible and fair to the public and the school employees, and fringe benefits that, together with the pay, make and keep the schools competitive with other employing agencies

Objects of Research. Every aspect of the personnel activity—from the earliest preliminary recruitment of youngsters to consider sometime entering school employment, through all the routine personnel activities, and including every step by which all who are to be influenced by the personnel activity come to have confidence in it, to the separation from service or retirement of the employee—is the proper object of personnel research aimed at improving school functioning.

Bases for Research

Personnel research has as its ultimate objective the improvement of the teaching-learning situation in the schools. Its approach to that objective is in part by way of an immediate objective to improve worker competencies and the conditions for capitalizing upon them.

The foundation for much of personnel research lies in disciplines other than education which play a role in understanding people and their behavior. These disciplines include particularly anthropology, biology, chemistry, history, mathematics, neurology, philosophy (including logic), physics, psychology, and sociology. These—especially psychology, sociology, and logic at this time—may be termed supporting disciplines for education.[8]

Basic research by a personnel division would most likely take place in terms of one or more of the supporting disciplines and would be, for example, psychological. By contrast, applied research would take place through efforts to use the findings of the supporting disciplines to improve school functioning. All basic and applied research findings that have pertinence for education, together with personnel records and reports, constitute the basis for conducting research relating to school personnel administration.

Techniques of Research

Basically, the technique of research is that of the scientific method. The scientific method is one of progression from knowledge to reflective thinking, to theory, to hypothesis, to testing of hypotheses, and to either disillusionment and a new beginning or the extension of the knowledge that was.

The scientific method employs observation, fact finding, experimentation, verification (e.g., tests of reliability and validity), analysis, and interpretation (involving generalization). It emphasizes objectivity and the negation of tendencies toward the personal involvement that turns investigation into promotion.

The means by which research is conducted include approaches that may be described as predominantly experimental, historical (research into the past), philosophical (emphasis upon value judgments derived by reflective thinking and logic), sociological (dealing with human relations), statistical, and survey (descriptive of what is current). A research design in terms of one of these approaches does not preclude the concomitant use of one or more of the others.

One consequence of the use of the scientific method in personnel research will undoubtedly be a de-emphasizing of personalities and a focussing upon issues. Analysis of the system by which employees are governed, rather than personal attacks upon employees, give promise of research that is conducive to improved functioning. "Efforts to correct misgovernment have too frequently failed . . . because men not methods were changed or attacked."[9]

[8] See Myron Lieberman, *Education as a Profession* (Englewood Cliffs, N.J., Prentice-Hall, Inc., 1956), pp. 192–195.

[9] Luther Gulick, *The National Institute of Public Administration: A Progress Report* (New York, The National Institute of Public Administration, 1928), p. 13, and *Proceedings of the Pittsburgh Conference for Good City Government and the Fourteenth Annual Meeting of the National Municipal League*, 1908, p. 127. These sources are quoted in John M. Pfiffner and Robert V. Presthus, *Public Administration* (New York, The Ronald Press Company, 1960), p. 187.

SUMMARY

Forms are used in personnel administration to facilitate the gathering and submission of individual and group information. What forms to use, the number of copies, and the content are realistically determined by the planned use to which the forms are to be put.

When completed, the forms used may be made a part of the personnel record, or items of information may be selected for transcription to the record. The major purpose for having personnel records is the furthering of organizational objectives. This purpose is supplemented by internal and external communications, fiscal, legal, and management purposes.

Maintained in the central office for personnel administration, personnel records are the responsibility of the employee, the person to whom he is immediately subordinate, and the staff of the personnel division. To be of value, personnel records must be kept continuously up to date,, readily available, and easy to use. A number of filing systems, mark-sense and punch-card recording techniques, and security measures contribute to the usability and value of personnel records.

Reports, drawn up from information provided through personnel forms and records, are generally descriptive. They may broaden perspective through comparisons. They serve as a means of morale building communication to employees and of supervision and control to the administration. In addition, some reports are archival, having the purpose of preserving information in convenient form.

Information gathered, recorded, and reported on provides a basis for the research that is the means for gaining the knowledge and better understanding of cause and effect relationships that are necessary to prediction and the progress of improved operation.

Research may be basic, i.e., of the kind that produces gains for the fund of knowledge; or it may be applied, i.e., of the kind that is concerned with finding ways by which to make use of the reservoir of knowledge. Both kinds of research are important to personnel administration. However, disciplines other than that of education—e.g., currently philosophy, psychology, and sociology—are the disciplines in which the research techniques for basic research are evident. Except to the degree that practitioners in the field of education make use of the research techniques of other disciplines they have no other alternative at this time than that of engaging in applied research. This pertains also to the area of school personnel administration.

Underlying the research activity, and buttressing it, is the use made of the objectivity of the scientific method, the emphasis upon fact finding, experimentation, verification, analysis, and interpretation. Stress is placed upon issues rather than upon personalities.

SELECTED READINGS

BENSON, Charles S., *The Economics of Public Education* (Boston, Houghton Mifflin Company, 1961), Chapter 12.

BORG, Walter R., *Educational Research* (New York, David McKay Co., Inc., 1963), Chapters 2, 4, 6–8, 12, 13, 15–17.

CHANDLER, B. J., and PETTY, Paul V., *Personnel Management in School Administration* (Yonkers-on-Hudson, N.Y., World Book Company, 1955), Chapter 19.

ELSBREE, Willard S., and REUTTER, E. Edmund, *Staff Personnel in the Public Schools* (Englewood Cliffs, N.J., Prentice-Hall, Inc., 1954), Chapter 10.

GOOD, Carter V., *Introduction to Educational Research* (New York, Appleton-Century-Crofts, 1963), Chapters 1, 2, 5–9.

HALSEY, George D., *Handbook of Personnel Management* (New York, Harper and Row, 1947), Chapters 29, 30, 31.

LIEBERMAN, Myron, *Education as a Profession* (Englewood Cliffs, N.J., 1956), pp. 191–195.

PFIFFNER, John M., and PRESTHUS, Robert V., *Public Administration* (New York, The Ronald Press Company, 1960), Chapter 12.

RUMMEL, J. Francis, *An Introduction to Research Procedures in Education* (New York, Harper and Row, 1958), Chapters 1–12.

TRAVERS, Robert M. W., *An Introduction to Educational Research* (New York, The Macmillan Company, 1958), Chapters 1–4, 13–15.

WHITE, Leonard D., *Research in Public Personnel Administration* (New York, Social Science Research Council, 1939).

WHITNEY, Frederick Lamson, *The Elements of Research* (Englewood Cliffs, N.J., Prentice-Hall, Inc., 1950), Chapters 1, 2, 6–13, 15, 16.

WOLFLE, Dael (Editor), *Symposium on Basic Research* (Washington, D.C., American Association for the Advancement of Science, 1959), pp. 1–185.

YODER, Dale, and HENEMAN, H. G., TURNBULL, John G., STONE, C. Harold, *Handbook of Personnel Management and Labor Relations* (New York, McGraw-Hill Book Company, Inc., 1958), Sections 22–25.

.21.

Personnel Administration and Employee Organization

SCHOOL personnel administration is a function of school administration. An omniscient school personnel administration that observes the principles developed throughout preceding chapters might conceivably satisfy the interests of education and all groups concerned therewith. However, lacking omniscience, even the best school administration may be expected to be at times myopic with respect to some issues, exploitative of personnel, and lethargic about innovation.

One antidote to some of the limitations and malpractices of administrators is supplied through the pressure of social change and employee prodding. However, regardless of eloquence or logic, the lone prodder may be expected to achieve improvement for himself and the group only rarely, and then at considerable risk to himself. The probability of making gains for education and those employed in effectuating it is enhanced by the collective action of the employee group.

Collective group action implies organization by which to supply that impressive group solidarity which commands the attention and respect of the administrator, board of education, and community. Just as employees in private enterprise and in government have gained for themselves the right to organize and to use their organizational strength, so also have school employees united in organizations designed to strengthen their stands.

Under the unit concept of school functioning, the justification for being on the school payroll is the contribution the employee makes to education. Every employee, then, may be expected to have an interest in promoting education, improving the competency of workers in the field of education, and working for the welfare of school employees. Hence, the most logical school employee organization ought to provide for membership by all school employees. The over-all school employee organization may be expected to have two major branches, the professional and the nonprofessional, each with a number of departmental subdivisions according to function.

Probably because of the identification of the school function with the teacher, the number of teachers, and the professionalism for which teachers strive, the connotation of school employee associations is pretty much limited to teacher associations. School employees other than teachers are without organization, organized under the auspices of local labor unions, or, in the case of secretarial employees, organized under an association of educational secretaries. Both the National Education Association and the American Federation of Teachers tend to place primary emphasis and focus upon the organization of the teacher employee group.

This chapter will be devoted to an exploration of what kinds of interests the school system may expect the organization—in which the school employee has membership and which speaks for him—to exhibit. This exploration will take place with reference to objectives, membership, ethics, representation, joint relations, discrete activities, and the means for asserting itself as an employee organization.

OBJECTIVES

Convinced of the function and importance of education, particularly in and for the democratic society, teachers and all other employees who contribute to the facilitation of instruction ought to be expected and encouraged to organize for the advancement of education. In fact, it may be considered the sole objective of school employee organization to serve the people by efforts to further and improve education.

The one objective, to further and improve education, is flanked and supported by corollary objectives that have major implications for the attainment of the prime objective. Among the corollaries are the objectives of employee improvement, employee welfare, and establishment and maintenance of independence.

Employee Improvement

Conscious of its stake in and responsibility for the education enterprise, the school employee organization may be expected to take measures directed toward improving the effectiveness of its membership. Among the measures through which the membership of the employee organization is stimulated to improve individual and personal competency are the establishment and enforcement of selective membership standards, provisions for exchange of ideas, highlighting of different practices, encouragement of experimentation, research, and a posture of openminded-ness toward innovation.

Employee Welfare

There is no doubt that the generally uninvitingly low level of the personal welfare of the school employee is at the root of school vulner-ability to criticism by various segments of the public.

The pay level and working conditions of nonprofessional school employees have in many instances been such that the schools have had to settle for the secretarial, clerical, custodial, and other personnel that were of such a level of competency as to be undesired by other govern-mental or private enterprises.[1]

The competent school teacher—who entered school employment in spite of low pay, a work week of approximately 48 hours, working condi-tions that left much to be desired, and little recognition—finds himself placed on a par with some who were academically unacceptable in the noneducation departments of their colleges or universities, some who have no understanding of the theories underlying learning because they are not teacher trained, and some who are "emergency" certified upon graduation from high school or the completion of part or all of a college program intended to meet objectives other than teaching.

It may be expected that a school employee organization will express interest in upgrading schools by advocating measures (pay, fringe benefits, and working conditions) calculated to attract to school employment high-caliber, adequately educated and trained men and women who merit recognition within and outside the school for their respective compe-tencies, professional and nonprofessional.

Organizational Independence

As an institution called into being by and for the people and wholly financed from public funds,

The public school is conceptually an impartial, nonsectarian, nonpartisan, and classless social institution in a society that has no rigid class structure and that subscribes to the idea of classlessness.[2]

It would be extremely difficult, if not impossible, for the schools to retain their conceptual posture if, for example, school employment were predicated upon adherence to some designated belief, membership in a

[1] There are fortunately also a goodly number of school employees, professional and nonprofessional, who are highly competent and who accept school employment in preference to other employment opportunities because of interests, location, or hours.

[2] Arthur B. Moehlman and James A. van Zwoll, *School Public Relations* (New York, Appleton-Century-Crofts, 1957), p. 536.

specified church, registration with a denoted political party, or identification with an indicated class. Any such requirement for school employment would undermine the confidence of the public as a whole, gain added support from some, and invite opposition from others. The school as an institution would be open to the suspicion of being representative of the points of view upon which employment was made conditional.

Whereas each employee as an individual has an equal right with other citizens to his personal beliefs and affiliations, the school employee, his organization, and the school become subject to the suspicion of bias if the school employee organization maintains a position other than that of impartiality, nonsectarianism, nonpartisanship, and classlessness.

Employment by a public institution places a limitation upon school employees, particularly the teacher group which has the especial obligation to be above suspicion as regards partiality in the classroom. Affiliation with existing interest groups, in effect inviting from competitive groups an opposition readily reflected upon the schools, threatens the school employee organization with impotency to further and improve education. It is therefore incumbent upon school employees in general and teachers in particular to establish their own employee organization, independent of other interest group organizations.

To be most effective, the professional interest group should maintain its independence by remaining aloof from entangling alliances and partisan effort. . . . The teaching profession cannot afford to be part of an alliance which is in opposition to the general public but which musters enough united strength to gain its ends in spite of the public. Neither can it obligate itself and feel compelled to support the cause of another interest group because of a debt to be paid rather than because of the merits of the cause.[3]

It would be extremely naive of school employees to imagine that they can gain strength and support through affiliation with nonschool-related interest groups without having to pay a price. To buy support without knowing the price tag to be placed upon it is unthinkably unintelligent when there are alternatives. And, to endanger the conceptual posture and status of public education in and for the democratic society is equivalent to jeopardizing the public institution and betraying the public trust conferred upon all who have a part in facilitating instruction.

MEMBERSHIP

Organization of school employees into one association in recognition of the unit concept of the functioning of the schools does have implications for recognizing the two major branches, professional and nonprofessional, and the departments within those branches. However, it is not to be inferred that such organization for all categories of school

[3] *Ibid.*, pp. 338, 339.

personnel implies automatic membership status concomitant to employment.

Irrespective of the branch or department of the school employee organization, automatic conferment of membership puts emphasis upon numbers rather than qualification. A stress upon numbers suggests reliance on the impressiveness of power-group size and whatever threat this may convey. By contrast, a stress upon membership standards that have implications for the qualifications of the employee is connotative of competency to serve the public interest. This latter is conducive to promoting the public confidence that is basic to the support required for improvement of education and all facets of school working conditions involved in such improvement.

The Professional Branch

Among the standards to be met to qualify for membership in the teaching profession today, the following would seem to be the minimum:[4]

1. Satisfactory completion of the program of studies prescribed for preparation to teach.
2. Full certifiability to teach in the state in which employed as a teacher.
3. Demonstrated competency established by satisfactory service throughout a probationary period during which adequate supervision was provided.
4. As applicable, the completion of programs of study, inservice training, and other prescribed preparation to qualify for certification to specialized tasks of administration, counselling, supervision, or teaching; and, certifiability for the specialty in the state in which employed to exercise it.

The title, *teacher,* ought to be reserved to those who meet all requirements for membership in a professional organization characterized by meaningful standards. Those who meet most, but not all, requirements might well be given differential titles in the schools and qualified membership in the association, receiving recognition through change of title and membership status upon qualification.[5]

Specialties as Professions. Particularly in the area of school administration, the question has been raised whether there ought not to be recognition of school administration as a profession in its own right.

4 The National Education Association, several state education associations (Among them Kansas, Maine, Maryland, and Michigan), and the American Association of School Administrators have set up membership requirements in terms of one or more of the following: level of education completed, state certifiability, and the accredited status of the institution of higher education at which academic work was taken.

5 Note the example of industry: "The Bay State Abrasive Products Company, Westboro, Mass., is the latest industrial firm to announce new policies restricting the title "Engineer" to legally qualified personnel . . . to only those . . . who are registered professional engineers." See, "Engineering Titles Restricted by Firm," *The American Engineer,* September, 1959, p. 19.

The point of view that has evolved historically and functionally[6] is that the school administrator is first of all a teacher and that his administrative assignment is the product of size and the consequent need for specialization. This point of view has emphasized the professional status of the school administrator as a teacher. It does not preclude the administrator, who qualifies as a member of the teaching profession, having also and concomitantly a *specialist* professional status as school administrator. School administrators, as well as other teachers who have left the classroom in order to serve in some professional specialist capacity, constitute a legitimate department within the over-all professional branch of the school employee organization.

The Nonprofessional Branch

All school employees who perform functions other than those requiring qualification as teachers may seek to qualify for membership in the nonprofessional branch of the school employee organization. This branch will have departments in accordance with the major categories of personnel, e.g., clerical, custodial, foodhandlers, health, maintenance, transportation, warehouse.

Membership in the over-all nonprofessional branch and in the departments thereof ought to follow the same principle of conformity to meaningful membership standards that have direct implications for the established competency of the employee.

It is postulated that as nonprofessional school employees conform to standards of membership in their branch of the school employee organization, they will come to see their jobs in the light of the contribution that each can make to the effectiveness of school functioning. Consequently they will work as employees of the schools and as members of the employee organization to do what is necessary to improve themselves and their lot in order that education may be furthered and improved.

ETHICS

Organization provides for an integration of individuals in terms of the spirit by which they are motivated and which underlies the functioning of their particular activity. This is true for all interest groups, professional and nonprofessional.

The spirit which binds together the individuals in organization finds some expression in a code of ethics. This code involves principles and attitudes that the individuals who come under it consider necessary to

---

6 Note that the multiple and dual administrative organization prevailing in many places early in the century have had to give way to the unit concept in which qualification as a teacher, classroom experience, and orientation to education transcended business and management competencies.

their functioning, take pains to define, deliberately adopt as expressly binding upon themselves, and endow with legal-type attributes and penalties for violation.

Group ethics may be expected to:

1. be the product of experience within the group and between the group and those it serves.

2. provide encouragement to the able to enter the profession (or for the nonprofessional, to qualify for employment and group membership) as long as the need for service exceeds the capacity to provide it.

3. promote functional balance between the general practitioner (as contrasted to the specialist) and the specialist.

4. elevate competence and meaningful criteria therefor above superficial conformities.

5. restrict tasks to those that are necessary and make prime demand upon the special competency of the member of the profession or the nonprofessional employee.

6. be conducive to the assumption and demonstration of personal responsibility appropriate to the nature and level of the task.

7. encourage the development of individuality as an offset to the danger presented by the organization man. (This is considered particularly important for those who, whether or not professional, are employees of any organization, governmental or private.)

Ethics for a Profession

The code of ethics for any profession represents the considered and purposeful application of the generally accepted social standard to the particular sphere of professional conduct, e.g., that of architect, doctor, engineer, lawyer, nurse, teacher. It is a group standard of conduct that must be reconciled to the matrix of community standards. It is a group standard that binds its members and has implications for the relationships of the group and its members with those outside the group.

Professional ethics for each of the professions subscribes, by statement or by the nature of the profession, to an ideal; the ideal of service.[7] This ideal transcends in concept reward or financial gain. Failure to come up to the ideal in practice does not negate its integrative effect, the prime basis for popular support of the professional group, and the value of the ideal as a referral point to gauge practice.[8]

[7] The ethics of public accounting, architecture, medicine, law, engineering, the clergy, teachers, organized labor, and public employees are discussed in *The Annals* (of the American Academy of Political and Social Science), Vol. 297, January, 1955, pp. 1–104.

[8] Milton Helpern, "A Doctor Criticizes '5 O'Clock Medicine,'" *U.S. News & World Report*, LIII:19, November 5, 1962, p. 8. This article by New York City's chief medical examiner and president of the Medical Society of the County of New York scores the practice of terminating the medical day at 4 or 5 o'clock and labels it as hazardous to those who suddenly get sick and damaging to the medical profession.

The Teaching Profession. For the most part professional education associations have insisted upon the functional unity of their members inasmuch as they are first of all teachers. Thus the interests of classroom teachers and administrators, together with other professional specialists, are regarded as identical, not opposed. On the basis of unity, teachers have an advantage enjoyed by the professions and not generally enjoyed by those outside their ranks, the advantage of not being involved in a management versus labor conflict over acquisitive interests.

The majority of teachers, those belonging to a professional association, hold to the ideals of 1) service of the public interest in education and 2) the group identification of its members irrespective of whether they serve by way of classroom teaching or some specialized professional function intended to facilitate instruction.

There is today no one organization to which all teachers belong. The state education associations combined would come close to accounting for all public school teachers. There is a National Education Association in which a majority of teachers have for some time held membership. The national association, organized in 1857, adopted a code of ethics in 1929. The NEA action came 33 years after the 1896 adoption of a code of ethics by the Georgia Education Association.[9]

In its code of ethics, as revised by its Ethics Committee and adopted by the NEA Representative Assembly, the National Education Association gives clear evidence of an integrative motivating spirit of service, of the obligations of members to each other, and of the duties of members to the public. It lacks an effective means of enforcement and consequently a compelling need to know or observe the code. There is an apparent need to develop, through emphasis upon the code and continuous efforts to recodify, a code that is truly expressive of the need of the teaching profession, the willingness of the profession to be bound by it, and the means for its enforcement.

Ethics for Nonprofessional School Employees

A corps of school employees not qualified to be members of the teaching profession has evolved. Their employment is justified wholly by the support they give to the teaching activity through their services. They constitute an interest group but are in a position unlike that of their counterparts in private industry. Their position is quite analogous to that of governmental employees. Thus their code of ethics may be expected to compare to that of public employees.[10]

[9] Written codes of ethics were adopted by other professions as follows: American Medical Association, 1848; American Bar Association, 1908; American Institute of Architects, 1909; American Institute of Accountants, 1917; Engineers' Council for Professional Development, 1947; and (nonprofessional, the Congress of Industrial Organizations, 1951). These data are derived from *The Annals*, 1955.

[10] Phillip Monypenny, "The Control of Ethical Standards in the Public Service," *The Annals*, Vol. 297, January, 1955, pp. 98–104.

Also, like teachers, the nonprofessional school employees enjoy the position of having the school administration allied with them to execute board policy for the effective operation of the schools. All agents of the board of education exist to serve the public interest in education. Public education is a nonprofit operation; therefore there are no profits for owner-management to withhold from labor or vice versa.

Being in a position analogous to that of teachers, nonprofessional school employees are also in a position to develop a code of ethics to govern their branch of the school employee organization. Their code may be expected to be developed along the lines of the seven steps listed earlier in this section.

REPRESENTATION

All public school employees, professional and nonprofessional, are distinct from the members of other somewhat comparable groups in that: as members of a profession, they are not private entrepreneurs who can control rather fully their own working conditions and remuneration; as public employees, they are morally or legally deprived of the right to assert themselves through the general strike; and as agents of the public, they are obligated to maintain their independence. This situation suggests at first blush a position of weakness and of lack of bargaining leverage.

One potent factor that militates in favor of school employees is the growing awareness that the public school is an institution of and in a democratic society. The implication is that, insomuch as possible, the school should operate democratically. This means that employees involved in the school operation should have a voice in the formation of the policies by which they are governed.

An organization to which school employees belong provides the means for considering issues, crystallizing opinion, agreeing upon action, designating spokesmen, and entering upon negotiations with the administration or, if necessary, the board of education.

Conscious of the nature of the school as a democratic public institution, desirous of being democratic rather than autocratic in his relationships with other school employees, and alert to his need for close liaison with all groups of school employees, especially those on the educational firing line where contacts with pupils and the public are a daily occurrence, the school administrator today as never before understands that he is expected to make use of the opportunities provided through employee organization to take the pulse of school operation, to diagnose the state of its health, and to prescribe in accord with the symptoms and complaints observed what seems necessary to produce improved functioning.

Since the present day administrator seeks and welcomes opportunities to work with those who represent the group(s) in an effort to find solutions to problems that have implications for the effectiveness of the schools, it would be convenient to deal with a single association of school employees. However, as long as employees are divided in their membership, it is incumbent upon the administration to have an effectively open door to representatives from each of the organizations in which employees have membership as employees.

JOINT RELATIONS

What has been said about employee organization suggests that just as the public, the administrator(s), teachers, and personnel auxiliary to teaching do play a role in controlling jointly the school operation,[11] so also the associations in which school employees have membership may be expected to identify their legitimate role in providing direction and motive power to school operation.

The exercise by the school employee association of control jointly with others has its basis in citizenship in the school community, the right to a voice in the determination of policies affecting one, the responsibility of any executive agent of the board of education, the special appraisal ability of those "on the inside," and assertion of defensible educational and self-interests.

Just as the employee now has, through his representatives at the round table, a voice in the policies and practices of private industry, so also should the school employee be expected to make himself heard relative to school operations through his representative(s). Whereas at one time the posture of the employee was expected to be one of servility, a more mature human relations attitude is to abhor servility and to recognize the dignity of man and his worth by assuring him his place in the joint effort to promote the welfare of the industry (school system) in which his own interests are also involved.

The school administration should expect the school employee association to strive for the attainment of an active role in those matters that it considers pertinent to the improvement of education, employee competency, and employee well being.

DISCRETE ACTIVITIES

There are a number of distinct activities in which the board of education and the school administration may expect the school employee association to take part and to make itself heard. Many of these activities will be of concern to the school administration because of their pertinence to instruction, directly or because of personnel implica-

11 See Chapter 12.

tions. A listing of a number of these activities, many of which have been discussed in some detail, will suffice.

School Employee Association Activities [12]

Establishment of membership standards

Development of codes of ethics, association and branch

Gathering information

Sponsoring experimentation

Engaging in statistical and other research

Professional development through workshops, conferences, and meetings

Appraisal of school operations

Dissemination of information, within the association and to the school system and the public

Encouragement of innovation

Recruitment, beginning at the junior high school level, to attract promising prospects to school employment

Efforts to influence the improvement of training and the raising of professional standards

Employment information

Placement services

Improvement of employee welfare with respect to:

work period	pay scales
assignment	fringe benefits
orientation	working conditions
transfers	grievance procedures
promotions	tenure
hours	appeal rights and procedures

Representation of educational and employee (professional and nonprofessional) interests at the administrative and board of education conference table

THE STRENGTH OF THE ASSOCIATION

Every interest group seeks its own advantage through a variety of means and agencies. Each has a number of sources of strength by which it seeks to advance its interests. Also, each has a major source of strength upon which it places great reliance. Thus, a dominant source of strength 1) for labor is its control of manpower through the threat and use of the strike. The strength of management has traditionally been its control over capital, including the material means for production, and the influence this control gives it. Public employees in the civil service, barred as government workers from using the strike, have found that "The most effective substitute for the strike in government service is the political power of the employees."[13]

[12] Many of these activities have been discussed in Chapters 4–11 and 16–19.

[13] Sterling D. Spero, "Collective Bargaining in Public Employment: Form and Scope," *Public Administration Review*, 22:1, Winter, 1962, p. 4.

School employees find themselves more analogous to government workers than to labor or management. They have tended to avoid use of the strike. They do not control capital. However, their position to emulate government workers in resorting to the use of political power is in question.

The Government Worker

Public employees under civil service have job protection. They remain relatively constant while those to whom they are subordinate are transient. The Achilles' heel of the transient government official is that he is directly or indirectly subject to partisan elections. Thus the government official has to react sensitively to public opinion lest he jeopardize his own position or that of the administration that appointed him.

The sensitive position of the elected official makes him susceptible to the pressures created by unfavorable public opinion produced through paid advertising, broadcasts, demonstrations, marches, rallies, etc. Government workers are conceptually strategically placed to capitalize upon the political sensitivity of the elected office. Their efforts need not be based so much on what is just or defensible as on the tactical advantage they hold.

The School Employee

In general, school employees, particularly teachers, have job protection through tenure. Ordinarily their chief executive, the superintendent, is the only professional whose job is truly vulnerable. However, the superintendent is not popularly elected; he is appointed by the board of education. The board, in turn, is most commonly popularly elected. However, being nonpartisan, the board is ordinarily not threatened by radical change. It is subject to gradual and progressive change in its membership in response to the public will.

The board of education is functionally placed as a buffer between the people and the school operation. The superintendent who observes this functional relationship has job security to the degree that the board of education regards his educational leadership sound and his execution of board policy satisfactory.

The board of education and the superintendent share with elected government officials an aversion to embarrassing situations and, like them, are likely to take what measures they can to avoid or overcome conditions conducive to awkwardness. They are abetted in their efforts to avoid public embarrassment by the attitude assumed by the large body of school employees, the teachers, and shared to some extent by other school employees.

School employees have generally regarded themselves as public employees debarred from the use of the strike. Teachers have for the most part tended to regard the strike as unprofessional. In addition, teachers and other school employees have expressed concern about the implications of their actions for the children. Thus teachers are inclined to lean backwards in an effort to meet a not wholly defined sense of professionalism. This leaning backwards results in generally disavowing techniques considered unsavory, such as exercising political power to bring into disrepute members of the board of education or the administration.

Barred as public employees, as well as by their sense of professionalism, from the use of the strike and scrupulous about using techniques considered unsavory, teachers are deprived of means readily relied upon by other interest groups. This leaves in question the source of strength and the means for asserting it that are supposed to be assured by organization.

School Employee Strength. Embodying the Jeffersonian point of view, the Northwest Ordinance of 1787 contained in its third article the statement, that has come to be a cornerstone to education throughout the United States, that

> Religion, morality, and knowledge, being necessary to good government and the happiness of mankind, schools and the means of education shall forever be encouraged.[14]

This perceptive statement has been confirmed by experience and supported by subsequent action during the evolution from the last days of the Congress of the Confederacy to the present. It affirms the function of the school to be the meeting of individual and societal needs.

The schools are necessary as a means to attain good government for and the well-being of the people. Thus school employees may expect that their strength lies in and is integral to the need of people, particularly in a democratic society.

However, the need of people does not automatically call forth the action suited to the need. Eventually, it is likely, intelligent people will evolve the means to fulfill their needs. This is a basic principle of democracy. However, the discovery of means can be hastened by individual effort and the eventual acceptance of ideas that seem to hold promise. It is possible for those who are specially trained in the field of education, who have dedicated themselves to the pursuit and dissemination of knowledge and who have a career interest in the advancement of edu-

[14] Henry S. Commager, *Documents of American History* (New York, Appleton-Century-Crofts, 1934), pp. 128–132.

cation as basic to the general welfare, to decrease the lag between need and the development of the means for fulfilling it through public relations activities that promote understanding of the community and its needs and of the school and its potentialities.

There are four clearcut ways in which the school employee organization can operate. First is that of a program of public relations; second is that of cooperative efforts to arrive at collective agreement; third is that of sanctions; and fourth is that of the limited strike. Each of these will be discussed briefly.

Public relations. The public relations activity is basically one of adult education. The adults of the community are faced with the responsibility for their social institution, the school. They can face their responsibility intelligently only to the extent that they understand themselves, their community, their needs, and the limitations upon and potentialities of their public schools.

The people of the school district have a right to expect that school employees, as their agents and as members of the community, will play a role in promoting understanding. School employees by reason of their involvement in the educational activity are in a position to provide perspective in terms of their vantage point. Teachers, masters in matters educational, are committed to the power of education as the key to knowledge, the control of man's environment (on earth and interplanetarily), and the furtherance of the well-being of mankind.

Those who are the masters of the educational art and technique have at hand so potent an instrument that dictators have attempted to regiment it to their own advantage in the realization that through education it is possible even to control the minds of men. Thus dictators have attempted to pervert education in order to capitalize upon its strength. However, the strength of education is fully as great, probably greater, when it is the education suitable for free men urged to explore freely in an effort to push back the frontiers of knowledge. It is essential that teachers realize the potency of the art and science that is theirs.

Teachers have the obligation to society and themselves to work with long range perspective for the future. Had this been recognized and observed throughout the past, many of the current problems of education would be nonexistent or at least noncritical. Among the factors pertinent to school public relations as an educational activity in which school employees, especially teachers, are operative are:[15]

. . . school public relations may be considered to be the two-way interpretive process between the society and its instrument, the public institution.

. . . school public relations has as its primary purpose the promotion of the social will as it is found in and expressed by the community.

[15] Arthur B. Moehlman and James A. van Zwoll, *School Public Relations* (New York, Appleton-Century-Crofts, 1957), pp. 152–155, 549.

School public relations must develop and retain its identity as distinct from the usual implications associated with public relations.

School public relations . . . and propaganda are at opposite poles.

The school public relations activity is typefied by a regard for the facts, an attempt to present them in unbiased fashion, and the encouragement of all who are interested to explore the issue under consideration as fully as possible.

The interpretive methods of school public relations are those of teaching or of education.

Exact knowledge, careful long-range planning, and efficient application of new evidence, as soon as it becomes available, aid in eliminating emergency situations.

Lack of alertness and flexibility produce conditions conducive to disintegrating revolution for both institution and society.

School public relations, conducted in accord with the point of view expressed in the foregoing quotations, is an activity by which school employees are able to pave the way for the enlightenment that is necessary in order to advance toward their legitimate interest group objectives. As a long-term activity, the public relations envisioned is conceived of as having far greater potential than any other means for the effective self-expression of a scrupulously professional interest group of integrity.

Collective agreement. Resistive to techniques identified with management-labor relations, boards of education and their chief executives on the one hand and teacher groups on the other have made all too little use of the promising aspects of the activities involved in collective bargaining.

Collective-bargaining activities do serve to bring face to face representatives of the interested parties. The result is a gain in understanding on the part of each group of the point of view held by the other. This is the necessary basis for arriving at agreement which will probably be at some point between those initially held by the respective groups.

Round-table discussion of the various parties that have an interest in education is not something to be feared, rather it is something to be promoted. It is most likely that the long range benefit of the collective approach is dual, accruing to the advantage of both the employing agency and the employee.

Boards of education and school administrators should expect that school employee organizations will seek confrontations which will permit an exchange of viewpoints and cooperative search for a satisfactory solution to the problems of the moment.

Sanctions. Public-relations activities hold promise for the long pull. The introduction belatedly of public-relations activities cannot, however, legitimately be expected to remedy immediately a situation that has reached critical proportions because of neglect of a continuous and long-term public-relations program. If in addition to past neglect of public relations there is failure to provide for collective agreement through co-operative efforts and round table conference, the failure to make progress toward their objectives may be expected to cause school employees to consider the possibility of invoking sanctions.[16]

When it is recalled that among the interests of school employee organizations were the provision of employment information and placement services, it becomes obvious that through these and the professional publication(s) of the association, it is possible to apply sanctions through which prospective employees are warned of the unfavorable working conditions in the school district and placement services are withheld from the school district.

The use of sanctions is a form of blacklisting, would ordinarily not be the function of the local school employees association, would operate on the broader level of state or national organization, is provided for and has been invoked by the California Teachers Association, and has been used for long by the American Association of University Professors. The invocation of sanctions is a drastic measure for exerting pressure in instances where reason has failed.

Limited strike. The right of public employees to strike "is universally denied by the courts, and such prohibitions are firmly fixed in the law."[17] Whereas opposition to the use of the strike on the grounds that striking is unprofessional is being undermined by strikes by doctors and the support of such strikes by medical associations, teacher concern for the implications of a strike for the children has served as a further deterrent to teacher strikes. This latter concern may be more commendable for its sentiment than for its realism.[18]

Among the interests of the school employee association there were listed a number of factors pertaining to working conditions and also the development of codes of ethics for the two major branches of the school employee organization. A code of ethics is a set of standards to regulate conduct.

It is expected that part of what will be in the code of ethics will be a definition of the essential responsibilities of the group in question and the provision for taking extreme action, short of an actual strike, should preferred efforts to resolve problems be unproductive.

Among the provisions for extreme action would be what, for lack of a better designation, is termed a *limited strike.* A limited strike is thought

[16] Arthur F. Corey, "Strikes or Sanctions," *NEA Journal,* 51:7, October, 1962, pp. 13–15.

[17] John M. Pfiffner and Robert V. Presthus, *Public Administration* (New York, The Ronald Press Company, 1960), pp. 333, 334.

[18] If pay or working conditions are such as to invite such last-resort tactics as a strike, they are also so bad as to discourage the talented and informed from preparing for school employment, from accepting it where conditions are notorious, and from remaining in school systems where improvement seems impossible. These results tend to perpetuate school inadequacies.

of as an operation during which basic and minimally essentially activities are carried on while all others are suspended. The limited strike has been used. Its status is not yet wholly clear. It may be outlawed or condoned in time.

Through an accretion of activities without a correlative expansion of staff (imposing added and often nonprofessional duties upon teachers) a considerable body of teacher "duties" have accumulated. This body of duties needs examination, evaluation of its merits, and provision for staffing of what is deemed essential. However, until these steps have been taken either by the school system or by the school employee association and the status of the limited strike is clarified, the suspension of adjunctive activities provides teachers with a leverage potential that can be put to effective use.

The scrupulousness with which teachers and other school employees have on the whole conducted themselves traditionally suggests that resort to the limited strike would be rare and restricted to highly provocative situations that have proved unamenable to other action and that invite extreme action just short of a *bona fide* strike. Following the employment of the other available ways of asserting organizational strength, the school employee association may be expected, in the face of failure, to resort to the limited strike in order to keep the school operating while exerting pressure for negotiation of the issues at stake.

SUMMARY

In carrying out his responsibilities with respect to the school employees, the administrator is faced with the need to reserve a place for interaction with the employees as such and also with the organization in which they associate themselves for various reasons, including the desire to gain strength through union.

The organization of school employees for strength is justified by its prime purpose to further and improve education. This purpose, however, is hedged about by others that support it—the improvement of employee competency, the well-being of the employee, and the maintaining of independence.

An organization of public school employees is limited, by the nature of the school as a public institution, to being independent, that is, free of entangling alliances or affiliations. Membership in the organization is subject to meeting the requirements therefor.

The quality and effectiveness of an employee association are to a degree conditional upon the code established to govern the membership and, as needed, to penalize members for infractions.

As a school employee association is comprised of two branches and a number of divisions or departments, it may be expected that each group will seek to be represented in conferences and negotiations that affect its interests. Increasingly, joint relations of the public through its representatives, the administrators, and the school employees by way of their representatives, may be expected to provide a means for cooperative action for the improvement of all conditions necessary to improved school functioning.

The strength of the school employee association lies not so much in sources relied upon by labor, management, and government workers as in the uniqueness of the educative function and enterprise. Thus the school employee finds his real strength in organization to be his mastery of and/or involvement in the art and science of educating or teaching.

However, education of the adult public—school-public relations—to its own values and needs and their implications for the schools is a long-term operation. More short-term and geared to quicker action are the power plays of negotiation or collective agreement, the invoking of sanctions, and the use in extreme instances of a suspension of all but specified essential functions. The suspension is termed a limited strike that in fact falls well short of being a *bona fide* strike, has the merit of preserving the major public interest, and exerts pressure for negotiation of the issues at stake.

SELECTED READINGS

BURRUP, Percy E., *The Teacher and the Public School System* (New York, Harper and Row, 1959), Chapters 12, 13.

CHANDLER, B. J., *Education and the Teacher* (New York, Dodd, Mead & Company, 1961), Chapter 10.

DUBIN, Robert, *Working Union-Management Relations: The Sociology of Industrial Relations* (Englewood Cliffs, N.J., Prentice-Hall, Inc., 1958), Chapters 3, 4, 6, 7.

MOEHLMAN, Arthur B., and VAN ZWOLL, James A., *School Public Relations* (New York, Appleton-Century-Crofts, 1957), Chapters 7, 16.

Research Division of the National Education Association, "Public School Teachers and Collective Bargaining," *Special Memo*, March, 1958, pp. 2–20.

The American Academy of Political and Social Science, "Ethical Standards and Professional Conduct," *The Annals*, Vol. 297, January, 1955, pp. 1–124.

———, "Labor Relations Policy in an Expanding Economy," *The Annals*, Vol. 333, January, 1961, pp. 1–152.

———, "The Ethics of Business Enterprise," *The Annals*, Vol. 343, September, 1962, pp. 1–140.

WARE, Martha, "Professional Negotiation," *NEA Journal*, 51:8, November, 1962, pp. 28–30.

YODER, Dale, HENEMAN, H. G., TURNBULL, John G., and STONE, C. Harold, *Handbook of Personnel Management and Labor Relations* (New York, McGraw-Hill Book Company, Inc., 1958), Section 4, pp. 2–54.

.22.

Postscript

IT IS AXIOMATIC that one thing of which we may be certain is change. This is true of every society and particularly of the democratic society which is responsive to the needs and the voice of the people. Change is inevitable. Resistance to and failure to provide for *orderly* change paves the road for revolt and radical readjustment. Acceptance of the normalcy of and provision for change set the stage for systematic, evolutionary change to which adjustment is easy.

The people have provided themselves with a government in which they maintain their voice through the elective process and representation. They have further assured responsiveness to their needs and wishes by setting up institutions that are conducive to the public well-being.

Among the institutions set up by the people are the schools through and by which the minds of men are opened, from early youth onward, to a regard for knowledge, appreciation of the tools and skills for gaining knowledge, understanding of themselves and their associates, and the tolerance that is the product of understanding and an earmark of the educated.

Education is regarded as important in all lands regardless of the forms of government under which they are ruled. It is regarded as the key to national progress and power. In a democracy, education has an added and transcendent importance. Education in and for the democratic society is the means by which men are made and kept free even during eras of great change.

It is the importance of education for the group and the individual that justifies the concern for, effort put into, and support given to the institutions—the schools—through which society and the individual are furnished guarantees to their freedom, growth, strength, prosperity, and general well-being at home and abroad.

The schools, together with other public institutions and agencies, are threatened by loss of functionality whenever they become resistive to change and find it comfortable to be static. The schools are representative of two groups in particular, the people of the school district and the employees of the board of education.

Through the educative process of school public relations the people are educated to the purposes, values, conditions, achievements, and needs of their schools. School public relations is a concern of all school personnel since each is potentially a public-relations agent for the schools. However, the chief concern of this book has been the school employee, not in terms of his public-relations responsibilities so much as in terms of his on-the-job effectiveness and what factors have implications for that effectiveness.

On-the-job effectiveness has implications for improvement in a changing society to which the functional school is integral.

Securing on-the-job effectiveness on the part of every school employee and providing conditions for improved on-the-job performance are particularly the functions of school personnel administration. Many of the factors pertaining to these two functions have been discussed in the preceding chapters. This postscript will bring into perspective the task of personnel administration under the three major headings of control, service, and cooperation.

CONTROL

Administration connotes control. Personnel administration, as a distinct activity within the administrative organization of the school system, has control aspects. The product of school district size and complexity, personnel administration as a specialized activity is a compensatory mechanism by which the administration seeks to bridge the gap between it and the individual employee so that the school system as a unit may operate harmoniously in the interests of the education function which is its reason for being. Control aspects of personnel administration which merit further consideration include human relations, deployment of the work force, and appraisal.

Human Relations

Throughout the consideration of school personnel administration, the dominant note is one of relationships between and among people. Early consideration was given to democratic versus autocratic administrative behavior toward those administered. There is general verbal commitment in the United States to democratic administration. Attempts are made in various ways to democratize administration, or at least to create the appearance of democratization.

During recent years the term "human relations" has been popularized. Conceptually a regard for human relations is an expression of the regard for the individual that is identified with democratic action. It may well be that the understanding of individual and group behavior under varying circumstances will truly contribute to improved democracy in the administration of public education. However, as with virtually every matter of genuine importance, so also in the realm of the democratization of school administration, new terms do not by themselves presage a difference in basic behavior patterns. There is no panacea by which maladies in interpersonal relationships may be remedied or difficulties overcome.

Democratization of administration is first of all a matter of the underlying spirit. Where the spirit of democracy is present and the urge to be democratic is strong, gains in the direction of democratic administration will take place through effort and perseverance and, when necessary, in spite of organization. When the spirit and urge are sufficiently general, organization will no doubt be affected in such a way as to reflect the democratic spirit.

However, a stress on human relations in no way of itself implies democratic rather than autocratic administration. Human relations are present in either kind of administration. As a matter of fact, there is great danger in identifying human relations as a term with democracy in administration.

The essence of autocratic administration is that those subject to it are subjugated. They lack freedom of expression or action in the area of concern. In extreme instances, even the control of their thoughts is attempted so that even in that area freedom is restricted or threatened.

It is just as possible that "human relations" as an activity may be, for the informed autocrat who relishes his power over people and his ability to exploit them to his own advantage, a somewhat sophisticated means for gaining his ends. Instead of using the raw power of his position to bludgeon others to do his bidding, the intelligent administrator who is committed to acting autocratically may, through his understanding of people and what makes them behave as they do under varying circumstances, manipulate them to serve his purposes and be denied freedom as surely as if he proclaimed his autocracy through brute force.

Thus, there is no magic in the currently popular term "human relations" nor necessarily in the practices associated with it. However, just as knowledge of human behavior may be used for autocratic purposes and in an autocratic way, so also it may be used for democratic purposes democratically. Again, it is the spirit in which the techniques of human relations are used that will determine whether administrative behavior is autocratic or democratic.

Appraisal

Organization exists as a means for achieving objectives. School administrative organization is no exception. Much in organization and administration is empirical, the product of experience. It is necessary continuously to appraise both organization and administration at all levels in order to determine whether they genuinely facilitate, as well as intended, the achievement of the school district's educational objectives.

Appraisal is the means for discovering both efficiency and deficiency. Understanding of the former permits its maintenance and extension. Understanding of the latter furnishes the basis for innovations to overcome it and to provide for improving efficiency. This is the purpose underlying many of the activities of the personnel division and of the research that is made possible by or accompanies them.

Deployment of the Work Force

The efficient operation of the education enterprise demands that the need for personnel be identified and analyzed, analyses be translated into descriptions of the jobs to be done, job descriptions be followed by specifications that must be met by the individual who is to be employed to do the job in question, recruitment procedures be operative to provide for a potential employee pool upon which to draw, those employed be placed or assigned in accordance with their major competencies, efforts be made to help them to adjust to their responsibilities, provisions be made for transfers and promotions as they are warranted, recognition be accorded as earned, and conditions—personnel and materiel—be conducive to the optimum realization of organizational and individual objectives.

Innovations in the subject matter curricular content, teaching techniques and the means by which they are made possible, and school plant (including building, grounds, and equipment) have implications for all facets of the employment and deployment of the personnel needed to staff and operate the schools.

As the operation of the personnel division becomes increasingly functional in terms of its practices and the innovations introduced, concern about incompetents may be expected to focus on a relatively inconsequential few. As a public agency, the schools may not legitimately serve as a refuge for incompetents. Those whose competencies are in no capacity conducive to the effective functioning of the schools must be stricken from the employee and payroll register. No administrator can be held responsible for the operation of a school system or a school in which a commendable regard for the individual uncommendably imperils the school operation to the disadvantage of the community and the youth whom the schools are obligated to serve.

SERVICE

Just as school personnel administration connotes control of the personnel situation, so also it has service implications. The control aspect of administration suggests management. The service aspect of administration suggests doing what is helpful, i.e., ministering to those who have needs to be fulfilled. The "ministering to" activity may find expression in the two areas labeled employee and personal although admittedly there will generally be an overlapping or identification of the two. Any separation of employee from personal will be in terms of how directly the service performed relates to the objectives of the school system.

Employee Services

Probably the outstanding services provided to individuals as employees are those of appropriate assignment, orientation, inservice training, supervision, and the reassignment that may be by way of transfer or promotion and sometimes even demotion. These services very clearly have direct implications for the on-the-job effectiveness of workers.

Other services that are closely related to worker productivity include 1) adjustments that result in a shifting of personnel so that they will be working in congenial association with those with whom they can work harmoniously, 2) assignment to work areas (of school building, classroom, office, building and grounds, operation, maintenance, warehouse, bus or truck routes, etc.) that are conducive to the employee's meeting as fully as possible the responsibilities associated with his job, and 3) provision of all necessary equipment by which to facilitate the productive service expected of the employee.

Personal Services

The personal services are those that have only an indirect or somewhat remote implication for on-the-job efficiency. These services are generated by circumstances outside the working environment. The provision of personal services is defensible from the school's point of view primarily because of their potential positive impact upon worker productivity, or conversely, of the potential negative impact upon productivity if the service is not provided.

From a social point of view—which may provide a legitimate additional justification for the provision of the personal services by the school and which appeals to many within and outside the schools—personal services are humane, help individuals to meet their problems and thus realize their own objectives for themselves, and are identified with the spirit of democracy in terms of regard for the individual.

Among the personal problems that affect personal efficiency in production and are to that extent the concern of the school system are those of health, social adjustment, legal matters, financial management, and security during employment, disability, and retirement.

Personal problems may be met in part by adequate provisions by the schools at the local, state, and perhaps even national levels through, e.g., insurances, leaves, consultative services, organization of needed social and recreational activities, loan funds and credit union operations, tenure, and old-age and disability retirement benefits.

COOPERATION

Meaning a joint action and implying that the joint action will be one that is in balance, cooperation is a concept to which virtually all subscribe and which puts any who oppose it into a defensive position.

There is scarcely an effort, even an individual one, the success of which does not depend to some extent on cooperation, the related efforts of others. Certainly, the operation of the public education enterprise—called into being and supported morally and financially by the people, governed by policies determined by the people via their board(s) of education, and made effective through the execution of the will of the people and board policy by all employees of the school system—is the product of cooperation, joint action, or the working together of many.

Despite all the positive aspects of cooperation, there are nevertheless facets to cooperation as it manifests itself in practice that are worthy of examination. Among these are the factors of balance, participation, and improvement.

Balance in Cooperation

In practice, cooperation comes often to be thought of as a one-way activity. On the one hand the employee who does cheerfully and without question what is wanted of him and on the other hand the administration that yields gracefully and with little resistance to employee demands are labelled cooperative. Cooperation comes to mean compliance, an activity judged by surface appearances rather than by an underlying spirit.

It is suggested that genuine cooperation in the schools has its basis in understanding and appreciation of the nature, functioning, and importance of education. Understanding and appreciation in turn serve as the foundation for a superstructure composed of a variety of the personnel services through which the unit function of the schools is served.

The different kinds of competencies are identified, jobs planned, personnel qualifications specified, and personnel employed and assigned in accord with the varied facets of the one over-all job of education. In a sense, all the personnel have a dual nature.

Every school employee is an individual and is expected to assume full responsibility for efforts and actions initiated by him. At the same time each employee is a component of the total operating mechanism, the school system. In the latter sense, he is expected to relate his activities to and coordinate them with those of his co-workers, professional and nonprofessional.

In both natures, individual and component, each employee of the board of education has the responsibility to carry all of the load he is reasonably capable of managing competently and effectively for the long haul. When each does so in terms of his duality, balance in cooperation is established and, instead of a one-way street, cooperation becomes a traffic interchange for the orderly channeling and conduction of the wide variety of endeavors that are essential to making the education enterprise desirably productive.

Participation

In recognition of the need for cooperation, much is made of participation or the involvement of individuals. Some of this is unquestionably the product of an earnest desire to democratize administration by enabling those who are to be governed by policies to have a voice in formulating them and recommending them for adoption.

The effort to promote participation has two major aspects, the functional and the nonfunctional, each of which is accompanied by action that does not of itself identify which aspect is operative. It is necessary to get below the surface of the evidences of participation to discover whether or not it is functional.

Functional Participation. The involvement of individuals because of the contribution they can make to improved school operation is the functional participation that justifies itself.

Functional participation is supported by the thesis that over an extended period of time judgments arrived at through group effort are more reliable than those arrived at through individual effort. This presupposes that the group members are truly participating in the best sense of the idea, generally requiring voluntary action in accord with genuine interest. Numbers alone have little significance. The thesis for participation is vindicated by those who are interestedly and therefore positively active in the group effort.

The primary product of participation is ideas and judgments which affect policy formulation and lay the foundation for action. A by-product of participation is the understanding generated in the process, having internal morale and external public relations implications.

Nonfunctional Participation. The involvement of individuals principally for the sake of having them involved is one form of nonfunctional participation. Such nonfunctional participation may be said to have the appearance but to lack the substance of involvement. Sometimes the result of a misconception of democratic action, nonfunctional participation substitutes a façade for the actuality of responsible group effort.

The compulsory presence of all for purposes of participation, irrespective of interest or desire, bodes ill for constructive involvement. Involvement that takes place under coercive conditions is accompanied by the danger that the harm done by those who do not enter into the spirit of participation will outweigh the positive outcomes of group effort.

Compulsory attendance at meetings, membership on committees, and enrollment in inservice training programs are sometimes defended for at least promoting understanding which will have positive values for productivity on the job and public relations in the community. There is some question as to whether positive values of understanding, morale, productivity, and desirable personal public relations are likely to be products of superficiality, coerciveness, lack of interest, and numbers present rather than those truly participating.

Occasionally, too, there is the school administrator who has a Machiavellian bent, using participation to his own advantage. He commits employees to involvement in a number of activities so that they will be kept busy with committee or other assignments and have a feeling of self-importance. His intent is to make involvement in minor matters the means by which he preserves for himself a free hand in major matters. In effect, participation becomes a process for keeping employees so occupied that they cannot become an annoyance to the administrator.

Cooperation for Tomorrow

The time to consider and initiate improvements in cooperation for the future is now. Everything good that has been or may be said in favor of cooperation probably will continue to justify it. Further improvement is possible by setting the concept of cooperation free from stigmas induced by nonfunctionality. However, important as it is to reinforce the good and eliminate the bad in cooperative effort, substantial improvement can be brought about chiefly by innovation.

Innovation often poses problems, e.g., of research and experimentation. However, in school personnel administration there is much room for innovation through adaptation from what has already been charted by social and economic developments in industry and government.

Robber Barons and Labor Unions. During an earlier era, the owners and managers of private enterprise earned for themselves the sobriquet of "robber barons." They sought from employees maximum service under marginal working conditions and for minimum reward. This, although largely in accord with the social concepts of the times, was a way of operating that could not endure and virtually invited a challenge.

The challenge to exploitation of labor came with the organization of workers into unions which had the courage and developed the strength to seek for employees a reward more nearly commensurate with their services.

For some time, labor unions and management have been poised in a struggle for power, each apparently seeking to dominate the other to its advantage. In the struggle for and the exercise of power, labor and management have evolved and resorted to a number of procedures by which they have kept open the doors of communication and avoided impasses that neither could afford.

The conceding of rights to each produced contracts. Contractual agreements became the product of consultations, negotiations, conciliatory activities, mediation and arbitration services, the armistice of a "cooling off" period, and improvements in communication. Through these activities a shut-down of operations by management or, through the strike, by labor has become a last-ditch operation.

Increasingly, labor and management are working their way to a recognition of their need for each other. Consequently, it seems only a matter of time before labor and management will have progressed to a reasoned settling of problems, at the conference table, in terms of socio-economic facts that neither can ignore without jeopardizing the industry in question and their own self-interests. The long-term interests of labor and management have too much in common for these two forces to be or remain in opposition to each other.

Government and Its Employees. A traditional preferred status for the government as employer, in which the organization of government employees was discouraged, stressed the sovereignty of the state and left the government employee defenseless in his employment. He was as open to exploitation as was his counterpart in private enterprise during the robber baron era of industry.

The introduction of civil service, not to benefit the government worker but to give government some assurance of continuity in and improvement of service, initially introduced some benefits to government workers, but not the power of organization.

The preferred status of government as employer is breaking down with changes in industrial practice and social consciousness. Consequently, government workers today are encouraged to join the worker organizations of their choice without prejudice to themselves. There is a disposition in government to make use of all of the techniques and procedures, barring the strike, which have been evolved in labor-management relations. The strike continues to be barred on the thesis that a strike by government workers against government as the employer constitutes the jeopardizing of the general welfare by a minority group, a thesis repugnant to the democratic concept.

In its willingness to sit at the council table to discuss and, so far as possible, negotiate with employee organizations, government has come to a position similar to that in which industry found itself. The interests of government as an employer are not basically in opposition to those of government employees. Government and government workers, just as industry and industrial employees, have much more reason to bring themselves into mutual alignment than to assume hostile postures toward each other.

The Schools and Their Employees. School administrators, with exceptions that are bound to become the rule, seem still committed to a robber-baron position relative to other school employees. Their reason for maintaining so outmoded a position sounds very like that of government before it liberalized the traditional preferred posture assumed by it.

To some extent school administrators may be aided in maintaining their anachronistic position to the degree that the professional education association is psychologically oriented toward management rather than labor, is unaware of changes that have taken place in management-labor relations or fails to see in those changes implications for the school scene, and seems at times in danger of making of professionalism a fetish by which teachers are abjured from regarding as applicable to their profession the techniques and procedures—barring, as in government, the general strike—evolved in labor-management relations.

The time is overdue for school systems and those who administer them to get into step with the socio-economic evolution of the times and to make use of the procedures by which administration and other employees of the board of education may be brought together to pull as a unit toward their common objectives and those of the people who maintain the schools. If the reasoned approach to the solution of problems in human relations can work in private enterprise and in government, surely the chances of its being successful in school administration are even better.

The schools have the advantage of the experiences and lessons of industry and government after which they can conceivably pattern procedures suited to the problems of the schools. Failing to do so, school administration-employee relations may be expected to deteriorate. Two hostile camps, that of administration and that of the other school employees (already existing to some extent and in some districts), may be expected to develop in power struggle opposition to each other. And, eventually school administration-employee relations too will have to evolve much as management-employee relations have outside the school scene, but out of first hand experiences that entail unnecessary delay and that further endanger the competitive position of the schools in the labor market.

CONCLUSION

Society and the school system in all its facets of organization and operation can no longer afford to ignore the need for the school system to be competitive with private enterprise and government in its recruitment and employment of professional and nonprofessional employees.

Particularly with reference to professional employees, if the schools are not effectively competitive, it is obvious that education will suffer. Just as obvious, but one step removed, is the price imposed upon industry and government, in fact upon all of society, if the level and effectiveness of education are not up to par because the schools are not competitive.

To the extent that industry and government exercise a priority over the schools in the recruitment, selection, and employment of workers, they are needlessly and unintelligently depleting and dissipating the major resource upon which their own effectiveness depends. By putting primary emphasis upon short-term goals rather than upon long-term objectives, private enterprise and government are killing the goose that lays the golden eggs.

Imperatives

It is imperative that 1) all responsible for the schools and their administration realize the fundamental importance of education, 2) private enterprise, government, and society as the great beneficiaries of education cooperate in taking the action necessary to guarantee to the schools the acquisition and maintenance of a top level work force, professional and nonprofessional, 3) the working conditions in the schools be ameliorated by implementation of personnel services and research along lines discussed throughout this text, together with those that have undoubtedly been neglected or are still emergent, and 4) the place of the United States be secured among the nations, by the democracy, strength, progress, prosperity, welfare of the individual and of society, and dedication to freedom and self-determination which are collectively possible only to a well-educated people who prize highly the enlightenment of education. School personnel administration is justified as an activity by its commitment to and contribution to the realization of the foregoing imperatives.

Appendix

Forms used in the Detroit, Michigan, Public School System in the administration of school employees.

Form 4036—(5-62. AR)

APPLICATION FOR   A DETROIT, MICHIGAN   TEACHING POSITION

Last Name	First Name	Middle Name	Maiden Name if married	Date	File Number

I. PERSONAL HISTORY

Social Security No.	Is the name on your Social Security card the same as the name given above? Yes ☐ No ☐	Date of Birth			Sex
		Month	Day	Year	

Permanent Address:			Tel.			Temporary Address:				Tel.	
No. and Street		City	Zone	State		No. and Street		City	Zone	State	

Underline marital status Unmarried Married Widowed Divorced Separated	Date of Marriage	Give length of residence in Michigan	Are you an American citizen?
	Date of Divorce	Years Months	Yes ☐ No ☐

Service in the Armed Forces, American Merchant Marine, or Red Cross. Branch _____ Discharge: Honorable _____ Other _____ Active Duty From:	Have you ever been arrested and/or convicted for violation of any federal or state law? Yes ☐ No ☐ If answer is YES, state nature and date of violation. Include traffic convictions resulting in damage of $50 or more.

To

Month	Day	Year	Month	Day	Year

II. EDUCATIONAL HISTORY

Name of High School		City	State	Date Graduated

LIST COLLEGES OR UNIVERSITIES IN CHRONOLOGICAL ORDER

Institution	City	State	From	To	Specific Degree	Date Granted
Majors	Sem. Hrs.	Minors			Sem. Hrs.	Total Sem. Hrs.
Institution	City	State	From	To	Specific Degree	Date Granted
Majors	Sem. Hrs.	Minors			Sem. Hrs.	Total Sem. Hrs.
Institution	City	State	From	To	Specific Degree	Date Granted
Majors	Sem. Hrs.	Minors			Sem. Hrs.	Total Sem. Hrs.
Institution	City	State	From	To	Specific Degree	Date Granted
Majors	Sem. Hrs.	Minors			Sem. Hrs.	Total Sem. Hrs.

Major Teaching Fields	Sem. Hrs.	Minor Teaching Fields	Sem. Hrs.

STUDENT TEACHING ASSIGNMENTS

College or University	School	Grade Level	Subjects	Semester Hours	Dates

Do you play the piano?	Type of Michigan Teaching Certificate held	By whom granted	Date Granted

III. TEACHING HISTORY BY YEARS

	School	Street Address	City	Zone	State	Grade or Subject	Dates
1							
2							
3							
4							

Present Teaching Position School	City	State	Grades or Subjects	Salary	Reason for leaving

IV. NON-TEACHING EXPERIENCE

Kind of Work	Name and Location of Firm	Dates of Employment	Earnings per Month

V. REFERENCES

Educational References—List names of instructors under whom you have had the major portion of your professional training.

	NAME	TITLE	INSTITUTION	CITY AND MAIL ZONE	STATE
1					
2					

Personal References—List two persons who know you as an individual.

	NAME	STREET	CITY AND MAIL ZONE	STATE
1				
2				

VI. TEACHING POSITION DESIRED

If you are interested *only* in substitute teaching and not in a contract position, list subjects and grades in order of preference and preparation.

	SUBJECT	GRADES	Do not write in this space SUBSTITUTE TEACHING				
			STATUS	YES	NO	ADMINISTRATOR	DATE
1			Emergency Substitute				
2			Emergency Substitute Regular Position				

Date available as a substitute teacher_____

CONTRACT POSITION DESIRED. In order of preference and preparation, list subjects and grades. A bachelor's degree and a Michigan Elementary Certificate are required for elementary school. A bachelor's degree and a Michigan Secondary Certificate are required for junior high school. A master's degree and a Michigan Secondary Certificate are preferred for high school.

	SUBJECT	GRADES	Do not write in this space SELECTION PROCESS				
			YES	NO	SIGNED	DATE	REMARKS
1					Supervisor		
					Personnel Dept.		
2					Supervisor		
					Personnel Dept.		
3					Supervisor		
					Personnel Dept.		

Date available as a contract teacher_____

I am not presently and have never been a member of the communist party, its front organizations, or any other subversive organizations. Further, I have not participated in the activities, or supported the principles of such organizations. (A "communist front organization" is any organization, the members of which are not all communists, but which is substantially directed, dominated, or controlled by communists or by the communist party, or which in any manner advocates, or acts to further, the world communist movement. Public Acts of Michigan—1952, No. 117)

I certify that the information given in this application is true and correct to the best of my knowledge.

Signature _____

PLEASE NOTE: After completing this detailed application, your next step is to request each college you have attended to send your transcripts to the Records and Certification Office, Detroit Board of Education, 5057 Woodward, Detroit 2, Michigan. The Personnel Department will evaluate your application for employment in the Detroit Public Schools as soon as complete credentials are on file. Additional information may be secured from the Teacher Evaluation Office, Room 1030, Schools Center Building, 5057 Woodward, Detroit 2, Michigan, or by telephoning 833-7900.

GRADE POINT AVERAGE

Name_____ Teaching Field_____

Date_____

Computed By_____

C = 1.0   B = 2.0   A = 3.0

		Undesirable	Doubtful	Average	Good	Superior
Total	_____Hrs.					
Teaching Field	_____Hrs.					
Professional	_____Hrs.					
Directed Teaching	_____Hrs.					

Remarks:

All credits are converted into semester hours. One quarter hour is equal to 5/8 or .625 semester hours.

Last Name   First   Middle   Maiden   Teaching Field

Present Address   Street   City   Zone   State

                                                                 Yes   No

Social Security Number _____

Do you want contract employment in Detroit? . . . . __ __

If so, give date available for contract placement_____

Would you consider substituting prior to contract placement?. . . . . __ __

Are you interested ONLY in substitute teaching? . . . . __ __

Give date available for substitute teaching_____

Circle days available for substitute teaching M T W T F

What Detroit school is nearest your home?_____

Do you have the use of a car? . . . . __ __

Are you under contract to another school system?. . . . . __ __

If so, give date contract expires_____   Years

Substitute teaching experience in Detroit Public Schools. . . . . _____

Contract teaching experience in Detroit Public Schools. . . . . _____

Contract teaching experience in other school systems. . . . . _____

Check how you *first* became interested in applying for a position in Detroit. Indicate *one* choice.

☐ Initiated my own application because_____

☐ Encouraged to apply by a Detroit School Employee (give name)_____

☐ Interviewed by representatives of the Detroit Public Schools on Campus of_____ College

    Date_____

☐ Received information from Teacher Placement Office of _____ College

☐ Other _____

MAKE NO ENTRY BELOW THIS LINE

I. Grade Point Average (C=1.0, B=2.0, A=3.0)   II. Committee Interview (Upper Half)

         Sem.   Honor
         Hours   Points

		Name	Date
A. Total	___ ___	Name	Date
B. Teaching Field	___ ___	Name	Date
C. Professional	___ ___	Name	Date
D. Directed Teaching ___	___		

III. Campus Interview by_____ Date_____

    ☐ Recommend placement on the Eligibility List if credentials are filed within one month.

    ☐ Scheduled for Teacher Selection Tests_____

    ☐ Recommend placement on Eligibility List if test results are satisfactory.

IV. Remarks:

	Robert E. LeAnderson	Speech
ELIGIBILITY LIST: ☐ Yes ☐ No	Chairman, Personnel Committee	Hearing

						☐ Contract		
Eligibility		Date Avail.				☐ Sub Only		
List Date	Subject	for Contract				☐ Sub until Contract		
Prob.	Date	Date	R	U	FC			
Contract No.	Offered	Accepted						
Date Placed on		Appointed						
Substitute List	Approved by	Prob. I: School		Subject			Date	

SUBJECT TO VERIFICATION OF DEGREE AND CERTIFICATE AND APPROVAL OF MEDICAL DIRECTOR.

Distribution of Copies: white - Personnel Assigning Office   buff   - Medical Office
                      pink   - Supervisor of Teaching Field   yellow - Teacher Evaluation Office
Form 4148 (12-61.3M.ML.)   green - Administrative Research

File No._____

Personnel Department
Detroit Public Schools
1354 Broadway
Detroit 26, Michigan

VERIFICATION OF PROFESSIONAL EXPERIENCE

_____ has indicated experience as a teacher ☐ social
worker ☐ physical therapist ☐ other_____ at _____
_____ from 19___ to 19___ , and is applying for a position in the Detroit Public Schools.
Please verify the service from your records and complete the personal qualification section.

EMPLOYMENT STATUS			LENGTH OF SERVICE		
☐ Teacher (Grade or Subject_____) ☐ Social Worker ☐ Physical Therapist ☐ Other (Give title)			From	To	Total
			Mo. Day Yr.	Mo. Day Yr.	Yrs. Mos.
Full-Time	Part-Time	No. of Days of Substitute Teaching	Reason for leaving		

QUALIFICATIONS	UNSATISFACTORY	SATISFACTORY	ESPECIALLY STRONG
*Classroom Teaching–preparation and presentation of work			
*Pupil Relationships–treatment of children and their response, handling of behavior situations			
Staff Relationships–co-operation with other teachers, staff, and superiors, professional interest			
Parent and Community Relationships–interest and participation in parent contacts and community activities			
Personal Qualities–care in personal appearance, speech; initiative			
Health			
Emotional Stability			

Would you rehire? Yes ☐ No ☐	If not, please state reason

Do you know of any specific reason why this person would NOT make a desirable staff member? Yes ☐ No ☐	If you do, please state reason below or on back of this form

Date	Signature of Official Completing Form	Title

*These items are to be completed for teachers only.

**Please return to the Department of Records and Certification, Detroit Public Schools,
1354 Broadway, Detroit 26, Michigan**

Form 4068 (Revised)—2-61—MLP

To Be Completed By Detroit Public Schools Personnel Department

☐ Approved for_____years' credit on salary schedule.   ☐ Not approved because:

_____

_____

☐ Process as appointment
☐ Process as reclassification

_____
Administrator, Personnel Department

Effective
Date_____ Salary_____ Financial Approval _____

419

DETROIT PUBLIC SCHOOLS
Detroit, Michigan

INTERVIEW SHEET

Date_____

Major Teaching Field	Minor Teaching Field

Mr.
Miss
Mrs.

_____

Name   Telephone Number

_____

Street Address

_____

City   Zone   State

The applicant listed above has been given the following material:

1. Application for a Detroit Teaching Position (Form 4036).
2. Teaching Applicant's Report of Work, Travel, and Community Experiences (Form 4149).
3. "Teach in Detroit." This pamphlet gives complete information concerning the filing of an application for a Detroit teaching position, transcripts, and recommendation folders.

Data:

☐ B. A.   ☐ B. S.   Granted from_____ Date_____

☐ M. A.   ☐ M. Ed.   Granted from_____ Date_____

Michigan Teaching Certificate granted_____ Date_____

Directed Teaching at_____ School—Grade_____ Date_____

Directed Teaching at_____ School—Grade_____ Date_____

Remarks:

Interviewed by:

Material presented by:

Material mailed by:

Form 4105—4-59—ML

Medical Director's Report

1. Name _____ Address _____
2. School _____ Department _____
3. Marital History _____
4. Present Illness _____

_____

5. Past History _____

_____

6. Family History _____

7. Have you a hernia? _____ Do you wear a truss? _____
8. Do you have headaches, dizziness or any nervous diseases? _____
9. Have you been vaccinated within the last five years? _____
10. Do you have heart trouble, asthma, or chronic cough? _____
11. When were you last examined here? _____
12. X-ray findings _____
13. Do you tire easily? _____ Have you ever had typhoid fever? _____

Physical Examination

Age _____ Height _____ Weight _____ G.A. _____

Temperature _____ Pulse _____ Respiration _____ B.P. Sys _____ Dias _____

Throat _____ Ears _____ R _____ L _____

Teeth _____ Eyes: with glasses _____ R _____ L _____

Skin _____ without glasses _____ R _____ L _____

Chest _____

Heart _____

Extremities _____

Reflexes _____

Abdomen _____

Pelvis _____

Endocrine System _____

Laboratory Finding _____

    Urinalysis _____ Reaction _____ Sp. Gr _____

    Albumin _____ Sugar _____

Recommendations _____

_____

Date _____   _____
                Medical Examiner

_____ Medical Director

Key rating; 1-Excellent 2-Good 3-Fair 4-Poor F-Failure

DETROIT BOARD OF EDUCATION

Form 4245—2-61—MLP

Side margin labels: Last Name | First Name | Middle Name | School | Date of Examination | Dr. Examining | Checked | Application Number | File Number

Teacher Selection
SPEECH AND HEARING REPORT

_____
                                        EXAMINER

Name_____ Date_____

Permanent Address_____ 'Phone_____

Detroit Address_____Zone_____ 'Phone_____

Teaching Field_____ Grade Preference_____

Present Position_____

Colleges or Universities Attended_____

HEARING

	125	250	500	1000	2000	4000	8000
Right Ear							
Left Ear							

☐   Passed

☐   Retest Necessary _____

☐   Medical Report Recommended   Received _____
                                                                    Date

Comments:_____

☐   Approved   ☐   Not Approved   Signed_____ _____
                                                        Board Medical Examiner   Date

SPEECH

☐   Satisfactory

☐   Defect:

     ☐   Articulation_____

     ☐   Stuttering   _____

     ☐   Voice   _____

☐   Medical Report Recommended   Received _____
                                                                    Date

Comments:_____

☐   Approved   ☐   Not Approved   Signed_____ _____
                                                        Board Medical Examiner   Date

☐   Approved   ☐   Not Approved   Signed_____ _____
                                                    Chairman, Personnel Committee   Date

Form 4059 1-58—ML   DETROIT PUBLIC SCHOOLS

Applicant's Self-Analysis

NAME_____ DATE_____

I. Describe various influences on you as follows:

a. Your own family background, relationship to members of family, etc.

_____

_____

_____

b. High school and college extra-curriculum and general activities.

_____

_____

_____

_____

c. Did you have to earn your way through college wholly or in part? What effect did this have on your life?

_____

_____

_____

_____

d. Social and friend relations when attending school or college and since that time:

_____

_____

_____

_____

e. Your present living arrangements and situations (alone, married, roommate, with parents):

_____

_____

_____

_____

_____

_____

Form 8646—10-59—3M—P

(OVER)

II. Describe briefly your most marked personality—

    a. Strengths: _____

_____

_____

_____

    b. Weaknesses: _____

_____

_____

_____

III. Describe any experiences which have given you insight into pupils and their problems: _____

_____

_____

_____

_____

IV. Why do you want to be a teacher?_____

_____

_____

_____

_____

V. What undesirable features are there about teaching? _____

_____

_____

_____

_____

_____

_____

_____

_____

CREDENTIALS SHEET

Last Name				First Name		Middle or Maiden Name	

DEGREE	INSTITUTION			CITY AND STATE	YEAR GRANTED	ENTERED	VERIFIED

Michigan Certificate	Elem.	Prov. Perm. Kdg.—8	9–12	7–8	Issued
					Expires
No._____	Sec.	Majors	Minors		Entered
					Verified

Michigan Certificate	Elem.	Prov. Perm. Kdg.—8	9–12	7–8	Issued
					Expires
No._____	Sec.	Majors	Miners		Entered
					Verified

Michigan Certificate	Elem.	Prov. Perm. Kdg.—8	9–12	7–8	Issued
					Expires
No._____	Sec.	Majors	Minors		Entered
					Verified

Michigan Certificate	Elem.	Prov. Perm. Kdg.—8	9–12	7–8	Issued
					Expires
No._____	Sec.	Majors	Minors		Entered
					Verified

Life Certificate	Institution		Date Granted	Entered
	City and State	Subjects		Verified

TEACHER OATH OF ALLEGIANCE ON FILE AT LANSING	FULL APPROVAL SPECIAL EDUCATION			
	SUBJECTS COVERED	DATE GRANTED	ENTERED	VERIFIED

LEGAL CHANGE OF NAME	Date	Court	Location	Case No.	Entered	Verified
DATE OF BIRTH	Month Day Year	Document Presented			Entered	Verified

Form 4037—Credentials Sheet (8-61.MLP.)

RED CROSS CERTIFICATE

TYPE	GRANTED	EXPIRES	ENTERED	VERIFIED

VOCATIONAL CERTIFICATE

SUBJECTS COVERED	GRANTED	EXPIRES	ENTERED	VERIFIED

SPECIAL CERTIFICATES

REASON REQUESTED	ISSUED	EXPIRES	ENTERED	VERIFIED

OTHER CREDENTIALS:

NOTICE AND RECORD OF PERSONNEL ACTION

NAME	FIRST	MIDDLE	LAST OR MAIDEN			MARRIED		SENIORITY		FILE NO.
DATE PROCESSED	ACTION	EFFECTIVE DATE	POSITION OR CLASSIFICATION	GRADE OR SUBJECT	SCHOOL OR DEPARTMENT	SALARY	INCREMENT; PAY PERIOD	CHARGE	ADDITIONAL INFORMATION

Form 4301--7-53--ML

DETROIT BOARD OF EDUCATION

427

Emergency Substitute Teaching Service

Last Name	First Name	Initial	Maiden Name	File No.

Date approved for substitute service _____

SUBJECT   DIVISION

_____   _____

_____   _____

_____   _____

_____   _____

Date
Approved: _____ Approved _____

RELEASE

Date released _____ Approved: _____

Date

Address _____ Approved _____

Date referred to Retirement Office by Personnel Records _____

Form 4007--7-53--2M--ML

REPORT ON QUALITY OF EMERGENCY SUBSTITUTE TEACHER SERVICE

Name of Substitute Teacher _____   File Number _____

Name of School _____   Subject or Grade _____

Dates of Service _____

Note to Rater: For evaluating the service of the substitute teacher working THREE OR MORE CONSECUTIVE DAYS in an assignment, the Personnel Department furnishes this rating form. It is requested that the principal or person designated by the principal discuss the quality of work with each substitute teacher before releasing him from the assignment. In special cases this rating form may be sent in following one day of service.

AREA	SATISFACTORY	UNSATISFACTORY
Classroom Teaching		
Pupil Relationships		
Staff Relationships		
Parent and Community Relationships		
Attendance-Promptness		
Personal Qualities		

It will be most helpful to explain your rating, if unsatisfactory, on the back of this sheet.

The information contained on this rating has been discussed with the substitute teacher.

_____   _____
Yes   No

_____   _____
Date   Principal or Other Rater

Please send one copy to the Substitute Office, Personnel Department, and keep one copy in your school.

Form 4076—3–60—MLP

Detroit Public Schools
Detroit, Michigan

PRINCIPAL'S RECOMMENDATION TO PERSONNEL DEPARTMENT
CONCERNING SUBSTITUTE TEACHERS

_____
Date

_____
Last Name   First Name

Do you recommend this person for a contract position in the Detroit Schools as a
teacher of

_____   _____   _____
                                                Yes   No

Please check general rating:

_____   _____   _____   _____   _____
Undesirable   Doubtful   Average   Good   Superior

Approximate time person has taught under my supervision _____   _____
                                                            Months   Years

REMARKS:

_____   _____
            Principal   School

Please complete this form and return to Catherine M. Malarney, Administrative Assistant', Personnel Department, not later than _____.

Form 4110—2-60—ML

430

NAME_____ FILE NO._____
       FIRST   MIDDLE OR MAIDEN   LAST

                                                  S. S. NO._____

☐ ASSIGNED   ☐ RECLASSIFIED   ☐ RELEASED
☐ APPOINTED   ☐ PROMOTED   ☐ TERMINATED   EFFECTIVE
☐ TRANSFERRED   ☐ RETURNED FROM LEAVE ☐ OTHER_____   DATE_____

FROM_____
         POSITION OR CLASSIFICATION   CODE   GRADE OR SUBJECT   SCHOOL   CODE

TO_____
         POSITION OR CLASSIFICATION   CODE   GRADE OR SUBJECT   SCHOOL   CODE

BOARD ☐   NOT BOARD ☐   SCHEDULE RATE ☐   SPECIAL RATE_____

                 HOURLY RATE ☐
SALARY $_____ BIWEEKLY ☐   FOR_____PAY PERIODS   INCREMENT PERIOD_____
                 DAILY RATE ☐

COMBINED ES AND ESRP DAYS.   MILITARY   TOTAL SALARY
AND FORMER DETROIT SERVICE____ OUTSIDE   SERVICE_____   CREDIT GRANTED_____
                               DETROIT SERVICE_____
                                              FINANCE
FINANCIAL APPROVAL_____ DATE_____ CODE____ /   /
                                              APPROPRIATION LOCATION   COST

DEGREE_____ CERTIFICATE_____ MEDICAL_____

                 ADDITIONAL SERVICE ☐   EMPLOYEE NOTIFIED_____
REASON FOR REQUEST: RELEASED SERVICE ☐ SCHOOL NOTIFIED_____

REPLACING_____

REMARKS_____

_____

REQUESTED BY_____ DATE_____

APPROVED BY_____ DATE_____ BY_____ DATE_____

      BY_____ DATE_____ BY_____ DATE_____

      BY_____ DATE_____ BY_____ DATE_____

                 RECEIVED BY PERSONNEL RECORDS_____

WHITE — PERSONNEL RECORDS   TAX CARD
YELLOW — BUDGET   TO PAYROLL ☐
PINK   — ASSIGNING OFFICE   TO PERSON ☐
                                                  INSURANCE
REQUEST FOR PERSONNEL ACTION   BROCHURE ☐
DETROIT PUBLIC SCHOOLS

FORM 4034 (4-62.FC)

RECOMMENDATION FOR PERMANENT CERTIFICATE

Date _____

I certify that _____

who was granted a Michigan_____Provisional Certificate in

_____ , has taught in the Public Schools of

Detroit, Michigan, as follows:

SCHOOL   GRADE AND/OR SUBJECT   FROM   TO

The records of the Board of Education indicate that the

candidate has been a satisfactory teacher for _____

_____. We recommend him for consideration

for permanent certification.

R.E. LeAnderson

Executive Administrative Assistant
Personnel Department

Form 4010—1-60—ML

AUTHORITY FOR SALARY DIFFERENTIAL FOR MASTER'S AND DOCTOR'S DEGREES
Personnel Department
Detroit Board of Education

NAME_____FILE NO._____

POSITION_____POSITION CODE_____SCHOOL_____

DEGREE_____ DATE GRANTED_____ COLLEGE_____ TRANSCRIPT RECEIVED_____

SALARY DIFFERENTIAL APPROVED_____EFFECTIVE_____

SALARY_____INCREMENT PERIOD_____CHARGE_____/_____/_____

FINANCIAL APPROVAL_____DATE_____

APPROVED FOR RETROACTIVE PAYMENT_____DATE_____
                                 Assistant Superintendent

_____DATE_____
                    Secretary and Business Manager

Form 4048 (8-61.ML.)

433

Detroit Public Schools

REQUEST FOR ADDITIONAL SALARY CREDIT FOR
30 HOURS BEYOND THE MASTER'S DEGREE

Last Name	First Name	Middle	Maiden	Date	File No.*

Home Address	City		Zone	Home Telephone

Present School or Department	Title	Grade or Subject Assignment	Current Annual Salary

I. GRADUATE DEGREES EARNED

INSTITUTION	CITY AND STATE	DEGREE	MAJOR FIELD OF STUDY	YEAR GRANTED

II. GRADUATE SEMESTER CREDIT HOURS EARNED BEYOND THE MASTER'S DEGREE

INSTITUTION	CITY AND STATE	MAJOR FIELD OF STUDY	SEMESTER HOURS EARNED	YEARS TAKEN

Signature of Applicant_____ Date_____

DO NOT WRITE BELOW THIS LINE

Transcript evidence of 30 Hours Beyond Master's Degree on file? ☐ Yes ☐ No	Verified by	Date
Salary Differential ☐ Approved ☐ Not Approved	By	Date

Remarks

Approved for Retroactive Payment	By				Date	
Reclassified Effective	Position Code	M____ Plus 30	Salary	Increment Period		
Approved by		Date	Appropriation	Location		Cost

Please return this application in triplicate to the Records and Certification Office, Personnel Department, Detroit Board of Education.

IMPORTANT: SEE REVERSE SIDE FOR STATEMENT GOVERNING REQUIREMENTS FOR ADDITIONAL SALARY CREDIT.

* May be secured from your pay-check stub.

Form 4005 (rev.) (8-61.MLP.)

ELIGIBILITY REQUIREMENTS FOR

ADDITIONAL SALARY CREDIT

Any contract employee who is on the teaching, supervisory, or administrative salary schedule, and who has completed 30 semester credit hours beyond the master's degree from an accredited college or university, is eligible for this additional salary credit.

1. The candidate must initiate his own request for consideration for additional salary credit beyond the master's degree by filing the application *Request for Additional Salary Credit* for 30 Hours Beyond the Master's Degree (Form 4005), which is available in the Personnel Department. (Persons already receiving additional salary credit for 30 hours beyond the master's degree need not file again.)

2. It is the candidate's responsibility to see that all official transcripts in support of this credit are filed with the Division of Records and Certification, Room 901, Phillips Building, 1346 Broadway, Detroit 26, Michigan.

3. The thirty (30) hours of credit must be earned at the graduate level, and must be directed toward the fulfillment of a doctorate in his major field, or in cognate studies designed to increase his effectiveness in his present or subsequent assignment. It is the intent of the policy that the work for this salary credit will be taken after the master's degree is granted.

DETROIT PUBLIC SCHOOLS
PERSONNEL DEPARTMENT

REQUEST FOR APPROVAL FOR EMPLOYMENT
IN SPECIAL EDUCATION CLASSES,
VISITING TEACHER PROGRAM,
AND THE PSYCHOLOGICAL CLINIC

1. _____ Request for first
    evaluation.
2. _____ Subsequent
    evaluation.

Last Name	First	Middle	Maiden	Date	File Number

Address: No. and Street	City	Zone	State	Telephone	Date of Birth

Present Detroit School or Assignment _____   ☐ Em. Sub. in Vacancy
Exceptional   Grades or   Date   ☐ Em. Sub. in Reg. Pos.
Type Child   Subject   Assigned   ☐ Contract Teacher

LIST ALL COLLEGES OR UNIVERSITIES ATTENDED IN CHRONOLOGICAL ORDER

	Institution	City	State	From	To	Sem. Hrs.	Degree	Date
1								
2								
3								
4								

TEACHING HISTORY BY YEARS

	School	Street Address	City	Zone	State	Grade or Subject	Date
1							
2							
3							
4							

Type of Michigan Teaching Certificate Held	Date Granted

Do you have full approval from the Michigan Department of Public Instruction for Special Education, School Diagnostician, or Visiting Teacher program?
☐ Yes ☐ No   Field_____   Date_____

If the answer is "No," please complete the following sections so that we can determine whether you qualify for temporary approval:

Please outline the courses you took from September, 1961 to August 30, 1962:

	Institution	Courses	Sem. Hrs.	From	To
1					
2					
3					
4					

Please outline the courses you plan to take from September, 1962 to August 30, 1963:

	Institution	Courses	Sem. Hrs.	From	To
1					
2					
3					
4					

REMARKS:

Please send reports to Miss Catherine M. Malarney, Administrative Assistant, Personnel Department, Detroit Public Schools.

Distribution of Copies: blue   — Records and Certification Office
                          white — Department of Public Instruction
Form 4162 (5-62.ML.)   yellow — College or University

REQUEST FOR LEAVE OF ABSENCE OR EXTENSION OF LEAVE

Name_____ File No._____ Date_____

Address (permanent)_____ Telephone_____

Zone

Address (temporary)_____ Telephone_____

Zone

☐ New Leave Present Assignment_____

School or Department   Grade or Subject

☐ Extension of Leave. Assignment before taking leave_____

School or Department   Grade or Subject

Reason for taking leave of absence or extension:

☐ Illness ☐ Study ☐ Maternity ☐ Personal Business ☐ Military

Leave or Extension to Begin_____ To End_____

Signature of Applicant_____ Date_____

Principal or Departmental Director_____ Date_____

District Administrator (Elementary Schools)_____ Date_____

Administrative Division Head_____ Date_____

MAKE NO ENTRY BELOW THIS LINE

DISPOSITION

Leave or Extension from_____ to_____ Type of Leave_____

Signature of Official Completing Case_____ Date_____

Signature of Personnel Official_____ Date_____

Personnel Change Notice (Form 4301) granting official approval of the Superintendent and the Board of Education for your leave of absence or extension is enclosed.

IMPORTANT

SEE REVERSE SIDE FOR STATEMENT GOVERNING LEAVES OF ABSENCE

Form 4043—(3-61.5M.FC.109.OL.)   DETROIT BOARD OF EDUCATION

POLICY GOVERNING LEAVES OF ABSENCE, EXTENSIONS OF LEAVE, AND RETURN

A request for a leave of absence or extension of leave is to be made out in duplicate and both copies sent to the Personnel Department. The yellow copy is filed in the Office of Personnel records and the white copy is returned to the employee.

The effective date of a leave is the day FOLLOWING the last day for which the employee is paid.

It is the responsibility of the employee to notify the Personnel Department in writing one month preceding the expiration of a leave if he wishes to return to employment, request an extension, or resign. AT THE EXPIRATION OF A LEAVE, IF AN EMPLOYEE DOES NOT RETURN AND NO EXTENSION IS GRANTED, HIS REMOVAL BECOMES AUTOMATIC.

THE MAXIMUM ALLOWANCE FOR LEAVES OF ABSENCE FOR ALL PURPOSES, EXCEPT AS INDICATED BELOW, SHALL BE THREE CONSECUTIVE YEARS.

Employees returning from leave are expected to remain in Board employment for at least one year.

Requests warranting special consideration beyond the limitations indicated may be referred to a Reviewing Committee for recommendation.

TYPES OF LEAVES

1. ILLNESS. An employee may be granted a leave of absence for prolonged illness subsequent to the termination of his sick leave bank. An extension of illness leave beyond one year must be accompanied by Form 431, Physician's Certificate, filled out by the employee's physician. Any further extension may be granted only upon recommendation of the Board Medical Examiner.

Return from illness leave can be effected as soon as approval of the employee's doctor and the Board Medical Examiner is secured. (Form 431, Physician's Certificate, may be obtained from the school office or from the Personnel Department and completed by the employee's doctor.) In general, the position will be held one year pending return.

2. MILITARY. An employee entering any of the armed services of the United States—including the Red Cross and the Merchant Marine—will be granted a leave without pay when enrolled and assigned to active duty. Upon termination of such active duty, the employee shall be reinstated in his former position or a like position in the department in which he was serving when his leave was granted, provided:

    a. He shall make application for reinstatement within 90 days of the date of his separation from the armed services, and

    b. He is still qualified and competent to perform the duties of his position.

The employee will return at the salary rate which he would have attained had he not been on leave.

*3. STUDY. A study leave will be granted to an employee planning to complete ten semester hours of credit or its equivalent each semester (work taken during the summer not included) in a university or college accredited by the North Central Association of Colleges and Secondary Schools or an equivalent agency. The schedule increase in salary is allowed upon return provided an official transcript is on file in his personnel record covering the work taken while on study leave.

*4. MATERNITY. When an employee requests a leave of absence for maternity, she shall file her request not later than the end of the third month of pregnancy. The date of leaving shall be agreed upon by the employee and her administrative head based upon the best interests of the school and the employee. In general, she shall be prepared to leave her position not later than the fifth month, or four months before the expected birth of the child. The date of leaving shall be determined by the Personnel Department in consultation with the Board of Education Medical Staff, with due consideration given to the closeness to a vacation period or to the end of the semester. The continuity of instruction and the personnel needs of a school, as well as the health of the employee, are factors which will be considered in establishing the termination date.

Maternity leaves of absence are granted for two years. An extension of a leave for personal business for one year may be granted following a maternity leave to care for the child. Any combination of maternity and personal business cannot exceed three years.

*5. PERSONAL BUSINESS. Leaves of absence for personal business shall be limited to one year and no leaves shall be granted, other than Sabbatical leaves, to Board employees primarily for the purpose of engaging in similar employment elsewhere, with the following exceptions:

    a. Leaves, not to exceed four years, shall be allowed for teaching in foreign lands under U. S. Government auspices.

    b. Leaves, recommended by the Reviewing Committee indicated above, shall be considered for limited assignments in federal, state, county, or city governments.

RETURN FROM LEAVE

1. An employee may request his return to Board employment before the expiration of his leave.

2. An employee is required to notify the Personnel Department in writing one month preceding the expiration date of a leave of his wish to return. Return from an illness leave of absence can be effected as soon as approval of the employee's doctor and the Board Medical Examiner is obtained.

3. An employee returning from a leave of absence must have the approval of the Medical Examiner of the Board of Education, and teaching employees must furnish chest x-rays from a physician, a city or county health department, or a college or university health service.

4. Return from a leave is dependent upon a suitable vacancy. Special consideration is given to employees returning from military or illness leaves.

* A LEAVE OF ABSENCE FOR STUDY, MATERNITY, OR PERSONAL BUSINESS IS NOT GRANTED DURING THE FIRST YEAR FOLLOWING APPOINTMENT TO A POSITION. Requests for leaves of absence for study or for personal business must be made not later than three calendar months prior to the proposed effective date of the leave.

PROGRESS REPORT ON
SATISFACTORY PROBATIONARY TEACHERS

Detroit Public Schools
Detroit, Michigan

Name of Teacher			File Number
School	Subject and/or Grade		Months in Assignment

Characteristics Considered	Especially Strong	Satisfactory	Indicate Steps taken to help teacher improve
Classroom Teaching—Preparation and presentation of work			
Pupil Relationships—Treatment of children and their response, handling of behavior situations			
Staff Relationships—Co-operation with other teachers, office and custodial staff, administrators and supervisors; professional interest			
Parent and Community Relationships— Interest and participation in parent contacts and community activities			
Personal Qualities—Care in personal appearance, speech; emotional stability, health, initiative			
Operating Procedures—Promptness and accuracy of reports, punctuality, care of room, supplies, equipment, 'carrying out of assigned duties			

Date of Report	Signature of Principal	Signature of District Administrator	Date

Principals are requested to indicate their evaluation of the special strengths and help they have given to a Probationary Teacher who is doing satisfactory work. If the teacher is unsatisfactory a report should be made on Form 4045, Special Report of Services of a Certificated Employee. Additional comments may be placed on the back of this sheet if the Principal desires. The report is to be completed for Probationary I Teachers at the end of each semester and the white and blue copies sent to the District Administrator.

Form 4044—4-61—MLP

White—Personnel Department; Blue—District Administrator;
Pink—Principal; Buff—Teacher

INSTRUCTIONS FOR FORM 4045

The Form 4045, Special Report on Services of a Certificated Employee (unsatisfactory report), has been completely revised. The principals and the supervisors will file separate reports, forwarding all copies of the completed form to the district administrator.

It is important that the principals and the supervisors indicate in writing that they have attempted to help the teacher by visits and by means of conferences. The front of the form has specific questions on this point, and the reverse side provides space for careful documentation, including specific dates. If necessary, additional sheets may be stapled to the form.

These ratings should be completed and filed by the school or other initiating unit by *November 1* to take effect at the end of the first semester, and by *April 1* to take effect at the end of the second semester of each school year.

The district administrator, after signing the forms, will route the copies as follows:

    Pink   To employee

    Salmon To principal or supervisor, respectively

    Yellow Retained by district administrator

    Blue   To division head

    White   To Personnel Department via the division head

Detroit Board of Education
1354 Broadway
Detroit 26, Michigan

SPECIAL REPORT
OF SERVICES OF A CERTIFICATED EMPLOYEE

Detroit Public Schools
Detroit, Michigan

Name of Employee		Title		File No.
Subject and/or Grade	School or Department	Division		Date Assigned to Present Position

How long have you been in an administrative or a supervisory relationship to the employee? _____
About how many times have you observed the work of the employee? _____
About how many times has the employee voluntarily conferred with you? _____
About how many times have you discussed the employee's work with him? _____

Underline the characteristics on which your evaluation is based. Detailed remarks should be written on the back of this form.

	SATIS-FACTORY	UNSATIS-FACTORY	REMARKS
PERFORMANCE ON THE JOB Effectiveness of planning, methods and techniques; care and organization of working area; equipment and materials; interest; resourcefulness; initiative; self-reliance; thoroughness; promptness and accuracy of reports; foresight.			
PERSONAL ATTRIBUTES Stability, cooperation, integrity, professional interest, dependability, care in personal appearance, relations with others (pupils, parents, community, staff, supervisors, administrators).			

GENERAL EVALUATION. The service of this employee is ☐ satisfactory ☐ unsatisfactory.

	Signature of Employee	Date
This evaluation has been discussed with me.		
Signature of Principal or Supervisor	School or Division	Date
Signature of District Administrator	Date	Signature of Division Head	Date

Copies: White - Personnel Department
         Blue   - Division Head
         Yellow - District Administrator
         Salmon - School or Department
         Pink   - Employee

Form 4045 (Revised) (2-62.MLP.)

441

ADDITIONAL REMARKS: Will you make reference in your comments to the type and amount of help given this employee; i.e., observation of work, conferences, employee visits to comparable situations, etc. Please give dates of visits and conferences, type and amout of help given and by whom.

_____

_____

_____

_____

_____

_____

_____

_____

_____

_____

_____

_____

_____

_____

_____

_____

_____

_____

_____

_____

_____

_____

_____

_____

_____   _____
Principal or Supervisor   Date

RECORD OF SATISFACTORY SERVICE
ADMINISTRATIVE-SUPERVISORY PERSONNEL

Detroit Public Schools
Detroit, Michigan

Last Name	First Name	Initial	Date of Report	File No.
Title of Position		School or Department		Months in Assignment

	Especially Strong	Satisfactory	Indicate Steps taken to help person improve
Professional or Job Competence Knowledge of the job and ability to identify and find appropriate solutions to problems. Promptness and efficiency in carrying out assignments.			
Personal Qualities Warmth, understanding and the ability to work co-operatively and effectively with pupils, teachers, administrators, parents, and other personnel.			
Communication Skills Ability to speak and write well.			
Leadership Initiative and ability to make sound decisions acceptable to others, with a high standard of professional ethics.			
Community Relations Tact and understanding in dealing with problems of parents, community agencies and other groups.			

I have discussed the contents of this report with the person indicated. Yes No Date _____	
	Signature of Rater
	Title
	School, Department or Division
Date	Signature of District Administrator or Division Head

In case of unsatisfactory work, Form 4045, Special Report of Services of a Certificated Employee, should be submitted.

The Record of Satisfactory Service for Administrative-Supervisory Personnel is to be completed by the immediate superior of all employees who have completed their first year in a supervisory or administrative position in the Detroit Public Schools. This includes Department Heads, Counselors, Supervisors, and all others who have direct supervisory or administrative responsibility for staff personnel. Use the reverse side for additional comments. Please return the completed form to the appropriate District Administrator or Division Head who will sign and return to the Personnel Department. This report should be completed at the end of the first year following promotion to the new classification.

First year persons should feel free to ask for a conference with their administrative superior.

Form 4047—11-60—ML   White—Personnel Department; Salmon—District Administrator or Division Head; Yellow—School or Department; Pink—Person

Detroit Public Schools
Detroit, Michigan

PRINCIPAL'S RECOMMENDATION TO PERSONNEL DEPARTMENT
CONCERNING RESIGNED TEACHERS

_____
Date

_____
Last Name   First Name

Do you recommend this person for a contract position in the Detroit Schools as a teacher of

_____   _____   _____
                                                            Yes   No

Please check general rating:

_____   _____   _____   _____   _____
Undesirable   Doubtful   Average   Good   Superior

Approximate time person has taught under my supervision _____   _____
                                                              Months   Years

REMARKS:

_____   _____
          Principal   School

Please complete this form and return to Catherine M. Malarney, Administrative Assistant, Personnel Department, not later than _____.

Form 4109—2-60—ML

444

PRELIMINARY APPLICATION: NON-TEACHING

Board of Education   Detroit, Michigan

LAST NAME			FIRST NAME	POSITION APPLIED FOR		DATE
STREET ADDRESS		ZONE	PHONE NUMBER (own or neighbor's)	DATE OF BIRTH: Month	Day Year	
SOCIAL SECURITY NUMBER			ARE YOU A CITIZEN?	MALE ☐ (check one) SEX: FEMALE ☐		YOUR HEIGHT _____Ft. _____In.
Check one:	UNMARRIED ☐ MARRIED ☐	WIDOWED ☐ DIVORCED ☐ SEPARATED ☐	AGES OF CHILDREN (write in squares below)			YOUR WEIGHT _____Pounds
WHAT DETROIT PUBLIC SCHOOL IS NEAREST YOUR HOME?				HOW MANY PEOPLE DEPEND ON YOU FOR SUPPORT?		
ARE YOU WORKING NOW?		WHERE ARE YOU WORKING?				
WHAT WORK EXPERIENCE HAVE YOU HAD?						

REMARKS:

Form 4241 (1-62.MLP.)   DEPARTMENT OF PERSONNEL

EMERGENCY SUBSTITUTE SERVICE RECORD

REMARKS	SCHOOL OR DEPARTMENT	TITLE	DATE STARTED	DATE RELEASED

NAME	ADDRESS	ZONE	PHONE NUMBER	FILE NUMBER

APPLICATION FOR EMPLOYMENT: NON-TEACHING

Board of Education—City of Detroit

5057 Woodward

Detroit 2, Michigan

POSITION APPLIED FOR	FILE NUMBER

LAST NAME (PLEASE PRINT)	FIRST NAME	MIDDLE NAME	MAIDEN NAME (IF MARRIED)	DATE TODAY

ADDRESS	CITY	ZONE	PHONE	SOCIAL SECURITY NUMBER

DATE OF BIRTH	DATE OF MARRIAGE	HEIGHT	AGES OF YOUR CHILDREN	HOW LONG HAVE YOU LIVED IN THE DETROIT AREA?
SEX (CHECK ONE)		____ FT. ____ IN.		
MALE ☐ FEMALE ☐	DATE OF DIVORCE	WEIGHT		WHAT DETROIT PUBLIC SCHOOL IS NEAREST YOUR HOME?
ARE YOU (CHECK ONE) SINGLE ☐		____ POUNDS		
MARRIED ☐ WIDOWED ☐ DIVORCED ☐ SEPARATED ☐	REMARKS:			

ARE YOU AN AMERICAN CITIZEN?   ☐ YES   ☐ NO

HAVE YOU EVER BEEN ARRESTED FOR VIOLATION OF LAW?   ☐ YES   ☐ NO
WERE YOU EVER CONVICTED OF VIOLATION OF A STATE OR FEDERAL LAW?   ☐ YES   ☐ NO

I am not presently and have never been a member of the communist party, its front organizations, or any other subversive organizations. Further, I have not participated in the activities, or supported the principles of such organizations. (A "communist front organization" is any organization, the members of which are not all communists, but which is substantially directed, dominated, or controlled by communists or by the communist party, or which in any manner advocates, or acts to further, the world communist movement. Public Act of Michigan–1952, No. 117)

I certify that the information given on this application is true and correct to the best of my knowledge.

_____

Signature

Do Not Write Below This Line

BIRTH REGISTRATION:	DATE OF BIRTH	MONTH	DAY	YEAR	DOCUMENT REGISTERED	REGISTERED BY	DATE REGISTERED
DIVORCE REGISTRATION:	DATE		COURT		LOCATION	NUMBER	REGISTERED BY	DATE REGISTERED

FORM 4240 (6-62.MLP.)   **Revised**   (OVER)

446

Educational History

TYPE OF SCHOOL	NAME OF SCHOOL	LOCATION	NO. OF YEARS	DATE GRADUATED	COURSE OR CURRICULUM
ELEMENTARY SCHOOL					
JUNIOR HIGH SCHOOL					
HIGH SCHOOL					
BUSINESS, TECHNICAL, OR TRADE SCHOOL					
COLLEGE OR UNIVERSITY					

PIANO INSTRUCTION:	INSTRUCTORS	LOCATION	NO. OF YEARS

SERVICE IN THE ARMED FORCES, MERCHANT MARINES, OR RED CROSS:	BRANCH	DATE ENTERED ACTIVE SERVICE	DATE RELEASED

HAVE YOU EVER BEEN EMPLOYED BY THE DETROIT BOARD OF EDUCATION?

☐ YES   ☐ NO

WHAT CLASS ENGINEER'S LICENSE DO YOU HOLD?

☐ FIRST   ☐ THIRD
☐ SECOND   ☐ H. P. BOILER OPERATOR

Employment Experience
(LAST 3 PLACES OF EMPLOYMENT)

NAME OF FIRM	ADDRESS OF FIRM	TYPE OF WORK	PAY RATE	DATES OF EMPLOYMENT (GIVE MONTH AND YEAR)	
				FROM	TO

REMARKS:

447

Report on Physical Condition

1. Have you ever had any occupational illness or injury while employed or in Military Service? Yes ☐ No ☐

2. Have you any physical disability or deformity that would in any way disqualify you from full discharge of duties of the position to which you seek appointment? Yes ☐ No ☐

3. Are you receiving, or have you ever received a disability pension? Yes ☐ No ☐

4. Are you ruptured? Yes ☐ No ☐

5. Have you ever had a nervous breakdown? Yes ☐ No ☐

6. Are you receiving, or have you ever received Workmen's Compensation payments for any occupational illness or injury? Yes ☐ No ☐

7. Have you, to your knowledge, ever had any of the following?

   Arthritis or Rheumatism Yes ☐ No ☐   Back Trouble Yes ☐ No ☐

   Diabetes Yes ☐ No ☐   Heart Trouble Yes ☐ No ☐

If answer to any of the above is yes, state date, type of injury or illness, and where employed at time of injury or illness. If there was a payment under Workmen's Compensation Act, state approximate amount of such payment.

_____

_____

_____

_____

I hereby certify that the above answers are true to the best of my knowledge.

_____   _____
Signature of Applicant   Date

This application is to be sent to the Medical Office, reviewed by the Doctor, and returned to the Non-Teaching Personnel Office.

(SEE OVER FOR EXTRA LINES)

448

BOARD OF EDUCATION
1354 Broadway
Detroit 26, Michigan

Detroit Police Department
Canfield Station
Woodward Avenue--between Forest and Hancock
Detroit, Michigan

Gentlemen:

Mr._____ at_____.

Social Security No._____, is a candidate for a

position as_____ with the Detroit Board of

Education. We are referring him to you that you may take his

fingerprints.

                    Date of Birth:_____

Please refer to Criminal Information Bureau--Subversive Detail.

                              Very truly yours,

                              H. W. Meagher ao

                              H. W. Meagher
                              Administrative Assistant

HWM/ao

Remarks:_____

_____

_____

_____

APPLICANT

LEAVE THIS SPACE BLANK

	SEX	
LAST NAME FIRST NAME MIDDLE NAME	RACE	

SIGNATURE OF PERSON FINGERPRINTED	SUPERINTENDENT POLICE DEPARTMENT DETROIT, MICH. ATTENTION, CHIEF OF DETECTIVES	COMPANY AND ADDRESS	HT. (IN.)	WT.
			DATE OF BIRTH	
RESIDENCE OF PERSON FINGERPRINTED			HAIR	EYES

SIGNATURE OF OFFICIAL TAKING FINGERPRINTS	NUMBER	LEAVE THIS SPACE BLANK
TYPE OR PRINT ALL REQUESTED DATA	DATE FINGERPRINTED	CLASS. _____
	PLACE OF BIRTH	
	CITIZENSHIP	REF. _____

SEE REVERSE SIDE FOR FURTHER INSTRUCTIONS

1. RIGHT THUMB	2. RIGHT INDEX	3. RIGHT MIDDLE	4. RIGHT RING	5. RIGHT LITTLE

6. LEFT THUMB	7. LEFT INDEX	8. LEFT MIDDLE	9. LEFT RING	10. LEFT LITTLE

LEFT FOUR FINGERS TAKEN SIMULTANEOUSLY	LEFT THUMB	RIGHT THUMB	RIGHT FOUR FINGERS TAKEN SIMULTANEOUSLY

450

FEDERAL BUREAU OF INVESTIGATION
UNITED STATES DEPARTMENT OF JUSTICE
WASHINGTON 25, D. C.

APPLICANT

To obtain classifiable fingerprints:

1. Use printer's ink.
2. Distribute ink evenly on inking slab.
3. Wash and dry fingers thoroughly.
4. Roll fingers from nail to nail, and avoid allowing fingers to slip.
5. Be sure impressions are recorded in correct order.
6. If an amputation or deformity makes it impossible to print a finger, make a notation to that effect in the individual finger block.
7. If some physical condition makes it impossible to obtain perfect impressions, submit the best that can be obtained with a memo stapled to the card explaining the circumstances.
8. Examine the completed prints to see if they can be classified, bearing in mind the following:

Most fingerprints fall into the patterns shown below (other patterns occur infrequently and are not shown here):

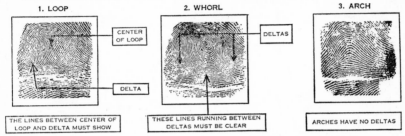

Law-enforcement agencies using this card for pistol permits, licenses, etc., should indicate type of permit or position in space "COMPANY AND ADDRESS."

Department of Defense activities and contractors initiating this card will make no entries in "CONTRIBUTOR AND ADDRESS" and "NUMBER." Such entries will be made by the Department of Defense investigative agencies concerned. Department of Defense activities using this card for military personnel or civilian employees will enter designation and address of requesting activity in "COMPANY AND ADDRESS." Department of Defense contractors will enter contractor's name and address in "COMPANY AND ADDRESS."

The space "NUMBER" should contain the number designated for the particular case or code designation. The number appearing in this space will be quoted on answers to the fingerprint search.

FD–258
(5–22–57)

U. S. GOVERNMENT PRINTING OFFICE, 1957—O–431750

451

BOARD OF EDUCATION
City of Detroit

Last Name	First Name	Initial	File No.

Position	School or Department

OATH OF ALLEGIANCE AND FIDELITY

I do solemnly swear (or affirm) that I will support the constitution of the United States and the constitution of this state, and that I will faithfully discharge the duties of my position in employment of the Board of Education of the City of Detroit according to the best of my ability.

_____
Signature

Subscribed and sworn to before me this _____ day of _____

_____
Notary Public, Wayne County, Michigan
Adele Ohmer

My commission expires January 14, _____, 19 63.

FORM 4320

452

REPORT ON PROBATIONARY EMPLOYEE

Mr.
Mrs.
Miss_____ was assigned to your building on_____

as Probationary_____. Please evaluate this employee on

the following factors:

		UNSATISFACTORY	SATISFACTORY	EXCELLENT
Work	QUALITY			
	QUANTITY			
Job Attitude (Co-operation)				
Adaptability				
Vitality				
Personal Habits				
		FREQUENT	SELDOM	NEVER
Absence				
Tardiness				

Based on the above rating, I recommend ☐ Permanent Appointment

                                          ☐ Retention on Probation

                                          ☐ Release

The above-named employee has seen this report and I have discussed it with him. / her.

Date:_____   _____
                                      Signature of Rater   Title

School:_____   _____
                                      Signature of Principal or Head of Unit

Please return to the Non-Teaching Personnel Department not later than_____

(You may use reverse side for comments.)

REPORT ON QUALITY OF NON-TEACHING EMERGENCY SUBSTITUTE SERVICE

NOTE TO RATER: The maintenance of good substitute service in the schools is the responsibility of the Personnel Department, working in co-operation with principals and supervisors in the schools and departments. Toward this end, it is requested that principals and supervisors discuss the quality of work with each substitute before releasing him from an assignment. For evaluating the service of substitutes working three or more consecutive days in an assignment, the Personnel Department furnishes this rating form. In special cases this rating form may be requested following one day of service when the situation so warrants.

Please complete the following report on the services of:

_____   _____ Cleaner   _____ Janitor
             Substitute   _____ Lunchroom Employee   _____ Clerk
                                       _____ Bath Attendant   _____ Accompanist

in the _____ Dept.
                                School from _____ to _____

CHARACTERISTICS	UNDESIRABLE	DOUBTFUL	AVERAGE	GOOD	SUPERIOR
Personal Appearance					
Vitality - Health					
Attendance - Promptness*					
Co-operation					
Quality of Work					
Quantity of Work					
Job Attitude					
Desirability as a Permanent Employee in Your School					

It will be most helpful if you explain or exemplify your rating in the space below.

_____

_____

_____

*Arriving late, leaving early

The information contained in this rating has been discussed with the substitute.

Signed_____

_____   _____   _____
          Date   School   Title

Form 4220-;3-58--ML

Detroit, Michigan, Public Schools

RATING FORM FOR CANDIDATES FOR PROMOTION TO CLERICAL ASSISTANT

<table>
<tr><td>RATING BY</td><td>CANDIDATE</td></tr>
</table>

On the following rating form please indicate your individual, independent judgment of the above-named candidate for promotion to the position of Clerical Assistant in the Detroit Public Schools. Clerical Assistant assignments involve acceptance of responsibility for specialized work and for the direction of a group of workers. This form should be filled out independently and not in collaboration with other raters. Furthermore, this form must be completed in strict confidence; the candidate must not be advised directly or indirectly of this rating.

Before making any ratings, it may be helpful to bear in mind the best possible candidate for Clerical Assistant with whom you are acquainted, and also a person who might be considered the opposite to the first one in every way. Sometimes it is possible to think of one or more individuals who would fall between these extremes.

You are to rate the characteristic of each candidate in three areas. Within each area, characteristics are described in a scale ranging from average (left) to excellent (right). Numbers ranging from 3 (low average) to 10 (very high) appear below the descriptions. You are to rate the candidate in each of the twenty traits by circling the number that seems appropriate for each trait.

The descriptive statements in each of the areas are intended to aid you generally in making your judgment. For example, under "Ability to work with people" consider the descriptive statement "Helps to create teamwork with colleagues and other staff members." Although this statement describes the highest level of "Ability to work with people", some candidates will be stronger than others even at this high level. Therefore, among candidates at this level some candidates may be given a numerical rating of nine, others, ten.

Rate each trait independently without reference to the rating given for any other trait. It is possible to rate a candidate three in one trait and ten in another. It is suggested also that you consider the candidate's potentiality as a Clerical Assistant as well as her effectiveness in her present assignment.

Please return, in a sealed envelope, this rating form to Mr. William C. Joy, Junior Administrative Assistant, Detroit Board of Education, Phillips Building, 1346 Broadway, Detroit 26, Michigan, not later than _____.

	Average	Good	Excellent
ACCURACY	Strives for accuracy; not always able to find own mistakes.	Has developed attitude of thoroughness in all details; few errors.	Devises methods of verifying work. Work done with precision.
	3 4 5	6 7 8	9 10
TECHNICAL SKILLS	Acceptable ability; rework necessary occasionally.	Quality and output of work consistently above average.	Unusual skills resulting in rapid production of uniformly neat, well-arranged work.
	3 4 5	6 7 8	9 10
KNOWLEDGE OF PROCEDURES	Able to understand and follow directions with some supervision.	Familiar with present procedures. Able to perform most new duties with minimum of directions.	Thorough knowledge of present work. Grasps new procedures easily. Resourceful in carrying out new procedures.
	3 4 5	6 7 8	9 10
ATTITUDE TOWARD SUPERVISION	Usually able to accept criticisms and suggestions without resentment.	Always able to accept criticisms and follow through on suggestions.	Responds readily and with enthusiasm to suggestions on work. Amenable to change.
	3 4 5	6 7 8	9 10
PERSEVERANCE	Needs occasional reminder to follow through on work.	Usually determined to see a job through.	Will not give up on job even under extreme difficulty.
	3 4 5	6 7 8	9 10
PROMPTNESS	Usually punctual. Work usually finished on time.	Rarely late. Meets deadlines without difficulty.	Schedule planned so that usually ahead of time in all work.
	3 4 5	6 7 8	9 10
ABILITY TO WORK WITH PEOPLE	Usually able to work well with fellow employees.	Always co-operative with fellow staff members, members of other departments, and visitors.	Helps to create co-operative teamwork with colleagues and other staff members.
	3 4 5	6 7 8	9 10

	Average	Good	Excellent
ACCEPTANCE OF RESPONSIBILITY	Prefers to be supervised.	Accepts responsibility willingly and usually needs little supervision.	Assumes responsibility and leadership readily. Sees work to be done.
	3 4 5	6 7 8	9 10
ABILITY TO ORGANIZE WORK	Able to develop satisfactory routine for daily tasks only.	Able to incorporate emergency work in daily routine with ease.	Skilled in analyzing problems, planning routine, executing plans, evaluating results.
	3 4 5	6 7 8	9 10
ABILITY TO MAKE DECISIONS	Tendency to jump to conclusions without forethought.	Makes decisions after considering facts; judgment usually good.	Able to consider evidence and reach excellent decisions without undue delay.
	3 4 5	6 7 8	9 10
ABILITY TO INSTRUCT OTHERS	Willing to help others. Lacks skill in putting her ideas across.	Able to give directions clearly and follow through on completion of work.	Patient with beginners. Can recognize and develop capabilities in others. Able to delegate work to others.
	3 4 5	6 7 8	9 10
INTEREST IN SELF-IMPROVEMENT	Ambitious to move forward but does little to improve skills or knowledge of job.	Industrious. Makes suggestions for improving work. Welcomes chance to learn new work.	Enthusiastic about work. Interested in assuming more responsibility. Continues to grow in knowledge and breadth of interest.
	3 4 5	6 7 8	9 10
INTEREST IN JOB	Accepts benefits and secure working conditions as her right as an employee.	Good appreciation of Board personnel policies. Understands role of the school in the community.	Interested in welfare of her employer. Proud of her association with the Detroit School System.
	3 4 5	6 7 8	9 10
SKILL IN HUMAN RELATIONS	Occasionally in disagreement with fellow employees. Allows personal feelings to enter discussion.	Rarely at odds with fellow employees. Able to adjust to many types of personalities.	Tactful. Can take objective view in controversy. Inspires confidence and good will.
	3 4 5	6 7 8	9 10

	Average	Good	Excellent
DISPOSITION	Outlook varies but usually cheerful and pleasant.	Optimistic outlook; likable person.	Unusually well-liked; keen sense of humor; alert and very cheerful.
	3 4 5	6 7 8	9 10
STABILITY	Usually self-controlled in not extremely provocative situations.	Shows good emotional control without tension in most situations.	Well-developed control of emotions; not affected by stress of many interruptions and difficult problems.
	3 4 5	6 7 8	9 10
POISE	Some skill in meeting the public. Acceptable telephone manners and voice.	Welcomes opportunity to deal with people. Pleasant telephone manners.	Able to deal with difficult people, telephone calls, and problem situations with graciousness and ease.
	3 4 5	6 7 8	9 10
PERSONAL APPEARANCE	Usually neat and clean. Not always properly dressed for office.	Almost always well groomed and appropriately dressed.	Always wears attractive, appropriate clothing; excellent grooming.
	3 4 5	6 7 8	9 10
VITALITY	Energy adequate for day's work; usually uses sick leave allowance.	Occasionally absent; usually vigorous health.	Rarely absent; extremely energetic; stamina for extended work periods.
	3 4 5	6 7 8	9 10
INTEGRITY	Sometimes fails to keep confidences; conduct may change in absence of supervision.	Knows and strives to maintain high ethical standards in all situations.	Absolutely trustworthy in use of her time and in the handling of money and confidential records and matters.
	3 4 5	6 7 8	9 10

SUMMARY: I have known this individual from _____(year) to _____(year) in my capacity as her:

▱ Employer or superior _____   ▱ Fellow Employee
                                  (My title at that time)

▱ Subordinate   ▱ Teacher   ▱ Other _____

Signature _____
                                     Title

DETROIT PUBLIC SCHOOLS

SUBJECT: **Special Service Report**

FROM   : Principal or Department Head

TO   : Non-Teaching Personnel Department

DATE   :

_____ has been employed in
Employee's Name

_____ since _____ as
School   Date

_____
Classification

We are making the following report on this employee's services.

RECOMMENDATION FOR:	IMPORTANT CHARACTERISTICS					
		UNSATIS-FACTORY	POOR	AVERAGE	GOOD	EXCELLENT
☐ Retention pending further trial	Adaptability					
	Vitality					
	Co-operation					
☐ Transfer	Quality of work					
	Quantity of work					
☐ Dismissal	Job Attitude					
	Personal Habits					
	Work Habits					

I have seen this rating. I understand I may state my position in writing for entry in my personnel file at the Board of Education.

_____   _____
Signature of Employee   Date

_____ _____ _____ _____
Person Making Rating   Position   School   Date

_____ _____ _____ _____
Person Making Rating   Position   School   Date

_____ _____ _____
Approved   Position   Date

See Back of Page

Form 4208--2-55--ML

Give complete data justifying your recommendation:

_____

_____

_____

_____

_____

_____

_____

_____

_____

_____

_____

_____

_____

_____

_____

_____

_____

_____

_____

_____

Date	Principal or Department Head

Form 4208 should be completed in triplicate. Principal or Department Head retains yellow copy.

When this form is signed, the green copy should be given to the employee and the white copy is to be sent to the Non-Teaching Personnel Department.

NON-TEACHING PERSONNEL DEPARTMENT

RATING—TEMPORARY OR SEASONAL EMPLOYEE

Name_____Classification_____File No._____

☐ Was Laid Off   ☐ Was Transferred

☐ Quit   ☐ Was Discharged

Last day on payroll was_____

We would appreciate your rating him on factors shown below. This will help us in obtaining satisfactory help for you at future dates.

	(1) Poor	(2) Average	(3) Good	(4) Excellent
Quality of Work				
Mechanical Ability				
Quantity of Work				
Attendance Include both tardiness and absenteeism when considering rating.				
Attitude Toward job and fellow workers				
Is he co-operative?				
Vitality Was he physically able to do jobs assigned to him?				

If rating in column number 1, please explain completely. (Use back of form if necessary.)

_____

_____

_____

I have seen this rating. I understand I may state my position in writing for entry in my personnel file at the Board of Education. My signature merely indicates I have seen the rating and have been given a copy.

_____   _____   _____
Signature of Person Making Rating   Signature of Employee   Date

_____   _____   _____
Signature of General Foreman   Position   Date

_____   _____
Signature of Department Head   Date

                                                                          _____
                                                                              Date

FORM 4204 (4-61. 1M. AR. 47. OL.)

Name Index

• Topical Index